# Bourne on Company Law

An ideal introduction for a student facing the challenges of company law for the first time, this excellent textbook lucidly examines the fundamental areas of company law that are covered in most undergraduate law courses.

The fourth edition of *Bourne on Company Law* has been extensively revised and updated in the light of the **Companies Act 2006**. It retains all of the most popular features from previous editions, including the understandable style, pedagogical support, and easy to use structure which enables readers to grasp the complexities of this fast moving subject.

*Bourne on Company Law* is

- one of the only textbooks on the market to include analysis and impact of the Companies Act 2006
- pitched at an appropriate introductory level for undergraduate law students and non-law students taking modules in company law – text is broken down into short, clear sections separated by subheadings for ease of navigation
- includes advice on further reading to point students towards sources for further study
- supported by a companion website offering twice annual updates to the law, helping to keep content current between editions

Bourne examines the impact of the changes in the Enterprise Act 2002, the Companies (Audit, Investigations and Community Enterprise) Act 2004, the Directors' Remuneration Report Regulations 2002, and the Combined Code on Corporate Governance. Providing a comprehensive and precise account of this dynamic area of law, this book will be invaluable to both undergraduate law and non-law students taking courses in company law.

The Companies Act 2006 is to be brought into effect in stages and is likely to be fully in force by October 2008. Readers are advised to check whether the relevant sections are in force or not.

References in the text book are to the Table A, Companies Act 1985 unless the context shows otherwise.

**Nicholas Bourne** is Leader of the Conservatives in the Welsh Assembly and teaches Company Law in Hong Kong.

# Bourne on Company Law

## Fourth Edition

Nicholas Bourne

Routledge·Cavendish
Taylor & Francis Group

Fourth edition published 2008
by Routledge-Cavendish
2 Park Square, Milton Park, Abingdon, Oxon, OX14 4RN

Simultaneously published in the USA and Canada
by Routledge-Cavendish
270 Madison Avenue, New York, NY 10016

*Routledge-Cavendish is an imprint of the Taylor & Francis Group, an informa
business*

© 2008, 1998, 1995, 1993 Nicholas Bourne

Previous editions published by Cavendish Publishing Limited

First edition            1993
Second edition           1995
Third Edition            1998

Typeset in Times by Keyword Group Ltd
Printed and bound in Great Britain by MPG Books Ltd, Bodmin,
Cornwall

*British Library Cataloguing in Publication Data*
A catalogue record for this book is available from the British Library

*Library of Congress Cataloging-in-Publication Data*
Bourne, Nicholas.
   Bourne on company law / Nicholas Bourne. – 4th ed.
      p. cm.
   ISBN-13: 978-1-84568-031-2
   ISBN-10: 1-84568-031-6
   1. Corporation law – Great Britain. I. Title. II. Title: Company law.
   KD2079.B685 2007
      346.41'066–dc22
2007021702

ISBN10: 1-84568-031-6 (pbk)
ISBN13: 978-1-84568-031-2 (pbk)

To the memory of my dear parents, Joan Bourne and John Morgan Bourne.

# Contents

# Preface

The Companies Act 2006 is the longest statute on any subject ever to pass through the Westminster Parliament. That is the measure of the challenge, both for an author and for students of Company Law.

The pace of change in Company Law is sometimes bewildering but the subject matter is always fascinating.

This book is written primarily for students. It is hoped, however, that some of the ideas will be of interest to the researcher and some of the analyses relevant for the practitioner.

As always, I am grateful to colleagues and to students past and present for their help. I am very grateful to my editorial team for their patience and assistance, and I am also extremely grateful to Sandra Morgan for decoding manuscripts and dictated discs.

The law may be complex and increasing in volume and complexity, but since Jonathan Swift commented as long ago as 1711 that, 'If books and laws continue to increase as they have done for 50 years past; I am in some concern for future ages, how any man will be learned or any man a lawyer', perhaps we have, in reality, no reason to fear that volume and complexity!

# Table of Cases

# Table of Statutes

# Introduction

## 1.1 A company or a partnership

When a group of people get together and decide to start a business, one decision that they will need to make early on is whether to operate as a company or as a partnership. There are certain advantages, and indeed certain disadvantages, that attach to incorporation, that is the process of creating a company. The following are, therefore, matters which those setting up a business will need to consider. The essence of the company is that it is a separate person in law, see *Salomon v A Salomon & Co Ltd (1897)* (see section 2.1). From this very basic difference between the company and the partnership flow many of the advantages and disadvantages of incorporation.

The most obvious advantage in incorporation is the access to limited liability. Not all companies are limited companies. Unlimited companies do not need to file accounts so sometimes this is an attraction for those setting up a business. However, the possibility of limiting the liability of the participators to the amount of the issued shares is an attractive one. Sometimes this advantage is, of course, more apparent than real. If a small private company goes to a bank and asks to borrow a large sum of money, the bank is unlikely to be satisfied with the possibility of recourse against the company's assets. In practice, the bank manager will require some collateral security from the company's directors. In a partnership, however, all the partners will have unlimited liability for the business's debts and liabilities. This is the case except in a limited partnership governed by the Limited Partnerships Act 1907. In a limited partnership, however, only sleeping partners may have limited liability and it is not possible to form a partnership made up entirely of limited partners. There must always be somebody who is 'picking up the tab' with no limitation of liability.

Under the Limited Liability Partnerships Act 2000, it is possible to opt for a new form of business association. The relationship between the members is like that of a general partnership but the institution has to be registered with the registrar of companies. Members of a limited liability partnership are not responsible for its debts. Limited liability partnerships are regarded as legal persons.

A further advantage of the company is the possibility of separating ownership from control. In a partnership, all of the partners are agents for the firm. In a company, and this is particularly the case in public companies, the ownership and the control are separated. Those people owning the share capital will not generally be the people who are running the business (however, in private companies, the owners and the managers may well be the same).

An attraction of incorporation is what is sometimes termed perpetual succession. This means that the company need never die. Companies do go into liquidation but they need not do so. There is no theoretical reason why a company cannot go on for ever. The Hudson's Bay Company has been running for well over 300 years, for example. In the case of partnerships, however, wherever there is a change of partners, there has to be a drawing up of partnership accounts and a re-formation of the partnership.

Incorporation is an attractive business medium where the participators wish to be able to transfer their shares at some later stage. In a company, shares are freely transferable, subject to the terms of the company's constitution (section 7.4). In a partnership, by contrast, a partner's share is not so transferable unless the agreement so provides. The advantage of transferability is seen at its clearest where a company is quoted on the Stock Exchange or the Alternative Investment Market (AIM). At this stage, there will be a market mechanism for disposing of and purchasing shares.

It is said to be easier to raise finance where a company is formed as opposed to a partnership. Clearly, if a company is quoted, it has access to the Stock Exchange to raise finance by issuing its shares and debentures (collectively called securities) to the public (Chapter 19). In the case of debentures, these may be secured by a floating charge over all of the company's assets and undertaking (section 19.5). Although this does not in general provide advantages for companies on or after 15 September 2003. The device of the floating charge is open to the company and a general partnership cannot take advantage of this means of raising finance, although it is open to limited liability partnerships to create floating charges.

It is probably the case that there is more prestige attached to the company than to the partnership. There is no reason that this should be the case but probably the trading and investing public sees a company in a more favourable light than a partnership.

A further consideration, although it might not be an advantage for companies, is taxation. Companies will pay corporation tax on their profits. In the case of partnerships, the profits of the partnership business are attributable to the partners of the firm, who will pay schedular income tax on those profits. It is not possible to say in isolation from factors concerning the circumstances of the participators and their other sources of income whether this is an advantage or not. It will depend on the circumstances.

The disadvantages that attach to incorporation are not numerous. There are clearly formalities to be complied with. A partnership agreement need not even be written. Clearly, it is desirable to have a written agreement for evidential purposes but there is no legal reason why the agreement should be in writing. Companies are subject to a comprehensive code of rules contained in the Companies Act 2006 and elsewhere; the partnership is not subject to a detailed statutory regime although the Partnership Act 1890 does set out some rules.

In the case of a company, there are various formalities to be complied with. A constitution has to be drafted. Articles of association (the constitution) have to be delivered to the Registrar at Companies House in Cardiff in the case of English and Welsh companies, together with a statement of capital and a statement of compliance. A certificate of incorporation will then be issued to the company. There are various ongoing formalities for a company, including the filing of an annual return, the filing of annual accounts (unless the company is unlimited) and the filing of various forms connected with changes of directors, issue of shares, issue of debentures, change of company secretary, etc. Companies also have to comply with formalities regarding the holding of meetings which is not the case in a partnership. Private companies are not required to hold AGMs but may do so if they wish.

Together with these formalities, there is the disadvantage of publicity in the case of the company. This is generally seen as a disadvantage as a company has no option but to make certain of its affairs public. These would include the company's directors, company secretary, the accounts of the company (unless unlimited), the annual return of the company, the company's constitution and various registers that have to be kept at the company's registered office.

Together with formalities and publicity, one may add expense as a disadvantage. However, the expense of setting up a company is not great. There is a charge for the issue of a certificate of incorporation and an annual fee for filing the company's annual return but few other charges are made by the company's registry. The cost of the annual audit may well be a deterrent, however, in the case of a limited company, although small companies are exempted from the statutory audit.

Two other disadvantages of incorporation may be mentioned here. These are the rules on the maintenance of capital that apply to companies and which are much stricter than in relation to partnerships and the remaining vestigal rules on *ultra vires* that limit a company's freedom of manoeuvre. Partnerships by contrast are free to do what is legal within the law of the land.

## 1.2 Types of companies

There are various classifications of companies that may be made.

### 1.2.1 Chartered company

A company may be chartered, that is, set up by a charter from the Crown, and may then derive its powers from the charter. The very first companies were of this variety, for example, the East India Company, the Massachusetts Bay Company, the Hudson's Bay Company. Today, chartered companies are not of economic significance but they still exist. Generally, they are not trading concerns. They may be professional organisations – the Institute of Chartered Accountants of England and Wales is an example. They may be local government corporations, for example, the Corporation of Chesterfield. Perhaps the most famous chartered company of them all is the British Broadcasting Corporation.

### 1.2.2 Statutory company

A further type of company is the statutory company. In Victorian England, there was a great plethora of incorporations. Each company had to be set up by a separate Act of Parliament. During this period of industrial revolution, the great mass of companies involved public utilities such as gas and water, or transportation such as canal companies and railway companies. Today, there are few statutory companies. The process is too cumbersome for periods of massive economic activity, as each company is incorporated by a separate act of Parliament.

### 1.2.3 Registered company

The third type of company in this classification is the most common of all. This is the registered company. There were problems with incorporation by charter or by statute in that these forms of incorporation were cumbersome and inconvenient. This ultimately led Parliament to act to make it simpler to incorporate. Registered companies originated with the Joint Stock Companies Act of 1844 when Gladstone was President of the Board of Trade. Limited liability was not introduced until the Limited Liability Act 1855. The current Companies Act under which registration may be sought by companies is the Companies Act of 2006. Provided a company complies with the formalities set out in the Act, it will be registered, that is, its name will be added to the list of registered companies and a file will be opened in its name at Companies House in Cardiff. In fact, today, clearly a manual register is not opened, the company's registered details are kept and are available for inspection at Cardiff and in London (and in Edinburgh for Scottish companies).

The Registrar of Companies for England and Wales is situated at Crown Way, Cardiff, CF14 3UZ. The Registrar is Head of a Government agency called Companies House.

The Registrar of Companies for Scotland is based at 37 Castle Terrace, Edinburgh, EH1 2EB.

As noted, in order to register a company, the company's constitution, the Articles of Association, must be delivered to the Registrar. This is submitted together with an application for registration providing information such as the company's name, the part of the United Kingdom where the registered office is to be situated, and whether members have limited liability, and, if so, whether it is limited by shares or by guarantee. It will also state whether the company is public or private. If the company is to have a share capital then a statement of capital and initial shareholdings must also be filed together with the application for registration. If the company is a company limited by guarantee, then a statement of the guarantee must be filed.

There needs to be a statement of who the directors are and if the company is a public company then there must be a statement of who is to be the secretary.

These documents must be accompanied by a statement of compliance to the effect that the requirements of the Act have been complied with.

Companies can be incorporated by electronic filing. This is likely to become more significant.

### 1.2.4 Limited and unlimited company

Another form of classification of companies is the distinction between a company limited by shares, a company limited by guarantee, a company limited by guarantee with share capital and an unlimited company.

Most companies are limited by shares. Trading companies will need to raise share capital with which to purchase assets which they need for running their businesses. Companies limited by guarantee are the media, usually utilised by charities, including educational institutions such as the London School of Economics. Such companies do not need capital with which to trade but may wish to have some of the other advantages of incorporation such as the ability to hold property in their own name. Since the Companies Act 1980, it has not been possible to create new companies limited by guarantee with a share capital but there are some companies falling into this category which existed in 1980 and remain registered companies. If the company is an unlimited one, as has already been mentioned, there will be no obligation to file annual accounts. However, this advantage must be balanced against the disadvantage that the members of the unlimited company will have unlimited liability and may be called upon to contribute to the company's assets if the company goes into liquidation.

### 1.2.5 Public and private company

Long in gestation, the Companies Act 2006 has finally reached the statute book. One of the declared aims of the statute is to cater for private companies as a priority. Thus, for example, there is a provision for model articles for private companies limited by shares and by guarantee, quite distinct from model articles for public companies.

A fundamental distinction pervading the whole of company law is the distinction between public and private companies and this, of course, is retained. Most companies are private but the more important larger companies are public companies. The basic distinction is that a public company may offer its shares and debentures to the public whilst a private company may not do so (see s755 CA 2006).

S757 CA 2006 provides for a prohibition order restraining a proposed contravention of the section. If a company acts in contravention of s755 then it may be required to re-register as a public company under s758 CA 2006. Whilst, if the court does not make an order for re-registration, it may either make a remedial order under s759 requiring any person knowingly concerned in the contravention of the section to offer to purchase any of the securities on appropriate terms where a person is affected by the contravention, or may make an order for the compulsory winding up of the company.

A further distinction is the capital requirement first introduced in the Companies Act 1980 which requires that a public company must have a minimum subscribed share capital of £50,000 (s763 CA 2006). This must be paid up to at least 25% so at least £12,500 must already have been raised by the issue of shares. A public company must furthermore have a trading certificate before it begins trading in addition to its certificate of incorporation (s761 CA 2006). This trading certificate will only be issued once the registrar of companies is satisfied that the company has fulfilled the formalities of the Act and raised the required minimum capital.

The name of the company will indicate whether the company is public or private. The description 'public limited company' or as abbreviated 'plc' (or Welsh equivalent 'ccc' and 'cwmni cyhoeddus cyfyngedig') will indicate that the company is a public one. By contrast, if the company is expressed to be 'limited' or as abbreviated 'ltd' or 'cyfyngedig' or as abbreviated 'cyf', the company is a private company (see ss58 and 59 CA 2006).

### 1.2.6 Community interest companies

A new form of company was created by the Companies (Audit, Investigations and Community Enterprise) Act 2004 (see s6 of the Companies Act 2006). The Companies (Audit, Investigations and Community Enterprise) Act 2002 provides in s26 that this is a new type of company for those wanting to establish social enterprises. The community interest company must set out an object in its memorandum such that a reasonable person might consider that the carrying on of the object would be for the benefit of the community (s35(3)). Furthermore, surpluses should normally be reinvested for the purposes of the community interest company rather than being distributed to shareholders (s30).

Such companies will not have charitable status, even if their objects are wholly charitable. A community interest company should register with Companies House as a company limited by guarantee or a company limited by shares, and then will apply for community interest company status to the community interest company regulator (ss27 and 36 of the Act). They must adopt a suitable constitution providing for the pursuit of the community interest object and provisions consistent with community interest companies such as restrictions on the transfer and distribution of the company's assets, and if the Regulator is satisfied that the company will pursue purposes beneficial to the community, then the company will be registered as a community interest company.

Community interest companies must produce an annual community interest report. This report will set out what the company has done during the year to benefit the community.

Some companies such as party political institutions may not gain community interest company status, by virtue of regulation.

Community interest companies will be more lightly regulated than charities but do not enjoy charitable status. It may be the appropriate vehicle for social enterprise if it is felt appropriate to incorporate with limited liability, and if flexibility is desired along with an organisational structure, membership and governance.

The name of the community interest company, if it is private, must end with 'Community Interest Company' or 'C.I.C.', or 'Cwmni Buddiant Cymunedol' or 'C.B.C.' for companies registering documents in Welsh, whereas if it is a public limited community interest company, then the appropriate company names will end with 'Community Interest Public Limited Company' or 'Community Interest P.L.C.', or 'Cwmni Buddiant Cymunedol Cyhoeddus Cyfyngedig' or Cwmni Buddiant C.C.C.', if it is desired to register documents in Welsh.

### 1.2.7 Legislation

Over the years Company Law has become increasingly complex and there is a very large and detailed set of rules governing Company Law in addition to the great welter of cases that affects this area.

The Companies Act 2006 is the current consolidation measure of Company Law. It is the longest piece of legislation on any subject to have passed through the British Parliament.

Additionally, there are other pieces of legislation, for example, the Insolvency Act 1986, as well as the Financial Services and Markets Act 2000, which are also important.

### 1.2.8 European law

Lord Denning has described the Treaty of Rome as being 'like an incoming tide which flows into the estuaries and up the rivers of English law' *(HP Bulmer v J Bollinger SA (1974))*.

Although this tide has not flowed into the channels of Company Law, it has gushed into its streams and affected English Company Law.

There is provision in the European Union's treaties for the harmonisation of the laws of member states in certain areas. The Council and the Commission are authorised to co-ordinate 'to the necessary extent the safeguards which, for the protection of the interests of members and others, are required of companies or firms ... with a view to making such safeguards equivalent throughout the Community' (art. 44(2) (g) Treaty of Rome).

This process of harmonisation is carried out by means of Directives. These are measures addressed to member states of the European Union to enact their provisions as law, leaving it to the member state to determine exactly how this is to be achieved. Of thirteen proposals so far, three draft directives have not yet been implemented, the fifth, tenth and thirteenth, and the ninth, has been withdrawn.

In 2001, the European Commission set up a High Level Group of Company Law Experts to consider the modernisation of Company Law in Europe. A report was produced by the Group: A Modern Regulatory Framework for Company Law in Europe. This may be found at the European Commission Internal Market website: www.europa.eu.int/com/internal. This website contains fuller details about current developments in EU Company Law.

### 1.2.9 Societas Europaea

From October 2004, it has been possible under Regulation (EC) No. 2157/2001 to set up a European public limited-liability company or 'Societas Europaea'. Such companies can be set up where there is co-operation between at least two European companies from different member states.

A Societas Europaea can be set up by merger, as a holding company or as a subsidiary. Once registered a Societas Europaea has legal personality. It must have a registered office and the head office must be in the same member state. Companies House produces an introductory guide on the Societas Europaea. It is available on the Companies House website: www.companieshouse.gov.uk.

## SUMMARY

## A company or a partnership

A company is a separate entity in law and certain advantages flow from this:

(a) access to limited liability;
(b) separation of ownership from control;
(c) perpetual succession;
(d) transferability of shares;
(e) raising finance.

A partnership may be set up without formalities, without publicity and without expense.

The profits of a company are subject to corporation tax, the profits of a partnership are subject to schedular income tax in the hands of the partners.

## Types of company

There are various classifications of companies:

(a) companies may be chartered, statutory or registered. The vast majority are registered;
(b) companies may be limited by shares, limited by guarantee or unlimited. A few are limited by guarantee with a share capital. Unlimited companies do not need to file annual accounts;

(c) an important distinction is between private companies and public companies. Most companies are private, but only public companies can offer their shares or debentures to the public. All companies quoted on the Stock Exchange are public.

(d) companies engaged in social enterprise may engage in activity via incorporation by becoming community interest companies.

## Further reading

Cath, IGF, 'Freedom of establishment of companies: a new step towards completion of the internal market' 6YEL 1986 247.

Freedman, J, 'Small business and the corporate form: burden or privilege?' (1994) 57 MLR 555.

Hicks, A, 'Corporate form: questioning the unsung hero' (1997) JBL 306.

Howell, C, 'The Company White Paper: a descriptive overview (2005) 26 Co Law 203.

Jacobs, FG, 'The Basic Freedoms of the EEC Treaty and Company Law' (1992) 13 Co Law 4.

Kahn-Freund, O, 'Some reflections on company law reform' (1944) 7 MLR 44.

Konard, AF, 'The European Alternative to Uniformity in Corporation Laws' (1991) 89 Mich L Rev 2150.

Sheikh, S, 'UK company law reform: towards a 21st century corporate revolution' (1996) 7 ICCLR 119.

# The *Salomon* principle and the corporate veil

## 2.1 Introduction

As has been noted, a key feature of the company is that it is a legal person with a separate existence from the company's members (i.e. shareholders where the company has shares) or its directors. From this separate personality flow many consequences.

The House of Lords' decision in *Salomon v A Salomon & Co Ltd (1897)*, established the separate identity of the company.

Aron Salomon and his boot and shoe business have done for company law what Mrs Carlill and her smoke ball did for the law of contract and what Mrs Donoghue and her adulterated ginger beer did for the law of tort.

Mr Salomon transferred his business to a limited company and he and six other members of his family subscribed the company's memorandum; the purchase price was £38,782. Salomon took 20,001 shares and the six other family members took one share each. Debentures (loan stock) of £10,000 and £8,782 cash were paid to Salomon as the balance of the purchase price. The business floundered and was wound up with liabilities in excess of its assets by £7,733. The company's liquidator claimed that the company's business was still Salomon's, in that the company was merely a sham to limit Salomon's liability for debts incurred in carrying it on and the repayment of Salomon's debenture should be postponed until the company's other creditors were satisfied. At first instance, Vaughan Williams J agreed with the liquidator. He held that Salomon's sole purpose in forming the company was to use it as an agent to run his business for him.

The Court of Appeal reached the same conclusion but for different reasons. It took the view that the principle of limited liability was a privilege conferred by the Companies Acts only on genuinely independent shareholders and not on 'one substantial person and six mere dummies'.

The House of Lords unanimously reversed the Court of Appeal. Lord Halsbury LC in *Salomon v A Salomon & Co Ltd* said:

> I must pause here, to point out that the statute enacts nothing as to the extent or degree of interest which may be held by each of the seven (subscribers) or

as to the proportion of influence possessed by one or the majority of the shareholders over the others. One share is enough. Still less is it possible to contend that the motive of becoming shareholders or of making them shareholders is a field of enquiry which the statute itself recognises as legitimate, if there are shareholders, they are shareholders for all purposes; and even if the statute was silent as to the recognition of trust, I should be prepared to hold that if six of them were the cestuis que trust of the seventh, whatever might be their rights *inter se*, the statute would have made them shareholders to all intents and purposes with their respective rights and liabilities, and dealing with them in their relation to the company, the only relations which I believe the law would sanction would be that they were corporators of the body corporate.

This case thus established one of the basic articles of faith of British company law, indeed of company law of all common law systems, that a company is a legal person independent and distinct from its shareholders and its managers.

This, at least, was the theory. However, the principle in *Salomon's* case has not been without its detractors. Otto Kahn-Freund in 'Some Reflections on Company Law Reform' in (1944) MLR 54, was critical of the principle in the case. He says, 'However, owing to the ease with which companies can be formed in this country, and owing to the rigidity with which the courts applied the corporate entity concept ever since the calamitous decision in *Salomon v Salomon & Co Ltd*, a single trader or a group of traders are almost tempted by the law to conduct their business in the form of a limited company, even where no particular business risk is involved, and where no outside capital is required.

This state of affairs would not necessarily call for reform, if it were not for the fact that the courts had failed to give that protection to the business creditors, which should be the corollary of the privilege of limited liability'.

Kahn-Fruend continues (page 57), 'What can be done? How is it possible to check the one-man company and other abuses of company law for purposes which it was never meant to serve? Is it conceivable that *Salomon's* case can be abrogated by legislation? Could the interests of outside creditors be protected by a general clause under which persons owning a controlling interest in a company would be liable for its debts? Or could there be a provision according to which a company would be deemed to act as agent for the owners of controlling interests'?

Nor is Kahn-Freund alone. Clive Schmitthoff in 'The Wholly Owned and the Controlled Subsidiary' [1978] JBL 218, considers problems that present themselves in connection with wholly owned and controlled subsidiaries (see section 2.2.2.2).

Schmitthoff looks at the decision in *Salomon* in the narrower context of subsidiary companies, although he analyses the decision and points out some difficulties that it presents.

He looks specifically at two separate problems; one concerns the problem of jurisdiction where the courts of the host country (of a subsidiary) may wish to exercise jurisdiction over the parent company in the home country. He also considers the separate problem of the liability of the parent for the debts of subsidiaries.

'As regards jurisdiction', he suggests 'the courts and authorities of the host country should assume jurisdiction over the parent company if it carries on substantial business in the host country by means of wholly owned or controlled subsidiaries, or by means of branch offices'.

'As regards liability, the parent company should be liable for the debts of wholly owned and controlled subsidiaries if it employed these dependent companies as agents, and it should be rebuttably presumed that it used these subsidiaries in that manner'.

Schmitthoff continues, 'If the subsidiary is wholly owned, there should be a conclusive presumption that it is controlled by the parent, and if the parent holds more than 50% of the voting power of the subsidiary, but does not own the subsidiary wholly, there should be a rebuttable presumption to the effect that the subsidiary is controlled' (p. 229).

Notwithstanding such statements and occasional exceptional judicial instances apart the principle of separate identity has been consistently applied.

In the New Zealand case of *Lee v Lee's Air Farming Ltd (1961)*, which went to the Privy Council, Lee owned all the shares but one in the company that he founded. His wife held the other share. Lee was governing director of the company whose business was spraying crops from the air. When he was killed in a flying accident while on company business, his widow was held to be entitled to recover compensation from the company for his estate as the company was quite separate and distinct from her husband its employee.

It has sometimes been said that the American realist school in jurisprudence explains far more about how judicial decisions are made than the system of precedent. Thus decisions may be put down to whether the judge has a fondness of, or aversion to red heads, and what the judge has had for breakfast. This may explain some of the cases in this area of law, which are notoriously difficult to reconcile one with another.

It is proposed to contrast some cases here. The case of *Lee v Lee's Air Farming (1961)*, can be contrasted with *Malyon v Plummer (1964)*. Here the plaintiff's husband had been killed in a fatal accident. This has been caused by the admitted negligence of the defendant. The husband owned all but one of the shares in a company. He worked a six day week for the company and was the only breadwinner. The plaintiff owned the other share and received a substantial salary for a limited amount of part-time work, which she performed on a casual basis. The wife sought to claim for the loss of her livelihood, asserting that when the husband was killed, the company was also effectively killed.

In the Court of Appeal, Sellers LJ said, 'In my opinion, the inter-position of FP Malyon Ltd, if that is how it should be regarded, does not prevent the court assessing truly the loss which the wife has suffered. The husband's business, FP Malyon Ltd, has been destroyed by the loss of the husband, and it is clear that the revenue was, in substance, derived from him. The decision in *Salomon v Salomon Co* need not blind one to the essential facts of dependency and require a finding of fact that is contrary to the true financial position as distinct from an artificial or ficticious one'.

The common feature in *Lee v Lee's Air Farming* and *Malyon v Plummer* is that in a loose sense justice can be seen to be done in both cases. In *Lee*, by asserting the separate identity of the company, the widow was able to benefit from the New Zealand Workman's Compensation Act and obtain compensation. In a similar way, by destroying the corporate façade in *Malyon v Plummer*, the widow was able to assert that when the husband died the company also died, and that they were one and the same thing, and thus she was able to recover compensation for the loss of livelihood. Two widows recovering compensation by opposite legal arguments. Judges of a certain age may well have an instinctive sympathy to widows.

It is often difficult to reconcile the cases and to find a coherent body of doctrine in this area.

Two further cases may be contrasted: *Buchan v Secretary of State for Employment and Ivey v Secretary of State for Employment (1997)*, on one hand and *Secretary of State for Trade & Industry v Bottrill (2000)* on the other hand.

In *Buchan v Secretary of State for Employment* and *Ivey v Secretary of State for Employment (1997)*, the Employment Appeal Tribunal distinguished the Privy Council decision in *Lee* in two joined appeals. The two directors involved held a half and a controlling interest respectively in their companies. It was held that they were not employees for the purpose of making a claim against the National Insurance Fund.

The tribunal considered that such directors could block decisions at board level, including decisions relating to their dismissal and that this was not consistent with being an employee. No doubt, the context of the dispute influenced the decision as the directors were seeking compensation as employees for dismissal. The Employment Appeal Tribunal took the view that it is not the purpose of the legislation to fund compensation for those whose businesses have failed.

However, in *Secretary of State for Trade and Industry v Bottrill (2000)*, the veil was not lifted. Bottrill was managing director of Magnatac UK Ltd. He held the only share. There was one other director. Bottrill had a contract of employment which set out all his duties, his hours, sick pay, etc. He paid tax and NI. The company became insolvent and he applied for a redundancy payment. It was held by the Court of Appeal, with Lord Woolff MR presiding, that it was a question of fact whether Bottrill was an employee or not. The fact that he was a controlling shareholder was not decisive. The question was whether there was a genuine contract. In the instant case the tribunal had been entitled to conclude that there was a genuine contract.

Two further cases may be contrasted.

In *Macaura v Northern Assurance Company Ltd (1925)*, where the owner of a timber business incorporated the business but continued to insure the property in his own name, it was held when the property was destroyed that he had no insurable interest and so could not claim on the policy. The property was no longer his, it now belonged to the company. It may well have been relevant in this case that the fire occurred soon after the insurance policy had been renewed. There was at least a hint in the case that this may have been a relevant factor in the decision. Is this a hint of arson?

Nevertheless, the case may be contrasted with the Supreme Court of Canada decision in *Constitution Insurance Co of Canada v Kosmopoulos (1987)*. Kosmopoulos was the sole shareholder and director of a company, Kosmopoulos Ltd, which carried on a retail business. He conducted the business as a sole proprietorship (as it had formerly been), and was himself the lessee of the business premises. He took out insurance in his own name. Damage was caused by fire to the assets of the company, and the insurers denied liability. Kosmopoulos' actions succeeded at trial and in the Ontario Court of Appeal. On further appeal by the insurers to the Supreme Court of Canada, the appeal was dismissed. It was held that it was not necessary that the insured should have a legally enforceful interest in the property. It was sufficient if he had a relation to, or concern, in the subject matter of the insurance, whereby he would suffer a loss upon the occurrence of the insured risks. Wilson J in the Supreme Court said that, 'Mr Kosmopoulos, as a sole shareholder of the company, was so placed with respect to the assets of the business as to have benefit from their existence and prejudice from the destruction. He had a moral certainly of advantage or benefit from those assets but for the fire. He had, therefore, an insurable interest in them, capable of supporting the insurance policy and is entitled to recover under it'.

There is no suggestion that the law in Canada is materially different from the law in the United Kingdom. Common law countries all seem to suffer from the same confusion of clinging to the *Salomon* principles of the basic separation of the company from its controllers, whilst at the same time undermining it with a variety of exceptions and qualifications which are considered in this chapter. Those hoping for a clear consistent message in this area will hope in vain, as the three case couplets above demonstrate.

### 2.1.1 Lifting the veil

Whilst the decision in Salomon's case has certainly been open to criticism, and the cases are far from consistent, in *Adams v Cape Industries plc (1990)*, the Court of Appeal held that an English company, whose business was mining asbestos in South Africa, was not present in the United States through another member of the corporate group. Slade LJ had said: '... save in cases which turn on the wording of particular statutes or contracts, the court is not free to disregard the principle of *Salomon v A Salomon & Co Ltd* merely because it considers that justice so requires'.

However, the Court of Appeal's view in *Adams v Cape Industries plc* has not always been followed faithfully. In *Creasey v Breachwood Motors Ltd (1993)*,

Richard Southwell QC, sitting as a deputy High Court judge, allowed the substitution of one company for another as defendant holding the second company liable for the debts of the first. This decision, however, was itself disapproved in *Ord & Another v Belhaven Pubs Ltd (1998)* by the Court of Appeal. The defendant, Belhaven Pubs Ltd, appealed against a decision of Judge Alton whereby the deputy judge ordered that the plaintiffs be granted leave to substitute Ascot Holdings plc as the defendant in an action brought by the plaintiffs against Belhaven Pubs Ltd, claiming damages for misrepresentation and breach of warranty. The Court of Appeal held that, in the absence of any impropriety, sham or concealment in the restructuring of the Group, it would be wrong to lift the corporate veil in order to make the shareholders of the defendant company liable instead of the company itself.

The principle of separate identity was also restated by Lightman J in *Acatos and Hutcheson plc v Watson (1995)*. He considered that the principle of separate identity should be upheld unless there was a specific statutory provision or some other contractual term or established common law principle to the contrary. He said 'outside these exceptions [the company] is entitled to organise and conduct its affairs in the expectation that the court will apply the principle of *Salomon v A Salomon & Co Ltd* in the ordinary way'. The case concerned the company acquiring all the issued share capital of a company called Acatos Ltd and Acatos and Hutcheson plc sought a declaration that the proposal did not fall foul of the provision prohibiting a company from purchasing its own shares, where Acatos Ltd's sole asset was a 29% holding in *Acatos and Hutcheson* plc. It was held that there was no breach of the provision.

## 2.2 Exceptions to the *Salomon* principle

However, the principle in *Salomon's case* does give way to exceptions. These are of two types: statutory and judicial.

### 2.2.1 Statutory exceptions

It was formerly the case that if an officer of the company did not use the company name in full on any letter, order for goods or money, etc, then that company officer was liable to the other party and also liable to a fine (s349 (4) CA 1985). However, the Companies Act 2006 alters this provision. S82 CA 2006 provides that the Secretary of State may make regulations requiring companies to display specified information at specified locations on documents, and on request to those with whom they deal. This information would include the name of the company. If the company then sought to enforce contractual rights against the other party, then these proceedings would be dismissed if the other party had a claim against the company which he was unable to pursue by reason of the company's breach of regulations, or if he had suffered some financial loss by reason of the company's breach of the regulations unless the court considered it just and equitable to permit the proceedings to continue (s83 CA 2006). Breach of the regulations under s82 would also amount to a criminal offence on the part of the company and on the part of every officer in default (s84 CA 2006).

If the company's business has been carried on with intent to defraud creditors or for any fraudulent purposes, the court, on the application of the liquidator, may declare that the persons who were knowingly parties to the fraud are liable to make such contributions (if any) to the company's assets as the court thinks proper (s213 of the Insolvency Act 1986). Whatever contributions the court orders will be distributed amongst the company's creditors and should therefore compensate for the loss caused to creditors by the fraudulent carrying of the business (Morphitis v Bernasconi (2003)). This section has a criminal counterpart in s993 of the Companies Act 2006. The section is applicable not merely to directors but to other persons who are trading through the medium of the company. By contrast, s214 of the Insolvency Act 1986, which deals with wrongful trading, empowers the court to make a declaration in the situation of insolvent liquidation against a person who was a director or shadow director who knew, or ought to have known, that there was no reasonable prospect of the company avoiding insolvent liquidation.

In *Re Produce Marketing Consortium (No 2) (1989)*, Knox J drew attention to two material differences from s213:

> ... First, the requirement for an intent to defraud and fraudulent purpose was not retained as an essential, and with it goes what Maugham J called 'the need for actual dishonesty involving real moral blame'.

He continued:

> The second enlargement is that the test to be applied by the court has become one under which the director in question is to be judged by the standards of what can reasonably be expected of a person fulfilling his functions, and showing reasonable diligence in doing so.

On the facts of the case, two directors of a fruit importing business were held liable. The directors of the company had been warned by the company's auditors of the company's serious financial plight.

In this case, the judge ordered that the directors should contribute to the company's assets the amount by which they had been depleted by the directors conduct, i.e. once again the aim is compensatory.

In *Re Purpoint Ltd (1991)*, the judge decided that the right measure of liability for wrongful trading was the increase in the net liabilities of the company which had been occasioned by the continuance of trading after the director should have known that the company was destined for liquidation. (See wrongful trading.)

There are some other situations in respect of insolvency where the veil is lifted. Section 216 of the Insolvency Act makes it an offence for a person who is a director, or shadow director, of a company that has gone into insolvent liquidation to be in any way concerned in the next five years in the formation or management of a company with a name similar to that of the original company. Section 217 makes such persons personally liable in such a situation.

A further provision applicable in situations of insolvency is s15 of the Company Directors Disqualification Act 1986, which provides that a person who has been disqualified from acting in the management of a company is personally liable for the company debts if he acts in contravention of this order.

In the case of a public limited company, if it acts before it has obtained its trading certificate, then the company and its officers are liable to fines. Furthermore, if the company fails to comply with its obligations within 21 days, the directors of the company are jointly and severally liable to indemnify any other party to the transaction in respect of any loss or damage suffered by reason of the company's failure to comply with its obligations (s767(3) CA 2006).

Group accounts have to be filed where companies are in a group. This is in addition to the separate sets of accounts that have to be filed for each of the constituent companies. In order to determine if a company is part of a group, clearly the veil is being lifted. To determine if a holding/subsidiary relationship exists, it is necessary to examine ownership of the shares, membership of the board of directors, or control of the board or company in general meeting (s399 CA 2006).

There are many other statutory examples. For example, under s6 of the Law of Property Act 1969, it is provided that an individual landlord is able to resist the renewal of a tenancy if he can show that he needs the premises for his own commercial purposes. This is extended to cover the situation where he needs the premises for the purposes of a company which he controls. See *Tunstall v Steigmann (1962)*.

### 2.2.2 Judicial lifting of the veil

It is difficult to identify a consistent thread running through the decided cases indicating when the veil will be lifted. It seems to be, as the American Realists (commenting on the nature of legal decisions) indicate, dependent on the particular judge and what the judge has had for breakfast! However, it is possible to identify certain consistent themes in the cases.

As Murray Pickering in 'The Company as a Separate Legal Entity' (1968) 31MLR 481 has demonstrated, there is a remarkable range of judicial expletives used where difficulties are experienced by the courts in separating the company as a legal entity from its members. These include, as Pickering notes, for example, 'a mere nominee', 'a mere fraud', 'an agent', 'a trustee', 'a mere device', 'a myth and a fiction' (*Broderib v Salomon (1895)*), 'a pretended association' (*Salomon v Salomon & Co (1897)*), 'a bubble' (*Re Carl Hirth (1899)*), 'an unreal' procedure (*Attorney General for Dominion of Canada v Standard Trust Co of New York (1911)*), 'an alias', 'a name' (*Re Darby (1911)*), 'an artificial legal thing', 'a legal abstraction' (*Continental Tyre & Rubber Co (GB) Ltd v Daimler Co Ltd (1915)*), 'mere machinery' (*Daimler Co v Continental Tyre & Rubber Co (1916)*), 'a metaphysical conception' (*Lennards Carrying Co Ltd v Asiatic Petroleum Co Ltd (1915)*), 'a sham or bogus' (*R v Grubb (1915)*), 'an abstract conception' (*Houghton & Co v Nothard Lowe & Wills Ltd (1928)*), 'a simulacrum' (*EBM Co Ltd v Dominon Bank (1937)*), 'a cloak' (*Gilford Motor Co Ltd v Horne (1933)*), 'a mere alter ego' (*Pegler v Craven (1952)*), 'an abstract being' (*Austin Reed Ltd v Royal Assurance Co Ltd [18 July 1956 CA]*), 'a creature' (*IRC v Lithgows Ltd (1960)*), 'a screen'. (*Barclays Bank v IRC (1960)*), and even 'a blacksheep' (*IRC v Sansome (1921)*).

### 2.2.2.1 Fraud situations

The court will lift the veil to prevent fraud or sharp practice. In *Jones v Lipman (1962)*, a vendor of land sought to evade a decree of specific performance of a contract for the sale of a piece of land by conveying the land to a company which he had purchased for the purpose of sidestepping the obligation.

The court held that the acquisition of the company and the conveyance of the land to it was a mere 'cloak or sham' to evade the contract of sale. The veil was lifted.

By contrast, in the Australian case of *Electric Light and Power Supply Co Ltd v Cormack (1911)*, the veil was not lifted. Here the New South Wales Supreme Court neglected to lift the veil. The defendant contracted to use the plaintiff's power in his business for two years exclusively. During this time he sold his business to a company which he managed which used another source of power. Rich AJ refused to lift the veil saying there was no intention to create injustice. It seems that the intention aspect was the determining factor in the case. This, of course, was not held to be significant in *Jones v Lipman*. In the opinion of the author, the *Jones v Lipman* decision is preferable. It should not be necessary to show an intention to create injustice in such cases, merely that injustice has been the result of the defendant's actions.

In *Gilford Motor Co v Horne (1933)*, an employee who was subject to a restraint of trade clause set up a company to circumvent the restriction. He claimed that the company was not bound by the restrictive covenant as it was a separate legal person distinct from himself and was not a party to the contract between him and his former employer. He proceeded to operate a garage in Highgate, London through the company in competition with his former employer. The company's shares were allotted to his wife and an employee of the company who were appointed directors. The court held that, since the defendant in reality controlled the company, its formation was a sham. An injunction was therefore issued against him restraining him from competing through the medium of the company.

A similar desire to prevent abuse is evident in *Re Bugle Press Ltd (1961)*. The issued capital of Bugle Press Ltd was £10,000. £4,500 each was held by two directors, Jackson and Shaw. The applicant Treby held the other £1,000 of shares. Jackson and Shaw formed another company of which they were the only two members and this company offered to acquire all the shares of Bugle Press Ltd.

The intention of Jackson and Shaw was to compulsorily acquire the shares of Treby under what are now the 'squeeze-out' and 'sell-out' provisions contained in Part 28 Chapter 3 of the Companies Act 2006. In short, they were using the takeover provisions to rid themselves of a difficult dissentient member. The court held that Treby was entitled to a declaration that Jackson and Shaw could not acquire his shares as the offeror and the holders of 90% of the acquired company were the same and the section was being used to expropriate a minority shareholder.

Fraud was also at issue in *Wallersteiner v Moir (1974)*. In this case, the defendant Moir had accused the plaintiff of a number of fraudulent acts. The court had to consider whether a loan made by a company to another company which was under the control of its director was illegal under s197 fo the Act which prohibits the giving of a loan to a director. Lord Denning MR considered that the company was the puppet of Dr Wallersteiner as the company was his creature and therefore that the loan should be treated as a loan made to him.

### 2.2.2.2 Group situations

Another situation where the veil is often lifted is in group situations where the parent company and a subsidiary are treated as one entity if they carry on the same business. The principle does not seem to be consistently applied, however. In *Smith, Stone and Knight Ltd v Birmingham Corporation (1939)*, the court treated a subsidiary company as the agent of its holding company (an approach that is at odds with the decision in the *Salomon* case itself).

Similarly, in *Firestone Tyre & Rubber Co Ltd v Lewellin (1957)*, an American company which operated through a wholly owned subsidiary in England was held liable to pay United Kingdom tax as the American company was carrying on business in the United Kingdom through the subsidiary.

In contrast, in *Harold Holdsworth & Co (Wakefield) Ltd v Caddies (1955)*, the question arose as to whether the director of a holding company could be assigned duties in relation to subsidiary companies. The House of Lords held that this was indeed possible on the basis that the companies were part of the same group enterprise.

In *DHN Food Distributors Ltd v Tower Hamlets London Borough Council (1976)*, the Court of Appeal had to consider a case involving the expropriation of property. A company, DHN Food Products, was formed to carry on the business of importing and distributing groceries. The premises the company traded from were in fact owned by Bronze, a wholly owned subsidiary of DHN. Bronze and DHN had the same directors. The London Borough of Tower Hamlets acquired the property to build houses on the site. Compensation was payable under the relevant legislation for loss of title. Compensation was also payable for disturbance of the business. However, compensation for disturbance of the business was only payable if the business disturbed belonged to the title holder. The operator of the business here was the holding company, the title holder was the subsidiary company.

The Court of Appeal treated the companies as one entity. Lord Denning MR said:

> We all know that, in many respects, a group of companies are treated together for the purpose of general accounts, balance sheets, profit and loss account. They are treated as one concern ... This is especially the case when a parent company owns all the share of the subsidiaries, so much so that it can control every movement of the subsidiaries.

Lord Denning MR relied heavily on the House of Lords decision in *Harold Holdsworth & Co (Wakefield) Ltd v Caddies* in *DHN (1976)* at page 860. He claimed it was a striking instance 'of the tendency to ignore the separate legal entities of various companies within a group'. In fact, Viscount Kilmuir LC, Lord Morton of Henryton and Lord Reid all arrived at their decisions because the appellant company owned all the shares in the subsidiary and could therefore precure the appointment of the respondent as managing director of the subsidiary company. There is nothing in their judgement to suggest that the separate identities of parent and subsidiary companies in a group should be disregarded.

The approach is not consistent. In *Lonrho Ltd v Shell Petroleum Company Ltd (1981)*, the House of Lords considered a claim by the plaintiff for discovery of documents in the possession of companies that were wholly owned subsidiaries of the defendant companies. The wholly owned subsidiaries were incorporated and resident in South Africa and Zimbabwe (or Southern Rhodesia as it then was). The House of Lords took the view that even though these companies were wholly owned subsidiaries, there was a degree of autonomy consequent upon these companies operating overseas. It felt that it was inappropriate to lift the veil in such a situation distinguishing *DHN Food Distributors Ltd v Tower Hamlets London Borough Council*. Interestingly, the Court of Appeal had taken the same view as the House of Lords and Lord Denning MR had stated that the parent companies had no 'power' over the subsidiaries. He considered the case to be quite different from the *DHN Food Distributors case*.

Similar issues were raised in *Woolfson v Strathclyde Regional Council (1978)*. The House of Lords in this case considered the situation where a compulsory purchase order had been made over certain shops in Glasgow. The shops were owned by Solomon Woolfson and by Solfred Holdings Ltd, the shares of which were held at two thirds by Woolfson and one third by Woolfson's wife. The shop premises were occupied by a company called M and L Campbell (Glasgow) Ltd which operated the business of costumiers of wedding garments. The share capital of Campbell was 1,000 shares of which 999 of these shares were held by Woolfson, the remaining share by his wife. Woolfson was the sole director of Campbell and he managed the business. His wife also worked for Campbell and provided valuable expertise in relation to the selling of the garments. Woolfson and Solfred Holdings Ltd claimed compensation for disturbance of the business. They argued that the business carried on on the premises was truly their business, conducted by Campbell as their agent so that, since they were the true occupiers of the premises, they were also entitled to compensation for disturbance. They placed reliance upon the decisions in *Smith, Stone and Knight Ltd v Birmingham Corporation* and *DHN Food Distributors Ltd v Tower Hamlets London Borough Council*.

Lord Keith, in the course of his judgment in the House of Lords, considered that the case was distinct from the decision in *DHN Food Distributors*. The position in that case, his Lordship said, was that compensation for disturbance was claimed by a group of three limited companies. In the case before him, the company that carried on the business, Campbell, had no control whatever over the owners of the land, Solfred and Woolfson. It may be seen that it is sometimes difficult to reconcile the decisions in this area.

Generally the decision in DHN has been seen as an 'aberration' (Rixon 'Lifting the veil between holding and subsidiary companies' (1986). It has been said that the separate entity principle is 'unchallengable by judicial decision' (in *Re The Albazero (1977)*).

Although Salomon is generally applied in group situations, problems do arise where there has been undercapitalisation within a group situation. Lynn Galagher and Peter Ziegler in 'Lifting the corporate veil in the pursuit of justice' [1990] JBL 292, analysed some American cases where undercapitalisation has been the ground for lifting the veil.

In *Chatterley v Omnico (1971)*, the Supreme Court of Utah held a parent company liable for the unpaid wages owed to the employees of a subsidiary company. Similarly, *Herman v Mobile Homes Corporation (1947)* provides an example of the undercapitalisation factor being applied. The Supreme Court of Michigan held that the subsidiaries were merely the alter ego of the parent company as they were undercapitalised. The action had been brought by the plaintiff against Mobile Homes for defective workmanship. Even here, however, the decisions are not uniform. In *Bartle v Home Owners Co-operative (1955)*, the veil was not lifted.

One United States Supreme Court decision where the veil was lifted, where there was undercapitalisation, is *Taylor v Standard Gas and Electric Company (1939)*. Deep Rock Oil Corporation was involved in the production of oil and gas and was a subsidiary of Standard Gas and Electric Company, the defendant. The defendant held virtually all the shares in Deep Rock and controlled its board of directors. The subsidiary was placed in liquidation and the holding company claimed as a creditor. This claim was challenged by the preference shareholders of Deep Rock who argued that Deep Rock was merely the alter ego of Standard. The United States Supreme Court agreed.

In the US it was possible therefore to discern a separate doctrine, where the veil of incorporation is often lifted where there is undercapitalisation within a group. This does not appear to have been a factor in the cases in the United Kingdom, where much seems to depend upon the particular judge or court involved, and there cannot be said to be a coherent thread through the cases. Such is the impact of Lord Denning that the *DHN Food Distributors* case is often cited as the leading case in this area, although the House of Lords has, as has been noted above, on occasion taken a completely different line refusing to lift the veil where the Court of Appeal, particularly when Lord Denning was active, showed a very different approach and was much more willing to lift the veil in group situations.

It seems pretty clear to the author that the *DHN decision* is the aberration rather than the decision setting out the general rule in relation to disregarding the separate identity of companies within a group. An intersting analysis of decided cases from before 1960 up to 1999 is provided in Charles Mitchell's analysis in 'Lifting the Corporate Veil in the English Courts, An Empirical Study' (1999) 3CFILR 15. Mitchell's analysis demonstrates that in decided cases between 40% to 57% of cases involved situations where the veil is lifted. The rate of lifting the veil in decided cases is highest in the 1970s. This could well be the influence of Lord Denning in the Court of Appeal, but interestingly the number of decided cases where the veil is lifted goes up again in the 1990s despite the dicta in the Court of Appeal decision in *Adams v Cape Industries plc.*

Other countries may arrive at different results from the UK. This appears to be the case in continental Europe. For example, in Italy, Article 2362 of the Civil Code of 1942 provides that in cases of insolvency of companies limited by shares the single person who holds the shares of the company will be liable for the debts of the company. This would seem to apply to both natural and legal persons.

Section 322 of the German Code provides that the parent shall be liable jointly and severally for the debts of the wholly owned subsidiary. Similarly, as noted by Schmitthoff in the 'The Wholly owned and the Controlled Subsidiary' [1978] JBL 218, the final draft of the statute for European companies (Bulletin of the European companies 4/75) the debts and liabilities of dependent companies within the group is provided for.

### 2.2.2.3 Miscellaneous situations

There are numerous other decisions where the veil has been lifted. It is difficult to classify these cases. It is therefore appropriate to examine this pot pourri of cases.

A decision of all the members of a company may be binding as a company decision notwithstanding that the decision has not been taken at a company meeting. To determine if the decision is one of all the members the veil has clearly to be lifted; see, for example, *Re Express Engineering Works Ltd (1920)*.

The veil may also be lifted to determine a company's nationality by reference to the nationality of its members. This occurred in *Re FG Films Ltd (1953)*, where the court held that the film *Monsoon* (never an international blockbuster!) was not a British film.

Although the company producing it was incorporated in England, it was controlled by an American corporation.

In *Daimler Co Ltd v Continental Tyre & Rubber Co (GB) Ltd (1916)*, the House of Lords decided that the company, although it was incorporated in England, was an enemy alien as all of its shareholders were German. In *Trebanog Working Mens Club & Institute Ltd v Macdonald (1940)*, the device of the trust was used to circumvent the principle of separate personality. A club incorporated to provide leisure facilities for its members purchased alcohol. The alcohol was sold to the members. The club was prosecuted for selling alcohol without a licence. The court acquitted the club of the charge since it was held that there was no sale as the members in reality owned the alcohol, which was purchased on their behalf by the committee of the club. It was held that the club held the alcohol as trustee for its members and that therefore the beneficial ownership in the alcohol was vested in the members collectively with the result that there was not a sale at all and therefore no criminal offence.

## 2.3 Companies – crimes and torts

Companies may be found liable for offences of strict liability.

This approach requires the precise interpretation of statutes to determine whether a strict liability offence is in issue. This is of importance in areas of licensing, pollution, food safety, etc. However, often, there it a due diligence defence and if the company can demonstrate that it practised due diligence defence and that the lack of diligence was on the part of a person who was not the true embodiment of the company it will escape liability. In *Tesco Supermarkets Ltd v Nattrass (1972)*, the company was charged with an offence under the Trade Descriptions Act 1968 in that certain goods stated to be available were not. The company demonstrated that it had introduced a system to try to ensure that this did not happen. The failure was held to be that of the store manager and not of the company and the company was held not liable.

In *R v Gateway Foodmarkets Ltd (1997)*, a company was held liable under s2(1) of the Health and Safety at Work etc Act 1974. This provides for liability where there is a failure to ensure the health, safety and welfare at work of any employee unless all reasonable precautions have been taken by the company or on its behalf.

The company had failed to provide for the safety of a duty manager at one of its Sheffield branches. He fell to his death into a lift shaft where a trap door had been left open in the control room floor.

In *R v British Steel (1995)*, the court held that it was no defence for the company that the senior management had taken all reasonable care to avoid a breach of the statutory duty, even though the strict liability was qualified by a defence if all reasonably practical steps had been taken. The court took the view that this reasonably practical defence applied not just to senior management but also to those in charge of the dangerous activity.

In *Tesco v Nattrass*, the principle of identification had been established. This means that the state of mind and will of the director can be attributed to the company.

Shortcomings in the identification approach were recognised in the Privy Council case of *Meridian Global Funds Management Asia Ltd v Securities Commission (1995)*. The Privy Council held that in certain cases the court has to determine whose act or knowledge was the company's. Generally, this would be the directing mind and will of the company, but not necessarily so.

*Meridian* was unusual in that a company was convicted of a crime where the individual, whose knowledge was attributed to the company, was not part of the company's directing mind and will. As Lord Hoffman said:

> Whose act (or knowledge or state of mind) was for this purpose intended to count as the act, etc of the company? One finds the answer to this question by applying the usual canons of interpretation, taking into account the language of the rule (if it is a statute) and its content and policy.

The policy of the New Zealand Securities Amendment Act 1988 which was at issue in *Meridian* was to require the immediate disclosure of a substantial security holder. The person here whose knowledge was attributed to the company was the person who acquired the relevant interest with the company's authority.

Sometimes decisions may be surprising, as in *Richmond on Thames Borough Council v Pinn and Wheeler (1989)*, where the company was found not guilty of driving a lorry without a permit.

However, the principles are reasonably straightforward. Difficulties do arise, however, where the crime requires mens rea on the part of the company. Here the courts have traditionally required that the guilty mind should be that of the company's directing mind and will, or as was said by Lord Denning MR in *Bolton Engineering v TJ Graham & Sons (1957)*, 'The brain and nerve centre of the company'.

Thus in *Lennard's Carrying Co Ltd v Asiatic Petroleum Co Ltd (1915)*, the House of Lords based identification on a person 'who is really the directing mind and will of the corporation, the very ego and centre of the corporation'.

These decisions should now be interpreted in the light of the *Meridian* decision.

Three cases in the 1940s established that companies could commit crimes involving dishonesty. *DPP v Kent and Sussex Contractors Ltd (1944)*; *R v ICR Haulage Ltd (1944)*; and *Moore v Bresler (1944)*.

Debate rages on the potential extent of a company's criminality. Some offences cannot be committed by a company. It seems clear that companies are incapable of committing offences of a sexual nature, or the offence of bigamy. Companies cannot commit murder. This is not because of a technical problem but because the offence carries a statutory sentence of life imprisonment, and companies cannot be imprisoned. There is no conceptual problem with holding a company liable for manslaughter. There have been very real practical difficulties in securing convictions, however, and this has been the subject of fierce debate in recent years.

In passing it is worth noting that in some common law jurisdictions a company may not be convicted of manslaughter. In *R v Murray Wright Ltd (1970)*, in the New Zealand Court of Appeal, the appellants were chemists and supplied the wrong medicine to Miss Keepa. She died as a result of taking the medicine. The appellants tried to quash an indictment issued in relation to this. Henry J refused, saying the company could be convicted of manslaughter. However, in the New Zealand Court of Appeal this was reversed, as s58 of the Crimes Act 1961 says that homicide is the killing of a human being by another, and on that basis a company could not be found guilty of homicide.

There is no such problem in the UK. However, in *Re Attorney-General's (No 2 of 1999) (2000)*, the Court of Appeal refused to apply the *Meridian* approach to identification in relation to manslaughter by negligence. This means a company can only be convicted if an identifiable human being, who is the directing mind and will of the company, can be shown to have committed the crime. It is therefore difficult to obtain convictions in relation to larger companies. Where there have been convictions, the companies have been small, as in *R v Kite (1996)*, where the managing director of the company that had organised a leisure trip for teenagers was found guilty of manslaughter, as was the company, where four teenagers died in a canoeing disaster in Lyme Bay.

In *R v Jackson Transport (Ossett) Ltd (1996) (unreported)*, the company concerned was somewhat larger, employing about 40 people. James Hodgson was killed in May 1994 while he was cleaning behind a tanker vehicle containing chemicals. He died when he used steam equipment to clean a valve in the tanker blocked with toxic chemicals. The company had not provided proper equipment, training or supervision. The company was convicted of manslaughter.

In August 2001, English Bros Ltd, a Wisbech construction company, pleaded guilty to the manslaughter of Bill Larkman, an employee who died in June 1999 (unreported), when he fell through a fragile roof to his death. The company had been warned previously about failing to provide correct safety equipment. The company was fined £25,000.

In October 2002, Dennis Clothier & Sons and one of its directors were found guilty of the manslaughter of Steven Hayfield (unreported). He had died when he was hit by a 20 tonne trailer which became detached from a tractor because it was dangerously loaded.

In April 2000, Teglgaard Hardwood (UK) Ltd (unreported) and one of its directors pleaded guilty to the manslaughter of a labourer, Christopher Longrigg, who died when a stack of timber fell on him while he was working for the company in a shipyard.

In Scotland, there has only ever been one company charged with homicide. This was Transco plc, the gas supply company. It was charged with the homicide of four people who died in December 1999 when a massive explosion destroyed a family house in Larkhall. Scotland's Court of Criminal Appeal dismissed culpable homicide charges against the company.

It seems that the argument for enacting a new offence of corporate killing applies equally in England, Wales and Scotland.

It has so far proved impossible to convict larger companies of manslaughter. There has been, and remains, considerable pressure for reform. The background to this pressure has been some horrific disasters like the Southall rail crash (1997) and the Herald of Free Enterprise disaster off Zeebrugge (1987). See also the Fennell Report into the Kings Cross Underground Fire (1988), and the Cullen Report into the Piper Alpha Disaster (1990).

The Law Commission consulted on the law of corporate manslaughter in Consultation Paper No 135 (1994). The Law Commission recommended a new offence based on whether the company's conduct fell significantly below what could reasonably be expected of it in the context of the significant risk of death or injury of which it should have been aware.

In a later report, Legislating the Criminal Code: Involuntary Manslaughter (1996), (Law Commission Report No. 237), the Law Commission in its final report calls for a new offence of corporate killing comparable to killing by gross negligence. The focus of this offence would be on the quality of the company's operating systems rather than on the guilt of individuals. In 2000 a Private Members Bill was introduced on corporate killing. It was introduced by Andrew Dismore MP. The Corporate Homicide Bill proposed to create a new criminal offence of corporate killing where the conduct of the company falls well below what could reasonably be expected. This was not pursued when the government announced its intention to bring forward legislation.

Legislation was announced in May 2003 by the Home Secretary, David Blunkett. The new offence will be of death caused by management failure if the way in which the company's activities are managed or organised fails to ensure the health and safety of persons employed in it, or affected by its activities. The maximum penalty will be an unlimited fine.

The Queen's Speech in November 2003 made no mention of the reform of the law of corporate manslaughter. In March 2005, the government published a White Paper on the matter (see Corporate Manslaughter: The Government's Draft Bill for Reform (CM6497).

Attitudes have changed, as noted by Celia Wells in 'Corporate Manslaughter: A Cultural and Legal Form', 6 Criminal Law Forum 45. In *R v Cory Brothers (1927)*, Cory Brothers put up an electrified fence, fearing pilfering in the coal strike of 1926, and an unemployed miner who was out ratting was electrocuted and killed. There was a prosecution for manslaughter but the trial judge directed that the company could not be indicted.

Deaths in major construction projects were once regarded as routine. In Radnorshire, in the area represented by the author in the National Assembly for Wales, over 100 people were killed in the construction of the reservoirs of the Elan Valley at the start of the twentieth century.

In the opinion of the author, it is high time that the law is reformed in this area and put on a statutory basis. There had been far too much talking about this area of law by successive governments and little or no action. The proposals contained in the Law Commission Reports should have been acted upon before the reports gathered dust on the ministerial bookshelves in the Home Office. At last reform is forthcoming (see section 2.3.1).

Companies may also commit torts. Not only will a company be liable for the torts of employees committed in the course of their employment on the basis of vicarious liability but they may also be liable in their own right. Thus a company may be liable for nuisance, etc.

### 2.3.1 Corporate manslaughter – proposals

In March 2005, the government issued a White Paper, Corporate Manslaughter: The Government's Draft Bill for Reform (CM6497).

The Home Secretary, in the foreword to the White Paper, states 'This government is committed to delivering safe and secure communities, at home and in the work place, and to a criminal justice system that commands the confidence of the public. A fundamental part of this is providing offences that are clear and effective. The current laws on corporate manslaughter are neither, as a number of unsuccessful prosecutions over the years stand testament'.

The proposals are designed to strike a balance. Companies and other organisations must be held properly to account for gross failings by their senior management which have fatal consequences. However, as an offence of homicide, corporate manslaughter charges must be reserved for the very worst cases of management failure. It is intended that the offence will complement rather than replace other forms of redress such as prosecutions under health and safety legislation.

A draft Bill set out proposals for a new specific offence of corporate manslaughter. An organisation would be prosecuted if a gross failing by its senior managers to take reasonable care for the safety of their workers and members of the public caused a person's death. The new offence would apply as now to all companies, and also to other types of incorporated body including many bodies in the public sector, such as local authorities. Government departments and other Crown bodies would also be liable to prosecution.

It is considered by the White Paper that the current problem with the law is the need to find a very senior individual personally guilty of gross negligence, manslaughter before the company itself can be convicted. At the heart of the new offence, therefore, is a more effective means of attributing failures in the way its activities are organised or managed at a senior level to an organisation. There remains the case that an organisation must owe a duty of care to the victim and the high threshold that conduct must have been grossly negligent is maintained.

Clear and explicit links are also built into the offence to duties that organisations must already comply with under health and safety legislation, providing clarity about the standards against which conduct will be judged. Consultation on the proposals ended on 17 June 2005. The Bill became law on 26 July 2007 and will come into force on 6 April 2008.

The proposals in the draft Bill had their starting point in the Law Commission's 1996 report 'Legislating the Criminal Code: Involuntary Manslaughter' (Law Com No. 237) (http://www.lawcom.gov.uk/files/lc237.pdf). The government subsequently issued a consultation paper in 2000 'Reforming the Law on Involuntary Manslaughter: The Government's Proposals' (http://www.homeoffice.gov.uk/docs/invmans.html).

### 2.3.1.1  The offence

The offence set out in the Corporate Manslaughter and Corporate Homicide Act 2007 is designed to tackle the difficulties created by the identification principle. The problem is addressed through a new test focussing on management failure.

An organisation to which the Act applies is guilty of an offence if the way in which its activities are managed or organised:

(a)  causes a person's death, and
(b)  amounts to a gross breach of a relevant duty of care owed by the organisation to the deceased.

The Act further provides that an organisation is guilty of an offence under the Act only if the way in which its activities are managed or organised by its senior management is a substantial element in the breach (s1(3)).

The heart of the new offence lies in the requirement for a management failure, a substantial element of which must be a gross failure at a senior management level. It focuses on the way in which a particular activity is being managed or organised. Organisations are not to be liable on the basis of any intermediate operational negligence causing death, or indeed for the unpredictable, maverick acts of its employees. Instead, the Act focuses responsibility on the working practices of the organisation. It also allows senior management conduct to be considered collectively as well as individually.

The definition of senior management is drawn to capture only those who play a role in making management decisions about or actually managing the activities of the organisation as a whole or a substantial part of it. In addition, the definition requires that the person play a 'significant' role (s1(4)).

The new offence is targeted at the most serious management failings that warrant the application of a serious criminal offence. It is not the intention of the legislation to catch companies or others making proper efforts to operate in a safe or responsible fashion, or where efforts have been made to comply with health and safety legislation but appropriate standards are not quite met.

The sanction to be applied is a financial penalty. The Act makes provision for this and organisations found guilty of manslaughter would face an unlimited fine (s1(6)).

## SUMMARY

### Introduction

The company is a separate entity in law. It is capable of owning property, concluding contracts and committing torts and crimes.

On occasion, the so called corporate veil is lifted and the deeds of the company are identified as those of its directors or shareholders.

### Exceptions to the *Salomon* principle

The situations where the veil is lifted may be classified as statutory or judicial.

#### Statutory exceptions

Statutory exceptions include:

(a) ss82 and 83 of the Companies Act 2006 – criminal liability for misdescription of the company;
(b) s213 of the Insolvency Act 1986 and s993 of the Companies Act 2006 – fraudulent trading;
(c) s214 of the Insolvency Act 1986 – wrongful trading by a company director;
(d) s216 of the Insolvency Act 1986 – prohibition on directors of insolvent companies being associated with a company with a similar name;
(e) s15 of the Company Directors Disqualification Act 1986 – personal liability of a disqualified person who acts in the management of a company;
(f) s777(3) of the Companies Act 2006 – liability of officers where a public company trades without a trading certificate;
(g) s399 of the Companies Act 2006 – the obligation to file group accounts;
(h) there are many situations under the companies' legislation where obligations are placed on groups, or where rules apply to directors of companies within the same group. Wherever there is a group situation the veil is being lifted;
(i) s6 of the Law of Property Act 1969 – landlord refusing to renew a tenancy where he needs the premises for the purposes of a company which he controls.

#### Judicial exceptions

It is difficult to categorise the judicial exceptions to the *Salomon* principle.
Certain themes can be identified, however:

(a) the veil is generally lifted to prevent fraud;
(b) sometimes, the veil is lifted in a group situation, treating companies within the same group as part of the same enterprise. This is particularly true where

a company is a wholly owned subsidiary of a holding company. Even here, there is no universal rule;

(c) sometimes the device used to lift the veil is agency, sometimes the trust, sometimes in a group situation the group enterprise;

(d) some cases turn on their special facts, eg the consent of all members is the consent of the company – *Re Express Engineering Works Ltd*, all the shareholders of a company were German, therefore the company was an enemy alien – *Daimler Co Ltd v Continental Tyre & Rubber Co (GB) Ltd* decided during the First World War.

## Companies and crimes and tort

Companies may commit crimes, although some crimes by their nature such as bigamy cannot be committed by companies. In relation to strict liability offences, if there is a defence of due diligence in the statute, the company may escape liability by demonstrating that the lack of care was that of an employee who was not part of the directing mind or will of the company. Companies may also commit torts.

Legislation is now providing for a clearer approach to corporate manslaughter.

## Further reading

Bromilow, D, 'Creasey v Breachwood Motors: mistaken identity leads to untimely death' (1998) 19 Co Law 198.

Burles, D, 'The criminal liability of corporations' (1991) 141 NLJ 609.

Clarkson, CMV, 'Kicking corporate bodies and damning their souls' (1996) 59 MLR 557.

Elliott, DW, 'Directors' thefts and dishonesty' [1991] Crim Law Review 732.

Gallagher, L, and Ziegler, P, 'Lifting the corporate veil in the pursuit of justice' [1990] JBL: 292.

Gobert, J, 'Corporate Killing at Home and Abroad – Reflections on the Government's proposals' (2002) 118 LQR 72.

Gobert, J, 'Corporate criminality: four models of fault' (1994) 14 LS 393.

Griffin, S, 'Section 349(4) of the Companies Act 1985 – an outdated Victorian legacy' [1997] JBL 438.

Kahn-Freund, O, 'Some Reflections on Company Law Reform' (1944) 7MLR 54.

Law Commission, 'The law of corporate manslaughter', Consultation Paper No 135, 1994, London: HMSO.

Law Commission, 'Legislating the criminal code: involuntary manslaughter', Consultation Paper No 237, 1996, London: HMSO.

Mitchell, C, 'Lifting the corporate veil in English Courts, An Empirical Study' [1999] 3CFILR 15.

Ottolenghi, S, 'From peeping behind the corporate veil to ignoring it completely' (1990) 53 MLR 338.

Pickering, MA, 'The company as a separate legal entity' (1968) 31 MLR 481.

Rixon, FG, 'Lifting the veil between holding and subsidiary companies' (1986) 102 LQR 415.

Samuels, A, 'Lifting the veil' [1964] JBL 107.

Schmitthoff, CM, 'Salomon in the shadow' [1976] JBL 305.

Schmitthoff, CM, 'The wholly owned and the controlled subsidiary' [1978] JBL 218.

Slapper, G, 'Corporate punishment' (1994) 144 NLJ 29.

Sullivan, GR, 'The attribution of culpability to limited companies' [1996] 55 CLJ 515.

Talwar, A, and Dawson, A, 'Corporate Killing' (2003) 153 NLJ 908.

Virgo, G, 'Stealing from the small family business' [1991] CLJ 464.

Wedderburn, KW, 'Corporate Personality and Social Policy: the problem of the quasi-corporation' (1965) 28 MLR 62.

Wells, C, 'Corporate Liability and Consumer Protection: Tesco v Nattrass revisited' (1994) 57 MLR 817.

Wells, C, 'The Corporate Manslaughter Proposals: Pragmatism, Paradox and Peninsularity' [1996] Crim Law Review 545.

Whincup, M, 'Inequitable Incorporation – the Abuse of a Privilege' (1981) 2 Co Law 158.

Wickins, RJ, and Ong, CA, 'Confusion worse confounded: the end of the directing mind theory?' [1997] JBL 524.

# Promoters and pre-incorporation contracts

## 3.1 Introduction

Somebody has to set up the company and, in order to set up a company, there have to be promoters. The promoters will purchase property from which the company is going to operate and undertake the preliminary steps to set the company up. They will thus be acting before the company has been formed.

In Victorian Britain there used to be professional company promoters. These promoters were often dishonest and acted fraudulently. The Anglo-Bengalee Disinterested Loan and Life Assurance Company, mercilessly lampooned by Dickens in *'Martin Chuzzlewitt'*, is typical of the sort of situation that arose. Indeed Albert Grant, who features in some of the prominent late Victorian cases concerning company promotion, is assumed to be the inspiration for the villain, Augustus Melmotte in Trollope's *'The Way We Live Now'*. A code of rules therefore developed to ensure that promoters acted with integrity in setting up the company.

There are few statutory rules in this area and indeed no satisfactory statutory definition of a promoter. Section 67 of the Companies Act 1985 formerly defined the promoter in s67(3) as a person who is 'a party to the preparation of the prospectus of a portion of it'.

In the absence of any precise definition in statute, resort must be had to judicial statements relating to promotion. As Gross notes in 'Who is a company promoter?' [1970] 86LQR 493, the term 'promoter' is ill defined by companies legislation. The usual *dictum* referred to in defining a promoter is that of Cockburn CJ in *Twycross v Grant (1877)* where he said that a promoter is 'one who undertakes to form a company with reference to a given project and to set it going and who takes the necessary steps to accomplish that purpose'. This definition is clearly somewhat general. In *Whaley Bridge Calico Printing Co v Green (1880)*, Bowen J said:

> The term promoter is a term not of law, but of business, usefully summing up in a single word a number of business operations familiar to the commercial world by which a company is generally brought into existence.

The old, Victorian rogue promoters responsible for finding directors to manage a company and for drafting prospectuses to raise capital from the public are largely a thing of the past. Most companies are promoted as private companies by those who will subsequently be managing the business. Rules are still necessary to protect those investing in the business and to protect creditors.

## 3.2 Promoters' duties

A company promoter owes fiduciary duties to the company which he is setting up. Fiduciary duties are basically duties of good faith and integrity. Most obviously, where a promoter is selling property to a company, he must ensure that he discloses any profit that he is making on the deal. The disclosure may be made to all of the shareholders, actual and potential, as was the case for example in *Salomon v A Salomon & Co Ltd (1897)*. Disclosure to the shareholders was also the method employed successfully in *Lagunas Nitrate Company v Lagunas Syndicate (1899)*. Alternatively, the disclosure may be made to the company's directors. However, in such an instance the disclosure can only be effective if it is to an independent board of directors. In *Erlanger v New Sombrero Phosphate Co (1878)*, a syndicate had purchased a lease of a Caribbean island called Sombrero. The syndicate was selling the island to a company which had been formed for the purpose.

The syndicate owed promotional duties in relation to the sale. They disclosed the profit that was being made in selling the island to the company to the board of directors. There were five directors; two were abroad at the material time, two were associated with the syndicate and the fifth was the Lord Mayor of London who was too busy to give proper attention to the affairs of the company. It was held in the circumstances that this was not a full disclosure to an independent board of directors. The company was able to rescind the contract.

When a promoter discloses a profit that he is making upon a deal, he must take care to ensure that he is disclosing the entire profit that he is making from the arrangement. In certain cases, there may well be some collateral profit as well as the direct profit from the sale. It was thus in *Gluckstein v Barnes (1900)*, where a syndicate had purchased the exhibition hall, Olympia. The syndicate disclosed the profit that it was making in re-selling the hall to the company but failed to disclose a profit that it was making in relation to certain mortgages over the hall which it had purchased at a discount. This meant that, when the syndicate purchased the hall, there was a further reduction of £20,000 since the price of the purchase also included an amount to be set off against debts which were now owed to the syndicate. Lord MacNaghten said:

> They issued a prospectus representing that they had agreed to purchase the property for a sum largely in excess of the amount which they had, in fact, to pay. On the faith of this prospectus, they collected subscriptions from a confiding and credulous public. And then comes the last act. Secretly, and therefore

dishonestly, they put into their own pockets the difference between the real and the pretended price.

The case clearly represents a breach of promoters' duties and the promoter in question, Gluckstein, was ordered to repay his share of the secret profit.

Particular problems may arise where a promoter has acquired property before the promotion began. In such a situation, where the promoter then sells the property to the company without fully disclosing the profit that is being made upon the transaction, there is a difficulty in awarding an appropriate remedy. If the company were to seek an account of profits in such a case, the question would arise as to what portion of profits properly belongs to the pre-promotion period and so would be rightfully the property of the promoter and what part of the profit could be said to belong to the post-promotion period and so belong to the company. In such cases, therefore, the view of the courts is that it is not possible to sue for an account of profits but merely for rescission of the contract, always assuming that the right to rescission has not been lost. See *Re Cape Breton Co, Cavendish-Bentinck v Fenn (1887)* and *Ladywell Mining Co v Brookes (1887)*. These decisions have been criticised notably by Xuereb in 'Secret Profit – *Re Cape Breton Company* revisited' *(1987)* 5 CLD 9 on the basis that some apportionment of the profit could be made by the court.

## 3.3 Remedies for breach of promoters' duties

Promoters owe fiduciary duties to the company which they are promoting. The duty is akin to the duty owed to the unborn child as no company is yet in existence. However, there is a range of remedies that will be available against a promoter who has breached his duty and failed to disclose the extent of the profit that he is making where he has sold property to the company. A possible remedy is for rescission of the contract of the sale between the promoter and the company. The usual bars to rescission will apply: so rescission is not available where there has been affirmation, where it is impossible to restore the parties to their pre-contractual positions or where third party rights have intervened.

An alternative remedy is for the company to sue for a return of the profit. If the company wishes to keep the property in question and merely recover the profit, this is clearly the appropriate remedy to seek. This was the remedy awarded, for example, in *Gluckstein v Barnes (1900)*.

These are the two usual alternative remedies. However, in one case, the remedy of damages was awarded against a promoter. This occurred in *Re Leeds and Hanley Theatre of Varieties Ltd (1902)*. In this case, the claim was for breach of duty of care in the promoter selling property to the company at an overvaluation. Damages were awarded against the promoter. This is a rare instance of damages being awarded against a promoter, but it is interesting to note that the measure of damages was the same as the profit made by the promoter.

It may be on occasion that a single shareholder can bring a claim as a derivative action on behalf of the company. The shareholder must fit within one of the exceptions to the rule in *Foss v Harbottle (1843)*. This could occur where the promoters are in control of the company and are using their management and/or voting powers in general meeting to prevent an action being brought in respect of an undisclosed profit that has been made by promoters.

A further remedy may be available in the particular instance of the company's liquidation. Section 212 of the Insolvency Act 1986 permits the court to order in a liquidation that a promoter restore to the company any property or money obtained in breach of duty. This may be done on the petition of the liquidator or on the petition of a creditor or member.

## 3.4 Payment for the promoters' services

A promoter cannot have a contract with the company which he is going to form. The company is not yet in existence and, therefore, is unable to contract. In *Re National Motor Mail Coach Company Limited, Clinton's Claim (1908)*, it was accepted that there could be no contract between a promoter and his unformed company such that a promoter could claim reimbursement of expenses incurred in setting up the company. Furthermore, the court held that there could be no quasi contractual remedy in this case, based on the company's having received a benefit.

Generally, in such cases, no problem will arise. The promoters who have been setting up the company will also be the first directors and will take care to ensure that they are reimbursed for their expenses and receive payment for the services that they have performed. However, where problems do arise, a fresh contract after incorporation may be the answer. It is important that this new contract should be supported by some element of fresh consideration or be concluded under seal, as otherwise the contract will be invalid for want of consideration since the consideration is past.

In Scottish law, past consideration for the payment of promoters' expenses is permissible as past consideration is good consideration in Scottish law. See *Park Business Interiors Ltd v Park (1991)*.

## 3.5 Pre-incorporation contracts

Where a person enters into a contract on behalf of an unformed company, a conceptual problem arises. It is clear in such instances that the company itself cannot be bound since the company does not exist.

### 3.5.1 Common law

In *Kelner v Baxter (1866)*, the plaintiff had delivered goods to the defendants. The goods had been ordered on behalf of the proposed Gravesend Royal Alexandra Hotel Co Ltd. The question arose as to whether the company was liable upon this contract. The Court of Common Pleas held that the company could not be liable since it did not exist at the time of the contract. In fact, the defendant, who had acted on behalf of the unformed company, was held liable on this contract.

Gross states in 'Pre Incorporation Contracts' [1971] 87 LQR 367, that it is rare to hear such widespread and common opposition against any aspect of company law as that against the rule in Kilner v Baxter.

This is the position at common law before statute intervened. The position was not uniform, however, and in some cases it was held that there was no contract. In *Newborne v Sensolid (Great Britain) Ltd (1954)*, Leopold Newborne (London) Ltd purported to sell a quantity of ham to the defendant. The defendant refused to take delivery of the ham. The company sued for breach of contract. It transpired that the company had not been registered until the day after the contract was concluded.

The plaintiff continued the action in his own name. The plaintiff was a promoter and director of the company. It was held in the Court of Appeal that there was no contract in this case. The fact that the agreement had been signed 'Yours faithfully, Leopold Newborne (London) Ltd' and the signature of the director added beneath indicated that there was no intention that person liability should attach to the director. It was therefore held that there was no contract. Similarly, in the Australian case of *Black v Smallwood (1966)* (High Court of Australia), it was held that where a contract was concluded where the purchaser was described as Western Suburbs Holdings Pty Ltd with the signatures of Robert Smallwood and J Cooper added subsequently as directors, there could be no contract between the plaintiff Black and the defendant Smallwood. In this case, all the parties believed that the company did exist whereas in fact at the time of the contract it did not. The court held that in the circumstances there could be no contract. Although a contract may take effect between the person purporting to act for the unformed company and the other contracting party, it is clear from the cases that there can be no adoption or ratification of that agreement by the company once it comes into existence. This is clear from the opinion of the Privy Council in *Natal Land and Colonisation Co Ltd v Pauline Colliery and Development Syndicate Ltd (1904)* (an appeal from the Supreme Court of Natal). The appropriate course of action in such a situation where a person acting for the company is bound is that, once the company comes into existence, it should enter into a new contract on the same terms.

### 3.5.2 Statutory provision

When the United Kingdom joined the European Communities by the European Communities Act 1972, s9(2) of the European Communities Act implemented part of the first EC Company Law Directive. Section 9(2) is now contained in s51(1) of the Companies Act 2006.

> A contract which purports to be made by or on behalf of a company at a time when the company has not been formed has effect, subject to any agreement to the contrary, as one made with the person purporting to act for the company or as an agent for it, and he is personally liable on the contract accordingly.

This statutory provision will mean that, in both *Kelner v Baxter* and *Newborne v Sensolid*, the person purporting to act for the company will be liable upon the contract as well as being able to hold the other party to the contractual agreement. In *Phonogram Ltd v Lane (1982)*, the court had to consider the effect of what is now s51(1) where a company called Fragile Management Ltd was in the process of being incorporated. The company was to manage a pop group called Cheap, Mean and Nasty.

The defendant was the manager of the pop group. He agreed with the plaintiffs that the plaintiffs would supply finance. He signed an agreement undertaking to re-pay the monies that had been advanced on behalf of Fragile Management Ltd if the contract were not completed before a certain time. Subsequently, the plaintiffs sued the defendant for the money that had been advanced. The defendant argued he was not personally liable. It was suggested on his behalf that the contract was not 'purported' to be made by the company as it was known that the company was not in existence. Indeed, it was known by both parties that the company had not yet been formed. However, Lord Denning MR took the view (a view shared by Shaw and Oliver LJJ) that a contract can purport to be made on behalf of a company even though the company is known by both parties not to have been formed. He took the view that, although what is now s51(1) can be excluded by contrary agreement, this contrary agreement should be express. This view was shared by the other members of the Court of Appeal.

It is possible in certain situations that a promoter may act on behalf of a company to be bought 'off the shelf'. In such a situation, the company does exist where the promoter is acting so that it is open to the company subsequently to ratify what the promoter has done provided that the promoter made it clear that he was acting on behalf of the company. It may be that the company subsequently alters it name; this will not change the legal situation.

In *OshKosh B'Gosh Inc v Dan Marbel Inc Ltd (1989)*, an off the shelf company was acquired. The company resolved to change its name to Dan Marbel Inc Ltd but no certificate of incorporation recording the change of name was obtained.

The Court of Appeal took the view that the company had been formed although trading under a different name. What is now s51(1) was therefore inapplicable.

Similarly, in *Badgerhill Properties Ltd v Cottrell (1991)*, the company was already in existence although its name had been wrongly stated. The Court of Appeal took the view that the section did not apply.

*Cotronic (UK) Ltd v Dezonie (1991)* is a rather different situation. The plaintiff company sued for monies owed in relation to work done as sub-contractors for a company Wendaland Builders Ltd controlled by the defendant. The defendant joined the owner of the property as third party.

The owner of that land argued that, when it entered into the agreement, Wendaland Builders Ltd had been struck off the register and, so, did not exist, so that there was no contractual liability. The defendant argued that what is now s51(1) applied. The Court of Appeal took the view that this was not a pre-incorporation situation. The defendant did not purport to be concluding a contract on behalf of a new company. (Note that the defendant did succeed on the basis of a *quantum meruit*.)

In *Rover International Ltd v Cannon Film Sales Ltd (1987)*, it was held that what is now s51(1) did not apply to companies not registered in the UK.

As noted above pp 36–37 the person purporting to act for the company will be able to hold the other party to the contractual agreement. The matter was put beyond doubt in *Braymist Ltd v Wise Finance Co Ltd (2002)*. Here a contract had been made on 28 January 1993 by the vendor, Braymist Ltd, which had not yet been incorporated. It was purporting to sell land. The title was held by another company, Plumtree Ltd. Braymist was to become a 100% subsidiary of Plumtree.

Mr Poole, who had management control of Plumtree, instructed solicitors, William Sturgess, to act. The solicitors signed for Braymist Ltd.

A notice to complete the contract was subsequently given, and it was attempted to enforce the contract against Wise by or on behalf of the unformed company.

Etherton J held that what is now s51(1) operated with mutuality so that it could be enforced against Wise. The proper person to enforce was the person who was acting for the unformed company, Braymist, namely William Sturgess, solicitors. This was upheld by the Court of Appeal.

Savirimuthu analyses this decision in 'Pre Incorporation Contracts and the problem of Corporate Fundamentalism – Are Promoters Proverbally Profuse' [2003] Co Law 196. Further reform of the law to allow ratification of pre-incorporation contracts by statute would be a sensible move. Prentice in 's9 of the European Communities Act' [1973] 89 LQR 518 believes that the opportunity should be taken to deal with this problem by permitting ratification of pre-incorporation contracts. This view is echoed by Green in 'Security of Transaction after Phonogram' [1984] 47 MLR 671, and Griffiths' 'Agents without Principals: Pre Incorporation Contracts in s36 C(1) of the Companies Act 1985' (1993) 13 LS 241.

Another case involving what is now s51(1) is the unreported decision of *Hellmuth, Obata and Kassabaum Inc. v Geoffrey King (unreported 29 September 2000)*. HOK had carried out planning work for a proposed sports arena in Hannover. They claimed fees against King who had acted for Arena Hannover AG (a company in formation). The action was allowed in respect of the work being undertaken. The judge, Colin Reese QC, held obiter that the section applied to quasi contractual claims for a quantum meruit as well as to contractual claims.

## SUMMARY

### Promoters

There is no statutory definition of promoters. One must therefore turn to the cases. A promoter is a person 'who undertakes to form a company with reference to a given project and to set it going and who takes the necessary steps to accomplish that purpose', *per* Cockburn CJ in *Twycross v Grant (1877)*.

Promoters owe fiduciary duties to the companies they are forming. They must disclose any profit they are making from the promotion – either to the members of the company or to an independent board.

The company may sue for disgorgement of the profit or for rescission (if this is not barred) where there is a breach of this duty.

## Pre-incorporation contracts

A conceptual problem arises where a person concludes a contract for the as yet unformed company. At common law, the position was confused. Sometimes, the person acting for the unformed company was held to be contractually bound but much depended on the form of words used. Since the European Communities Act 1972 the position has been standardised. Section 51(1) of the Companies Act 2006 now provides that where a person acts for an unformed company, that person is contractually bound unless there is an agreement to the contrary.

## Further reading

Gold, J, 'The Liability of Promoters for Secret Profits in English Law' (1943) 5 UT LJ 21.

Green, NN, 'Security of transaction after *Phonogram*' (1984) 47 MLR 671.

Griffiths, A, 'Agents Without Principals: Pre-incorporation Contracts and Section 36C of the Companies Act 1985, (1993) 13 LS 241.

Gross, JH, 'Who is a company promoter?' (1970) 86 LQR 493.

Gross, JH, 'Pre-Incorporation Contracts' (1971) 87 LQR 367.

McCrea, B, 'Disclosure of Promoters' Secret Profits' (1969) Univ of BCLR 183.

McMullen, J, 'A casenote on Phonogram v Lane' [1982] CLJ 47.

Prentice, DD, 'Section 9 of the European Communities Act' (1973) 89 LQR 518.

Roberts, A, 'Three Ring Circus' (on S36C(1) CA85) (2003) 147 SJ 458.

Savirimuthu, J, 'Pre-Incorporation Contracts and the Problems of Corporate Fundamentalism – Are Promoters Proverbally Profuse?' (2003) Co Law 196.

Xuereb, PG, 'Secret Profit – Re Cape Breton Revisited' (1987) 5 CLD 9.

# Issue of shares to the public

## 4.1 Background

As has been noted section 1.2.4, most companies are limited by shares. Public companies may issue shares to the public section 1.2.5.

The Financial Services and Markets Act 2000 has replaced the Financial Services Act 1986 and related legislation in regulating the financial services industry. There is now a single regulator, the Financial Services Authority, which is a company limited by guarantee. This was formerly the Securities and Investments Board. Details of the operation of the Financial Services Authority can be found on its website – *www.fsa.gov.uk*.

Sections 1-6 of the Financial Services and Markets Act 2000 provide that the Financial Services Authority should fulfil four objectives:

(i) maintaining confidence in the financial system (s3);
(ii) promoting public understanding of the financial system (s4);
(iii) securing the appropriate degree of protection for consumers (s5);
(iv) reducing the extent to which it is possible for businesses to be used for a purpose connected with financial crime (s6).

The Financial Services Authority, as the United Kingdom Listing Authority, is responsible for maintaining an Official List of securities which are admitted to trading on at least one recognised investment exchange. An investment exchange becomes a recognised investment exchange by obtaining a recognition order from the Financial Services Authority under s290 of the Act. The London Stock Exchange is the principal recognised investment exchange in the United Kingdom. It admits listed company securities to trading on its listed market. It also operates the Alternative Investment Market providing a market place for shares of medium sized and less mature companies. Its website address is *www.londonstockexchange.com*. There are other UK based recognised investment exchanges, such as the London Metal Exchange, as well as recognised overseas exchanges.

## 4.2 The London Stock Exchange

The London Stock Exchange is a recognised investment exchange. It deals with the buying and selling of government stocks and the securities of British and foreign companies amongst other things.

The London Stock Exchange operates three important markets. These are the Main Market, the Alternative Investment Market for less mature stock, and the Professional Securities Market which is a market for professional traders dealing in debt securities.

## 4.3 Regulation

There are various aspects relating to the public offer of shares which are regulated. These are the recognised investment exchanges themselves, the market for the sale and purchase of shares, the issue of securities, as will all the involvement of those buying and selling securities.

## 4.4 Prospectuses

The principle of the Prospectus Directive (203/71/EC) is to provide that where there is a public offer of securities or a request for admission of securities to trading on a regulated market then a prospectus must be published (Article 3 of the Directive). The prospectus in question must be approved by the appropriate authority in the issuer's state. As noted, the Financial Services Authority is the competent authority in the United Kingdom (s85(7) FSMA 2000).

## 4.5 Content

The obligatory content of a prospectus is specified in the Directive. It must contain all information necessary to enable investors to make an informed assessment of the assets and liabilities, financial position, profits and losses, and prospects of the issuer of the securities and the rights attaching to them. This is provided for in FSMA s87A (1)(b) and (2).

The prospectus should contain information about the issuer of the securities, about the securities themselves, and should also contain a summary.

A supplementary prospectus has to be forwarded to the FSA and published where appropriate if there arises something of significance relating to the information in the prospectus before the offer of securities has closed, and after the approval of a prospectus.

## 4.6 Exemptions

An offer of securities that is addressed to qualified investors may be made without the publication of a prospectus (FSMA 2000 s86(1)(a)). Furthermore, there is no obligation to publish a prospectus if the offer is made to fewer than 100 persons who are not qualifed investors (FSMA 200 s86(1)(b)).

Certain small issues are also exempt from the requirement for a prospectus:

If the total consideration for the offer is less than 2.5mn Euro, provided that this exemption can only be used once in every 12 months (FSMA ss85(5)(a) and 87, and sch 11A, para.9). This is an EU limit across the whole of the EU and would not apply to each member state separately.

Additionally, there is no obligation to publish an approved prospectus if the consideration cannot exceed 100,000 Euros. Again, this exemption can only be used once in every 12 months. (s86(1)(e)).

Large issues of shares, where the minimum consideration paid by each investor is 50,000 Euros are also exempt from the requirement to publish a prospectus. (s86(1)(c) and (d)).

It is worth noting in the case of each of these exemptions, other than the one exempting the publication of a prospectus where the offer is solely to qualified investors, that although publication of a prospectus is not needed in relation to the offer, if the securities are to be admitted to trading on a regulated market then a prospectus will normally be required.

## 4.7  Powers of the Financial Services Authority

The Financial Services Authority has powers under ss87K and 87L to suspend or prevent a public of securities, or an application for trading of securities on a regulated market, if it discovers or reasonably suspects that there has been a contravention of the relevant provisions of Part 6 of the Act or of prospectus rules, or of other obligations under the Prospectus Directive.

It may also impose financial penalties (s91(1)(A)) or issue a public statement of censure (s91(3)) for contravention of the Act or of the prospectus rules or of any provision in the Prospectus Directive. The following persons may be penalised:

   (i) an issuer of transferable securities;
  (ii) a person offering transferable securities to the public or seeking their admission to trading on a regulated market;
 (iii) an applicant for the approval of a prospectus;
 (iv) a person upon whom an obligation has been imposed under s87K or s87L;
  (v) any other person to whom the Prospectus Directive applies; and
 (vi) a director of any of the above knowingly concerned in the contravention that is in issue (s91(2)).

## 4.8  Remedies for misleading prospectuses

### 4.8.1  Common law and statute – misrepresentation in contract

If a plaintiff has been induced to purchase securities on the strength of a misrepresentation in the listing particulars, he may have a remedy for the misrepresentation.

The plaintiff may seek rescission of the contract against the company. He must demonstrate a material misrepresentation of fact which has induced him to enter into the contract. Non-disclosure of a relevant fact may amount to a misrepresentation if it can be demonstrated that the omission renders the listing particulars misleading. Thus, in *Coles v White City (Manchester) Greyhound Association Ltd (1928)*, a prospectus described land as eminently suitable for greyhound racing. The prospectus failed to state that the local authority would have to give planning permission for the erection of stands for viewing and for greyhound kennels.

A shareholder sought rescission on the basis of the omission. It was held that the description was misleading in that the omission distorted what was actually stated.

Rescission is not dependent upon whether the person making the statement or omission is fraudulent or not and is available for fraudulent, negligent and innocent representations. However, the court has a discretion to refuse to order rescission and to award damages in lieu of rescission if it considers this appropriate (s2(2) of the Misrepresentation Act 1967).

The right to rescission is lost in certain circumstances. Thus, a plaintiff may not rescind a contract if it is not possible to restore the parties to their pre-contractual position. This is sometimes stated as *restitutio in integrum impossibile est*. This bar to rescission will apply if the company is in liquidation; see *Oakes v Turquand (1867)*. Another bar to rescission is if the plaintiff affirms the contract after discovering the misrepresentation. This may occur, for example, if the plaintiff votes at a meeting of members after discovering the misrepresentation; see *Sharpley v Louth and East Coast Railway Company (1876)*. In a similar way, if the plaintiff fails to set the contract aside promptly after discovering the misrepresentation, he will not be able to rescind.

In addition to the remedy of rescission, damages may also be awarded under s2(2) of the Misrepresentation Act 1967, unless the misrepresentor can prove he had reasonable grounds to believe and did believe up to the time the contract was made that the facts represented were true. This section only applies if the misrepresentor is a party to the contract. This, therefore, can only apply against the company itself. Additionally, in contract, it is sometimes the case that a misrepresentation is incorporated into the resulting contract. Where this occurs, it will then be open to the injured party to frame a claim for contractual damages.

### 4.8.2 Common law and statute – damages in the tort of deceit

Damages may be claimed against a person who has accepted responsibility for a part of the listing particulars or authorised the contents of part or all of the listing particulars for a statement of fact which that person made knowing it to be false or reckless as to its truth. In *Derry v Peek (1889)*, a prospectus was issued by a tramway company. The company was empowered to use horse-drawn trams in Plymouth. The prospectus stated that the company was empowered to use steam-driven vehicles. In fact, this was not the case though application had been made to the Board of Trade for permission to do so. Permission was not granted and an investor who had relied on the prospectus brought an action for damages for fraud against the directors. It was held that since the directors honestly believed the statement to be true, they were not liable in fraud.

Although an action in the tort of deceit may be brought against the company itself as well as against the directors, since an action may be brought under s2(1) of the Misrepresentation Act 1967, where the company itself has made the misrepresentation, the action in tort is not relevant in such a situation. An exception to this, however, is where a later market purchaser brings an action in tort. Generally, actions will be brought by those who have subscribed for shares or debentures directly from the company. However, if a later purchaser can show that the listing particulars were directed to encouraging purchases on the open market, he may be able to sustain an action in tort where clearly no action in contract would be possible. Generally, the view used to be taken that listing particulars and prospectuses were intended to encourage subscription for shares rather than purchases on the stock market; see, for example, *Peek v Gurney (1873)*. However, in *Possfund Custodian Trustees Ltd v Diamond (1996)*, Lightman J refused to strike out a claim that the court should recognise that prospectuses are intended to encourage purchases in the aftermarket (here, on the USM – the old second market).

### 4.8.3 Common law and statute – damages in the tort of negligent misstatement

An action will lie in damages against a person who makes a negligent statement which causes economic loss provided there is a relationship of sufficient proximity. The range of potential defendants certainly includes the company and its directors and experts who have consented to the contents of part or all of the listing particulars.

The case establishing potential liability in this area is *Hedley Byrne & Co Ltd v Heller & Partners Ltd (1964)*. As in the case of the tort of deceit, it is possible that the range of potential plaintiffs in the tort of negligent misstatement will include not just those who have subscribed for shares or debentures direct from the company but also those who have purchased securities on the open market. In such a situation, the tortious remedy may be relevant against the company but otherwise, where a contractual relationship exists, s2(1) of the Misrepresentation Act 1967 is the appropriate remedy. However, it seems that the scope of liability in the tort of negligent misstatement is limited. The House of Lords in *Caparo Industries plc v Dickman and Others (1990)* held that no duty of care was owed to potential investors in relation to the auditing of the company's accounts. Lord Bridge of Harwich said:

> To hold the maker of the statement to be under a duty of care in respect of the accuracy of the statement to all and sundry for any purpose for which they may choose to rely on it is not only to subject him, in the classic words

of Cardozo CJ to 'liability in an indeterminate amount for an indeterminate time to an indeterminate class' [*Ultramares Corporation v Touche (1931)*] it is also to confer on the world at large a quite unwarranted entitlement to appropriate for their own purposes the benefit of the expert knowledge or professional expertise attributed to the maker of the statement.

This principle was applied in *Al-Nakib Investments (Jersey) Ltd v Longcroft (1990)*, where there was a claim against the directors of a company in relation to a share purchase on the stock market following an allegedly misleading prospectus. The court considered that the prospectus was intended to encourage subscriptions for shares so that there was no remedy for purchasers on the open market. There seems to be no settled rule in this area. *Caparo plc v Dickman (1990)* and *Al-Nakib Investments Ltd v Longcroft (1990)* lean in favour of a restrictive approach while the statutory provisions in the Financial Services and Markets Act 2000 and in the Public Offers of Securities Regulations 1995 and the more recent decision in *Possfund Custodian Trustees Ltd v Diamond (1996)* lean in favour of a more inclusive view of the purposes of a prospectus.

### 4.8.4 FSMA 2000 – remedies

S90 provides that any person responsible for a prospectus (s86) is liable to pay compensation to a person who has (a) acquired securities to which the particulars apply; and (b) suffered loss in respect of them as a result of:

(i)  any untrue or misleading statement in the particulars; or
(ii) the omission from the particulars of any matter required to be included by s80 or s81. (The general duty of disclosure and the duty to supplement it with details of any significant new matter or change.)

Compensation may be payable by:

(i)   the issuer of the shares;
(ii)  every director of the issuer, unless published without the director's knowledge or consent, as where on becoming aware of its publication the director gives reasonable public notice that it was published without his knowledge or consent;
(iii) every person named in the document as a director or as having agreed to become a director, provided this was done with the person's authorisation;
(iv)  every person who accepted and is stated in the document as accepting responsibility for the document or part of it, and every person who has authorised the contents of the document or any part of it. Where a person is responsible for only part of a document, liability can only arise in respect of that part.

### 4.8.4.1 Defences

Various defences are available:

1. **Reasonable belief:** If, after making reasonable enquiries the defendant reasonably believed that the statement in question was true and not misleading, or that the matter which was omitted was properly omitted. One of the following four circumstances must also be proved:

   (i) the defendant continued in that belief until the shares were acquired; or

   (ii) they were acquired before it was reasonably practicable to bring a correction to the attention of persons likely to acquire the shares in question; or

   (iii) before the shares were acquired, the defendant took all reasonable steps to secure that a correction was brought to the attention of persons likely to acquire the shares; or

   (iv) the shares were acquired after such a lapse of time that the defendant ought, in the circumstances, to be reasonably excused, provided that the defendant continued to believe the statement or omission was proper until after dealings in the shares commenced.

   (Financial Services and Markets Act 2000, Sch 9, para 5 and Sch 10 para 1).

2. **Expert's statement:** If the defendant reasonably believed on reasonable grounds that the expert was competent to make the statement and had consented to its inclusion in the form and context in which it was included. One of the following four circumstances must also be proved:

   (i) that the defendant continued in that belief until the shares were acquired; or

   (ii) they were acquired before it was reasonably practicable to bring the fact that the expert was not competent or had not consented to the attention of persons likely to acquire the shares in question; or

   (iii) that before the shares were acquired, the defendant had taken all reasonable steps to secure that the fact of the non competence or non consent was brought to the attention of persons likely to acquire the shares in question; or

   (iv) the shares were acquired after such a lapse of time that the defendant ought, in the circumstances, to be reasonably excused, provided that the defendant continued to believe in the expert until after dealings in the shares commenced.

   (Financial Services and Markets Act 2000, Sch 9, para 5 and Sch 10 para 2).

3. **Reasonable steps to correct defect:** If the defendant took reasonable steps to bring a correction or the fact of an expert's lack of competence or consent to the attention of potential investors, then this is a defence.

   (Financial Services and Markets Act 2000, Sch 10, paras 3 and 4).

4.  **Official statements and documents:** It is a defence to show that the statement which caused the loss accurately and fairly reproduces a statement made by an official person or contained in an official document.

(Financial Services and Markets Act 2000, Sch 10, para 5).

5.  **Claimant's knowledge of the situation:** It is a defence to prove the person claiming compensation acquired the shares in question with knowledge that the statement was false or misleading, or that there was a material omission.

(Financial Services and Markets Act 2000, Sch 10 para 6).

## 4.9  Invitations to invest

S21 of the Financial Services and Markets Act 2000 provides that a person must not in the course of business communicate an invitation or inducement to engage in investment activity, unless that person is an authorised person or unless the content of the communication is approved by an authorised person. The section does not apply to communications originating outside the United Kingdom (s21(3)). Where the section is contravened a criminal offence triable, either way, is committed by the person who makes the communication (s25). On contravention, a person is guilty of an offence and liable:

(a)  on summary conviction, to imprisonment for a term not exceeding six months or a fine not exceeding the statutory maximum, or both;

(b)  on conviction on indictment, to imprisonment for a term not exceeding two years or a fine, or both.

It is a defence for a person to demonstrate that:

(a)  he believed on reasonable grounds that the content of the communication was prepared or approved under s21 by an authorised person; or

(b)  that he took all reasonable precautions and exercised all due diligence to avoid committing the offence.

The Financial Services and Markets Act 2000 (Financial Promotion) Order 2001, elaborates on the financial promotion restriction and exemptions from it (SI2001/1335).

Article 19 of the Order provides that the financial promotion restriction does not apply to a communication which:

(a)  is made only to recipients whom the person making the communication believes on reasonable grounds to be investment professionals; or

(b)  may reasonably be regarded as directed only at such recipients.

The financial promotion restriction is not applicable to 'non-real time communications' or to 'solicited real time communications' made by a company to certain persons. A non-real time communication is a communication other than one made in the course of a personal visit, telephone conversation or other interactive dialogue (Article 7).

A real time communication is solicited where it is made in the course of a personal visit, telephone call or other interactive dialogue if the call, visit or dialogue: (a) was initiated by the recipient of the communication, or (b) takes place in response to an express request from the recipient of the communication (Article 8).

In relation to non-real time communications or solicited real time communications, the restriction does not apply to communications by a company to creditors or members concerning its own investments or those of another undertaking in the same group (Article 43). Furthermore, the restriction does not apply to such communications made to a 'common interest group'. A common interest group is a group in relation to a company made up of persons who at the time the communication is made might reasonably be regarded as having an existing and common interest in each other and the company in:

(a) the affairs of the company, and (b) what is done with the proceeds arising from any investment to which the communication relates (Article 52).

The financial promotion restriction does not apply to communications by a director or employee of a company speaking on a television or radio broadcast, or webcast (Article 20A).

The financial promotion restriction does not apply either to any non-real time communication or any solicited real time communication made by a supplier to a customer of his in relation to the sale of goods or supply of services or a related sale or supply (Article 61).

The financial promotion restriction does not apply to communications made between companies in the same group (Article 45).

The financial promotion restriction does not apply to one-off communications (Article 28 & 28A).

The financial promotion restriction does not apply to communications to what are termed 'certified high network individuals' (Article 48). Such individuals must have a certificate signed by their accountant or employer certifying an annual income of a specified amount or the holding of net assets or a specified value.

The financial promotion restriction does not apply to the publication of a company's annual accounts and directors' report provided it does not contain any invitation or advice to underwrite, subscribe for, or otherwise acquire or dispose of the company's shares or debentures (Article 59).

The financial promotion restriction does not apply to publication in relation to listing particulars, prospectuses or supplementary versions of these (Articles 70–73).

The financial promotion restriction does not apply to communications in relation to participation in employee share schemes (Article 60). Furthermore, the restriction does not apply to communications for the purpose of selling a controlling interest in a company (Article 62), or in connection with the takeover of certain unlisted companies (Articles 63–66 and Schedule 4).

## SUMMARY

### Issue of shares to the public

The Financial Services and Markets Act 2000 provides for the publication of a prospectus where shares are issued to the public. It enacts into the United Kingdom's law the provisions of the Prospectus Directive (Directive 2003/71/EC).

The Financial Services Authority is the single regulator under the Act and is responsible for maintaining confidence in the financial system, promoting public awareness of the financial system, securing the appropriate degree of protection to consumers, and reducing the extent to which it is possible for financial services businesses to be used in connection with financial crime.

Recognised investment exchanges, which include the London Stock Exchange, are recognised by the Financial Services Authority for the purposes of transactions in securities.

### Content of prospectuses

Prospectuses should contain information to enable investors to make an informed assessment of the assets and liabilities, financial position, profits and losses, and prospects of the issuer of the securities and the rights attaching to them. This information must be presented in a clear and comprehensible format.

There are certain exemptions from the requirement to publish prospectuses, such as if the only potential investors are qualified investors, broadly speaking those who are steeped in trading in securities. Certain small and large issues are also exempted from the requirements of publication, though in these cases a prospectus is still needed if the securities are to be traded on a recognised investment exchange.

### Remedies

Remedies are available under statute and at common law in relation to misleading prospectuses.

### Further reading

Alcock, A, 'Public offers in the UK: the new regime' (1996) 17 Co Law 262.
Page, AC, 'Self-regulation: the constitutional dimension' (1986) 49 MLR 141.
Sealy, LS, 'The "disclosure" philosophy and company law reform' (1981) 2 Co Law 51.

# 5

# The company's constitution
## some vital considerations

The Companies Act 2006 makes a fundamental change to the company's constitution.

Henceforth the company will effectively have a single constitution. The articles of association will become the company's constitution. Formerly there were two components to the constitution; the memorandum of association (which covered matters like the company's name and its objects) and the articles of association.

The memorandum of association is now defined in s8 of the Act. It is a much shorter document and is in prescribed form, simply stating that the subscribers wish to form a company and agree to become members of that company and take at least one share each.

The memorandum of association must be delivered to the registrar, together with an application for registration, stating the company's proposed name, situate of the registered office, whether England and Wales, Wales, Scotland or Northern Ireland, whether the liability of the members of the company is to be limited and, if so, whether by shares or by guarantee, and whether the company is to be a private or public company (s9 CA 2006).

If the company is to have a share capital there should also be submitted a statement of capital and initial shareholdings (s10 CA 2006).

If the company is a company limited by guarantee there should be a statement of guarantee submitted (s11 CA 2006).

Additionally, there should also be a statement of the company's proposed officers (s12 CA 2006) delivered together with the application for registration.

The application must also contain a statement of the intended address of the company's registered office and a copy of any proposed articles of association (s9(5) CA 2006).

A statement of compliance is also required to be delivered to the registrar stating that the requirements of the Act as to registration have been complied with (s13 CA 2006).

The articles of association now form the company's constitution and those provisions of an existing company's memorandum that do not come within the ambit of a new style memorandum (such as the objects of the company and the name of the company) will be treated as if they were provisions of the company's articles (s28 CA 2006).

## 5.1 The name of the company

In general, those setting up a company are free to choose any name they wish. They are, however, constrained by certain rules.

### 5.1.1 Indications of type of company

A limited company must generally indicate this at the end of its name by the words 'Public Limited Company' or 'plc', or in the case of a Welsh company 'cwmni cyhoeddus cyfyngedig', or 'ccc', although this does not apply to community interest companies; see ss33(3) and (4) of the Companies (Audit, Investigations and Community Enterprise) Act 2004 (s58 Companies Act 2006). If the company is a community interest company which is public, then the appropriate company names will end with 'Community Interest Public Limited Company', or 'Community Interest PLC', or 'Cwmni Buddiant Cymunedol Cyhoeddus Cyfyngedig' or 'Cwmni Buddiant CCC'.

Private limited company names should end with 'Ltd', or in the case of Welsh companies with 'cyf' (s59 CA 2006). Certain companies are exempt from this requirement.

A private company is exempt from s59 if:

(a) it is a charity;
(b) it is exempted from the requirement of that section by regulations made by the Secretary of State; or
(c) it meets the conditions specified in s61 (continuation of existing exemption for companies limited by shares), or s62 (continuation of existing exemption for companies limited by guarantee).

S61 and s62 provide for exemption if the company was previously exempt and did not include the word 'Limited' or any other permitted alternatives, and the objects of the company are the promotion of commerce, art, science, education, religion, charity or any profession, and anything incidental or conducive to any of those objects, and the company's articles require its income to be applied in promoting its objectives, prohibit the payment of dividends or return of capital to its members and require all the assets otherwise available to the members to be transferred on its winding up, either to a similar body or to another body, the objects of which are the promotion of charity and anything incidental or conducive thereto.

### 5.1.2 Permitted characters

S57 CA 2006 provides that the Secretary of State may make provision by regulation:

(a) as to the letters or other characters, signs or symbols (including accents and other diacritical marks) and punctuation that may be used in the name of a company registered under the Act; and

(b) specifying a standard style or format for the name of the company for the purposes of registration.

The regulations may prohibit the use of specified characters, signs or symbols, when appearing in a specified position (in particular at the beginning of a name).

### 5.1.3 Prohibited and restricted use of names

S53 of the Companies Act 2006 prohibits the use of certain names. A name must not, in the opinion of the Secretary of State, be offensive or such that its use by the company would constitute an offence.

In *R v Registrar of Companies ex p Attorney General (1991)*, Lindi St Claire, the famous prostitute, formed a company to carry out the service of prostitution. She initially attempted to call the company 'Prostitutes Ltd', 'Hookers Ltd' and 'Lindi St Claire (French Lessons) Ltd'. All of these titles were rejected by the registrar of companies. Subsequently the company was registered as 'Lindi St Claire (Personal Services) Ltd' and this action was then brought to challenge the registration of the company since the company's purposes were unlawful. In the upshot, the company was struck off the register.

The practice of creating 'phoenix' companies with similar names to companies which have gone into liquidation is outlawed by s216 of the Insolvency Act 1986. Contravention of the section leads to civil and criminal consequences.

### 5.1.4 Index of names

The name must not be the same as one already appearing on the index of names kept by the registrar of companies (s66 CA 2006).

The Secretary of State may make provision by regulation supplementing the section. The regulations may make provision:

(a) as to the matters that are to be disregarded; and
(b) as to words, expressions, signs or symbols that are, or are not, to be regarded as the same, for the purposes of the section.

The regulations may provide:

(a) that registration by a name that would otherwise be prohibited under this section is permitted

   (i) in specified circumstances, or
   (ii) with specified consent, and

(b) that if those circumstances obtain or that consent is given at the time a company is registered by a name, a subsequent change of circumstances or withdrawal of consent does not affect the registration.

S67 provides that the Secretary of State may direct a company to change its name if it has been registered in a name that is the same as, or, in the opinion of the Secretary of State, too like:

(a) a name appearing at the time of the registration in the registrar's index of company names; or
(b) a name that should have appeared in that index at that time.

Any such direction must be given within 12 months of the company's registration by the name in question and must specify the period within which the company is to change its name. Failure to comply with the direction constitutes an offence by the company and every officer of the company in default (s68 CA 2006).

### 5.1.5 Specific permission required

The approval of the Secretary of State is required for a company to be registered under the Act by a name that would be likely to give the impression that the company is connected with:

(a) Her Majesty's Government, any part of the Scottish Administration or Her Majesty's Government in Northern Ireland;
(b) a local authority; or
(c) any public authority specified for the purposes of this section by regulations made by the Secretary of State (s54 CA 2006).

Other sensitive words or expressions are covered by s55 of the Companies Act 2006. The approval of the Secretary of State is required for a company to be registered under the Act by a name that includes a word or expression for the time being specified in regulations made by the Secretary of State.

The Secretary of State may, by regulations made under either s54 or s55, require that in connection with an application for approval of the Secretary of State, the applicant must seek the view of a specified government department or other body (s56 CA 2006).

### 5.1.6 Tort of passing off and company names adjudicators

The choice of name may also be limited by the possibility of an action being brought against the company for the tort of passing off. If the name chosen by the company is similar or the same as the name used by an existing business, then the proprietor of that business may bring an action to injunct the company from using the name and may also seek an account of profits. Thus, in *Ewing v Buttercup Margarine Co Ltd (1917)*, the plaintiff, who operated as a sole trader under the name of The Buttercup Dairy Company, sought to restrain the defendants from using the name Buttercup Margarine Co Ltd. The action was successful. To succeed in an action for passing off, the plaintiff would have to show evidence of confusion and that he had suffered economic loss from this confusion. In *Salon Services Hairdressing Supplies Ltd v Direct Salon Services Ltd (1988)*, there was no evidence of economic loss and therefore no injunction was applied.

Provisions in the Companies Act 2006 allow for the first time for objections to a company's registered name where there is similarity to a name in which a person has goodwill.

A person (the applicant) can object to a company's registered name on the grounds:

(a) that it is the same as a name associated with the applicant in which he has goodwill; or
(b) that it is sufficiently similar to mislead by suggesting a connection between the company and the applicant (s69).

The objection must be made by application to a company names adjudicator (see s70).

The respondents must then demonstrate if the ground specified in (a) or (b) above is established by the applicant that:

(a) the name was registered before the commencement of the activities on which the applicant relies to show goodwill; or
(b) that the company

    (i) is operating under the name, or
    (ii) is proposing to do so and has incurred substantial start up costs in preparation, or
    (iii) was formerly operating under the name and is now dormant, or

(c) that the name was registered in the ordinary course of a company formation business and the company is available for sale to the applicant on the standard terms of that business; or
(d) that the name was adopted in good faith; or
(e) that the interests of the applicant are not adversely affected to any significant extent.

If none of these is shown, the objection shall be upheld.

The Secretary of State shall appoint persons to be company names adjudicators (s70 CA 2006), and one of the adjudicators shall be appointed chief adjudicator (s70(4) CA 2006).

The Secretary of State may make procedural rules in relation to proceedings before a company names adjudicator (s71 CA 2006).

The adjudicator may make an order requiring the respondent company to change its name, and requiring all the respondents to take such steps as are within their power to facilitate the making of that change, and not to cause or permit any steps to be taken calculated to result in another company being registered with a name that is an offending name.

The order must specify a date by which the respondent company's name is to be changed, and may be enforced as a court order (s73 CA 2006).

An appeal lies from the adjudicator's decision to the court (s74 CA 2006).

## 5.2  Change of name

S77 of the Companies Act 2006 provides that a company may change its name by special resolution or by any other means provided for by the company's articles. This is significant as the company's articles may provide, for example, that the company's name could be changed by a board resolution. Whether the change is by a special resolution, by a board resolution or by other means, the company must give notice to the registrar (s78).

A change of name may be made conditional upon the happening of an event, and on the happening of the event the company must then give notice to the registrar (s78(2) CA 2006).

When a new certificate of incorporation with the new name is issued, the change of name is effective (s81).

In addition, the name of a company may be changed:

(a)  by resolution of the directors under s64 (change of name to comply with a direction of the Secretary of State where a company ceases to be entitled to exemption from using the word 'Limited' or permitted alternative); or

(b)  by order under s73 (the order of an adjudicator following objection to a company name) (see above).

Mention has already been made of the Secretary of State's power to require a company with a name that is similar to an existing name to change its name (s67 above). In addition, the Secretary of State has the power, within five years of the registration of a company, where it appears that misleading information has been given for the purposes of registration of a particular name, or that an undertaking or assurance has been given for that purpose and has not been fulfilled, then the Secretary of State may direct the company to change its name (s75 CA 2006).

Furthermore, if, in the opinion of the Secretary of State, the name by which a company is registered gives so misleading an indication of the nature of its activities as to be likely to cause harm to the public, the Secretary of State may direct the company to change its name. Such a direction must be complied with within a period of six weeks from the date of the direction, or such longer period as the Secretary of State may think fit to allow. There is no time limit in relation to exercise of this power (s76 CA 2006).

In *Re Association of Certified Public Accountants (1997)*, Jacob J refused to set aside a direction issued by the Secretary of State for Trade and Industry who had directed the company to change its name. The Association of Certified Public Accountants had been set up to provide a professional association for accountants. Membership of the Association was chiefly drawn from people who did not have formal accountancy qualifications. The Secretary of State took the view that use of the word 'certified' indicated some type of formal qualification.

Jacob J agreed that the name was misleading and that since people would be likely to pay more to qualified accountants the name was likely to cause harm.

Companies may trade under names other than their corporate ones. Consent is still required, however, if a connection is suggested with HM's Government or any local authority, as if the word is one of the sensitive ones set out in regulations.

## 5.3 Business names

Part 41 of the Companies Act 2006 deals with business names, i.e. names adopted by businesses and not just companies. This part of the Act is applicable additionally to any business carried on by a sole trader or by any business carried on as a partnership (see s1192 CA 2006).

A person may not, without the approval of the Secretary of State, carry on business in the United Kingdom under a name that would be likely to give the impression that the business is connected with:

(a)  Her Majesty's Government;
(b)  any part of the Scottish administration;
(c)  Her Majesty's Government in Northern Ireland;
(d)  any local authority or public authority specified in regulations made by the Secretary of State (s1193 CA 2006).

Any person who contravenes the section commits an offence.

Furthermore, a person may not, without the approval of the Secretary of State, carry on a business in the United Kingdom under a name that includes a word or expression for the time being specified in regulations made by the Secretary of State under this section (s1194 CA 2006). Once again, a person who contravenes this section commits an offence.

S1195 CA 2006 provides that the Secretary of State may, under s1193 or s1194, require that in connection with an application for approval to the Secretary of State, the applicant should seek the view of a specified Government department or other body. If such a requirement applies, the applicant must request the specified department or other body in writing to indicate whether it has any objections to the proposed name and, if so, why. He should submit to the Secretary of State a statement that such a request has been made and a copy of any response that is received.

The Secretary of State, after giving approval, may withdraw the approval under s1193 or s1194 if it appears to the Secretary of State that there are overriding considerations of public policy that require such approval to be withdrawn.

S1197 covers names that are misleading and considered inappropriate because they are associated with a particular type of company or form of organisation, or are similar to words, expressions or other indications associated with a particular type of company or form of organisation.

A person who uses a name in contravention of regulations under this section once again commits an offence.

S1198 provides that a person must not carry on business in the United Kingdom under a name that gives so misleading an indication of the nature of the activities of the business as will be likely to cause harm to the public. Once again contravention of the section involves the commission of an offence.

S1199 provides that in relation to ss1192–1196 (sensitive words or expressions), and s1197 (inappropriate indication of company, type or legal form) where a person carries on a business under an existing name immediately before the coming into force of this chapter and the use of the name is lawful, then it will remain lawful. Where a business is transferred to a person on or after the date on which the chapter comes into force, and the business is carried on under the same name, then the name for a period of 12 months continues to be lawful, and after that time the transition of lawfulness will end.

Chapter 2 of Part 41 of the Act deals with disclosure that is required in the case of individuals or partnerships.

The Chapter applies to an individual or partnership carrying on business in the United Kingdom under a business name (s1200 CA 2006). The information that is required to be disclosed in the case of an individual is his name, and in the case of a partnership is the name of each member of the partnership (s1201 CA 2006).

S1202 provides that the information is required on:

(a)  all business letters;
(b)  written orders for goods or services to be supplied to the business;
(c)  invoices and receipts issued in the course of the business; and
(d)  written demands for payment of debts arising in the course of the business (s1202 CA 2006).

S1203 allows for exemption for certain large partnerships if they have more than 20 persons if the following conditions are met:

(a)  that the partnership maintains at its principal place of business a list of the names of all the partners;
(b)  no partner's name appears in the document except in the text or as a signatory;
(c)  the document states in legible characters the address of the partnership's principal place of business and that the list of the partners' names is open for inspection there (s1203 CA 2006).

Additionally s1204 requires that a person to whom the Chapter applies must, at the business premises, display in a prominent position so that it may easily be read by customers or suppliers, a notice containing the information required, i.e. the name of the sole trader or the names of all the partners.

S1205 provides for the criminal consequences of failure to make the required disclosure, and s1206 provides for the civil consequences of failure to make disclosure. S1206 provides that in any legal proceedings brought by a person arising out of a contract made in the course of a business in respect of which, at the time the contract was made, there was a breach in failing to disclose in business documents or disclose at business premises, the required information, then the proceedings shall be dismissed if the defendant shows:

(a) that he has a claim against the claimant arising out of the contract that he has been unable to pursue by reason of the latter's breach of the requirements of disclosure; or

(b) that he has suffered some financial loss in connection with the contract by reason of the claimant's breach of those requirements.

## 5.4 A company's registered office

A company must, at all times, have a registered office to which all communications and notices may be addressed (s86 CA 2006).

A company may change the address of its registered office by giving notice to the registrar (s87 CA 2006).

The registered office is important in relation to inspection of registers, indexes and documents and also as to statement of the address of the registered office on company documents (s87(3) CA 2006). This subsection provides that when a company has given notice to the registrar the change in the address of its registered office it may act on the change from that date and, in any event, no later than 14 days from notice in relation to changing the place for inspection and changing the address of the registered office on relevant documents.

Welsh companies may register as such if their registered office is situated in Wales. This allows such companies to file documents in Welsh although translations into English must be made available.

## 5.5 Changes of status

### 5.5.1 Re-registration of a private company as a public company

Ss90–96 of the Companies Act 2006 provide for re-registration of private companies as public companies.

A special resolution for re-registration must be passed, s90(1).

The company must have a share capital and the nominal value of the allotted share capital must be not less than the authorised minimum, and each of the company's allotted shares must be paid up at least as to one quarter of the nominal value plus the whole of any premium. If the shares have been fully or partly paid up by an undertaking given by the person to do work or perform services, then that undertaking must have been performed or otherwise discharged, and if the shares have been allotted as fully or partly paid, otherwise than in cash, and the consideration includes an undertaking other than the one referred to above, then that undertaking must have been performed or discharged, or there must be a contract between the company and the other individual that the undertaking is to be performed within five years of the date of the special resolution (s91 CA 2006).

Additionally, there must be a balance sheet prepared for no earlier than seven months before the date on which the application is delivered to the registrar, an unqualified report by the auditors on the balance sheet, a written statement by the auditors that, in their opinion, at the balance sheet date the amount of the company's net assets was not less than the aggregate of the called up share capital and undistributable reserves, and between the balance sheet date and the date on which the application for re-registration is delivered there must be no change in the company's financial position, resulting in the net assets becoming less than that aggregate (s92 CA 2006).

If shares are allotted by the company in the period between the balance sheet date and the passing of the resolution otherwise for cash, then any valuation required on property in return for non cash consideration must be appropriately carried out (s93).

The application for re-registration must be accompanied by a statement of the company's proposed name on re-registration (s94) and of the company's proposed secretary (s95), together with a copy of the special resolution, a copy of the company's amended articles as proposed, a copy of the balance sheet and other documents required under s92, and if s93 applies a copy of the valuation report. A statement of compliance should accompany the documents that the relevant requirements of this part of the Act have been complied with as to re-registration as a public company (ss94–95).

On an application for re-registration as a public company, the registrar, if satisfied that the company is entitled to be so re-registered, shall re-register it and issue a certificate of incorporation (s96).

### 5.5.2 Re-registration of a public company as a private company

A public company may re-register as a private limited company if a special resolution is passed and if the conditions below are met (s97 CA 2006).

The conditions are that first there must be no application for cancellation of the resolution. S98 provides that there may be an application to cancel a resolution by the holders of not less than 5% in nominal value of the company's issued share capital or any class of the company's issued share capital, or if the company is not limited by shares by not less than 5% of its members or by not less than 50 of the company's members. The members must be dissenting members, i.e. they must not have consented to or voted in favour of the resolution.

The application must be made within 28 days of the passing of the resolution. The court may then make an order cancelling or confirming the resolution.

The application should contain a statement of the company's proposed name on re-registration and a copy of the company's articles as proposed to be amended, together with a statement of compliance that the requirements of the Act have been complied with (s100 CA 2006).

On application for re-registration the registrar, if satisfied that the company is entitled to be re-registered, shall re-register it and issue a new certificate of incorporation (s101 CA 2006).

### 5.5.3 Re-registration of a private limited company as unlimited

S102 of the Companies Act 2006 provides that a private limited company may re-register as an unlimited company if:

(a)  all the members of the company have assented to its being so re-registered, and
(b)  an application is delivered for re-registration in accordance with s103 of the Act; and
(c)  the company has not previously been re-registered as limited.

The application must be accompanied by a statement of the company's proposed name on re-registration, the prescribed form of assent authenticated by or on behalf of all of the members, and a copy of the proposed amended articles, together with a statement of compliance which must contain a statement by the directors that the persons by whom or on whose behalf the form of assent is authenticated constitute the whole membership of the company and, if members have not authenticated the forms themselves, that the directors have taken all reasonable steps to satisfy themselves that each person who acted as agent was lawfully empowered to do so (s103 CA 2006). S104 provides for a certificate of incorporation to be issued on re-registration.

### 5.5.4 Unlimited private company becoming limited

S105 of the Companies Act 2006 provides that an unlimited company may re-register as a private limited company if a special resolution is passed for re-registration, and if the application is made with the accompanying documents provided by s106 of the Act, provided that the company has not previously been re-registered as unlimited. The section provides that the application must be accompanied by a statement of the company's proposed name on re-registration, together with a copy of the resolution, and if the company is to be limited by guarantee, a statement of the guarantee, and, in either case, a copy of the proposed new articles of the company.

A statement of guarantee must state that each member undertakes that if the company is wound up while he is a member, or within a year of his ceasing to be a member, he will contribute to the assets of the company as may be required for:

(a) payment of the debts and liabilities contracted before he ceases to be a member;
(b) payment of the costs, charges and expenses of winding up; and
(c) any adjustment of the rights of the contributories among themselves, not exceeding a specified amount (s106(3)).

A statement of compliance must accompany the documents (s106(4)) and a new certificate of incorporation on re-registration will then be issued if the documents are in order (s107 of the Act).

A company which, on re-registration under s107, already has allotted share capital must, within 15 days after the re-registration, deliver a statement of capital to the registrar setting out the number of shares of the company, the aggregate nominal value of the shares, and for each class of shares:

(i) prescribed particulars of the rights attached to the shares
(ii) the total number of shares of that class
(iii) the aggregate nominal value of shares of that class; and
(iv) the amount paid up and the amount (if any) unpaid on each share (s108).

Failure to comply with the section is an offence committed by the company and every officer of the company who is in default.

### 5.5.5 Re-registration of a public company as a private and unlimited company

S109 of the Act provides that a public company limited by shares may be re-registered as an unlimited private company with a share capital if:

(a) all the members agree;
(b) an application for re-registration is made in accordance with s110 of the Companies Act 2006; and
(c) the company has not previously been re-registered as limited or unlimited.

The application must contain a statement of the company's proposed name on re-registration and must be accompanied by the prescribed form of assent by or on behalf of all the members, and a copy of the company's proposed amended articles.

The statement of compliance made with the application must contain a statement by the directors that:

(a) the persons by or on whose behalf the form of assent is authenticated, constitute the whole membership of the company; and

(b) that if it is authenticated by any agents that the directors have taken reasonable steps to satisfy themselves that they are lawfully empowered to act on behalf of the people they are purporting to act for.

S111 provides for the issue of a certificate of incorporation on re-registration.

## 5.6 Objects of the company

A company henceforth will have unrestricted objects unless the company's articles specifically restrict its objects (s31). Therefore a company will be able to do anything that is lawful except to the extent that its articles state otherwise. Many companies will, of course, wish to have restricted objects and those companies that already have restricted objects clauses may continue with them.

What was previously the memorandum of the company would contain a statement of the company's objects. Historically, this statement of objects was envisaged as a short, crisp statement of what the company was set up to do. It will be seen that this turned out to be extremely wide of what occurred in practice.

The registrar of companies does not exercise any supervisory role in relation to a company's objects except to ensure that those objects are legal. Mention has already been made of *R v Registrar of Companies ex p Attorney General (1991)* (see section 5.1.3). Registration of the company is not, however, conclusive evidence of the fact that its objects are legal: see *Bowman v Secular Society Ltd (1917)*.

However, the statement of a company's objects is important for other reasons. A company may be restrained from doing something which is outside the scope of its objects clause. Thus, in *Simpson v Westminster Palace Hotel Co (1860)*, a shareholder sought to restrain the hotel company from letting out rooms as office space. In the event, it was held that this was not *ultra vires* the company's objects but it was held that had it been so an injunction could have been issued. In *Stephens v Mysore Reefs (Kangundy) Mining Co Ltd (1902)*, a goldmining company which was set up to mine in India was restrained from mining for gold in West Africa as this was beyond its objects clause (see now s40(4) CA 2006).

A second reason why a company's statement of objects is important is that if the substratum of the company (its *raison d'être*) is destroyed, then a petitioner may apply to wind the company up on the just and equitable ground under s122(1)(g) of the Insolvency Act 1986. Thus, in *Re German Date Coffee Company (1882)*, a company was set up to work a German patent to manufacture coffee from dates. The German patent was not granted. The company did, however, obtain a Swedish patent. A petition brought by two shareholders to wind the company up on the grounds that its objects had failed was successful despite the fact that some shareholders wished to continue with the company's activities in Sweden. Such petitions are a rarity.

An important area in relation to a company's objects clause is the question of to what extent a contract beyond the capacity of the company is enforceable, either against the company or by the company. It was formerly the case that such contracts were void at common law. Thus, in *Ashbury Railway Carriage & Iron Co Ltd v Riche (1875)*, the company's objects were stated to be making, selling and hiring railway carriages. The company entered into a contract to build a railway in Belgium. The contract was approved by the shareholders at a general meeting of the company. It was held that the contract was *ultra vires* the company and that it made no difference that the shareholders had affirmed the contract as it was void *ab initio*. The company was thus able to avoid the contract and was not liable for damages to the other party to the agreement. The validity of *ultra vires* contracts has been altered dramatically by statute, as will be demonstrated below.

## 5.7 Drafting the objects clause

Although not as crucial as formerly when *ultra vires* contracts were void, the drafting of a company's objects clause is still clearly important where companies elect to have objects clauses. The consequences of a company engaging in activities outside of its objects clause have just been examined. The history of objects clauses and their interpretation is largely a history of conflict between the judiciary on the one hand, which wished to confine objects clauses to short crisp statements of the company's activities and entrepreneurs on the other hand, who wished to provide companies with as much latitude as possible in their activities. In *Re Crown Bank (1890)*, North J held that a company's *intra vires* activities were limited to its main economic activity and that other matters stated in the company's objects clause could only exist in relation to that main economic activity. The effect of this decision was at issue in *Cotman v Brougham (1918)*. In this case, the House of Lords had to consider the objects clause of Essequibo Rubber & Tobacco Estates Ltd. The objects clause enabled the company to carry on virtually every type of activity. In the Court of Appeal, Lord Cozens Hardy MR had said:

> Now we are familiar with an enumeration of objects which extends the full length of the alphabet, and sometimes beyond it, so that you get sub-clauses (aa) and (bb) after you have exhausted all the other letters.

The last sub-clause of the objects clause provided that every sub-clause should be construed as a substantive object of the company and that none of the sub-clauses should be deemed to be subsidiary or auxiliary to the principal object. At issue was the matter of underwriting certain shares in an oil company. Applying the principle in *Re Crown Bank*, underwriting could only exist as an *intra vires* business in relation to rubber and tobacco. However, the statement in the company's objects clause was held to be valid, with the result that the activity was held to be *intra vires*. The House of Lords thus reluctantly held the provision in the memorandum to be valid.

Another drafting device used to extend the scope of a company's permitted activities was at issue in *Bell Houses Ltd v City Wall Properties Ltd (1966)*. The company was engaged in acquiring land and building houses. A sub-clause of the objects clause permitted the company 'to carry on any other trade or business whatsoever which can, in the opinion of the board of directors be advantageously carried on by the company in connection with or as ancillary to any of the above businesses or the general business of the company'.

The plaintiff company had introduced a financier to the defendant company for an agreed fee. In this case, the plaintiff company was suing for this fee. The defendants meanwhile alleged that the contract was *ultra vires* as the plaintiffs were in the business of developing property not helping others to do so. At first instance, the action of the plaintiffs for their fee was dismissed on the ground that the contract was *ultra vires*. The plaintiffs appealed to the Court of Appeal. The appeal was successful. It was held that the objects clause permitted the directors to carry on any business which they considered could be advantageously carried on with the main business. It is, however, worth stressing that this decision of itself does not permit a company to register an objects clause where the directors can simply decide that some other activity is advantageous and profitable. This is because there are limiting words in the sub-clause, namely 'in connection with or as ancillary to'. Therefore, there must be some nexus between the new business and the company's principal business.

The interpretation of an objects clause was also in issue in *Re New Finance and Mortgage Company Limited (in liquidation) (1975)*. The object clause of this company provided that the company could act 'as financiers, capitalists, concessionaires, bankers, commercial agents, mortgage brokers, financial agents and advisers, exporters and importers of goods and merchandise of all kinds, and merchants generally'. The company in fact ran two garages and garage shops. The company went into voluntary liquidation and Total Oil (Great Britain) Ltd sought to prove in the liquidation in relation to the sale of motor oil to the company. The liquidator rejected the proof as he contended that the purchase of the oil was *ultra vires*. The court held that the words 'and merchants generally' were broad enough to cover all types of commercial transactions and that therefore the purchase of the motor oil was *intra vires*.

The impresario, Sir David Frost, has also indirectly contributed to the law in this area. In *Newstead (Inspector of Taxes) v Frost (1983)*, the objects clause of a memorandum of a company authorised to carry on and execute all kinds of financial, commercial, trading or other operations was held to be valid. Some doubts were expressed on this by Viscount Dilhorne in the House of Lords but the objects clause was nevertheless upheld. At issue was the validity of a tax savings scheme entered into by David Frost with the company. The case is analysed by Pettet in 'Unlimited Objects Clauses' [1981] 97 LQR 15.

The combined effect of the jurisprudence of these various cases is to indicate that by ingenious drafting it is possible to give a company an extremely wide capacity within which to act. Such decisions inevitably led to a questioning of the law in this area and prompted reform. This will be examined below.

As noted above, unless a company's articles specifically restrict the objects of the company, its objects are unrestricted (s31(1) CA 2006).

Where a company amends its articles to add, remove or alter a statement of the company's objects, it must give notice to the registrar and the registrar on notice will register the amendment, and once entered on the register the amendment is effective (s31(2) CA 2006).

## 5.8 *Ultra vires* contracts and common law

It has already been noted that, at common law, contracts that were outside of a company's objects clause were *ultra vires* and void. Such contracts could not be enforced by the company or against the company: see *Ashbury Iron and Railway Carriage Company v Riche*. It made no difference whether the person dealing with the company knew what the company's objects were or not.

The whole doctrine of *ultra vires* rested on the principle of constructive notice, the rule in *Ernest v Nichols (1857)*, whereby a person dealing with a company was deemed to know what was in its constitution. A person dealing with a company was however entitled to assume that where an activity could have been executed in an *ultra vires* or an *intra vires* way it would be executed in an *intra vires* way. Thus, in *Re David Payne & Co Ltd (1904)*, where a company borrowed money that was in fact applied to its *ultra vires* business, the lender of the money was entitled to sue on the contract as he was entitled to assume that the loan was to be used for *intra vires* activities. This did not help the outsider if he actually knew the purpose of the loan, even though he might not have realised it was *ultra vires*. The combination of actual knowledge of the activity and constructive notice of its *ultra vires* nature would be fatal. Thus, in *Re Introductions Ltd (1970)*, where the company went into the *ultra vires* business of pig breeding, the lender of money, knowing that the purpose of the loan was for pig breeding, was unable to enforce the loan (nor could the lender rely upon a substantive provision permitting the company to borrow contained in the objects clause, as the court held that borrowing of itself could not stand as a substantive separate object of a company). In *Re Jon Beauforte (London) Ltd (1953)*, a supplier provided a company with coke. In fact, the coke was used for the *ultra vires* activity of manufacturing veneered panels. The *intra vires* business was stated in the company's objects clause *inter alia* as costumiers, gown, robe, dress and mantle makers. At common law, the supplier had constructive notice of the objects clause. The order for the coke was placed on notepaper that showed that the company was in the business of manufacturing veneer panels. The court held that this combination of actual notice (by virtue of the notepaper) and constructive notice was fatal to the supplier's claim.

The whole area of *ultra vires* contracts and unauthorised acts of directors (an area that will be examined below) came up for consideration in *Rolled Steel Products (Holdings) Ltd v British Steel Corporation and others (1986)*. The state of the law could scarcely be said to be satisfactory before the decision in *Rolled Steel Products*. The decision in this case further adds to the mosaic of rules in relation to *ultra vires* acts of a company and unauthorised acts of directors.

Rolled Steel Products owed money to S Ltd. One of the directors of Rolled Steel Products (S) was also a director of S Ltd. S Ltd owed money to Colvilles Ltd which was a subsidiary of British Steel Corporation. This debt was guaranteed personally by S, the director of Rolled Steel Products and S Ltd. Colvilles believed that S and S Ltd would have insufficient assets to pay back their debt. They therefore proposed that they would lend money to Rolled Steel Products, who would use this money to pay off S Ltd, who could then pay part of the debt owed to Colvilles and that Rolled Steel Products would guarantee payment of the remainder of the debt, creating a debenture to secure the debt.

Rolled Steel Products had a provision in its constitution permitting it to give guarantees and security. The board resolution passed by Rolled Steel Products to grant the guarantee was only quorate by virtue of S's presence. S should have declared an interest and should not have counted in the quorum. The meeting was therefore insufficient for these purposes.

At first instance, Vinelott J held that the guarantee and the debenture were void as they were for purposes other than those authorised by the constitution. This reasoning is consistent with the reasoning in *Re Introductions Ltd*.

On appeal, however, the Court of Appeal held that since the company had the power in its constitution to give guarantees and to provide security, the company had contractual capacity to make the guarantee and debenture and that therefore the acts were not *ultra vires* the company. This clearly casts doubt on the decision in *Re Introductions Ltd* although it was not overruled.

The Court of Appeal went on to say, however, that the directors were acting beyond their powers in providing a guarantee and security for purposes other than those authorised by the constitution and since the defendant knew of this lack of authority, they could acquire no rights under the guarantee or the debenture.

It is to be noted that, although the decision in *Rolled Steel Products* was made in 1985, the relevant facts arose in 1969 and, therefore, were unaffected by the first statutory intervention in this area under the European Communities Act 1972. The whole issue of judicial control of objects clause and *ultra vires* activity is considered by Rajak in 'Judicial Control: Corporations and the decline of *Ultra Vires*' (1995) Camb.LR 9, where Rajak notes that the high water mark of the doctrine of *ultra vires* was in the 1870s, and that by the end of the 1980s it had largely ceased to exist in any meaningful way.

The somewhat confused and arbitrary decisions in relation to what contracts were enforceable and what contracts were not, together with the decisions on the interpretation of objects clauses, prompted the government to consider statutory reform of the *ultra vires* rule and led to the commissioning of the Prentice Report, which is considered below. In the meantime, however, British membership of the European Communities had necessitated reform of British company law in line with the first directive on EC company law which had been passed in 1968 (68/152).

## 5.9  Section 9(1) of the European Communities Act 1972

Article 9 of the first EC directive on company law provides as follows:

(i)  Acts done by the organs of the company shall be binding upon it even if those acts are not within the objects of the company, unless such acts exceed the powers that the law confers or allows to be conferred on those organs.

However, Member States may provide that the company shall not be bound where such acts are outside the objects of the company, if it proves that the third party knew the act was outside those objects or could not in view of the circumstances have been unaware of it; disclosure of the statute shall not of itself be sufficient proof thereof.

(ii)  The limits on the powers of the organs of the company, arising under the statutes from a decision of the competent organ, may never be relied on as against third parties, even if they have been disclosed.

Section 9(1) of the European Communities Act passed on the UK becoming a member of what is now the European Union accordingly provided that in favour of a person dealing with a company in good faith any transaction decided on by the directors shall be deemed to be one which it is within the capacity of the company to enter into and the power of the directors to bind the company shall be deemed to be free of any limitation under the memorandum or articles of association, and a party to a transaction so decided on shall not be bound to enquire as to the capacity of the company to enter into it, or as to any such limitation on the power of the directors, and shall be presumed to have acted in good faith unless the contrary is proved.

Several points should be noted in relation to s9(1) of the ECA 1972 (later re-enacted as s35 of the Companies Act 1985) and what is now s40 CA 2006. These are as follows:

(a)  The provision only operated in favour of a person dealing with the company. Thus, the company itself could not take advantage of the section to enforce an *ultra vires* contract.
(b)  The section only operated where the person dealing with the company was acting in good faith.
   The section failed to contain a definition of good faith but, as is stated, there is a presumption of good faith that stands unless the contrary is proved. In *Barclays Bank Ltd v TOSG Trust Fund Ltd (1984)*, Nourse J stated *obiter* that a person acts in good faith if he acts genuinely and honestly in the

circumstances of the case and that it is not necessary to show that he acted reasonably to demonstrate that he acted in good faith.

In *Wrexham Association Football Club Ltd v Crucialmove Ltd (2006)* it was held that a contractor who did not deal with the board was required to check the authority of the person purporting to act for the company where circumstances suggested that enquiry should be made.

(c) The transaction had to be decided on by the directors.

There was no guidance given as to how this was to be determined but it seems from the decision in *International Sales and Agencies v Marcus (1982)* that, provided the chain of delegation can be traced back to the board of directors, this was sufficient for satisfying the condition in the section.

## 5.10 The Prentice Report and the Companies Act 1989

In light of the obvious anomalies in the law and the ease with which companies could avoid falling into the *ultra vires* trap, the government asked Dr Dan Prentice of Oxford University to investigate the area of objects clauses and *ultra vires* with a view to the possible abolition of the *ultra vires* doctrine and recommending any necessary safeguards for investors and creditors.

The report recommended the abolition of the doctrine with few provisos, although the resulting Companies Act 1989 provisions did not go as far as some of the more radical recommendations of the Prentice Report.

The Companies Act 1989 did provide for alteration of objects clauses in any circumstances by special resolution and for the adoption of a general objects clause permitting a company to operate as a general commercial company. As has been noted, these provisions have now been overtaken by s31 CA 2006 providing that companies have unrestricted capacity unless they adopt restricted objects clauses. A provision relating to objects contained in the company's articles is now alterable by special resolution in a similar way to other provisions in a company's articles.

## 5.11 A company's capacity under the Companies Act 2006

The general thrust of the provisions contained in the Companies Act 1985, as amended by the Companies Act 1989, are retained in the Companies Act 2006.

S39 of the Companies Act 2006 provides that the validity of an act done by a company should not be called into question on the ground of lack of capacity by reason of anything in the company's constitution.

This section is therefore wider than merely encompassing provisions relating to the company's objects. In *Re Cleveland Trust (1991)*, the constitution restricted the payment of dividends. The restriction, despite being outside of the objects clause, would be caught by s39.

S40 of the 2006 Act provides that in favour of a person dealing with a company in good faith, the power of the directors to bind the company, or authorise others to do so, is deemed to be free of any limitation under the company's constitution.

A person deals with a company if he is a party to any transaction or other act to which the company is a party. A person dealing with a company is not bound to enquire as to any limitation on the powers of the directors to bind the company or authorise others to do so and is presumed to have acted in good faith unless the contrary is proved, and is not to be regarded as acting in bad faith by reason only of his knowing that an act is beyond the powers of the directors under the company's constitution (s40(1), (2), (3)).

The section does not, however, affect any right of a member to restrain the company from doing something that is beyond the power of the directors, but no such proceedings lie in respect of an act to be done in fulfilment of a legal obligation arising from a previous act of the company (s40(4)) (see section 14.2.1).

The section does not affect any liability incurred by the directors or any other person by reason of the directors exceeding their powers (s40(5)).

## 5.12 Transactions involving directors or their associates – CA 2006

S41 provides that where a company enters into a transaction and the parties to the transaction include:

(i)  a director of the company or its holding company, or
(ii) a person connected with any such director

the transaction is voidable at the instance of the company.

Whether or not the contract is voided, any director of the company or of its holding company, or a person connected with any such director, and any director of the company who authorised the transaction, is liable to account to the company for any gain he has made directly or indirectly from the transaction, and to indemnify the company for any loss or damage resulting from the transaction.

However, the transaction ceases to be voidable if:

(a) restitution of any money or other asset which was the subject of the transaction is no longer possible, or
(b) the company is indemnified for any loss or damage resulting from the transaction, or
(c) rights acquired bona fide for value without notice of the directors exceeding their powers by a person who is not a party to the transaction would be effected by the avoidance of the transaction, or
(d) the transaction is affirmed by the company.
    It should be noted that transaction in this context includes any act (s41 CA 2006).

## 5.13 Directors' power to bind the company – CA 2006

Where a person deals with a company in good faith, the power of the directors to bind the company shall be deemed to be free of any limitation under the company's constitution. The outsider is not to be regarded as in bad faith by reason only of his knowing the act was beyond the directors' powers (s40).

It should be noted that s40 protects an outsider who deals with a company and that 'deals' is now defined as where a person is a party to any transaction or other act. This would seemingly encompass gifts and the receipt of cheques (see *International Sales and Agencies Ltd v Marcus (1982)* under the old law).

In *Smith v Henniker-Major & Co (2002)*, the question of whether a director of a company as opposed to an entirely independent third party could rely on what is now s40. The section provides that a company may be bound by the actions of its directors in favour of a person dealing with the company in good faith.

A joint venture company (SPDL) was formed to acquire a site with development potential. The plaintiff held 30% of the shares in the company and was also one of its four directors. Two of the company's directors used another company (SPL) to accomplish the deal with help from SPDL's solicitors, the defendants Henniker-Major & Co. The plaintiff alleged that the defendant's solicitors had accepted a retainer on behalf of SPL in breach of their fiduciary duties, as SPDL had already instructed them. The plaintiff, as a creditor of SPDL through guarantees for loans, decided to assign himself the cause of action against the solicitors and to sue them. Notice of a board meeting to carry out this assignment was given to the other remaining director (the other two directors having resigned). The other remaining director, however, did not attend the board meeting. The plaintiff went ahead with the meeting and, against the articles (as the meeting was not quorate), resolved to assign himself the cause of action. The defendant's firm of solicitors argued the assignment of the cause of action was void as the board was inquorate. The plaintiff sought to rely on what is now s40 protecting those dealing with a company by shielding them from the provisions of the company's constitution, i.e. here the provision relating to the quorum.

The Court of Appeal agreed that the plaintiff could not rely on the section to assign himself the company's cause of action. The policy of the section was to protect somebody from outside of the company and certainly somebody who wasn't a director who has no reason to doubt the authenticity of a particular act of the company. This could not be said to be the case here the court said. The court considered that in principle the section was wide enough to include a director as a person dealing with the company, but in this case the plaintiff was not merely a director, he was also chairman, and as such it was his duty to ensure the constitution was properly applied. He could not, therefore, rely on the section where he, himself, was responsible for the company's constitution not being followed.

## 5.14 Charities

S39 and s40 relating to corporate capacity and the power of directors to bind the company do not apply to the acts of a company that is a charity except in the following circumstances:

(a) in favour of a person who does not know, at the time that the Act is done, that the company is a charity, or
(b) a person who gives full consideration in money or money's worth in relation to the Act in question and does not know (as the case may be)

    (i) that the act is not permitted by the company's constitution, or
    (ii) that the act is beyond the powers of the directors.

In these two situations s39 and s40 will apply.

Where a company that is a charity purports to transfer or grant an interest in property, the fact that (as the case may be) the act was not permitted by the company's constitution or that the directors exceeded any limitation on their powers under the constitution, does not affect the title of a person acquiring the property or any interest in it for full consideration without notice of the circumstances affecting the validity of the company's act (s42(2) CA 2006).

## 5.15 Capital

As noted, s59 of the Companies Act 2006 provides that a statement of capital must be delivered at the time of registration. The statement of capital and initial shareholdings must state:

(a) the total number of shares of the company to be taken on formation by the subscribers to the memorandum;
(b) the aggregate nominal value of those shares;
(c) for each class of those shares prescribed particulars of the rights attached to them, the total number of shares of that class and the aggregate nominal value of shares of that class;
(d) the amount to be paid up and the amount (if any) unpaid, on each share.

Companies are no longer required to have an authorised share capital, although they may do so and may include such a restriction in their articles.

In consequence of this, whenever a company's share capital changes, whether by reduction or by an allotment of new shares, then in addition to other formalities the company must deliver to the registrar of companies a statement of capital. Thus, for example, under s555 of the Companies Act 2006, when a limited company makes an allotment of shares, there must be delivered to the registrar for registration a return of the allotment within one month which must be accompanied by a statement of capital. The statement of capital parallels that set out in s10 above.

It must therefore state the total number of shares of the company, the aggregate nominal value of the shares, for each class of shares:

(i) prescribed particulars of the rights attached to the shares;
(ii) the total number of shares of that class;
(iii) the aggregate nominal value of shares of that class

as well as the amount paid up and the amount (if any) unpaid on each share. This statement of capital should thus provide an up-to-date resumé of the capital of the company at any given time.

## SUMMARY

### The company's constitution: Some vital considerations

The Companies Act 2006 makes a fundamental change to Company Law in regard to the constitution. Henceforth the memorandum of association is an application to the registrar for registration. The application will state the company's proposed name, the situate of the registered office, the potential liability of members, and whether the company is to be private or public. It will be accompanied by a statement of capital if this is appropriate or a statement of guarantee if this applies. Additionally there will be a statement of the company's proposed offices, together with the application for registration.

These matters are considered in this chapter.

### Further reading

de Gay, S, 'Problems surrounding use of the new single objects clause' (1993) 137 SJ 146.
Farrar, JH, '*Inquorate Boards, Organs and Section 35A of the Companies Act 1985*' [2003] CLJ 45.
Ferran, E, 'The reform of the law on corporate capacity and directors' and officers' authority' (1992) 13 Co Law 124 and 177.
Frommel, SN, 'Reform of the *ultra vires* rule: a personal view' (1987) 8 Co Law 11.
Hanningan, BM, 'The reform of the *ultra vires* rule' [1987] JBL 173.
Heatherington, P, and Knapp, J, s35A CA 85 (2003) 153 MLJ 640.
Howell, C, 'Companies Act 1985' s35A and s322A (2003) 24 Co Law 264.
Pettet, BG, 'Unlimited objects clauses?' (1981) 97 LQR 15.
Poole, J, 'Abolition of the *ultra vires* doctrine and agency problems (1991) 12 Co Law 43.
Rajak, H, 'Judicial control: corporations and the decline of *ultra vires*' (1995) CLR 9.
Twigg-Flesner, C, 'Sections 35A and 322A revisited: Who is a 'person dealing with a company'?' (2005) 26 Co Law 195.
Wedderburn, KW, '*Ultra vires* in modern company law' (1983) 46 MLR 204.
Wedderburn, KW, '*Unreformed Company Law*' (1969) 32 MLR 563.

# 6

# The articles of association

The company has been formed and as noted must have articles prescribing regulations for the company (s18 CA 2006).

With the Companies Act 2006, a company will effectively have a single constitution rather than the two components of memorandum and articles that prevailed before the Companies Act 2006. This will be the articles. As noted in Chapter 5, the new style memorandum is a document in a prescribed form stating that the subscribers intend to form a company and undertake to become members and to take at least one share each (s8 CA 2006). The previous chapter considered some of the vital provisions of the constitution and also how a company may change its status.

Since 1856 model articles have been provided for certain types of companies, for example, Companies Act 1985 Table A provides model articles for companies limited by shares. This operates as a 'default' set of articles for all such companies. If a company therefore devises its own Articles of Association, Table A will not apply except to the extent that the table adopted by the company is not comprehensive. The view was taken that Table A, which has been revised several times over the last 150 years, but essentially remains a product of the Victorian era both in terms of language and substance, was in need of a rethink. It is essentially drafted in terms of public rather than private companies and successive revisions have tended to include increasingly complex provisions designed to cover every conceivable event or set of circumstances.

The result is that the vast majority of the provisions in Companies Act 1985, Table A are irrelevant to the vast majority of companies. The 'one size fits all' approach has a number of problems. The 1985 Act Table A is user unfriendly, poorly laid out, and often unintelligible to non-specialists. Most of it concerns matters which are remote from the concerns of smaller companies, and it does not take account of relatively recent changes in the law, e.g. the introduction of single member companies.

Following the recommendations of the Company Law Review, the government considered that reform of Table A was an important part of updating company law for a modern economy. It proposed in future that there should be:

- a radically simplified set of model articles for private companies limited by shares

- for the first time a full set of model articles for private companies limited by guarantee
- comprehensive, clear and concise guidance for small companies who are using or thinking of using model articles.

To companies set up under the new legislation, the default provisions will apply in relation to the new types of model articles in the same way as they did for Companies Act 1985 Table A. Existing companies will be able to replace their current articles with the new model articles if their members pass a special resolution to do so.

S19 of the Companies Act 2006 provides that the Secretary of State may, by regulations, prescribe model articles of association for companies. Different model articles may be prescribed for different descriptions of company. Draft model articles for private companies limited by shares, and for public companies have already been produced. Sometime in 2007 the final state of the model articles will become known.

S20 applies the default principle to the extent that a company's registered articles do not cover every situation the relevant model articles will fill the gap. Additionally, this section makes it clear that the model articles that are in existence at the time a company is formed will be the articles that apply in default (s20 CA 2006).

## 6.1  Resolutions or agreements affecting a company's constitution

S30 of the Companies Act 2006 provides that copies of resolutions or agreements, or written memoranda setting out the terms of such which affect a company's constitution, must be forwarded to the registrar within 15 days and recorded by him.

S29 sets out the resolutions and agreements to which s30 applies. These are:

(a)  any special resolution;
(b)  any resolution or agreement agreed to by all the members of a company (which otherwise would only have passed as a special resolution);
(c)  any resolution or agreement agreed to by all the members of a class of shareholders (which otherwise would only have passed by resolution with a specified majority);
(d)  any resolution or agreement that binds all members of a class of shareholders though not agreed to by all those members;
(e)  a resolution to give, vary, revoke or renew authority in relation to the allotment of shares by directors (s551(9) CA 2006);
(f)  a resolution to redenominate share capital or a class of share capital under s622(8) CA 2006.;
(g)  a resolution of the directors of a company in connection with re-registration in consequence of a company acquiring its own shares, under s664(1) CA 2006;

(h) a resolution conferring varying revoking or renewing authority under s701(8) of the Companies Act 2006 (market purchase of a company's own shares);

(i) a resolution for voluntary winding up; (s84(1)(a) of the Insolvency Act 1986)

(j) a resolution of a director of an old public company that the company should be re-registered as a public company; (s2(1) of the Companies Consolidation (Consequential Provisions) Act 1985).

(k) a resolution passed by virtue of regulations made under s790 of the Companies Act 2006 (transfer of title to securities).

Such resolutions and agreements should be embodied in or annexed to the company's articles.

## 6.2 Companies' objects

S31 CA 2006 provides that, unless a company's articles specifically restrict the objects of the company, its objects are unrestricted.

Where a company amends its articles so as to add, remove or alter a statement of the company's objects, it must give notice of this to the registrar (s31(2)).

The provisions of this section have effect subject to the special position of charities (s42 CA 2006) (see section 5.14).

## 6.3 Constitutional documents and members

S32 provides that a company must, on request by any member, send him a copy of the up-to-date articles of the company, together with a copy of any resolution or agreement that has been recorded under s30 as described above.

The provisions of a company's constitution, when registered, bind the company and its members to the same extent as if they were covenants, signed and sealed on behalf of the company and of each member, to observe those provisions (s33 CA 2006). (See below.)

## 6.4 Alteration of the articles of association

S21 of the Companies Act 2006 provides that a company may amend its articles by special resolution.

S22 of the Act provides that a company's articles may provide that specified provisions of the articles may be amended or repealed only if conditions are met or procedures are complied with that are more restrictive than those applicable to the case of a simple special resolution, i.e. provisions in a company's constitution may be entrenched.

If a company's articles on formation contain entrenchment provisions or are subsequently altered to include entrenchment provisions, the company must give notice to the registrar (s23 CA 2006). Similarly, if a company removes provisions for entrenchment, the registrar must be given notice of that fact (s24 CA 2006).

With regard to existing companies, s28 provides that the provisions that immediately before the commencement of this part of the Act (Part III) were contained in a company's memorandum are to be treated after the commencement of this part of the act as provisions of the company's articles.

This applies not only to substantive provisions but also to provisions relating to entrenchment.

As has been noted, a company may alter its articles of association by special resolution (s21 of the Companies Act 2006). Indeed, any article that seems to restrict a company's freedom to alter its articles is invalid (see *Allen v Gold Reefs of West Africa (1900)*), although a separate shareholders' agreement may validly restrict the alterability of the company's articles on the part of shareholders. In *Russell v Northern Bank Development Corporation Ltd (1992)*, four shareholders of a company had agreed not to vote in favour of increasing the company share capital unless all the shareholders and the company agreed in writing. The House of Lords held that the company could not be bound by this agreement. However, the agreement could stand as it was valid amongst the shareholders without the company's participation. Had the agreement merely involved the company, this would have been void, whether it had been included in the company's constitution or as part of an external agreement, as it would involve the company fettering its statutory powers.

A company cannot be restricted from altering its articles even if this results in a breach of contract between the company and a third party (see *Southern Foundries (1926) Ltd v Shirlaw (1940)*).

There are various considerations for a company to bear in mind in relation to changes of articles. Now the minority remedy in ss994–996 CA 2006 (remedy for unfairly prejudicial conduct) is likely to be used by a party wishing to challenge a change of the company's articles.

The power of a company to alter its articles is subject to certain conditions:

(a) A company cannot alter its articles to contravene the provisions of the Companies Act. Thus, for example, any provision in the articles which would seek to exempt a director from liability for negligence is void by virtue of s232.

(b) Any alteration of the articles which conflicts with an order of the court is, of course, void. Thus an order of the court under s996 relating to the remedy for unfairly prejudicial conduct cannot be overridden by a change of articles.

(c) If the alteration of articles involves an alteration or abrogation of class rights, then, in addition to the special resolution required under s21, the company must follow the regime appropriate to variation of class rights set out in ss629–634. (This will be considered below – see section 6.5).

(d) In addition to the statutory restrictions, the power to alter a company's articles is subject to the principle that any alteration must be *bona fide* for the benefit of the company as a whole. In *Allen v The Gold Reefs of West Africa Ltd (1900)*, the company's articles of association gave the company a lien upon all partly paid shares held by a member for any debt owed to the company.

A member who held some partly paid shares was also the only holder of fully paid shares in the company. Upon his death, he owed money in relation to the partly paid shares. The company altered its articles by special resolution to provide for a lien over fully paid shares. This alteration was questioned. The Court of Appeal held that the company could alter its articles provided that the alteration was in good faith. Lord Lindley MR said:

> ... the power conferred by it [s21] must, like all other powers, be exercised subject to those general principles of law and equity which are applicable to all powers conferred on majorities and enabling them to bind minorities. It must be exercised, not only in the manner required by law, but also bona fide for the benefit of the company as a whole, and it must not be exceeded.

Much of the case law has centred upon a discussion of how it is to be determined whether an alteration is for the benefit of the company as a whole. In *Greenhalgh v Arderne Cinemas Ltd (1951)*, it was proposed to delete a provision in the company's articles which gave members a right of pre-emption over shares that a member wanted to sell. It seemed that the majority shareholder, Mr Mallard, was prompted not by what was in the company's best interest but out of malice towards a minority shareholder. The question arose as to whether the alteration was for the benefit of the company as a whole. Lord Evershed MR said that:

> ... the phrase 'the company as a whole' does not (at any time in such a case as the present) mean the company as a commercial entity, distinct from the corporators; it means the corporators as a general body. That is to say, the case may be taken of an individual hypothetical member and it may be asked what is proposed, in the honest opinion of those who voted in its favour, for that person's benefit.

In this case, the Court of Appeal held that the alteration was valid.

This analysis does raise difficulties in determining the benefit of the individual hypothetical member. It is clear that hardship to a minority will not of itself invalidate an alteration of articles. In *Sidebottom v Kershaw Leese & Co Ltd (1920)*, a minority shareholder in the company carried on a business that was competing with the company. It was proposed to alter the company's articles to insert a clause whereby a shareholder who competed with the company would be required to transfer his shares at a fair value to the directors. It was held that the alteration was valid even though it was carried out specifically against one particular member. The clause in question, of course, could apply in relation to any member.

By contrast, in *Brown v British Abrasive Wheel Co Ltd (1919)*, where 98% majority shareholders wished to insert a provision in the articles requiring the minority who were not prepared to invest further capital to sell their shares as a condition of the majority's providing further capital, the alteration was held invalid. It was noted that such a provision could be used to require a minority to sell its shares at the will of the majority.

The cases do appear to be inconsistent. If the question is not what is for the benefit of the company as a separate corporate entity, it is difficult to conjure up a hypothetical shareholder in whose interest the alteration must be. Malevolence did not prevent Mr Mallard succeeding in *Greenhalgh v Arderne Cinemas*, why should the majority's view be overridden in *Brown v British Abrasive Wheel Co Ltd*? A possible interpretation is offered by Lord Evershed MR in the *Greenhalgh* case where he argues that if the effect of the alteration is to discriminate between the majority shareholders and the minority shareholders to give the majority an advantage, then the alteration should not be permitted.

(e) It is now the case that ss994–996 will provide a possible remedy to a shareholder who has been unfairly   prejudiced in the conduct of a company's affairs by the use of majority voting power. This may be in relation to altered articles, see e.g. *Re D R Chemicals (1989)* – dilution of voting power, and *Re a Company (No. 005685 of 1988) exp Schwarz (1989)* – deletion of pre-emption rights. In addition courts have sometimes been willing to act to protect minority shareholders from the oppressive use of majority voting power. See *Clemens v Clemens Brothers Ltd and Another (1976)*, *Estmanco (Kilner House) Ltd v Greater London Council (1982)*. Ways in which disgruntled shareholders can object to alterations of articles are considered by Rixon in 'Competing Interests and Conflicting Principles: An Examination of the Power of Alteration of Articles of Association' [1986] MLR 446.

(f) A final point should be noted in relation to alteration of the articles. Notwithstanding that an alteration of the articles may result in a breach of contract by the company, an injunction will not issue to stop the alteration taking place, see *Southern Foundries (1926) Ltd v Shirlaw (1940)*. The innocent party will, of course, be able to pursue a remedy in relation to the breach of contract.

## 6.5 Variation of class rights

Variation of class rights was formerly of the more complex areas in company law. It was an intricate web of legal technicalities and judicial nuances. The basic principle is that an alteration of rights attached to a particular class of shares involves a special regime, which generally means that separate class consent has to be given. The principle is to protect the holders of those special rights.

The statutory rules are set out in ss629–634 of the Companies Act 2006.

Often, a company may have just one class of shares with uniform rights. In such a situation, questions of class rights obviously do not arise. Often, however, there will be additional classes of shares, such as preference shares or management shares.

### 6.5.1 Class Rights

S629 of CA 2006 provides that, for the purposes of this chapter, shares are of one class if the rights attached to them are in all respects uniform. For this purpose the rights attached to shares are not regarded as different from those attached to other shares by reason only that they do not carry the same rights to dividends in the 12 months immediately following their allotment.

Despite the statutory provision, defining a class of shares remains difficult, statutory provision is as broad. Vaisey J offered a workable definition in *Greenhalgh v Arderne Cinemas Ltd (1945)* where he said 'although the word "class" is not a word of technical art, you cannot put people, whether they be shareholders or policy holders, into the same class if their claims or rights diverge. Rights may well be attached to certain shares such as a right to a preferential dividend or a right to be paid off first in a liquidation'.

The traditional view is that the rights must attach to the shares and not to the shareholders. Thus, in *Eley v The Positive Government Security Life Assurance Co Ltd (1876)*, where the articles conferred the right to be a company solicitor on a shareholder, the right could not be construed as a class right – it was a personal right attaching to the shareholder. Such a case is a clear example but the rule has hardly been applied uniformly. In the Australian case *Fischer v Easthaven Ltd (1964)*, which concerned a home unit company in which the unit holders were shareholders, the court considered that the relationship between a home unit owner and the company imposed a contractual duty on the company not to alter its articles so as to abrogate their rights, effectively treating them as class rights.

In *Cumbrian Newspapers Group Ltd v Cumberland and Westmorland Herald Newspaper and Printing Co Ltd (1986)*, the whole question of class rights was analysed. The case is analysed by Polack in a case note on Class Rights [1986] CLJ 399.

The case centred on the plaintiff's desire to maintain the Cumbrian newspaper's independence from large national chains. The plaintiff published the *Penrith Observer* whose circulation, largely confined to that market town, was about 5,500 per week. Their chairman, John Burgess (later Sir John) negotiated with the defendants, who published the *Cumberland and Westmorland Herald* with a circulation throughout Cumbria. The negotiations involved the provision of discounted advertising arrangements for the defendants which would enhance the defendants' ability to attract advertising and the closure of the *Penrith Observer*. Sir John was anxious to protect the independence of the Cumbrian Press and so it was agreed that his shareholding of 10.67% in the defendant company entitled him to the rights of pre-emption over other ordinary shares, rights over unissued shares and the right to appoint a director. Later, the defendants wanted to cancel these special rights. The plaintiffs contended that they were class rights and therefore subject to the special statutory provisions of the Companies Act 1985.

Scott J held:

> In my judgment, a company which by its articles, confers special rights on one or more of its members in the capacity of member or shareholder,

thereby constitutes the share for the time being held by that member or members, a class of shares. The rights are class rights.

The *Eley* case can therefore be distinguished on the basis that the right did not attach to Eley as shareholder.

### 6.5.2 Defining 'variation'

The next matter to be considered is whether the company's proposal amounts to a variation of the existing rights. Once again, fine judicial nuances abound in this area.

It should be said at the outset that not every act of a company which adversely affects the interests of a particular class of share amounts to a variation of the class rights of that share. Thus, in *White v The Bristol Aeroplane Co Ltd (1953)*, the company proposed to capitalise its profits and distribute them in the form of a bonus issue of ordinary and preference shares.

The court held that the bonus issue would not affect the existing preference shareholders' rights or privileges. These rights might be affected as a matter of business practice because of the new preference stock, but this would relate to the enjoyment of the rights and not the rights themselves. Such fine legalistic reasoning is also apparent in a case decided at about the same time, namely *Re John Smith's Tadcaster Brewery Co Ltd (1953)*.

Another famous case which analysed the concept of variation concerned the ubiquitous case of *Greenhalgh v Arderne Cinemas Ltd and Mallard* (1946). Mr Greenhalgh lent money to the company in exchange for 10 pence shares. These shares ranked *pari passu* with the ordinary 50 pence shares. The company later resolved to sub-divide the 50 pence shares into 10 pence shares which effectively quintupled the voting strength of the 50 pence shares.

The Court of Appeal held that the voting rights had not been varied by the resolution. The only voting right was one vote per share and this had remained the same throughout.

Such decisions demonstrate how restrictively the concept of variation of class rights has been interpreted in the cases. The area is riddled with the subtlest of distinctions. Lord Greene MR in *Greenhalgh* even said that:

> If it had been attempted to reduce that voting right (of the 10 pence share), for example, by providing or attempting to provide there should be one vote for every five of such shares, that would have been an interference with the voting rights attached to that class of shares. But nothing of the kind had been done: the right to have one vote per share is left undisturbed.

Nothing could better illustrate the fine legalistic distinctions that are made in the cases. It is clear from Lord Greene's *dictum* that it is the means rather than the end that is all important.

Sometimes, the company's constitution will set out clearly when a particular class of shareholders' consent is required. In *Re Northern Engineering Industries plc (1994)*, a company's articles of association stipulated that a reduction of capital required the consent of the company's preference shareholders. The Court of Appeal held that this included the situation where it was proposed to cancel the preference shareholders.

### 6.5.3 Statutory procedures

If the proposal is clearly to alter the substance of the rights of a class of shareholders, the procedure that is set out in the Act must be followed. It is worth noting that a provision to alter or insert a new procedure relating to class rights is itself a variation of class rights, as is abrogation of rights. Both will involve the statutory procedures (s630(5), (6) and s631(5), (6)).

In *Re House of Fraser Plc (1987)*, the issue of abrogation of class rights was discussed. In this case, the company applied for a court order to confirm a reduction of capital. The petition to reduce the capital was opposed by two preference shareholders. Capital was to be returned to the preference shareholders. The court confirmed the reduction as it was merely an application of their class rights, the court taking the view that the class rights of the preference shareholders, involving as they did priority in a winding up, had been fulfilled and not varied. The provision in the Act to the effect that an abrogation amounts to a variation does not cover such a case. It was stated in the Court of Session that:

> Abolition or abrogation are not appropriate expressions to describe the situation where a right and its corresponding obligation have been extinguished by performance.

The House of Lords upheld the Court of Session.

S630 deals with variation of class rights where companies have a share capital.

The rights attached to a class of a company's shares may be varied by the consent in writing of the holders of at least three quarters in nominal value of the issued shares of that class, or by a special resolution passed at a separate general meeting of the holders of that class.

Where the company has no share capital, s631 applies. This provides that the consent that is required is the consent in writing of at least three quarters of the members of the class, or a special resolution passed at a separate general meeting of the members of that class to sanction the variation.

In relation to the right to object to a variation where a company has a share capital, the holders of not less in aggregate than 15% of the issued shares of the class in question, being persons who did not consent to or vote in favour of the resolution, may apply to the court within 21 days to have the variation cancelled (s633 CA 2006). The variation has no effect then until it is confirmed by the court.

In relation to the right to variation where the company has no share capital, members amounting to not less than 15% of the members of the class in question, being persons who did not consent to or vote in favour of the resolution, may apply to the court within 21 days to have the variation cancelled. Similarly the variation does not take effect unless and until it is confirmed by the court (s634).

It must be said that, usually, the court will confirm the order, but it will cancel it if it considers that the alteration has been passed by a vote which neglects the interests of the class. This is what occurred in *Re Holders Investment Trust Ltd (1971)*.

In this case, Holders Investment Trust Ltd proposed to reduce its capital by cancelling its 5% cumulative preference shares in exchange for an equivalent amount of unsecured loan stock to the shareholders of that class. Almost 90% of the preference shares were vested in trustees and trusts set up by one, William Hill. They voted in favour of the resolution. They also held 52% of the ordinary stock and shares. Their vote was clearly influenced by the benefit they would receive as ordinary shareholders from the proposed variation. Megarry J held that the scheme was unfair and refused to sanction the reduction, saying 'it fell substantially below the threshold of anything that justly be called fair'.

Such cases are exceptional. It is more usual to find that what is acceptable to the majority will have to do for the minority as well.

## 6.6 Membership contract

Section 33 of the Companies Act 2006 provides that the provisions of a company's constitution bind the company and its members to the same extent as if there were convenants on the part of the company and of each member to observe those provisions. Previous incarnations of this provision were to similar effect, such as s14 CA 1985 and s20 CA 1948. There has been much controversy about the effect of what is now s33 CA 2006.

In *Hickman v Kent or Romney Marsh Sheep-Breeders' Association (1915)*, the Association which was a registered company provided in its articles that disputes between the Association and a member of the Association should be referred to arbitration rather than being the subject of litigation in the courts. Mr Hickman, who was in dispute with the Association about his expulsion, started proceedings in the High Court. An injunction was issued to prevent the proceedings in the High Court. Astbury J held that the effect of s33 was to create a contract between the Association and its members whereby the members agreed not to take a dispute to court.

Another illustration of the same principle is to be found in *Pender v Lushington (1877)*. In this case, the articles gave shareholders the right to vote. The articles also fixed a maximum amount of votes which each member could cast, namely 100. To evade this rule, Pender transferred some of his shares into the names of nominees who were bound to vote as directed by him. The shares were registered in their name. At a meeting the chairman refused to count their votes. Pender sued for an injunction to restrain the chairman from declaring the nominees' votes invalid.

He succeeded on the basis of the contract in the articles which bound the company to the shareholder. Shareholders had the right to vote as set out in the articles of association.

Thus far the principle seems straightforward. A member can sue in relation to matters set out in the articles and also can be sued by the company in the same way. However, it seems the matter is not so simple. In *Eley v Positive Government Security Life Assurance Co Ltd (1876)*, Eley had been named as company solicitor in the articles of association. He had been appointed as such but was subsequently removed. Eley was a member of the company and he sought to enforce the rights set out in the articles. He was unsuccessful. The court held that he was an outsider and could not enforce the contract in his capacity as a solicitor. The articles only gave him rights in his capacity as a member. It is not clear from the decision whether the position would have been different had he sued as a member. In the later case of *Beattie v E and F Beattie Ltd (1938)*, the articles of the company provided for any dispute between a member and the company to be referred to arbitration. A director of the company who also held shares in the company sought to restrain legal proceedings against him on the basis of this article. The Court of Appeal held that he must fail as he was seeking to enforce the terms of the articles as an outsider, that is, as a director rather than as a member. It is thus said that the articles of association cannot be enforced by a member or against a member in relation to outsider rights and obligations. In *Salmon v Quin and Axtens Ltd (1909)*, the company's articles gave the power of management to the board of directors but provided that joint managing directors each had a power of veto over certain key decisions. Salmon, one of the managing directors, sought to enforce this right of veto in relation to a board resolution. He sued the company on behalf of himself and other shareholders to restrain the company from acting on the resolution in breach of the article. The court held that he would succeed. He was thus able to enforce his right as a director by suing upon the membership contract. The case is clearly at odds with the later decision in *Beattie v E and F Beattie Ltd*.

### 6.6.1 The effect of s33

There has been much discussion about these cases and the effect of s33 and its predecessors. Professor Gower takes a traditional view that the membership contract is only enforceable in relation to membership rights and obligations in the narrow sense. Lord Wedderburn ('Shareholders' rights and the rule in *Foss v Harbottle' (1957)* 16 CLJ 194 and (1958) 17 CLJ 93), in contrast, takes the view that a member always has the right to have the articles and memorandum enforced. He takes the view that there is one basic membership right to have the articles and memorandum enforced. Wedderburn's view is endorsed by Drury in 'Relative Nature of the Shareholders Right to Enforce the Company Contract' [1986] CLJ 219. Other academics have joined the fray. GD Goldberg 'The Enforcement of Outsider Rights under s20(1) of the Companies Act 1948), (1972) 35 MLR 362, and then again in 'The Controversy on S20 Contract Revisited' (1985) 48 MLR 158, and Dr GN Prentice 'The Enforcement of Outsider Rights' ((1980) 1 Co Law 179) have put forward a qualified version of Wedderburn's thesis that a member can sue in respect of a right set out in the articles. Goldberg argues that a member has a contractual right to have the affairs of the company conducted by the appropriate organ while Dr Prentice contends that it is necessary to ask whether the particular provision affects the power of the company to function. These contentions may help to rationalise the decision in *Salmon v Quin and Axtens Ltd*. However, there is no evidence that the judges were thinking in this way.

A different view is put forward by Roger Gregory 'The S20 Contract' ((1981) 44 MLR 526) who argues cogently that there are two lines of cases supporting different views and that the cases are irreconcilable. This view is probably closest to the truth.

An interesting case that is perhaps consistent with either theory and which illustrates the breakdown that there has been between membership and management rights in small private companies is *Rayfield v Hands (1960)*. In this case, a provision in the articles stated that every member who wished to transfer his shares should notify the directors of this and that the directors would be obliged to purchase the shares at a fair value. In this company all of the shareholders were directors.

The plaintiff informed the directors of his wish to sell his shares and then when they refused to take them as stipulated under the articles he sought to enforce the article against them. The court held that the article imposed a contractual obligation against the directors in their capacity as members.

On occasion, the company's constitution may form the basis of a quite separate contract. This was the case, for example, in *Re New British Iron Company ex p Beckwith (1898)*, where directors were able to imply a contract on the same terms as the articles when suing for their remuneration.

However, if this is the case then the contract incorporating the terms of the company's articles may well be on alterable terms since the articles are freely alterable by the company. Thus, in *Swabey v Port Darwin Gold Mining Company (1889)*, the court took the view that the company could alter its articles and so affect the terms of the contract for the future.

In some cases, it may be that there is an implied term that the contract is concluded on the basis of the articles as they are at a particular date. Therefore, later variation of the articles will not affect the terms of the contract. Thus, in *Southern Foundries (1926) Ltd v Shirlaw (1940)*, both the Court of Appeal and the House of Lords held that it was a breach of contract to alter the articles of the company so as to affect the contract of employment between the appellant and the respondent.

### 6.6.2 Special features

Quite apart from the controversy concerning the types of rights and obligations that can be enforced via the membership contract, the s33 contract has other special features. In some respects, it is quite unlike an orthodox contract.

The court has no jurisdiction to rectify the articles even though they do not represent the intention of those signing them, as was held in *Scott v Frank F Scott (London) Ltd (1940)* and *Bratton Seymour Service Co Ltd v Oxborough (1992)*. In this respect, the contract is quite different from a normal contract. However, if the understanding of the members differs materially from the constitutional arrangements of the company, this may be a basis for winding the company up on the just and equitable ground under s 122(1)(g) of the Insolvency Act 1986. In the New Zealand case of *Re North End Motels (Huntly) Ltd (1976)*, a retired farmer subscribed for half of the share capital of the company on the basis that he would have an equal say in its management. He found, however, that he was in a minority on the board of directors and he successfully petitioned to wind the company up on the just and equitable ground.

It used to be the case that a member could not sue for damages for breach of his membership contract while remaining a member. This was a rather unusual feature of the membership contract of a company. A member was limited to the remedy of an injunction or a declaration.

This was the rule in *Houldsworth v City of Glasgow Bank (1880)*. However, s655 of the Companies Act 2006 now provides that 'a person is not debarred from obtaining damages or other compensation from a company by reason only of his holding or having held shares in the company or any right to apply or subscribe for shares or to be included in the company's register in respect of shares'.

The s33 contract is, of course, subject to the provisions of the Companies Acts and so the articles cannot defeat the provisions of the legislation. Furthermore, the company's articles are alterable by special resolution and so this means that the terms of the s33 contract can also be altered.


## SUMMARY

## The articles of association

### The articles of association constitute the company's constitution

#### Alteration of the articles

Although the articles are said to be freely alterable – in fact, by special resolution under s21 of the Companies Act 2006 – there are various restrictions that apply:

(a) the alteration must not contravene the companies' legislation;
(b) the alteration must not be 'at odds with' a court order;
(c) a special regime applies if the alteration varies class rights;
(d) at common law, an alteration of the articles must be put forward *bona fide* for the benefit of the company as a whole.

## Variation of class rights

Where rights are attached to a particular class of share, a special procedure applies for varying those rights.

First, it must be determined that there is a separate class of shares involved. The courts adopt a broad approach to this question as in *Cumbrian Newspapers Group Ltd v Cumberland and Westmorland Herald Newspaper and Printing Co Ltd (1986)*.

Secondly, the question arises as to whether there is a proposed variation of rights attaching to those shares. Here the court adopts a restrictive approach so that if what is to be varied is the enjoyment of rights rather than the rights themselves then the variation of class rights regime does not apply. For example, a proposed reduction of a preference dividend would be a variation of class rights whereas a proposal to increase the voting strength of management shares as against ordinary shares would not be a variation of the rights of the ordinary shareholders.

Thirdly, if there is a proposed variation of class rights, then in addition to passing a special resolution of all of the shareholders there needs to be a separate class consent. This may be expressed by special resolution of the class concerned or by three quarters consent of the class concerned in writing.

Fourthly, even if there is a separate class consent given, it is open to a dissentient 15% of the class to apply to the court to seek to stop the variation. They may be able to do so, for example, by demonstrating that the holders of the shares of the class concerned have voted in a particular way as they are also shareholders of another class (see *Re Holders Investment Trust Ltd (1971)*).

## Membership contract

The provisions of the articles and also of the memorandum constitute a contract between the company's members and the company and between the members *inter se* (s33 of the Companies Act 2006).

There is controversy as to whether the contract is enforceable in relation to all rights and obligations set out in the constitution or merely so called membership rights and obligations.

There are other special features about the membership contract.

There can be no rectification even if there is a fundamental misunderstanding of the provisions of the company's constitution, although the circumstances may justify a winding up order.

It is no longer the case that a member cannot sue his company for damages whilst remaining a member.

## Further reading

Drury, RR, 'The relative nature of a shareholder's right to enforce the company contract' [1986] CLJ 219.

Ferran, E, 'The decision of the House of Lords in *Russell v Northern Bank Development Corporation Limited*' [1994] 53 CLJ 343.

Goldberg, GD, 'The enforcement of outsider rights under s20(1) of the Companies Act 1948' (1972) 35 MLR 362.

Goldberg, GD, 'The controversy on the s20 contract revisited' (1985) 48 MLR 158.

Gregory, R, 'The s20 contract' (1981) 44 MLR 526.

Mason, HH, 'Fraud on the minority. The problem of a single formulation of the principle' (1972) 46 ALJ 567.

Polack, K, 'Casenote on the Cumbrian Newspapers Group Case' [1986] CLJ 399.

Prentice, GN, 'The enforcement of "outsider rights"' (1980) 1 Co Law 179.

Reynolds, B, 'Shareholders' class rights: a new approach' [1996] JBL 554.

Rixon, FG, 'Competing interests and conflicting principles: an examination of the power of alteration of articles of association' (1986) 49 MLR 446.

Rutabanzibwa, AP, 'Shareholders' agreements in corporate joint ventures and the law' (1996) 17 Co Law 194.

Wedderburn, KW, 'Shareholders rights and the rule in *Foss v Harbottle*' [1957] CLJ 194 and [1958] CLJ 93.

Xuereb, PG, 'The limitation on the exercise of majority power' (1985) 6 Co Law 199.

# Shares and payment of capital

## 7.1 The nature of a share

Where a company is limited by shares, the capital of the company is divided into shares. These are units of a given amount defining a shareholder's proportionate interest in the company. The nature of a share was discussed in *Borland's Trustee v Steel Bros & Co Ltd (1901)* where Farwell J said:

The share is the interest of the shareholder in the company measured by a sum of money, for the purpose of liability in the first place, and of interest in the second, but also consisting of a series of mutual covenants entered into by all the shareholders *inter se* in accordance with (what is now s33 of the Companies Act 2006).

### 7.1.1 Main features

The main features of a share are as follows:

(a) a right to dividends declared on the shares;
(b) generally (unless it is a non-voting share) a right to vote at general meetings;
(c) on the liquidation of the company or on a reduction of capital the right to receive assets distributed to shareholders of that class;
(d) an obligation to subscribe capital of a given amount which will sometimes be the nominal value of the share if the share is issued at par and sometimes will be in excess of this if the share is issued at a premium (the issue of shares at par and at a premium will be discussed below in section 7.8);
(e) rights of membership attached to the shares as defined in the company's memorandum and articles (discussed above in relation to the s33 membership contract in section 6.6);
(f) a right to transfer the share in accordance with the articles of association at section 7.4.

## 7.2 Different classes of shares

Often, a company will only have one class of share. These will be ordinary shares or the equity of the company. On occasion, the company may have more than one class of share. The classes will be differentiated by reference to rights to dividend, rights to repayment of capital, rights to vote, etc. Where this is the case, matters of the variation of class rights may arise where it is proposed to alter the company's articles and that alteration varies the rights attaching to a particular class of share (these matters are considered under Variation of Class Rights in section 6.5).

### 7.2.1 Preference shares

It is perhaps appropriate here to say something about the nature of a preference share which is probably the most common type of share other than ordinary shares.

The most common feature of a preference share is that it confers a right to a preferential dividend up to a specified amount, for example, 8% of its paid up value. This dividend is paid before any dividend is paid on the ordinary or equity share capital of the company. Preference shares may also have other preferential rights such as preferential voting rights or a right to repayment of capital in priority to other shares on a winding up.

The rights of the preference shares will depend upon what is set out in the terms of issue or in the articles of association (or conceivably the memorandum) of the company.

In relation to dividends, the preference share holder is only entitled to a preferential dividend when this dividend is actually declared. Even if there are available profits there is no obligation upon the directors to declare a dividend (the question of dividends is considered separately (see Chapter 8). If, however, a dividend is not declared in any given year in relation to preference shares, the right to that dividend is carried forward. This presumption of the preference dividend being cumulative can be rebutted by a provision in the articles or in the terms of issue but, in the absence of any express statement, it is assumed that the right to a preference dividend is cumulative. Therefore, if a preference dividend of 8% is not paid in Year one, the right to that dividend carries forward into Year two and so on.

If the preference dividend is paid in full, there is no further right to any additional dividend unless the terms of issue or articles say so. If there is such a right to an additional dividend, the preference shares are termed participating preference shares.

In relation to capital, there is no automatic priority for preference shares in a winding up or in a reduction of capital. The right only exists if the terms of issue or the articles set out such a right. If preference shares are given a priority in a winding up, then once their capital has been returned, this is exhaustive of their rights unless the terms of issue or the provisions of the articles provide otherwise, that is, preference shares do not participate in any surplus assets on a winding up.

## 7.3  Other classes of shares

The possible types of class of shares are virtually infinite. It is not uncommon for a company to have *redeemable preference shares*. These shares are shares that mirror preference shares except they are redeemable at a set date or at the option of the company.

A company may issue *deferred* or *founders shares*. These shares rank after ordinary shares in respect of dividends and sometimes in relation to a return of capital. They will usually, however, have additional voting rights. Typically, they would be taken up by a company's promoters.

Many large public companies have separate management shares, for example, the Savoy Hotel Group. These shares carry additional voting rights and they are thus able to outvote the ordinary shares of the company. In other respects, their rights will often be the same as the ordinary shares, for example, in relation to dividends and return of capital.

## 7.4  Transfer of shares

Shares are freely transferable unless the company's articles impose restrictions on transfers. It was formerly the case before the Companies Act 1980 that private companies had to restrict the transferability of their shares in some way as a condition of their private status. This requirement was swept away by the Companies Act 1980.

If the articles contain no restriction at all, then the motive of the transferor in disposing of his shares is immaterial. In *Re European Bank, Masters case (1872)*, 12 days before a banking company stopped business, a shareholder transferred shares to his son-in-law. The shares were partly paid shares. The court held that the transfer could not be set aside. The court would not inquire into the *bona fides* of the transferor. In *Re Smith, Knight & Co (1868)*, the court held that the directors of the company have no discretionary powers except those that are given to them by the company's constitution to refuse to register a transfer which has been made *bona fide*.

### 7.4.1  Restrictions on transferability

What happens where there is some restriction on transferability? The restriction may take one of many forms. Articles of association may give the directors an absolute discretion to refuse to register a transfer of shares. This was the position in *Re Smith and Fawcett Ltd (1942)* (see section 12.4.2). In this case, the court held that the directors had a total discretion as to registering transfers. The only limitation on their discretion was that it should be exercised *bona fide* in the interest of the company. The Court of Appeal refused to draw an inference that it was being exercised *mala fide*. It is clear that, where the directors have an absolute discretion to refuse to register a transfer, the courts are reluctant to interfere. It should be noted, however, that a refusal to register a transfer of shares may justify a petition under ss994–996 (considered under Minority Protection, Chapter 14).

Sometimes the refusal to register may only be exercised on certain grounds. A familiar power is one that the directors can exercise if, in their opinion, it is contrary to the interests of the company that the proposed transferee should become a member.

In *Re Bede Shipping Co Ltd (1917)*, which concerned a Newcastle based steamship company, the court held that such a power only justifies a refusal to register on grounds that are personal to the proposed transferee. It does not, for example, justify a refusal to register transfer of single shares or shares in small numbers because the directors do not think it is desirable to increase the number of shareholders. The refusal to register was exercised on the ground that the directors did not want the shares to be held by many people. Lord Cozens-Hardy MR cited Chitty J in *Re Bell Bros (1891)* with approval:

> If the reasons assigned are legitimate, the court will not overrule the directors' decision merely because the court itself could not have come to the same conclusion, but if they are not legitimate, as, for instance, if the directors state that they rejected the transfer because the transferor's object was to increase the voting power in respect of his shares by splitting them among his nominees, the court would hold the power had not been duly exercised.

### 7.4.2 The issue of pre-emption

Often, the restriction on transfer may be one of pre-emption, giving other shareholders the right to purchase the shares of the transferor at a fair value before they are offered elsewhere. This situation arose in *Curtis v JJ Curtis & Co Ltd (1986)* in the New Zealand Court of Appeal. Here, the company's articles of association provided that a shareholder who wished to transfer his shares to an outsider had first of all to offer them to existing shareholders. This was not done. Cooke J held that a perpetual injunction would be granted against the transferor preventing him from transferring them other than in accordance with the articles.

A pre-emption clause was the restriction which was utilised in *Rayfield v Hands (1960)* to preserve control in a few people in a small company. Similarly in *Greenhalgh v Mallard (1943)*, an article provided that, if a member wished to transfer his shares to a non-member, they must first be offered to existing members. Another article provided that, if a member wished to sell his shares, he must notify the fact to the directors. A member transferred his shares to other members. Greenhalgh, another member, sought to have the transfers declared invalid on the ground that the restriction on transfer of shares applied to sales to existing members as well as to non-members and, in this case, the shares had not been first offered to members as a whole.

This argument was rejected by the Court of Appeal because the articles were not sufficiently clear to restrict a transfer to existing members. The restriction was held to apply only to the case of sales of shares to non-members.

Lord Greene MR stated:

> Questions of constructions of this kind are always difficult but, in the case of the restriction of transfer of shares, I think it is right for the court to remember

that a share, being personal property, is *prima facie* transferable, although the conditions of the transfer are to be found in the terms laid down in the articles. If the right of transfer, which is inherent in property of this kind is to be taken away or cut down, it seems to me that it should be done by language of sufficient clarity to make it apparent that this was the intention.

The issue of pre-emption also came up in *Tett v Phoenix Property and Investment Co Ltd and Others (1986)* where the articles of association of the company restricted the right of the shareholder to transfer his shares. On the facts of the case, it was held that the directors had offered the shares to existing shareholders and the offer had not been taken up so that sale elsewhere was effective. Registration of the transfer was appropriate.

The courts will lean against an interpretation of any power in the directors which hampers the right to transfer shares.

On the other hand, the courts will not carry out a literal construction so far that it defeats the obvious purpose of the provision. Thus, in *Lyle and Scott Ltd v Scotts Trustees (1959)*, where the articles provided for a right of pre-emption in the other shareholders where a shareholder was desirous of transferring his ordinary shares, and some shareholders sold their shares to a takeover bidder and received the purchase price and gave him irrevocable proxies to vote on his behalf, the House of Lords held that in the context 'transferring' meant assigning the beneficial interest and not the process of having a transfer registered. The shareholders had indicated their intention to sell their shares and could not continue with the sale without giving the other shareholders their right to exercise their pre-emption rights.

It is most important, if the company wishes to protect some shareholders from the effect of shares being held by others, to ensure that the power of refusal to register a transfer of share also applies on transmission (cases where shares pass on death or bankruptcy).

In *Safeguard Industrial Developments Ltd v National Westminster Bank Ltd (1982)*, a shareholder held the balance of control between two rival brothers. He died leaving the shares to one of the brothers' children. The question arose as to whether pre-emption applied on transmission or simply where a shareholder wished to transfer his shares during his lifetime.

The court held that the provision could only apply in respect of transfer not transmission. Careful wording is therefore needed to protect companies and their shareholders in such a situation.

### 7.4.3 Directors' rights to reject on prescribed grounds

If, on the true construction of the company's articles, the directors are only entitled to reject on certain prescribed grounds, and if it is proved that they have rejected on others, the court will interfere as in *Re Bede Steam Shipping Co Ltd*. Interrogatories may be administered to determine on which of certain prescribed grounds the directors have acted but not as to their reasons for rejecting on those particular grounds: see *Sutherland (Jute) v British Dominions Land Settlement Corporation Ltd (1926)*.

However, if the directors do state their reasons, the court will investigate them to determine whether they have acted on those grounds. They will over-rule their decision if they have acted on considerations which should not have influenced them.

Even where the right to refuse is a qualified one, in certain situations the directors may not be obliged to give their reasons. In a case concerning Tottenham Hotspur Football Club, it was established that, even if the directors can only refuse to register a transfer on certain grounds, they cannot be obliged to give the reason if the articles provide they need not do so (*Berry and Stewart v Tottenham Hotspur Football & Athletic Co Ltd (1935)*).

### 7.4.4 Positive act of board

In relation to transfer generally, it should be noted that a refusal to register a transfer must be a positive act of the board. In *Re Hackney Pavilion Ltd (1924)*, the two directors of the company were divided on the question of whether the proposed transfer should proceed. The company secretary was asked to write to the executrix's solicitors and return the transfer documents indicating that the transfer could not go ahead. The High Court ordered that the transfer must go ahead. Astbury J said:

> Now, the right to decline must be actively exercised by the vote of the board ad hoc. At the actual board meeting, there was a proper quorum but, as the board was equally divided, it did not and could not exercise its rights to decline.

In such situations, the transfer must, therefore, go ahead.

### 7.4.5 Refusal must be exercised within a reasonable time

Another restriction on refusal of registration of a transfer is that the refusal must be exercised within a reasonable time. This rule has statutory force from s771 CA 2006, which provides that when a transfer of shares in or debentures of a company has been lodged with the company, the company must either register the transfer or give the transferee notice of refusal, together with the reasons for the refusal as soon as is practicable, and in any event not later than two months after the date on which the transfer is lodged. Failure to comply with this section constitutes an offence. During the two month period, however, the transferee cannot claim to be registered as a member, even though there are no directors, so that the company cannot exercise the right to refuse to register: see *Re Zinotty Properties Ltd (1984)*.

S994 of the Companies Act 1985 probably enables members to apply for a remedy in cases where directors fail to register a transfer of shares and this failure constitutes unfair prejudice to the members concerned. This may now enable a member to obtain a remedy in cases such as *Re Smith & Fawcett Ltd (1942)* (see section 12.4.2). Other transfer situations may involve this section. S994 was involved in *Re a Company (No 007623 of 1984) (1986)*, where a rights issue was made which the petitioning shareholder was unwilling to accept.

Hoffmann J held that the remedy was to offer to sell his shares to the other members under pre-emption provisions. The pre-emption provisions of this company contained a mechanism for determining a fair value of the shares by means of a valuation conducted by auditors. This procedure should have been employed without recourse to the courts. The inference of the decision is that a remedy would have been available under s994 had there been no pre-emption provisions.

The area of law relating to share transfer, and particularly restrictions on transferability, is increasingly important as more and more people buy shares and as more and more set up their own businesses where they may wish to keep control and ownership within a tightly-knit group.

## 7.5  Share warrants

S122 of the Companies Act 2006 provides that on the issue of a share warrant, the company must enter in the register of members the fact of the issue of the warrant, a statement of the shares included in the warrant, and the date of issue of the warrant, and amend the register if necessary so that no person is named on the register as the holder of the shares specified in the warrant.

Subject to the company's articles on surrendering the share warrant for cancellation, the bearer is entitled to have his name entered as a member in the register of members.

## 7.6  Pre-emption rights

S561 CA 2006 provides that a company must not allot equity securities to a person on any terms, unless it has made an offer to each person who holds ordinary shares in the company to allot to him on the same or more favourable terms a proportion of those securities that is as nearly as practicable equal to the proportion in nominal value held by him of the ordinary share capital of the company, and the period during which any such offer may be accepted has expired or the company has received notice of the acceptance or refusal of every offer so made.

S562 provides for the need of communication of the pre-emption offer to shareholders and s563 provides that failure to comply with s561 and s562 constitutes an offence for which the company and every officer in default is liable to compensate any person to whom an offer should have been made in accordance with the provisions of the sections.

S564 provides an exception to the pre-emption right in relation to the allotment of bonus shares. S565 provides for an exception where shares are issued for non-cash consideration, wholly or in part, and s566 provides for an exception where securities are held under an employees' share scheme.

In the case of private companies with only one class of share, the right to pre-emption may be excluded generally in relation to the allotment by the company of equity securities generally, or in relation to allotments of a particular description (s569 CA 2006).

In addition to this, s570 provides for the disapplication of pre-emption rights where directors of a company (i.e. public and private) are generally authorised for the purposes of s551 (power of directors to allot shares, etc; authorisation by company), they may be given power by the articles or by a special resolution to allot equity securities as if s561 (right of pre-emption) did not apply to the allotment or as if it did apply subject to modification.

S571 provides for disapplication of pre-emption rights by special resolution in relation to a specified allotment of equity securities. Where the directors of a company are authorised, whether generally or otherwise, to allot shares, the company may, by special resolution, resolve that s561 (right of pre-emption) does not apply to a specified allotment or applies to such an allotment with modifications.

Finally, s573 CA 2006 disapplies pre-emption rights in relation to the sale of Treasury shares.

## 7.7 Payment for shares

S580 provides that shares may not be allotted at a discount. S581 provides for different amounts to be paid on shares. S582 provides that shares allotted by a company and any premium on them may be paid up in money or money's worth (including goodwill and know-how). S583 provides for the meaning of 'payment in cash'. S585 provides that public companies must not accept an undertaking to do work or perform services in return for shares. S586 provides that public companies' shares must be paid up to at least one quarter, and the whole of any premium.

S587 provides that public companies must not allot shares as fully or partly paid otherwise than in cash if the consideration for the allotment is or includes an undertaking which is to be, or may be performed, more than five years after the date of the allotment.

S593 provides that a public company must not allot shares as fully or partly paid up otherwise than in cash unless:

(a)  the consideration has been independently valued;
(b)  the valuer's report has been made to the company during the six months immediately preceding the allotment; and
(c)  a copy of the report has been sent to the proposed allottee.

This section does not apply to the allotment of shares in a company arrangement where Company A, in return for the transfer to that company of shares of Company B, or the cancellation of all or some of the shares of Company B allots shares (s594).

S595 provides that s593 does not apply to the allotment of shares by a company in connection with a proposed merger with another company. This is where one of the companies proposes to acquire all the assets and liabilities of the other in exchange for the issue of shares or other securities of that one to shareholders of the other, with or without any cash payment to shareholders.

Although the statutory provision (s593) only applies to public companies, there is a common law rule that all companies must only issue shares for non-cash assets if the value of those assets is at least equal to the value of the shares. In general, however, in a private company situation the courts will not interfere with the valuation placed upon those assets.

It may do so, however, if there is fraud, see *Re Wragg (1897)*, or if the consideration is clearly inadequate, e.g. the consideration is past consideration as in *Hong Kong and China Gas Co Ltd v Glen (1914)*.

This rule that shares cannot be issued at a discount is already clearly stated in common law. In *Ooregum Gold Mining Co of India Ltd v Roper (1892)*, the House of Lords held that shares could not be issued at a discount. That is to say, that the company must always obtain at least the nominal value (or par value) of the share in payment.

There are some exceptions to the rule that shares cannot be issued at a discount. It is possible to issue shares to underwriters under ss552 and 553 of the Act at a commission of up to 10% on the par value of the shares. Another exception is that a company may issue debentures at a discount (debentures are considered in Chapter 19). The debentures may be convertible into shares. Provided that the right to convert is not immediate, there will be no contravention of s580, see *Koffyfontein Mines Ltd v Mosely (1911)*.

## 7.8  Issue of shares at a premium

Shares may sometimes be issued at a premium. Shares are issued at a premium if they are issued at more than par or nominal value. The amount of any premium must be fully paid on allotment if an issue is in a public company. The amount of the premium is paid into a share premium account. For most purposes, the share premium account is treated just as if it were ordinary share capital. There are certain exceptions to this principle. They are that the money in a share premium account may be used to pay up fully paid bonus shares or to pay off the company's preliminary expenses or to pay up any commitment or discount allowable on the issue of shares or debentures of the company or in providing for the premium payable on redemption of debentures of the company.

There is no statutory rule requiring a company to obtain the best possible premium on an issue of shares in the way that there is a similar rule to obtain at least the par value and, therefore, not to issue shares at a discount. Yet if shares are issued at well below the price that they could attain in the market, this may constitute a breach of directors' duties.

S610 of the Companies Act 2006 provides that if a company issues shares at a premium, whether for cash or otherwise, a sum equal to the aggregate amount or value of the premiums on those shares must be transferred to an account called 'the share premium account'.

## 7.9 Return of allotments

S555 CA 2006 provides that a company limited by shares and a company limited by guarantee and having a share capital must, within one month of making an allotment of shares, deliver to the registrar a return of the particular allotment.

The return must set out the total number of shares of the company, the aggregate nominal value of the shares, and for each class of shares prescribe particulars of the rights attaching to the shares, the total number of shares of the class and the aggregate nominal value of that class, and also the amount paid up and the amount (if any) unpaid on each share.

S556 requires a return of allotment by an unlimited company where it is allotting new classes of shares. Here the company must, within one month of making such an allotment, deliver to the registrar a return setting out the prescribed particulars of the rights attached to the shares.

S557 provides that it is an offence to fail to comply with the requirement to make a return under s555 and s556.

## SUMMARY

## Shares and payment of capital

### Introduction

A share is the interest of the shareholder in a particular company. There are various different types of shares such as ordinary, preference, deferred and management shares.

### Transfer of shares

Shares are said to be freely transferable but, in the case of private companies, it is often the case that there are various restrictions on transferability.

Sometimes, the restriction on transferability will give the company's directors the power to refuse to register a transfer. The power may be a general power of refusal or it may be exercisable on specified grounds. It is a power to refuse – so, if the directors are evenly split, the transfer must go ahead. If the directors have a general power to refuse, they cannot be obliged to give reasons for their refusal to agree to the transfer.

Sometimes, the restriction provides that shares must first be offered for sale to existing members. If this is so, the provision will be construed strictly (as it will in all cases of restriction on transfer) so that, if it is desired to restrict shares being transmitted in cases of death and bankruptcy, this would have to be set out clearly.

### Issue of shares

When shares are issued, the directors must take care to ensure that the statutory pre-emption provisions are honoured. These pre-emption provisions may be excluded or modified in various ways.

When shares are issued, the directors must also take care to ensure that the company receives full payment for the shares. Here, again, there are statutory provisions to ensure that the company pays in full. In particular, shares must not be issued at a discount, i.e., at less than par value.

Once shares have been issued, a return of allotments has to be made to the registrar of companies setting out the shares that have been issued and the consideration that has been received.

## Further reading

Napier, C, and Noke, C, 'Premiums and pre-acquisition profits – the legal and accountancy professions and business combinations' (1991) 54 MLR 810.

Pennington, RR, 'Can shares in companies be defined?' (1989) 10 Co Law 140.

Pickering, MA, 'The problem of the preference share' (1963) 26 MLR 499.

Rice, DG, 'The legal nature of a share' (1957) 21 Conv (NS) 433.

# The payment of dividends

When companies distribute their profits to the company's shareholders, they do so by paying dividends on those shares.

## 8.1 Distributable reserves

The payment of dividends used to be a matter to be decided by commercial prudence and the company's constitution. The memorandum of association generally made no express provision, although almost invariably the articles of association did.

### 8.1.1 The company's constitution

Under articles of association it is generally provided that the basic power to pay dividends lies with the company in general meeting. It is granted the power to pay a dividend up to the amount recommended by the directors.

A typical provision would provide that the company may by ordinary resolution declare dividends in accordance with the respective rights of the members, but no dividend shall exceed the amount recommended by the directors.

Generally, directors will be granted the power to declare interim dividends. For example, it may be provided that:

> Subject to the provisions of the Act, the directors may pay interim dividends if it appears to them that they are justified by the profits of the company available for distribution.
>
> If the dividends are to be paid otherwise than in cash, express authority is required.

This point was at issue in *Wood v Odessa Waterworks Co (1889)*, where the company's articles empowered dividends 'to be paid' by directors. This was interpreted as meaning 'paid in money'. A member was then able to rely on this article in challenging a distribution that was made in a non-cash form by the issue of bonus debentures.

Dividends are payable, in the absence of any provision to the contrary, to those members who are on the register at the time the dividend is declared.

Another question that needs to be considered in relation to provisions in the memorandum or articles is from which profits are dividends payable. Some articles, for example, specify 'the profits of the business', which is taken to mean that dividends can only be paid out of trading profits and not out of capital profits.

As has been noted previously, preference shareholders are only entitled to a preferential dividend when the dividend is actually declared. However, a preferential dividend is presumed to be cumulative. This means that if the dividend is not paid in one year it must be paid in a later year (see section 7.2.1).

### 8.1.2 The Stock Exchange

In addition to the requirements set out in the company's constitution, The Stock Exchange provides rules for companies that are listed or are dealt with on the Alternative Investment Market. The Stock Exchange requires that the date of any board meeting at which the declaration or recommendation of payment of a dividend is expected to be decided must be notified to The Stock Exchange in advance; it will then publish the information. The Stock Exchange issues a schedule of suitable dates to assist in settlement of transactions and to permit securities to be traded 'ex-dividends' from a convenient date.

### 8.1.3 Statutory provisions

If the regime relating to the payment of dividends used to be somewhat lenient, that changed with the Companies Act 1980. Amendments were made by the Companies Act 1981 and the provisions are now contained in the Companies Act 2006.

A company may not make a distribution which includes paying a cash dividend except out of the profits available for distribution (s830 of the Companies Act 2006).

The statutory provisions of the Companies Act 2006 apply to distributions. These are defined in s829(1) to include any distribution of the company's assets to its members. The definition is an extremely wide one and covers any benefits in cash or in kind. However, the following are expressly excluded:

(a)  an issue of fully or partly paid bonus shares;
(b)  reductions of capital;
(c)  the redemption or purchase of any of the company's shares out of capital or out of unrealised profits;
(d)  distributions of assets to members of the company on its winding up (s829(2)).

The profits available for distribution in both private and public companies are accumulated, realised profits not previously distributed or capitalised, less accumulated, realised losses not previously written off in a reduction or reorganisation of capital (s830(2)). Two key points about this provision should be noted:

(a) The use of the word 'accumulated' in relation to profits and losses applies to a continuous account.

In particular, directors should ensure that previous years' losses are made good before a distribution is made. This reverses the position in *Ammonia Soda Co Ltd v Chamberlain (1918)*. In this case, a distribution of revenue profits was made in a trading year even though there was an accumulated deficit from earlier years which had not been made good.

The plaintiff company, which had been incorporated for the purpose of acquiring, developing and working as brineland an estate in Cheshire, sued to recover dividends which the company alleged had been wrongly paid. The Court of Appeal held that there was no law that prohibited a company from distributing the clear net profit of its trading in any year without making good trading losses of previous years.

(b) Profits must be realised.

Directors should ensure that any income whether from trading or from capital must have actually been received by the company. This reverses the decision in *Dimbula Valley (Ceylon) Tea Co Ltd v Laurie (1961)* which permitted the distribution of unrealised capital profits. (It is perhaps worth noting that, in a Scottish decision, the opposite result had been reached: see *Westburn Sugar Refineries Ltd v IRC (1960)*.)

A further restriction in s831 of the Companies Act 2006 only applies to public companies. Distributions may only be made so long as the value of the company's net assets does not fall below the aggregate of its called up share capital plus its undistributable reserves.

## 8.2 Undistributable reserves

Undistributable reserves are defined in s831(4) as:

(a) the share premium account;
(b) the capital redemption reserve;
(c) the amount by which the accumulated unrealised profits (so far as not previously utilised by capitlisation) exceed its accumulated unrealised losses (so far as not previously written off in a reduction or reorganisation of capital duly made); and
(d) any other reserve which the company is prohibited from distributing by any enactment or by its articles.

This means, in effect, that a public company must maintain its capital and take account of any changes in the value of its fixed assets.

Before the Companies Act 1980 a dividend could be paid out of realised profits without the need to make good any capital loss realised or unrealised, for example, as in *Lee v Neuchatel Asphalte Co (1889)*. This is now no longer the case in relation to public companies.

## 8.3 Investment companies

'Investment companies' was a new category created by the Companies Act 1980, and are subject to a special regime and may ask for a different basis of distribution of profits. The rules (ss832–835 of the Companies Act 2006) are only applicable if the company has a listing, and it must have notified the registrar of companies of its status.

An investment company must comply with the following conditions:

(a) its business consists of investing its funds mainly in securities with the aim of spreading investment risk and giving its members the benefit of the results of the management of its funds (s833(2)(a));
(b) none of its holdings in companies (other than in other investment companies) represents more than 15% by value of its total investment (s833(2)(b) and s834);
(c) the distribution of capital profit is prohibited by its articles (s833(2)(c));
(d) the company has not retained during any accounting reference period more than 15% of its investment income from securities (s833(2)(d)).

The aim of the different rules is to relieve investment companies of the problem they might encounter in connection with the net value test applicable to a public company. Securities, the assets of investment companies, are subject to fluctuation in value which might take the value of assets below the net value level. Yet, since such companies receive considerable income from dividends, due allowance must be made for this fact.

An investment company may make a distribution out of its accumulated realised revenue profits not previously used by distribution or capitalisation, less its accumulated revenue losses, whether realised or not, not previously written off in a reduction or reorganisation of capital if at that time the value of its assets is at least equivalent to one and a half times its total liabilities and to the extent that the distribution does not reduce the value of its assets below that amount (s832 of the Companies Act 2006). The advantage of this basis for distribution is that realised and unrealised capital losses do not have to be taken into account in determining the amount available for distribution. However, the company can only distribute realised capital profits on a winding up.

## 8.4 Insurance companies

Insurance companies (as defined in s843(7) and s22 of the Financial Services and Markets Act 2000) which carry on a long term business are also subject to special rules. Any amount which is properly transferred to a company's profit and loss account from a surplus or a deficit on its long term business funds is to be treated as a realised profit or a realised loss as appropriate (s843 of the Companies Act 2006).

## 8.5 Accumulated realised profit by reference to accounts

It is for the directors of any company, who will be the ones making a recommendation (if any) to pay a dividend, to ensure that these rules are complied with. A dividend will be based on a company's profits, losses, assets and liabilities as well as provisions (for example, for depreciation) and share capital and reserves. Basically, the directors must determine if there is an accumulated realised profit from which a dividend can be declared. In assessing whether there is such a profit, they should refer to the company's relevant accounts (s836 of the Companies Act 2006). Generally, the most recent audited annual accounts will be the relevant ones, and the last annual accounts must have been laid before the company in general meeting. The accounts must have been properly prepared or prepared subject only to matters which are not material, and the auditors must have made a report on the accounts to the members.

If the auditors' report is qualified, then they must state in writing whether, in their opinion, the substance of the qualification is material for determining the legality of the proposed dividend.

If the distribution infringes s830 or s831, the directors will need to refer to such 'interim accounts' as are necessary to decide whether a dividend can be paid (s838). A copy of the accounts must have been delivered to the registrar in the case of a public company.

If a distribution is to be made during a company's first accounting reference period, or before any accounts have been laid before a general meeting or delivered to the registrar, 'initial accounts' must be prepared to assess whether there is a profit available for dividend. The 'initial accounts' need not be audited but if the company is a public one, auditors must report on whether the accounts have been properly prepared. Furthermore, a copy of these initial accounts and an auditors' report must be delivered to the registrar (s839).

## 8.6 Distributions in kind

The decision in *Aveling Barford Ltd v Perion Ltd (1989)*, decided by reference to common law rules on distributions and maintenance of capital, is widely considered to have cast doubt on the validity of intragroup asset transfers carried out at book value rather than by reference to market value. The balance sheet of the plaintiff company (which was now in liquidation) showed that the company had more assets than liabilities but a deficit on its profit and loss account. The plaintiff sold property valued at £650,000 to the first defendant company which was controlled by Dr Lee Kin Tat from Singapore. Dr Lee also controlled the plaintiff company. The property was sold for £350,000, it was then resold within a year for £1.5 million. The plaintiff company obtained judgment in default on the grounds that the first defendant was a constructive trustee of the proceeds of sale. On appeal it was held to be a breach of Lee's fiduciary duties to arrange to sell the property for £350,000. The first defendant was accountable as constructive trustee.

It is understood that often such transactions are carried out by reference to book value rather than market value for business, administrative or tax reasons. S845 of the Companies Act 2006 provides that where the transferring company has distributable profits, its assets can be transferred at book value. This will remove the current uncertainty in the law, and avoid the need for companies to carry out complex asset revaluations requiring considerable professional advice and payment of fees.

## 8.7 Wrongful payment of dividend

There are various consequences of a wrongful payment of dividend. There are no criminal sanctions for a breach of the rules, but if a shareholder knows or has reasonable grounds for believing at the time of the distribution made to him that the distribution is in contravention of the Companies Act, then he is liable to repay it (or the offending part of it) to the distributing company (s847 of the Companies Act 2006). Thus ignorance of the legal position is no defence; see *It's a Wrap (UK) Ltd v Gula (2006)*.

In *Precision Dippings Ltd v Precision Dippings Marketing Ltd (1985)*, the plaintiff company, which was a wholly owned subsidiary of the defendant company, paid a cash dividend of £60,000 to the defendant. The relevant accounts, the company's last annual accounts, were qualified. The last annual accounts showed sufficient distributable profits to finance the dividend but no statement on the materiality of the qualification had been made by the auditors as the Act required.

Subsequently, the company went into creditors' voluntary liquidation and the auditors then issued a written statement to the effect that the qualification in their report was not material. The plaintiff company, through its liquidator, sued to recover the dividend on the ground that it was paid in contravention of the statute and was *ultra vires*. The Court of Appeal held that the company had paid a dividend in contravention of the statute. The auditors' written statement had to be available before a distribution was made, and the absence of such a statement was not a mere procedural irregularity that could be waived or dispensed with. The dividend payment was *ultra vires* and, as the defendant company received the money with notice of the facts as a volunteer, it held the money as constructive trustee for the plaintiff company.

### 8.7.1 Directors' liability

S847 of the 2006 Act does not deal with the position of directors responsible for the payment of dividends. A director who is responsible for an unlawful distribution could be liable to the company for a breach of duty. In *Flitcroft's* case (1882), the question of directors' liability for the wrongful payment of the company's dividends arose. For several years, the directors had presented to the shareholders in general meeting reports and balance sheets in which various debts the directors knew were bad were entered as assets, so that an apparent profit was shown in the company's accounts, although in reality there were no profits. The general meeting relied on the accounts to pass resolutions to declare dividends. The company was wound up and the liquidator sought to have the directors make good the wrongful payment of dividends. The Court of Appeal held that the directors were liable for these wrongful payments and must reimburse the company the full amount of the dividend.

However, this principle only applies where the director knows about the circumstances of the payment. An innocent director is not liable to repay a dividend that has been wrongfully paid.

In *Re Denham & Co (1884)*, Crook, a director whose name appeared on the company's reports, never attended board meetings nor took any active part in the preparation or issue of the company's reports or balance sheets, although, at one meeting, he did formally propose the resolution to declare a dividend. It was found that the company had been paying dividends out of capital. The court held, however, that Crook was not personally responsible for the company's reports and balance sheets and the dividends paid under them. He had no reason to suspect any misconduct and was not guilty of negligence. As Chitty J said:

> As regards Crook, who acted as a director throughout the period of the four years when the dividends were paid, it is not charged against him that he was guilty of actual fraud, or that he was in fact party or privy to the fraud committed, and I am satisfied, on the evidence, that he had not any suspicion of it ... The auditors are not before me on the present occasion, still I am bound to say that from the evidence, such as it is, it does appear that the auditors themselves were to some extent cognisant of and parties to the fraud. Mr Crook was, however, entitled to trust them, there was nothing at all to arouse his suspicions that they were not doing their duty.

Similarly, in *Dovey v Cory (1901)*, a director who agreed to the payment of dividends out of capital, and who relied on the advice of a fellow director and general manager of the company by whose statements he was misled and whose integrity, skill and competence he had no reason for suspecting, was held not to be liable in negligence. In the course of his judgment, the Earl of Halsbury LC made it clear that directors are also entitled to trust their auditors:

> I cannot think that it can be expected of a director that he should be watching the inferior officers of the bank or verifying the calculations of the auditors themselves. The business of life could not go on if people could not trust those who are put into a position of trust for the express purpose of attending to details of management.

### 8.7.2 Auditor's liabilities

In addition to directors, the company's auditor may also be liable for the wrongful payment of dividends. The auditors will only be liable to the company if he facilitated the improper payment of a dividend.

As Lindley LJ said of the auditor in *Re London and General Bank Ltd (No 2) (1895)*: 'It is nothing to him whether the dividends are properly or improperly declared provided he discharges his own duty to the shareholders'. In that case, dividends had been paid out wrongfully, and the company's assets were overstated in the balance sheet. The court found that the auditors had been negligent in respect of a particular year's report – certain loans which were not realisable were entered in the accounts at face value. The auditor was held liable to repay the dividends in question.

An auditor's liability is generally limited to situations where the auditors are in breach of their contractual duty in relation to the company's annual audit and where this negligence facilitates the payment of a dividend out of capital.

An auditor may be clearly liable to the company for breaches of his contract with the company which has resulted in the wrongful payment of dividends. Lopes LJ spoke of the auditor's contractual duties in those terms in *Re Kingston Cotton Mill Co (No 2) (1896)*:

> It is the duty of an auditor to bring to bear on the work he has to perform that skill, care and caution which a reasonably competent, careful and cautious auditor would use. What is reasonable skill, care and caution must depend on the circumstances of each case. An auditor is not bound to be a detective or … to approach his work with suspicion or with foregone conclusion that there is something wrong. He is a watchdog, but not a bloodhound. He is justified in believing hired servants of the company in whom confidence is placed by the company.

The rules have been made much stricter since 1980. No criminal liability attaches to directors or others simply for the wrongful payment of dividends. Any member knowingly receiving a dividend wrongfully paid is liable to repay it. Directors may, however, find themselves liable for breach of their duties to the company and auditors may also be in breach of their contractual duty to the company, their client.

## SUMMARY

## Payment of dividends

The payment of dividends used to be a matter to be decided largely by reference to the company's constitution. The Companies Act 1980 introduced statutory controls for the first time. Since that date, dividends can only be paid out of accumulated realised profits less accumulated realised losses. This applies to private and public companies. Public companies also have to maintain the value of their capital assets before paying any dividend but private companies are also obliged to make provision for depreciation under the accounting rules.

Special rules apply to investment companies and companies carrying on long-term insurance business.

Where dividends are paid wrongfully, recipients will be obliged to pay back the sum where they know of the circumstances. Directors who have recommended payment of an unlawful dividend may be responsible as may the company's auditor who has facilitated payment of an unlawful dividend.

## Further reading

Hutton, N, 'Declaring dividends' (1995) 19 CSR 86.
Instone, R, 'Realised profits: unrealised consequences' [1985] JBL 106.
Noke, C, 'Realised profits: unrealistic conclusions' [1989] JBL 37.

# 9

# The maintenance of capital

Certain aspects of maintenance of capital have already been considered. The rules relating to the issue of shares and payment for those shares have been considered. It is now proposed to consider certain other rules relating to the maintenance of capital, namely the provision of financial assistance to acquire a company's shares and the company purchasing its own shares.

The existing statutory prohibition is, in general, removed for private companies. The 2006 Act retains the prohibition of financial assistance by a public company or by its subsidiaries (which may be private) for the purpose of the public company's shares (s678 CA 2006).

A public company is also forbidden from providing financial assistance for the purpose of the purchase of its holding company shares where that holding company is a private company (s679).

Although this clearly represents a relaxation of the position in relation to private companies, directors will still need to consider their general duties as directors to the company, and particularly in the context of the company's potential insolvency.

## 9.1 Financial assistance towards the purchase of a company's own shares

S678 CA 2006 provides that where a person is acquiring or proposing to acquire shares in a public company, it is not lawful for that company or any of its subsidiaries to give financial assistance, directly or indirectly, for the purpose of the acquisition before or at the same time as the acquisition takes place.

S677 defines financial assistance. It means:

(a) financial assistance given by way of gift;
(b) financial assistance given:
    (i) by way of guarantee, security or indemnity (other than an indemnity in respect of the indemnifier's own neglect or default), or
    (ii) by way of release or waiver.

(c) financial assistance given

    (i) by way of a loan or any other agreement under which any of the obligations of the person giving the assistance are to be fulfilled at a time when, in accordance with the agreement, any obligation of another party to the agreement remains unfulfilled, or

    (ii) by way of the novation of or the assignment (in Scotland assignation) of rights arising under a loan or such other agreement, or

(d) any other financial assistance given by a company where:

    (i) the net assets of the company are reduced to a material extent by the giving of the assistance, or

    (ii) the company has no net assets.

S678 does not prohibit a company from giving financial assistance for the acquisition of shares if:

(a) the company's principal purpose in giving the assistance is not to give it for the purpose of any such acquisition, or

(b) the giving of the assistance for that purpose is only an incidental part of some larger purpose of the company

and the assistance is given in good faith in the interests of the company.

S679 deals with assistance by a public company for the acquisition of shares in its private holding company.

In such a situation it is not lawful for a public company that is a subsidiary of the company to give financial assistance directly or indirectly for the purpose of the acquisition before or at the same time the acquisition takes place. The same exceptions apply as in relation to s678.

If a company contravenes s678 or s679, an offence is committed by the company and every officer in default (s680 CA 2006).

S681 provides that the prohibitions do not cover:

(a) a distribution of the company's assets by way of:

    (i) dividend, or

    (ii) distribution in the course of a winding up.

(b) an allotment of bonus shares;

(c) a reduction of capital;

(d) a redemption of shares;

(e) anything done in pursuance of an order of the court under Part 26 (order sanctioning compromise or arrangement with members or creditors)

(f) anything done under an arrangement in pursuance of s110 of the Insolvency Act 1986 or Article 96 of the Insolvency (Northern Ireland) Order 1989 (liquidator in winding up accepting shares for the company's property);

(g) anything done under an arrangement made between a company and its creditors binding on the creditors by virtue of Part 1 of the Insolvency Act 1986 or Part 2 of the Insolvency (Northern Ireland) Order 1989.

S682 provides that certain transactions are not prohibited:

(a) in the case of a private company, or
(b) in the case of a public company if:

    (i) the company has net assets that are not reduced by the giving of the assistance, or
    (ii) to the extent that the assets are so reduced the assistance is provided out of distributable profits.

The transactions to which the section applies are:

(a) the lending of money in the ordinary course of business;
(b) the provision in good faith in the interests of the company of financial assistance for the purposes of an employee share scheme;
(c) the provision of financial assistance by the company for the purposes of or in connection with anything done by the company (or another company in the same group) for the purpose of enabling or facilitating transactions in shares in the first mentioned company or its holding company between and involving the acquisition of beneficial ownership of those shares by:

    (i) *bona fide* employees or former employees of the company (or of another company in the same group), or
    (ii) spouses or civil partners, widows, widowers or surviving civil partners or minor children or step children of any such employees or former employees

(d) the making by the company of loans to persons other than directors employed in good faith by the company with a view to enabling them to acquire fully paid up shares in the company or its holding company to be held by them by way of beneficial ownership.

### 9.1.1 Consequences of breach of the provisions

As has been noted, there are criminal sanctions applying where there is a breach of the sections (s680). In addition, the transaction itself is unlawful and void.
    There are various other consequences:

(a) any guarantee issued in connection with the transaction is itself void: see *Heald v O'Connor (1971)*;
(b) the company may sue its directors for breach of duty as they are liable in a similar way to trustees in relation to misapplication of trust funds: see *Selangor United Rubber Estates Ltd v Cradock (No 3) (1968)* and *Belmont Finance Corpn. Ltd v Williams Furniture Ltd (1979)*;

(c) furthermore, other persons receiving corporate property with knowledge that it is being applied for a wrongful purpose are liable to the company on the basis of constructive trust: see *Selangor United Rubber Estates Ltd Co v Cradock* and *Belmont Finance v Williams Furniture*;

(d) there is also the possibility that the company can sue for conspiracy if two or more persons have got together to accomplish the unlawful act: see *Belmont Finance v Williams Furniture*.

### 9.1.2 Financial assistance

It should be recalled that prior to the 2006 Act, private companies were also, in general, subject to a prohibition on the provision of financial assistance. Whilst this is no longer the case generally, unless they are facilitating the acquisition of shares in a public company, some of the earlier case law provides useful guidance on what constitutes financial assistance and which may, therefore, cause public companies in the future to fall foul of the law.

The question of the provision of financial assistance arose in *Parlett v Guppys (Bridport) Ltd (1996)*.

Mr and Mrs P, and their two sons, agreed that four companies controlled by them should provide P with salary, bonus and pension in return for P transferring his shares in Estates, one of the four companies into the joint names of himself and his sons. The sons subsequently challenged the agreement alleging that it was unenforceable as it gave financial assistance in breach of the Companies Act.

The court took the view that the agreement did not have to be performed in breach of the Act. It could reasonably have been believed that other companies in the group would bear the costs and there was accordingly no reduction in the net assets of estates and no financial assistance given within the section.

In *Brady and Another v Brady (1989)*, a scheme had been devised to break deadlock within a family business. The scheme was challenged on the basis that Brady was providing financial assistance for the purchase of its own shares. The two shareholders in Brady were two brothers, Jack and Bob, whose discord had led to the scheme. The brothers agreed to divide the business. Brady became a subsidiary of a new company called Motoreal, which issued to a new company Actavista loan stock equal to half the asset value of Brady. This debt was to be discharged by the transfer to Motoreal of half of Brady's asset value. It was accepted that this infringed the Act in that Motoreal had acquired shares in its subsidiary Brady and had incurred liability for the purchase of that acquisition. Brady had given financial assistance to discharge that liability.

A crucial issue in the case was whether the transaction was saved by what is now s678(4) CA 2006 in that the company's principal purpose in giving the assistance was not to reduce or discharge liability but to end the deadlock. The House of Lords took the view that there was no larger purpose. As Lord Oliver said:

> The acquisition was not a mere incident of the scheme devised to break the deadlock. It was the essence of the scheme itself and the object which the scheme set out to achieve.

Note: The scheme was not illegal as the company was private and therefore fell within the private company exception under the Companies Act 1985.

## 9.2 A company's purchase of its own shares and the issue of redeemable shares

S684 provides that a limited company with a share capital may issue shares that are to be redeemed or are liable to be redeemed at the option of the company or the shareholder (redeemable shares) subject to the following provisions.

The articles of a private limited company can exclude or restrict the issue of redeemable shares.

A public limited company may only issue redeemable shares if it is authorised to do so by its articles.

No redeemable shares may be issued at a time when there are no issued shares of the company that are not redeemable.

S685 provides that the directors of a limited company may determine the terms, conditions and manner of redemption of shares if they are authorised to do so:

(a)  by the company's articles, or
(b)  by a resolution of the company.

A resolution may be by ordinary resolution even though it amends the company's articles.

Where the directors are so authorised to determine the terms, conditions and manner of redemption of shares, they must do so before the shares are allotted and any obligation of the company to state in a statement of capital, the rights attached to the shares extends to the terms, conditions and manner of redemption.

If the directors are not so authorised, the terms, conditions and manner of redemption of any redeemable shares must be stated in the company's articles.

S686 provides that redeemable shares may not be redeemed unless they are fully paid. The terms of redemption of shares in a limited company may provide the amount repayable on redemption, and may, by agreement, between the company and the holder of the shares, be paid on a day later than the redemption date.

S687 provides for the financing of redemption. A private limited company may redeem redeemable shares out of capital in accordance with Chapter 5 of Part 18 of the Act (see section 9.4), but subject to that, redeemable shares in a limited company may only be redeemed out of distributable profits of the company or the proceeds of a fresh issue of shares made for the purposes of the redemption.

S688 provides that redeemed shares are to be treated as 'cancelled', and the amount of the company's issue share capital is diminished accordingly.

S689 provides that where a limited company redeems any redeemable shares it must within one month of doing so give notice to the registrar specifying the shares redeemed, and the notice must be accompanied by a statement of capital.

Although a company is prohibited subject to the provisions of the Act from purchasing its own shares, the company may, in certain circumstances, acquire its own shares. Thus, a company may acquire its shares as a gift. Furthermore, the company's articles may provide for the forfeiture of shares or the acceptance of shares in lieu of forfeiture where sums are owed to the company.

In addition to the rules that allow a company to purchase or redeem its shares in certain circumstances, a company may acquire its shares in a reduction of capital or in pursuance of a court order under, e.g. ss994–996 in relation to the remedy for unfairly prejudicial conduct.

## 9.3  The purchase by a company of its own shares

S690 provides that a limited company with a share capital may purchase its own shares including any redeemable shares subject to the provisions of the Act and any restriction or prohibition in the company's articles.

A limited company may not purchase its own shares if, as a result of the purchase, there would no longer be any issued shares of the company other than redeemable shares or shares held as treasury shares.

S691 provides a limited company may not purchase its own shares unless they are fully paid, and where a limited company purchases its owns shares the shares must be paid for on purchase.

S692 provides that a private limited company may purchase its own shares out of capital in accordance with Chapter 5 of Part 18 of the Act. Subject to that, a limited company may only purchase its own shares out of:

(i) distributable profits, or
(ii) the proceeds of a fresh issue of shares made for the purpose of financing the purchase.

and any premium payable on the purchase by a limited company of its own shares must be paid out of distributable profits of the company.

S693 provides that a limited company may only purchase its own shares:

(a) by an off market purchase in pursuance of a contract approved in advance in accordance with s694, or
(b) by a market purchase authorised in accordance with s701.

S694 deals with off market purchases. Either the terms of the proposed contract must be authorised by special resolution of the company before the contract is entered into, or the contract must provide that no shares may be purchased in pursuance of the contract until its terms have been authorised by a special resolution of the company.

S701 deals with authority for a market purchase. A company may only make a market purchase of its own shares if the purchase has first been authorised by resolution of the company. That authority may be general or limited to the purchase of shares of a particular class or description and may be unconditional or subject to conditions. The authority must specify the maximum number of shares autho-rised to be acquired and determine both the maximum and minimum prices that may be paid for the shares.

S706 deals with the treatment of shares where purchased. Where a limited company makes a purchase of its own shares in accordance with this chapter (Chapter 4 of Part 18 of the Act) then:

(a) if s724 (treasury shares) applies the shares may be held and dealt with in accordance with Chapter 6 of this part of the Act;
(b) if that section does not apply, the shares are treated as cancelled and the amount of the company's issued share capital is diminished accordingly.

S707 deals with a return to the registrar of a purchase of a company's own shares. Where a company purchases shares it must deliver a return to the registrar within the period of 28 days beginning with the date on which the shares are delivered to it.

## 9.4  Redemption or purchase by a private company out of capital

S709 provides that a private limited company may, subject to any restriction or prohibition in the company's articles, make a payment in respect of redemption or purchase of its own shares otherwise than out of distributable profits or the proceeds of a fresh issue of shares.

S710 sets out the permissible capital payment. The payment that may, in accor-dance with these provisions, be made by a company out of capital is such amount as, after applying for that purpose:

(a) any available profits of the company, and
(b) the proceeds of any fresh issue of shares made for the purposes of the redemption or purchase.

is required to meet the price of redemption or purchase.

S711 provides that any available profits mean any profits that are available for distribution and s712 sets out whether profits are available for distribution in accordance with this part of the Act.

S712 provides that profits should be determined by reference to the following items in the relevant accounts:

(a) profits, losses, assets and liabilities;
(b) provisions:

  (i) where the relevant company accounts are Companies Act accounts pro-visions of a kind specified for the purposes of this sub-section by regu-lations under s396
  (ii) where the relevant accounts are, IAS accounts, provisions of any kind.

(c) share capital and reserves (including undistributable reserves).

Having determined the profits, the amount should then be reduced by the amount of any distribution lawfully made by the company and any other payment lawfully made by the company out of distributable profits after the date of the relevant accounts and before the end of the relevant period.

The resulting figure is the amount of available profits.

S713 provides that the following actions are necessary if there is to be a payment out of capital by a private company:

s714 (directors' statement and auditor's report)
s716 (approval by special resolution)
s719 (public notice of proposed payment)
s720 (directors' statement and auditor's report to be available for inspection.

S714 provides for the directors' statement and the auditor's report. These must state that in their opinion the company will be able to continue to carry on business as a going concern and be able to pay its debts as they fall due throughout the year.

S715 provides that if the directors have no reasonable grounds for that opinion then their actions constitute an offence.

S716 provides that the payments are to be approved by special resolution to be passed on or within a week immediately following the date on which the directors make their statement.

S721 provides that where a private company passes the special resolution approving a payment out of capital for the redemption or purchase of its shares then any member of the company, other than one who assented to or voted in favour of the resolution, or any creditor of the company, may apply to the court for cancellation of the resolution. The application must be made within five weeks after the passing of the resolution. The court may order an arrangement for the purchase of dissentient members' interests or for the protection of dissentient creditors. In general, it may cancel or confirm the resolution and may do so on such terms as it thinks fit.

## 9.5 Treasury shares

S724 provides that a limited company, where it makes a purchase of its own shares, may, subject to conditions, hold the shares or deal with them. Where shares are held by the company the company must be entered in its register of members as the member holding the shares. These are treasury shares.

S725 provides that where a company has shares of only one class, the aggregate nominal value of shares held as treasury shares must not at any time exceed 10% of the nominal value of the issued share capital.

Where the share capital of a company is divided into different classes, the aggregate nominal value of each class of shares held as treasury shares must not exceed 10% of the nominal value of the relevant class.

S726 provides that a company must not exercise any right in respect of the treasury shares, and any purported exercise of such a right is void. This would apply in particular to the right to attend or vote at meetings for example.

S727 deals with the disposal of treasury shares. A company may sell the shares for a cash consideration or transfer the shares into an employees' share scheme.

S728 provides that where shares that are held by a company as treasury shares are sold or transferred, the company must deliver a return to the registrar not later than 28 days after the disposal. Failure to comply with this section is an offence committed by every officer of the company who is in default.

S729 provides that a company may cancel treasury shares and where there is such a cancellation the amount of the company's share capital is reduced accordingly by the nominal amount of the shares cancelled.

The company must deliver a return to the registrar not later than 28 days after the shares are cancelled (s730 CA 2006).

S731 provides for the treatment of proceeds of sale of treasury shares. If the proceeds of sale are equal to or less than the purchase price paid by the company for the shares then the proceeds are treated as a realised profit of the company. If the proceeds of the sale exceed the purchase price paid by the company, then an amount equal to the purchase price is treated as realised profit and the excess must be transferred to the company's share premium account.

## 9.6  The capital redemption reserve

Where shares of a limited company are redeemed or purchased wholly out of the company's profits, the amount by which the company's issued share capital is diminished on cancellation of the shares redeemed or purchased, or on cancellation of shares held as treasury shares must be transferred to a reserve called the Capital Redemption Reserve (s733 CA 2006).

The company may use the capital redemption reserve to pay up new shares to be allotted to members as fully paid bonus shares (s733(5)). Subject to that the capital redemption reserve is treated as capital.

## 9.7  Reduction of capital

It used to be the case that a company's articles had to authorise a reduction of capital. This is no longer necessary, although the articles may prohibit or restrict such a reduction (s641(6) CA 2006).

In the case of a private company it is possible to reduce the company's share capital by special resolution supported by a solvency statement. In the case of a public company, a special resolution confirmed by the court is necessary.

There are three types of reduction:

(a)  to extinguish or reduce liability on any of the company's shares in respect of share capital not paid up;
(b)  to cancel any paid up share capital that is lost or unrepresented by available assets; or
(c)  to repay any paid up share capital in excess of the company's needs (s641(4) CA 2006).

In cases (a) and (c), the company is actually giving something back to the shareholders, either an actual return of capital or cancelling an existing liability. In case (b), nothing is being returned to the shareholders, there is merely a recognition of the fact that the company's paid up share capital is unrepresented by the company's assets.

A company might wish to reduce capital in order to buy out a retiring member of the company or to pay money over to the personal representatives of a deceased member where there are insufficient profits available for distribution. In the case of a private company, this can be accomplished by purchasing the company's own shares out of capital (see section 9.4), but, in the case of a public company, a formal reduction of capital will often be used in such circumstances.

### 9.7.1  Procedure for a private company

The procedure for private companies reducing their share capital is set out in ss642–644 CA 2006.

A resolution for reducing the share capital is still needed. This is a special resolution, although it may be passed as a written resolution (s642 CA 2006).

A solvency statement must be made available to every elgible member at the time that a proposed written resolution is sent out and, where the resolution is passed at a general meeting, a copy of the solvency statement must be made available for inspection by members of the company throughout the meeting (s642(2) and (3) CA 2006).

The solvency statement is a statement that each of the directors has formed the opinion as regards the company's position that there is no ground on which the company could be found unable to pay its debts, and has also formed the opinion:

(a)  if it is intended to commence the winding up of the company within 12 months of that date that the company will be able to pay its debts in full within 12 months of the commencement of the winding up; or
(b)  in any other case that the company will be able to pay its debts as they fall due during the year immediately following that date.

If the directors make a solvency statement without having reasonable grounds, then an offence is committed by every director in default.

The solvency statement should be made no more than 15 days before the date of the resolution to reduce the company's capital.

### 9.7.2 Reduction of capital by a public company

A reduction of capital in a public company is carried out in accordance with ss645–651 CA 2006.

A special resolution must be passed and then the company must apply to the court for an order confirming the reduction.

If the proposed reduction involves either:

(a)  a diminution of liability in respect of unpaid share capital; or
(b)  the payment to a shareholder of any paid up share capital.

then s646 (creditors entitlted to object a reduction) applies unless the court orders otherwise.

In the case of s646 applying, every creditor of the company who is entitled to any debt or claim, that if the company were winding up would be admissible in proof against the company, is entitled to object to the reduction of capital.

The court will then consider objections and may refuse or order a reduction of capital and any order confirming a reduction of capital may be on such terms and conditions as the court thinks fit (s648(1)).

The court must not confirm the reduction unless it is satisfied with respect to every creditor of the company who is entitled to object to the reduction of capital that either:

(a)  his consent to the reduction has been obtained; or
(b)  his debt or claim has been discharged or has determined or has been secured (s648(2)).

Where the court confirms the reduction it may order the company to publish the reasons for the reduction of capital or such other information as the court thinks expedient (s648(3) CA 2006).

The court may, if for any special reason it thinks it proper to do so, make an order requiring the company to add at the end of the company name the words 'and reduced' for a specified period of time (s648(4) CA 2006).

It sould be noted that where a proposed reduction of capital of a public company means that the company will no longer have the authorised minimum capital, the registrar must not register the order unless either:

(a)  the court so directs; or
(b)  the company is first re-registered as a private company (ss650–651 CA 2006).

## SUMMARY

### Financial assistance towards the purchase of a company's own shares

There are restrictions on the provision of financial assistance for the purpose of acquiring shares in the company or of its holding company, particularly in the case of public companies. There are various exceptions to this prohibition.

### Purchase of a company's own shares and the issue of redeemable shares

All companies may, subject to satisfying certain conditions, issue redeemable shares and may also purchase their own shares. In the case of public companies, this can only be financed out of distributable profits or out of the proceeds of a fresh issue. In the case of private companies, the purchase may be financed out of capital.

### Reduction of capital

Companies may reduce their issued capital by special resolution followed, in the case of public companies, by application to the court. The court will consider the position of creditors in deciding whether to approve the reduction.

### Further reading

Pettet, BG, 'Developments in the law of financial assistance for the purchase of shares' (1988) 3 JIBL 96.

Pettet, BG, 'Financial assistance for the acquisition of shares: further developments' (1995) 10 JIBL 388.

Sterling, MJ, 'Financial assistance by a company for the purchase of its shares' (1987) 8 Co Law 99.

# Directors

## 10.1 Management of the company

The company is not a natural person. Therefore, somebody needs to act on behalf of the company. The division of powers between the shareholders in general meetings and the directors will be considered later. Suffice it to state at this juncture that the power of management is largely left with the directors. The purpose of this section of the textbook is to consider the role of directors, the appointment of directors, the removal of directors, the powers of directors, and directors' duties. There is no precise definition of a director. S250 CA 2006 merely states that a director 'includes any person occupying the position of director, by whatever name called'.

## 10.2 The appointment of directors

S7 of the 2006 Act provides that subscribers may form a company. In order to do so they must submit registration documents which include a statement of the company's proposed officers (s9(4)(c) CA 2006).

S12, which deals with the statement of the proposed officers, provides that the statement of the company's proposed officers required to be disclosed to the registrar, must contain the required particulars of:

(a) the person who is, or persons who are, to be the first director or directors of the company, together with
(b) details of any secretary or joint secretaries of a private company, if there is to be one, and
(c) in the case of public company the person who is, or the persons who are, to be the first secretary or joint secretaries of the public company.

The statement must also contain a consent by each of the persons named to act in the relevant capacity.

S154 CA 2006 provides that a private company must have at least one director, and a public company must have at least two directors. S155 goes on to provide that a company must have at least one director who is a natural person.

This requirement is met if the office of director is held by a natural person as a corporation sole or otherwise by virtue of an office. If it appears to the Secretary of State that a company is in breach of either s154 or s155, the Secretary of State may give the company a direction under s156 indicating what the company must do in order to comply, and the period within which it must do so.

A minimum age is introduced for directors by s157 CA 2006. A person may not be appointed a director of a company unless he has attained the age of 16 years. S158 provides that the Secretary of State may make provision by regulation for cases in which a person who has not attained the age of 16 may be appointed as a director of a company.

With regard to existing under age directors, any person who is under age will cease to be a director on s157 coming into force (s159).

S160 provides that in a public company the appointment of each individual as a director must be, by a separate resolution, unless a resolution that the votes may be composite, agreed to by the meeting without any vote being given against it (s160 CA 2006).

S161 provides that the acts of a person acting as a director are valid, notwithstanding that it is afterwards discovered that there is a defect in the appointment, that the person is disqualified from holding office, that the person has ceased to hold office, or that he was not entitled to vote on the matter in question. This applies too, even if the resolution is void under s160 (appointment of directors of a public company to be voted on individually).

Every company must keep a register of its directors (s162 CA 2006). The register must be kept available for inspection either at the company's registered office or at a place specified in regulations under s1136. The company must give notice to the registrar of the place at which the register is kept available for inspection and of any change in that place unless it has, at all times, been kept at the company's registered office (s162(3), (4) CA 2006).

The company's register of directors should contain details of each director including a service address. It was formerly necessary for a private address to be given but this is no longer the case. The service address that the director has to give may be stated as the company's registered office (s163(5) CA 2006).

A company is also obliged to keep a register of directors' residential addresses and to notify company house of its contents (s165 CA 2006). The contents of this, however, are, with few exceptions, kept private (see s240 CA 2006). The protection of privacy, however, ceases to apply if the director's service address is ineffective (s245 CA 2006).

These provisions do not apply to directors' residential addresses already on the public register at Companies House. However, the Act does enable regulations to be made requiring the registrar to make a specific address unavailable to public view if an application is made specifying the address that is to be removed, and its location on the register (s1088 CA 2006).

Subsequent directors may be appointed in accordance with the articles. The board of directors may generally appoint people to casual vacancies between annual general meetings, but where this is done the people appointed to such vacancies must stand down at the next annual general meeting and be subject to re-election by ordinary resolution.

Changes in directors and registered details of directors (for example, a change of address) must be notified to the companies registry within 14 days of the change (s167).

### 10.2.1 Shadow director

S251 defines a shadow director.

In the Companies Acts 'Shadow Directors', in relation to a company, means a person in accordance with whose directions or instructions the directors of the company are accustomed to act.

It is provided that a person is not to be regarded as a shadow director by reason only that the directors act on advice given by him in a professional capacity.

It is further provided that a body corporate is not to be regarded as a shadow director of any of its subsidiary companies for the purposes of:

Chapter 2 (General Duties of Directors),
Chapter 4 (Transactions requiring members' approval)
Chapter 6 (contract with sole member who is also a director)

by reason only that the directors of the subsidiary are accustomed to act in accordance with its directions or instructions.

The intention is to prevent controllers of the company from escaping legal responsibilities and liabilities.

S223 provides that for certain situations a shadow director is treated as a director. These are:

(a) ss188 and 189 (directors' service contracts)
(b) ss190–196 (property transactions)
(c) ss197–214 (loans, etc)
(d) ss215–222 (payments for loss of office).

It is further provided by the section that any reference in these provisions to loss of office as a director does not apply in relation to loss of a person's status as a shadow director.

It is important to stress that a person is a shadow director of a company only if 'the directors of the company' are accustomed to act in accordance with that person's directions or instructions. The shadow director must be 'the puppet master controlling the actions of the board' whilst the directors 'must be the "cats-paw" of the shadow director'. Furthermore, the reference to 'accustomed to act' indicates that the acts must be done not on one individual occasion but over a period of time and as a regular course of conduct (see *Re Unisoft Group Ltd (No 2) (1994) per* Harman J).

It seems clear from the judicial interpretation of s251 that a high degree of control of a company's business is necessary for a person to be adjudged to be a shadow director. In *Re PFTZM Ltd (1995)*, PFTZM ran a hotel. The hotel had some financial difficulties and the hotel's landlord company permitted the company to continue trading on the basis that a director and a manager of the landlord company attended the company's management meetings and decided which of the company's creditors would be paid. The court held that there was no *prima facie* case for deciding that the landlord company's director and manager were shadow directors.

Judge Paul Baker QC said, speaking of the term 'shadow director' at p. 367 [1995] 2BCLC 354, 367:

> This definition is directed to the case where the nominees are put up but in fact behind their strings are being pulled by some other persons who do not put themselves forward as appointed directors. In this case, the involvement of the applicants here was thrust upon them by the insolvency of the company. They were not accustomed to give directions. The actions they took, as I see it, were simply directed to trying to rescue what they could out of the company using their undoubted rights as secured creditors.

There is a distinction between shadow directors and those acting as directors but who have not been formally appointed – de facto directors. In *Re Moorgate Metals Ltd (1995)*, Warner J held that a Mr Rawlinson, who was acting as a director of Moorgate, was a de facto director. He was in sole charge of the company's trading and had brought the company into being.

## 10.3 Executive and non-executive directors

A distinction is often made between executive and non-executive directors. A non-executive director is a director who is employed under a contract for services and is not working full-time for the company and will receive, in exchange for his work for the company, a director's fee. By contrast an executive director is a director who is employed under a contract of service, i.e. an employment contract, and will be generally working full time for the company and will be receiving a salary in exchange for his work.

There is no great significance in the distinction between the two in Company Law. For example, they are subject to the same regime of directors' duties. However, in relation to corporate governance, discussed below (Chapter 25), non-executive directors have an important role to play in seeking to ensure that the board of a company acts in the interests of the company rather than of individual members of the board. The Combined Code provides for a balance of executive and non-executive directors, and in particular independent non-executive directors. It is their task to control the executive directors. At least half of the board of companies in the FTSE 350 should be independent, whilst smaller quoted companies should have at least two independent directors. Independent non-executive directors should form the majority on the nomination committee which recommends appointments of directors, and the remuneration and audit committees should consist entirely of independent non-executive directors. The role of non-executive directors (and particularly independent non-executive directors which are defined in the Combined Code – section 25.8.1) are vital in ensuring appropriate corporate governance therefore.

## 10.4 Qualification of directors

Unlike company secretaries, directors do not need to have a particular qualification to serve even in a public company. However, there are some negative conditions that must be considered.

Articles generally provide that a person may be disqualified from office if he becomes insane or bankrupt and also the board may remove a director who has been voluntarily absent from board meetings for a period of six months or more.

In addition, there are statutory disqualifications from office. By virtue of the Company Directors Disqualification Act of 1986, both undischarged bankrupts and those disqualified by the court are ineligible to serve. Disqualification of directors will be considered below, in section 10.7. In addition, persons aged over 70 can only be elected or re-elected as directors of public companies or private companies that are subsidiaries of public companies if special notice is given (special notice will be considered below, in section 15.4.1).

## 10.5 Removal from office

Section 168 of the Companies Act 2006 provides that a company may by ordinary resolution at a meeting remove a director before the expiration of his period of office, notwithstanding anything in any agreement between it and him.

This provision was first introduced in the Companies Act 1948 in response to the recommendations of the Cohen Committee of 1945. At first sight it seems to be a very powerful weapon in the hands of shareholders but its apparent power is subject to certain very real restrictions.

### 10.5.1 Weighted voting provisions

Although the section prohibits the exclusion of removal by ordinary resolution, it does nothing to counteract normal principles of company law that may make that power very difficult to exercise. Thus, in British company law, it has always been possible to weight votes attaching to shares. This may, therefore, be used to give a minority shareholder who is a director the power to block his removal. In *Bushell v Faith (1970)*, the House of Lords held that a weighted voting provision was valid in this context. Shares were held in a property company which owned a block of flats in Southgate, North London by two sisters and a brother. The shares were held equally. The sisters wished to remove the brother from the board of directors. In normal circumstances, they would have had no problem as they had more than half of the shares. However, there was a provision in the articles of association that stated on a resolution to remove a director, his shares would carry three votes each. The House of Lords held by a majority of four to one that this provision was valid. The effect of this was therefore to block the brother's removal as a director. It is perhaps worth noting that the senior Law Lord, Lord Morris of Borth-y-Gest dissented in this case. He said the effect of finding that weighted voting was permissible in such circumstances was to drive a coach and horses through the intention of the legislature. It is possible that a shareholder could, in appropriate circumstances, use such a weighted voting provision as the basis of a petition under ss994–996 of the Companies Act 2006.

### 10.5.2 Quorum provisions

By the same token, it would seem that other devices may be used. For example, a quorum provision that stated that the meeting was *inquorate* in the absence of the director threatened with removal would not be contrary to the Companies Act 1985. However, it may well be that a shareholder wishing to remove a director may be able to use such a provision as the basis of a petition under ss994–996 of the Companies Act 2006 as being unfairly prejudicial. In *Harman v BML Group Ltd (1994)*, there was a shareholders' agreement which contained a provision that the meeting was only quorate if B or his proxy was present. B was removed as a director in his absence and he issued proceedings under s994 contesting his removal. The Court of Appeal held that those wishing to remove the director could not use s168 as the section could not be used to override class rights. The shareholders' agreement attached rights to shares and this has the same effect as if the class rights were contained in the company's articles.

### 10.5.3 Compensation provisions

S168(5)(a) provides that a person who is removed under s168 is not deprived of compensation or damages payable to him in respect of the termination of his appointment as director or of any appointment terminating with that as director thereby. The section is without prejudice to the removed director's rights to compensation for breach of contract. It was formerly the case that directors would have lengthy service contracts at high remuneration and that therefore at least in private companies it would be extremely expensive to dispense with their services.

It was formerly the case that directors would have lengthy service agreements at high remuneration and that therefore, at least in private companies, it would be extremely expensive to dispense with their services. S188 provides that directors' long term services agreements need the approval of the members.

This is in relation to any term of a director's employment that is longer than two years. The company must agree to any provision longer than two years and must do so by resolution of the members of the company and, in the case of a director or a holding company, by resolution of the members of that company too.

A resolution cannot be passed unless a memorandum setting out the proposed contract incorporating the provision is made available to members:

(a)  in the case of a written resolution by being sent to every eligible member; and
(b)  in the case of a resolution at a meeting by being made available for inspection by members of the company both:

   (i)  at the company's registered office for not less than 15 days ending with the date of the meeting;
   (ii)  at the meeting itself.

Removal may still prove expensive for the company: see *Shindler v Northern Raincoat Co Ltd (1960)*; *Southern Foundries Ltd (1926) v Shirlaw (1940)*. It may be that the company has concluded a service agreement with the director in which there is a liquidated damages provision specifying how much is payable to the director in the event of breach of the service agreement. In such an instance, the director may sue for the sum as a debt provided it is not a penalty, see *Taupo Totara Timber Co Ltd v Rowe (1978)*, a Privy Council decision on appeal from New Zealand.

### 10.5.4 Voting agreements

A director may have entered into voting agreements with other shareholders whereby they agree to vote as directed by him in specific instances. If this is the case, the director may ensure that they vote as promised: see *Stewart v Schwab (1956)* (South Africa) and see, on voting agreements in a different context, *Russell v Northern Bank Development Corporation Ltd (1992)*.

### 10.5.5 Petition to complain of a removal

If the company is a quasi partnership company, it may be that the director if he is also a member can petition under ss994–996 of the Companies Act 1985 on the grounds that his removal from office is unfairly prejudicial to his interests as a shareholder. This was one successful ground for the petition in *Re a Company (1986)*, for example. In *Re Bovey Hotel Ventures Ltd (1981, unreported)*, an excluded director succeeded in a petition to purchase the shares of the excluding director. In *Re Bird Precision Bellows Ltd (1986)*, it was accepted by the parties concerned that the company was a quasi partnership. The petitioning shareholders had been excluded from office as directors. The court held that in the circumstances of the case the conduct amounted to unfair prejudice and it was ordered that the petitioner's shares be purchased by the respondents at a fair value.

In order to pre-empt a removal under s168, the director concerned would need to threaten that if removed he would seek a remedy under ss994–996.

### 10.5.6 Petition for a winding up order

In a similar way under s122(1)(g) of the Insolvency Act 1986, a director-member who is removed from a quasi partnership company may seek to wind the company up on the just and equitable ground. Such a petition was successful in *Ebrahimi v Westbourne Galleries Ltd (1973)*. In this case, Ebrahimi and Nazar had run a successful partnership business selling carpets and tapestries. They decided to incorporate. The business flourished. Later Nazar sought the entry of his son, George, into the business and it was so agreed. Some shares were transferred from Ebrahimi and some from Nazar. Discord soon followed and Nazar and George excluded Ebrahimi from the business and removed him as a director. Furthermore, the considerable profits of the business were paid out as directors' salaries rather than in the form of dividends. Exclusion as a director therefore kept Ebrahimi away from the profits. He sought a winding up order under the Act. The House of Lords held unanimously that his petition would be granted.

In most circumstances, director members in such a situation will now petition under ss459–461. The just and equitable winding up remedy is after all a 'sledge hammer' remedy. Furthermore, s125(2) of the Insolvency Act 1986 requires the court, if it is of the opinion that the petitioner is entitled to relief, to decide whether it is just and equitable that the company should be wound up, bearing in mind the possibility of other forms of relief. The court, if it comes to the conclusion that it would be just and equitable that the company should be wound up in the absence of any other remedy, must make a winding up order unless it is of the opinion that the petitioner is acting unreasonably in not pursuing that other remedy. In most circumstances, it will surely be unreasonable for a petitioner not to seek a remedy in such a situation under ss459–461 of the Companies Act 1985. However, in *Virdi v Abbey Leisure Ltd (1990)*, the court considered that a refusal by the shareholder to accept an offer to buy his shares where he feared that the valuation would be wrong was not unreasonable.

## 10.6 Special notice

Special notice is required in two situations in company law. The removal of a director is one of these circumstances (s168(2)). The other is the removal of the company's auditors (ss510–511 CA 2006).

If the resolution concerns the removal of a director, the resolution must be forwarded forthwith to the director in question (s169(1)). He may make representations in writing which are then to be circulated to every member of the company to whom notice of the meeting is to be sent. If for some reason it is not possible to circulate his representations, they must be read out at the meeting. An exception to this situation is where the representations are considered to amount to an abuse of the section, in which case application may be made to the court which would then decide if it thought appropriate that circulation was inappropriate.

Notice of the resolution to remove the director would then be included in the notice of the meeting that is to be called. The director who is threatened with removal would be allowed to speak in his defence at the meeting (s169).

In both situations where special notice is appropriate, the resolution that is needed is an ordinary resolution.

In general, if the requirements of special notice are not complied with, the meeting and the removal of the director at such a meeting will be void. However, this gives way to the principle that the court will not interfere with the decision that is reached at such a meeting if it is clear that, had the correct procedures been followed, the decision would have been the same: see *Bentley-Stevens v Jones (1974)*.

The mere serving of special notice by a member who wishes to propose a resolution to remove a director will not of itself entitle that member to have the resolution circulated. Were it otherwise, any vexatious member (perhaps planted by a rival company) could embarrass the company by requiring meetings to be held to discuss his proposed resolution. In *Pedley v Inland Waterways Association Ltd (1977)*, Pedley, who was a solicitor (and so should arguably have known better), proposed the removal of the entire board of the company. He served special notice. Not surprisingly, the board did not wish to call the meeting. They did not do so. Pedley argued that this was a contravention of the provisions of the Act. He was unsuccessful. In order to ensure that a meeting is held, a person serving special notice will need to fit within one of the categories of those able to call meetings. These circumstances will be considered subsequently at Chapter 15.

The Companies Act 1989 introduced a regime whereby private companies did not need to call meetings if members otherwise agreed on a particular course of conduct. These situations will be considered subsequently in section 15.10.4. At this stage, suffice it to say that there are certain exceptions where even in private companies' meetings will need to be held and these exceptions include the proposed removal of a director and the proposal to remove an auditor. The director (and auditor) has, after all, the right to speak in his own defence, a right that can only properly be secured if a meeting is held.

## 10.7 Statutory disqualification of directors

The Company Directors Disqualification Act 1986 governs the position on disqualification. Section 1 of the Act sets out the basic thesis whereby a person may be disqualified from being:

(a) a director; or
(b) a liquidator or administrator; or
(c) a receiver or manager; or
(d) in any way directly or indirectly concerned or taking part in the promotion, formation or management of a company.

There are various periods of disqualification which may be meted out depending upon the ground of disqualification. The period of disqualification runs from the date of the disqualification order.

### 10.7.1 Disqualification for general misconduct

Sections 2–5 of the Company Directors Disqualification Act 1986 deal with disqualification for general misconduct in connection with companies.

Section 2 provides for disqualification upon the conviction of an indictable offence which is in connection with the promotion, formation, management or liquidation of a company or with the receivership or management of a company's property.

The disqualification order may be passed by a court winding up the company or by a court before or upon a person being convicted of an offence. The maximum period of disqualification is five years in the case of a court of summary jurisdiction and 15 years in any other case.

Sections 3 and 5 of the Act permit disqualification for persistent breaches of companies' legislation. A person is to be taken to be persistent in default if it is conclusively proved that in the five years ending with the date of the application he has been adjudged guilty of three or more defaults in relation to Companies Act provisions. The default may either involve conviction of a particular provision or a default order being made against the person in question under one of the following:

(a) s242(4) – failure to deliver company accounts;
(b) s713 – failure to make returns;
(c) s41 of the Insolvency Act 1986 – failure of a receiver or manager to make returns;
(d) s170 of the Insolvency Act 1986 – failure of a liquidator to make returns.

The maximum period of the disqualification under s3 is five years.

Section 4 allows the court to disqualify for fraudulent trading (see section 24.3) or for fraud in relation to the company by an officer, liquidator, receiver or manager or breach of duty by such officer, liquidator, receiver or manager.

The maximum period of the disqualification under s4 is 15 years.

### 10.7.2 Disqualification for unfitness

Sections 6–9 of the Act provide for disqualification for unfitness.

It is provided that the court must make a disqualification order against a person when application has been made if it is satisfied that a person has been a director of a company which has become insolvent and that his conduct as a director of that company (either taken on its own or together with his conduct as a director of any other company or companies) makes him unfit to be concerned in the management of a company. Application under s6 is made by the Secretary of State for Trade and Industry or if the Secretary of State so directs by the official receiver.

A company is taken to be insolvent if:

(a)  the company goes into liquidation at a time when its assets are insufficient to pay its debts and liabilities and the expenses of the winding up; or
(b)  an administration order is made in relation to the company; or
(c)  an administrative receiver of the company is appointed.

There is a duty upon the official receiver, the liquidator, the administrator or a receiver as is appropriate to inform the Secretary of State for Trade and Industry if it is considered that a director is within the section. Schedule 1 of the Act provides for the matters that are relevant for determining the unfitness of directors. These are:

(a)  any misfeasance or breach of any fiduciary or other duty by the director;
(b)  misapplication or retention of property by the director or any conduct by the director giving rise to an obligation to account for money or other property;
(c)  the extent of the director's responsibility for the company entering into any transaction that is liable to be set aside under Pt XVI of the Insolvency Act which deals with provisions relating to debt avoidance;
(d)  the extent of the director's responsibility for failure by the company to comply with one of the various provisions that are set out relating to the keeping of records and the making of an annual return;
(e)  failure to approve and sign the company accounts;
(f)  the extent of the director's responsibility for the company entering into a transaction or giving a preference which is liable to be set aside under s127 of the Insolvency Act 1986 (as a disposition after the commencement of winding up) or a transaction which may be set aside as a transaction at an undervalue or a preference, see ss238–240 of the Insolvency Act 1986;
(g)  failure to comply with one or more of the obligations under the Insolvency Act relating to the provision of a statement of affairs, co-operation with the liquidator, etc.

Note: The matters set out in (f) and (g) above relate specifically to where the company has become insolvent. The other matters are applicable in all cases and may thus arise where the director's conduct in another (possibly solvent) company is being examined.

The maximum period of disqualification under the section is 15 years and the minimum period is two years.

Section 8 provides for disqualification of a director after an investigation of a company (see Chapter 21). If it appears to the Secretary of State from a report made by inspectors that it is expedient in the public interest that a disqualification order should be made against a person who is or has been a director or shadow director, he may apply to the court for such an order to be made against that person. The court may make such an order if it is felt that the director is unfit.

The disqualification period here is subject to a maximum of 15 years disqualification.

Section 9 of the Act provides that, where a court is to determine whether a person's conduct as a director or shadow director makes him unfit to be concerned in the management of a company, the court shall again have regard in particular to the matters mentioned in Pt I of the First Schedule to the Act, and, if the company is insolvent, the factors set out in Pt II of the Schedule which deals with matters applicable where the company has become insolvent are appropriate.

In *Re Sevenoaks Stationers (Retail) Ltd (1991)*, the Court of Appeal set out certain principles on disqualification for unfitness. Dillon LJ said at p. 328:

> I would for my part endorse the division of the potential 15 year disqualification period into three brackets, which was put forward by Mr Keenan for the official receiver to Harman J in the present case and has been put forward by Mr Charles for the official receivers in other cases, *viz*:

(i) the top bracket of disqualification for periods over 10 years should be reserved for particularly serious cases. These may include cases where a director who has already had one period of disqualification imposed on him falls to be disqualified yet again;
(ii) the minimum bracket of two to five years' disqualification should be applied where, though disqualification is mandatory, the case is relatively not very serious;
(iii) the middle bracket of disqualification for from six to 10 years should apply for serious cases which do not merit the top bracket.

In *Secretary of State for Trade and Industry v Gray and another (1995)*, the Court of Appeal allowed an appeal where the first instance judges had considered that the future protection of the public did not merit a period of disqualification. The Court of Appeal stated that if the respondents' conduct fell below the standard appropriate for persons considered fit to be directors then it was the judge's duty to make a disqualification order.

An example of a disqualification for unfitness is provided by *Re Firedart Ltd (1994)* where F, the director, had continued trading through the medium of the company when it was insolvent, had received excessive remuneration and had failed to keep proper accounting records. The appropriate period of disqualification was held to be six years.

### 10.7.3 Disqualification in other cases

Sections 10–12 deal with other cases of disqualification. Section 10 provides that where there has been participation in wrongful trading or fraudulent trading such that a person is held liable to make a contribution to a company's assets, then whether or not an application for an order is made, the court may if it thinks fit make a disqualification order against the person to whom the declaration of liability relates. The maximum period of the disqualification is 15 years.

Section 11 of the Act provides that it is an offence for a person who is an undischarged bankrupt to act as a director. Section 12 provides that where a person fails to make a payment as provided for in an administration order of the county court, the court may make a disqualification order against the person concerned in revoking the administration order. The period may not exceed two years.

Section 13 provides that a person who acts in contravention of a disqualification order is guilty of an offence which on conviction on indictment is punishable by up to two years' imprisonment and/or a fine and is punishable on summary conviction by imprisonment of not more than six months and/or a fine up to the statutory maximum.

Section 14 of the Act provides that where a company is guilty of an offence of acting in contravention of a disqualification order and it is shown that the offence occurred with the consent or connivance or is attributable to any neglect on the part of any director, manager, secretary or other officer of the body corporate or any person purporting to act as such, he shall be guilty of an offence as well as the body corporate.

Section 15 provides that a person who is disqualified and continues to act is personally responsible for all the relevant debts of the company.

There is a register of disqualification orders which is kept by the Secretary of State in pursuance of s18 of the Act.

### 10.7.4 Summary disqualification procedure

Sometimes, there is the possibility of a summary procedure for dealing with applications for disqualification of directors being utilised. This procedure, as set out in *Re Carecraft Construction Co Ltd (1993)*, was reviewed in *Secretary of State for Trade and Industry v Rogers (1997)* by Scott VC.

Scott VC said that the *Carecraft* summary procedure can be used where:

(a) the facts regarding the director's conduct are not disputed;
(b) the Secretary of State for Trade and Industry is willing for the case to be dealt with by the judge on those undisputed facts;
(c) the director is willing for the case to be dealt with by the judge on those facts;
(d) the Secretary of State and the director have reached agreement either on the length of the disqualification period or at least on the parameters which it should fall within.

This process enables disqualification to proceed expeditiously and with reduced costs. The DTI has launched a 24-hour Disqualification Hotline so the public can name misperforming disqualified directors. The hotline number is 0845 6013546 and is charged at local rates. Questionnaires are sent to those responding to the request for information by using the hotline.

## 10.8 Directors' loss of office and compensation payments

Where a director loses office, he may, nevertheless, be awarded a golden handshake sum. SS215–222 CA 2006 deal with this area.

S217 provides that a company may not make a payment for loss of office to a director unless the payment has been approved by a resolution of the members of the company. The section further provides that it cannot make payment for loss of office to a director of its holding company unless the payment has been approved by a resolution of the members of each of those companies. The payment may be organised in a slightly different way.

Under s218 it is not lawful in connection with the transfer of a business for payment for loss of office to be made unless the payment has been approved by a resolution of the members of the company. No payment for loss of office may be made by any person to a director of a company in connection with the transfer of the whole or any part of the undertaking or property of the company unless the payment has been approved by a resolution of the members of the company.

Further, no payment for loss of office may be made by any person to a director of a company in connection with the transfer of the whole or any part of the undertaking or property of a subsidiary of the company unless the payment has been approved by a resolution of the members of each of the companies.

S219 provides that, if a payment is proposed to a director by any person in connection with the transfer of shares in the company or in a subsidiary of the company resulting from the take over bid, it may not be made unless the payment has been approved by a resolution of the relevant shareholders. The shareholders who want to approve the payment are the holders of the shares to which the bid relates, and any holders of shares of the same class as any of those shares.

S222 deals with the consequences of payments in contravention of the golden handshake sections.

If a payment is made in contravention of s217 (payment by a company), the payment is held by the recipient on trust for the company making the payment, and any director who authorised the payment is jointly and severely liable to indemnify the company that made the payment for any loss resulting from it.

If a payment is made in contravention of s218 (payment in connection of transfer of undertaking, etc), it is held by the recipient on trust for the company whose undertaking what property is or is proposed to be transferred.

If a payment is made in contravention of s219 (payment in connection with share transfer),

   (a) it is held by the recipient on trust for the persons who have sold their shares as a result of the offer made; and

(b) the expenses incurred by the recipients in distributing that sum amongst those persons shall be borne by him and not retained out of that sum.

It should be noted that the provisions on golden handshakes do not apply to payment of compensation for breach of a contract of service by court order (s168(5)(a)) or to a *bona fide* settlement of a claim under s168, or where a director sues for a liquidated sum set out in the contract as payable in the event of breach: see *Taupo Totara Timber Co Ltd v Rowe (1978)*, a Privy Council decision on appeal from New Zealand (see s220).

There is also an exception for small payments in relation to the golden handshake provisions where approval is not required if:

(a)  the payment in question is made by the company or any of its subsidiaries, and
(b)  the amount or value of the payment, together with the amount or value of any other relevant payments, does not exceed £200 (s221).

## 10.9 Loans, quasi loans and credit transactions in favour of directors

The law in this area is not likely to set the pulse racing. The 2006 Act removes current prohibitions on loans etc, to directors and connected persons. There is now a general position where these may be made subject to the requirement of the shareholders' approval, which must be obtained before the particular transaction with the director etc is entered into (ss197–214 CA 2006).

S197 CA 2006 provides that a company may not make a loan to a director or give a guarantee or provide security in connection with a loan made by any person to a director unless the transaction has been approved by a resolution of the members of the company.

If the director is a director of the company's holding company, the transaction must also have been approved by a resolution of the members of the holding company.

S198 deals with quasi loans. Quasi loans are defined in s199 to mean transactions where one party (the creditor) agrees to pay or pays otherwise in pursuance of an agreement, a sum for another (the borrower) or agrees to reimburse that other in relation to expenditure incurred by another party for another (the borrower).

In relation to quasi loans to directors, s198 provides that if the company is a public company or a company associated with a public company, then the company may not make a quasi loan to a director of the company or of its holding company, or give a guarantee or provide security in connection with such a quasi loan, unless the transation has been approved by a resolution of the members of the company. If the director is a director of the company's holding company, the transaction must also have been approved by a resolution of the members of the holding company.

S256 CA 2006 and the definition of an associated company are relevant here. S256(b) provides that companies are associated if one is a subsidiary of the other or both are subsidiaries of the same body corporate.

S200 CA 2006 deals with loans or quasi loans to persons connected with directors.

The section applies to a company that is a public company or a company associated with a public company. In these circumstances a company may not make a loan or quasi loan to a person connected with a director of the company or of its holding company or give a guarantee or provide security in connection with such a loan or quasi loan unless the transaction has been approved by a resolution of the members of the company. If the connected person is a person connected with a director of the company's holding company, the transaction must also have been approved by a resolution of the members of the holding company.

S201 and s202 deal with credit transactions.

A credit transaction is a transaction under which one party, the creditor, supplies goods or sells land under a hire purchase agreement or conditional sale agreement or leases or hires land or goods in return for periodical payments, or otherwise disposes of land or supplies goods or services on the understanding that payment is to be deferred (s202 CA 2006).

S201 provides that in relation to a public company or a company associated with a public company, the company cannot enter into a credit transaction as creditor for the benefit of a director of the company or of its holding company or a person connected with such a director, or give a guarantee or provide security in connection with a credit transaction, unless the transaction or the giving of the guarantee or the provision of security has been approved by a resolution of the members of the company.

If the director of connected person is a director of its holding company, or a person connected with such a director, the transaction must also have been approved by a resolution of the members of the holding company.

S203 CA 2006 is a provision designed to plug a loophole such that the company may not enter into an arrangement with somebody else which would have required approval under ss197, 198, 200 or 201, where the other person entering the arrangement obtains a benefit from the company or a body corporate associated with it, or where the company arranges for the assignment to it, or assumption by it of any rights, obligations or liabilities under a transaction that if it had been entered into by the company would have required such approval.

In such situations the arrangement must be approved by a resolution of the members of the company, and of its holding company (if appropriate).

There are certain exceptions to these general rules:

(a) Expenditure in connection with regulatory action or investigation (s206 CA 2006)
(b) Expenditure, de minimis (s207 CA 2006)
(c) Intragroup transactions (s208 CA 2006)

(d)  Expenditure by money lending companies made on the normal terms of business (s209 CA 2006).

S213 deals with the civil consequences of contravention.

The transaction or arrangement in question is voidable at the instance of the company unless restitution is no longer possible, or the company has been indemnified for any loss or damage, or rights acquired in good faith for value and without notice of the contravention by a person who is not a party to the transaction, would be affected by the avoidance.

It is to be noted that the categories for a person 'connected' with a director for these provisions have been extended to include civil partners, cohabitants, and infant children of the cohabitant living with the director, the director's adult children and his parents (ss252–253 CA 2006).

It should be noted that certain transactions remain outside of the scope of the prohibition, thus quasi loans to and credit transactions with a director or connected persons by a private company that is not associated with a public company, and loans to such connected persons by such a company, do not require approval.

## SUMMARY

### Directors

#### *Appointment of directors*

The appointment of directors is a matter which is generally settled by the articles of association.

Public companies must have at least two directors and private companies must have at least one director.

There are various categerisations of directors; particuarly important is the distinction between executive and non-executive directors. Shadow directors, those in accordance with whose directions and instructing directors are accustomed to cut one subject too many of the same rules and principles as directors.

#### *Removal of directors*

Section 168 of the Companies Act 2006 provides for the removal of directors from the board of directors by ordinary resolution in general meeting.

There are various provisos which may affect the exercise of this power:

(a)  the possibility of weighted voting shares;
(b)  a carefully drawn quorum provision;
(c)  compensation payable for breach of contract;
(d)  voting agreements;

(e) a ss994–996 petition by a shareholder/director;

(f) a winding up petition on the just and equitable ground (s122(1)(g) of the Insolvency Act 1986) by a shareholder/director;

(g) the procedural niceties of the special notice procedure.

## Statutory disqualification

The Company Directors Disqualification Act 1986 provides for disqualification from office as:

(a) a director; or

(b) a liquidator or administrator; or

(c) a receiver or manager; or

(d) a person concerned in the promotion, formation or management of a company.

Disqualification may arise on various grounds. It may be from conviction of an indictable offence connected with the running of a company, persistent breach of filing provisions of the companies legislation, or for fraudulent trading. In addition, directors may be disqualified on the ground of unfitness following the insolvency of their company or following a company investigation. There are various guidelines which are set out in a schedule to the Act which are relevant in determining unfitness.

An undischarged bankrupt cannot act as a director.

## Directors' loss of office and compensation payments

Golden handshake payments for directors have to be disclosed to members and assented to.

## Loans, quasi-loans, etc

There are strict rules restricting loans, quasi loans and credit transactions in favour of directors and connected persons. Transactions in breach of the provisions are void and civil consequences may result.

# Further reading

Baker, PV, 'A casenote on *Bushell v Faith*' (1970) 86 LQR 155.

Griffin, S, 'The disqualification of unfit directors and the protection of the public interest' (2002) NILQ 207.

Hicks, A, 'Director Disqualification – the National Audit Office Follows Up', ILP, 15 (1999) 112.

Hicks, A, 'Disqualification of Directors – Forty Years On' (1988) JBL 27.

Hoey, A, 'Disqualifying delinquent directors' (1997) 18 Co Law 130.

Millman, D, 'Personal liability and disqualification of company directors: something old, something new' (1992) 43 NILQ 1.

Ong, KTW, 'Disqualification of directors: a faulty regime?' (1998) 19 Co Law 7.

Wardman, K, 'Directors and Employee Status: An examination of relevant Company Law and Employment Law principles' (2003) 24 Co Law 139.

Wheeler, S, 'Directors' disqualification: insolvency practitioners and the decision making process' (1995) 15 LS 283.

# Powers of directors

## 11.1 Introduction

Generally, companies will delegate considerable powers of management to the directors of the company. Table A of the Companies Act 1985 of Art 70, for example, provides:

> Subject to the provisions of the Act, the memorandum and the articles and to any directions given by special resolution, the business of the company shall be managed by the directors who may exercise all the powers of the company. No alteration of the memorandum or articles and no such direction shall invalidate any prior act of the directors which would have been valid if that alteration had not been made or that direction had not been given.

The company will obviously delegate only such powers as it itself has. Thus, the directors are not competent to engage in *ultra vires* transactions. As has been seen, however, *ultra vires* transactions may be ratified and the breach of directors' duties may be ratified by a separate special resolution. Furthermore, the directors can only validly act in the interests of the company and for the purposes for which the powers are conferred upon them: see *Hogg v Cramphorn Ltd (1967)*; *Bamford v Bamford (1970)* (see section 12.4.1).

The powers delegated to the directors are delegated to them collectively. It is open to the directors, of course, to sub-delegate powers to individual directors or, indeed, to others.

## 11.2 Control of the directors

In general, the directors are vested with management by the members. Their removal from office is by an ordinary resolution passed in general meeting following special notice: see s168 of the Companies Act 2006. Directors may exercise their powers of management while they are in office: see *Salmon v Quin and Axtens (1909)*. Where companies have articles like Art 70 of Table A of the Companies Act 1985 (above), however, this permits directions to be given by special resolution to the directors.

In *John Shaw & Sons (Salford) Ltd v Shaw (1935)*, the Court of Appeal refused to allow the members to override the decision of the directors to commence legal proceedings. In *Breckland Group Holdings Ltd v London and Suffolk Properties Ltd (1988)*, the company attempted to commence legal proceedings. The company had two members B Ltd and C Ltd. It had been agreed that C Ltd would appoint two directors and B Ltd one director. It had further been agreed that for legal proceedings to be commenced, both B Ltd and C Ltd would have to agree. The High Court restrained the parties from taking any further steps until a board meeting of the company could be held. The matter was one for the board of directors to determine under the equivalent of Table A of Art 70. Previously, in *Marshalls Valve Gear v Manning Wardle & Company (1909)*, it had been held that the board of directors could be overridden by the company in general meeting in relation to potential litigation involving one of the directors.

In other circumstances, the members may have to act to fill a void.

The House of Lords, in *Alexander Ward & Co v Samyang Navigation Co (1975)*, allowed two members to act to protect the interests of the company when the company had no directors. In *Re Argentum Reductions (UK) Ltd (1975)*, Megarry J declined to decide whether the members had reserve powers where the directors were unable to act, stating at p 189 'there are deep waters here'.

The cases are far from consistent. On occasion, the courts have permitted the members to act where there is deadlock on the board of directors. Thus in *Baron v Potter (1914)*, the company had two directors who were not on speaking terms. It was impossible to hold constructive board meetings. Canon Baron refused to attend board meetings with Potter. Potter tried to call a general meeting. Baron intended to boycott this meeting but his train was met by Potter at Paddington who proceeded to try to hold a meeting on the platform. He proposed Charles Herbert, William George Walter Barnard and John Tolhurst Musgrave as additional directors. Baron objected and Potter purported to use his casting vote as chairman. The court held that this was an ineffective meeting. In the circumstances, it was held that in view of the deadlock on the board of directors, the powers were exercisable by the members in general meeting. In a similar way, in *Foster v Foster (1916)*, there was a dispute over which of the two directors should be appointed as managing director of the company. There were three directors in all. The articles gave the power to appoint a managing director to the board of directors. However, directors could not vote on a matter in which they had a personal interest. It was, accordingly, not possible to pass the resolution. The general meeting accordingly could fill the vacuum.

It is open to the members of the company in general meeting to ratify matters that have been performed by the directors. It is possible to use this power of ratification in relation to *ultra vires* acts by special resolution. It is possible to use the power of ratification in relation to acts that are beyond the directors' authority by ordinary resolution provided that the directors are not acting fraudulently: see *Hogg v Cramphorn Ltd (1967)*; *Bamford v Bamford (1970)*; and *Grant v United Kingdom Switchback Railways Co (1888)*.

## 11.3 Managing director

The articles, such as Art 72 of Table A of the 1985 Act, permit the appointment of a managing director. The appointment of a managing director, however, is not a legal requirement.

The appointment of a managing director will cease if he ceases to be a director. If he has a separate service agreement and is removed as a director, he may of course sue upon this contract: see s168(5)(a) of the Companies Act 2006.

## 11.4 Validity of the acts of directors

If matters are delegated to the board of directors, this of course means directors who are properly appointed. On occasion, directors may be invalidly appointed and questions arise as to whether those dealing with them may hold the company bound. There are certain rules of law which tend to validate the acts of a director in spite of any irregularities in his appointment in such circumstances.

There is a statutory principle contained in s161 CA 2006 that the acts of a person acting as a director are valid, notwithstanding that it is afterwards discovered:

(a) that there was a defect in his appointment;
(b) that he was disqualified from holding office;
(c) that he had ceased to hold office;
(d) that he was not entitled to vote on the matter in question.

It should be noted that s161 covers defects of appoint or qualification, but as is made clear by *Morris v Kanssen (1946)*, the principle cannot apply where there has been a fraudulent attempt to appoint a director. It can only apply where there is a *bona fide* attempt to appoint a director, etc. It does not cover cases of fraud.

A quite separate principle is an application of the rule in *Turquand's Case* (1856) which is considered more fully below (section 11.5). If a person deals with a company through persons who are purporting to act as directors even though they have not been properly appointed, he may be entitled to assume that they are in fact directors and to hold the company bound by their acts: see *Mahony v East Holyford Mining Co (1875)*, where the directors who had concluded the transaction had not in fact been appointed. A company as an artificial person can only act through agents.

The principles of agency law dictate that an agent can only act within his actual or ostensible authority in binding the company. If an agent acts beyond his actual and ostensible authority and contracts with another the company is not bound. The remedy for the other party contracting with the non agent in these circumstances will be for breach of warranty of authority.

The outsider may be able to hold the company bound on the basis of actual authority or on the basis of ostensible (sometimes called 'apparent' authority, holding out or agency by estoppel).

Diplock LJ in *Freeman and Lockyer v Buckhurst Park Properites (Mangal Ltd)* [1964] 2QB 480 at p505, said 'the commonest form of respresentation by a principal creating an "apparent" authority of an agent is by conduct, namely, by permitting the agent to act in the management or conduct of the principal's business. Thus, if in the case of a company, the board of directors who have "actual" authority under the Memoramdum and Articles of Association to manage the company's business, permit the agent to act in the management or conduct of the company's business, they thereby represent to all persons dealing with such agent that he has authority to enter on behalf of the corporation into contracts of a kind which an agent authorised to do acts of the kind which he is in fact permitted to do, normally enters into in the ordinary course of such business'.

Thus, if the company makes it appear that an individual director or person has authority to conclude a particular transaction, an outsider can hold the company bound. A director simply by virtue of holding the office of director has no implied authority as agent of the company to conclude contracts. Yet, if the company allows the director to act as if he had such authority, then the company may be estopped from denying that he has the authority. It is no longer the case that the mere fact that the company's constitution makes it clear that there is no such authority is sufficient to render the authority non-existent (see section 5.11). There is no constructive notice of such restrictions (see s40 CA 2006). The question of agency by estoppel was discussed in *Freeman and Lockyer v Buckhurst Park Properties (Mangal) (1964)*. Diplock LJ said that there must have been a representation that a person had authority and that representation must have been made by those who had authority within the company. The other party must have relied on the representation in entering into the contract. He went on to say that there must be nothing in the constitution to countermand that authority. This last point of Diplock LJ is, of course, no longer applicable. In *Freeman and Lockyer* itself, the board of directors had permitted one director to act as if he had been appointed managing director. In fact he had not been appointed as managing director but the articles of association made provision for such an appointment. Accordingly the company was held liable. On occasion problems may arise as identified by Lord Pearson in *Hely-Hutchinson v Brayhead Ltd* [1968] 1QB 549 at p. 593, 'now there is not usually any direct communication in such cases between the board of directors and the outside contractor. The actual communication is made immediately and directly, whether it be expressed or implied by the agent to the outside contractor. It is, therefore, necessary in order to make a case of ostensible authority to show in some way as such communication which is made directly by the agent is made ultimately by the responsible parties, the board of directors. That may be shown by inferrence from the conduct of the board of directors in the particuar case by, for instance, placing the agent in a position where he can hold himself out as their agent and acquiesing in his activities, so that it can be said that they have in effect caused the representation to be made'.

In *Armagas Ltd v Mundogas SA (1986)*, Lord Keith of Kinkel said:

> Ostensible authority comes about where the principal, by words or conduct, has represented that the agent has the requisite actual authority, and the party dealing with the agent has entered into a contract with him in reliance on that representation.

Thus, in *First Energy (UK) Ltd v Hungarian International Bank Ltd (1993)*, the manager of a branch of the bank made an offer of facilities to First Energy. He did not have authority to make such offers himself, but it was held that he had ostensible authority to communicate such offers. The bank was, therefore, held liable.

If there is a representation by the principal (the directors) that the agent has the necessary authority, then the principal is stopped from ascerting that the agent did not have authority. Of course, the principal may withdraw a representation of authority but this is only effective when communicated.

## 11.5 The rule in *Turquand's* case

In *Turquand's* case (*Royal British Bank v Turquand (1856)*), the company's articles authorised the directors to borrow money if this had been sanctioned by ordinary resolution. A resolution was passed but it did not specify the amount which the directors could borrow. The directors borrowed money and the company became insolvent. Turquand was sued as the liquidator. It was held that the plaintiff's bank was deemed to be aware that the directors could only borrow up to the amount of the resolution as the articles were available at Companies House and, therefore, there was constructive notice of the contents of the articles of association. Yet, an outsider had no means of knowing whether an ordinary resolution had been passed. Ordinary resolutions were not registerable. In the circumstances, the bank was entitled to assume the fact of a resolution being passed and was not required (indeed not entitled) to investigate the internal workings of the company. The rule is sometimes called 'the indoor management rule'.

The rule does not apply in all circumstances. Thus, if the outsider actually knew or had strong grounds for suspecting that the act was not authorised, the rule cannot be relied upon: see *Underwood v Bank of Liverpool and Martins (1924)*. Furthermore, if the person dealing with the company is himself one of its directors, then it is reasonable to assume that he will know of the internal operations of the company and may therefore not be able to rely upon the principle: see *Hely-Hutchinson v Brayhead (1968)*.

Furthermore, it seems that the principle in *Royal British Bank v Turquand* cannot be relied upon if the document that is presented is a forgery: see *Ruben v Great Fingall Consolidated (1906)*.

The principle of indoor management is therefore useful to bind the company to acts of directors (or apparent directors) who are acting beyond their capacity.

Those dealing with the company no longer have constructive notice of the articles or memorandum if they should contain restrictions on the capacity of persons to act.

The rule is seemingly restricted to situations where the board as a whole is presumed to have authority rather than individual directors.

The area of agents' authority clearly overlaps with the area of corporate capacity and powers. S40 of the Companies Act 2006 will generally afford more protection to an outsider as even knowledge of the act being beyond the authority of the board will not amount to bad faith (s40(2)(iii)). On the other hand, *Turquand* probably applies where there is not a properly constituted board and so the principle in *Turquand's* case remains of importance.

## SUMMARY

### Introduction

Articles such as Companies Act 1985 Table A of Art 70 provide for the management of the company's business by the directors and most companies follow this format.

It is not generally open to the shareholders in general meeting to take on the functions of the directors. There are certain exceptions to this general rule, however. If the directors are unable to act for some reason, such as deadlock or if there are no directors, then the shareholders may act.

### Validation of directors' acts

If a person acts as director but there is some defect in his initial appointment, nevertheless, his acts are to be treated as valid.

Furthermore, where a person is held out as a director or as having authority to the outside world and this is relied upon where there is nothing to indicate the lack of actual authority, the outsider will be able to hold the company responsible on agency principles.

A further rule, called the indoor management rule or the rule in *Turquand's* case, provides that, if to an outsider the correct procedures appear to have been adhered to, then the outsider can hold the company responsible notwithstanding that there is some *internal* irregularity. An outsider is not bound, indeed not entitled, to enquire into the internal workings of the company.

### Further reading

Ferran, E, 'The reform of the law on corporate capacity and directors' and officers' authority' (1992) 13 Co Law 124.

Flynn, J, 'The power to direct' (1991) 13 DULJ 101.

Hirt, H, 'The company's decision to litigate against its directors: Legal strategies to deal with the Board of Directors' Conflict of Interest' [2005] JBL 159.

MacKenzie, J, 'Who controls the company? – The interpretation of Table A' (1983) 4 Co Law 99.

Sealy, LS, 'Agency principles and the rule in *Turquand's* case' (1990) 49 CLJ 406.

Sullivan, G, 'The relationship between the board of directors and the general meeting in limited companies' (1977) 93 LQR 569.

# Directors' duties

## 12.1 Introduction

One of the most significant changes brought about by the Companies Act 2006 is in relation to the statutory code of duties that a director owes to a company (ss170–177 CA 2006).

A person who ceases to be a director continues to be subject:

(a) to the duty in s175 (duty to avoid conflicts of interest) as regards the exploitation of any property, information or opportunity of which he became aware at a time when he was a director, and

(b) to the duty in s176 (duty not to accept benefits from third parties) in relation to things that were done or omitted by the director before he ceased to be a director.

S170(4) provides that the general duties shall be interpreted and applied in the same way as the common law rules or equitable principles regard should be had to the corresponding common law rules and equitable principles in interpreting and applying those general duties.

It is therefore proposed to consider pre-existing case law which impacts on the interpretation of these duties.

## 12.2 The nature of the duty owed

The traditional view in British company law was that directors owed their duties to the company which was interpreted as the providers of capital; that is to say to the shareholders. This duty was owed to the shareholders as a body and not to individual shareholders. Thus, in *Percival v Wright (1902)*, where certain shareholders approached the directors asking them to purchase their shares at a time when secret takeover negotiations were going on, the directors failed to mention this to the shareholders. In subsequent litigation, it was held that the directors were not in breach of duty to the shareholders. The directors owed their duty to the shareholders as a body and the court took the view that premature disclosure of the takeover negotiations would have been detrimental to the shareholders. The position is different if the approach is made by the directors to the shareholders. In such a situation, the directors constitute themselves as fiduciaries vis à vis the shareholders: see *Briess v Woolley (1954)*; *Allen v Hyatt (1914)*. In *Peskin v Anderson (2000)* the Court of Appeal confirmed that there needs to be special circumstances to justify the imposition of fiduciary duties on directors to particular shareholders.

The case involved the de-mutualisation of the RA Club in Pall Mall with payouts to members. Former members of the Club who retired prior to the cut off date argued that the directors were in breach of fiduciary duty for not disclosing the plans. The Court held there were no special circumstances requiring particular attention for those former members.

Other jurisdictions took a more liberal view of the duty owed to individual shareholders. Thus, in *Coleman v Myers (1972)*, the New Zealand Court of Appeal held that the managing director and chairman of a company owed fiduciary duties to the shareholders of the company in a takeover situation. Indeed, even in Great Britain, it seems that in certain situations the courts are willing to hold that a duty is owed to individual shareholders. This seems to be the case in takeover situations: see *Gething v Kilner (1972)*.

Note that the decision in *Percival v Wright* in relation to purchase of shares by directors is obviously now subject to legislative provisions on insider dealing and indeed the proposition that directors of a company may purchase the shares of other shareholders without disclosing pending negotiations for the purchase of the company has been doubted by Browne-Wilkinson VC in *Re Chez Nico (Restaurants) Ltd (1991)*.

'S172 of the Companies Act 2006 now provides that a director of a company must act in the way that he considers, in good faith, would be most likely to promote the success of the company for the benefits of its members as a whole'. This clearly preserves the principle in *Percival v Wright* in statutory form.

The section goes on to provide that in doing so the director must have regard amongst other matters to:

(a) the likely consequences of any decision in the long term;
(b) the interests of the company's employees;
(c) the need to foster the company's business relationships with suppliers, customers and others;
(d) the impact of the company's operations on the community and the environment;
(e) the desirability of the company maintaining a reputation for high standards of business conduct; and
(f) the need to act fairly as between members of the company.

This section has been stated to enshrine in statutory form the principle of 'englighted shareholder value'.

The previous common law rule in *Percival v Wright* with regard to a duty being owed to the providers of capital, had previously been extended by statute to include the interests of employees by the Companies Act 1980. However, this was the extent of the existing duty by directors when the new provisions in the Companies Act 2006 came into being. There was, for example, considerable doubt at common law as to whether a duty was owed to creditors (see e.g. in *Liquidator of West Mercia Safetywear Ltd v Dodd (1988)*, although s214 of the Insolvency Act 1986 did make it clear that a duty was owed to creditors of the company in the event of the company's insolvency by directors and shadow directors.

## 12.3 Nominee directors

S173 CA 2006 provides that a director of a company must exercise independent judgment. This puts it beyond doubt that a director who is placed on a board as a nominee of a substantial shareholder or otherwise must act in accordance with the interests of the company that he is serving rather than the interests of the nominator.

## 12.4 Directors' exercise of powers for a proper purpose

S171 CA 2006 provides that a director of a company must:

(a)  act in accordance with the company's constitution; and
(b)  only exercise powers for the purposes for which they are conferred.

This statement of duty reflects the pre-existing position in case law.

On occasion, the question of whether directors have exercised their powers for a proper purpose has arisen in decided cases. The most common example of the exercise of directors' powers that is subject to the fiduciary duty of directors in decided cases is the power to issue shares.

### 12.4.1 Power to issue shares

It is no longer necessary for private companies with one class of share to obtain authority from the company's shareholders before allotting shares. The Act permits directors of such companies to allot shares unless the articles provide otherwise (s550 CA 2006). This does not, however, apply to companies with more than one class of share, or to public companies. In such cases there must be authorisation for the exercise of the power of allotment in the company's constitution.

The power to issue shares is given for the purpose of raising necessary capital for the company. Any other purpose is not *prima facie* a legitimate exercise of that power. However, the courts have recognised that other purposes may be validated by the company in general meeting. Thus, for example, it is an improper purpose to issue shares to defeat a takeover bid but the exercise of the issue of shares for this purpose may be validated by the company in general meeting. In *Hogg v Cramphorn Ltd (1967)*, a takeover bid was proposed which the directors genuinely believed not to be in the best interest of the company. To block the takeover bid, the directors issued 5,000 additional shares which were to be held on trust for the employees of the company. The court held that the issue was not a proper exercise of the directors powers and therefore invalid. However, the court ordered that a meeting of the members should be held which could if it considered it appropriate validate the issue.

At this company meeting, the new shares would not be able to vote. In the event, the issue was ratified. A similar conclusion was reached in *Bamford v Bamford (1970)*. It is not every issue of shares for extraneous purposes that can be validated, however. If the purpose of the issue of shares is clearly to further the directors' or majority shareholders' own personal interests, the issue cannot be validated by the company in general meeting, see *Howard Smith Ltd v Ampol Petroleum Ltd (1974)* (a Privy Council case from Australia). In this case, there were rival bids for the share capital of a company. The majority shareholders favoured one bid. The directors who favoured a different bid issued additional shares to the bidding company to place the majority shareholders in a minority position. The Privy Council held that the issue was an improper exercise of their powers as it was designed to thwart the wishes of the majority shareholders.

In *Clemens v Clemens Brothers Ltd (1976)*, two shareholders held the entire share capital of a company and the majority shareholder used her voting power to pass a resolution authorising the issue of new shares to an employee trust scheme. This was held to be invalid. The effect of the new issue of shares was to reduce the other shareholders' holding (that of her niece) to less than the 25% stake where she had been able to block a special resolution. Foster J considered that the exercise of the majority's voting power in this case was being used inequitably against the minority shareholder and this was held to be invalid.

In an earlier unreported decision, *Pennell, Sutton and Moraybell Securities Ltd v Venida Investments Ltd (1974)* (noted in (1981) 44 MLR 40 by Burridge), the majority proposed to increase the share capital of the company. The minority had sought a declaration that this constituted a fraud on the minority and asked for an interlocutory injunction. The minority succeeded. Templeman J held that there was a *prima facie* case of abuse of powers by the company's directors and the judge considered that the company was a quasi-partnership company based on mutual trust and confidence.

In *Criterion Properties plc v Stratford UK Properties (2004)* a director of the claimant company caused it to enter into an agreement whereby an excessive payment had to be made if control of the company changed or if some of the management team left. It was said in the case to be excessive and it was questioned as to whether the director in question could conclude the contract.

### 12.4.2 Power to refuse to register a transfer of shares

There are, however, other examples of the exercise of directors' powers that are subject to the same fiduciary duty. In *Re Smith and Fawcett Ltd (1942)*, the question arose as to the exercise of the directors' power to refuse to register a transfer of shares. By the articles of association, the directors had unlimited discretion to refuse to register a transfer. The appellant sought to register 4,001 shares in his name after the death of his father who had previously held the shares. The directors refused to register the transfer but offered to register a transfer of 2,001 shares, provided that the applicant sold the other shares to one of the directors at a price proposed by the directors of the company. The High Court held that the directors were acting within their discretion and this was upheld by the Court of Appeal.

### 12.4.3 Power to enter into management agreement

In a similar way, the question of the exercise of directors' powers arose in *Lee Panavision Ltd v Lee Lighting Ltd (1992)*. In this case, the plaintiffs had acquired an option to purchase the defendants. The plaintiffs also had a management agreement by which they ran the defendants' business and they also nominated the company's directors. It was clear that the option to purchase the business was not to be exercised and that the management agreement would therefore be terminated. Since the plaintiffs wished to continue managing the business, they ensured that the directors of the defendants voted in favour of a second management agreement perpetuating the plaintiffs' control of the company. Subsequently, the directors of the defendants were removed from office and the defendants announced that they did not consider themselves bound by the second management agreement. The plaintiffs sought an injunction to prevent breach of the second agreement. The defendants alleged that the directors had not disclosed their interest in the agreement. Harman J held that the agreement was void at the instance of the defendants and that the agreement had not been entered into in the interests of the defendants. This was upheld by the Court of Appeal. Harman J had also held that it was voidable on the basis of the failure of the directors to declare their interests to a board meeting. The Court of Appeal took the view that there was no breach of what is now s177 since the interest of the directors was known to all members of the board.

### 12.4.4 Other powers

The powers of directors that are subject to directors' fiduciary duties also extend to other areas:

(a) the power to borrow money and grant securities: see *Rolled Steel Products (Holdings) Ltd v British Steel Corporation* (1986);
(b) the power to call general meetings;
(c) the power to provide information to shareholders; and
(d) the power to make calls on partly paid shares.

Even where there is no breach of duty in relation to the exercise of powers by directors, there is the possibility of a petition alleging unfair prejudice under ss994–996 of the Companies Act 2006.

## 12.5 The duty of care and skill

This duty is now provided for in statute by s174 CA 2006.

It is provided that a director of a company must exercise reasonable care, skill and diligence. This means the care, skill and diligence that would be exercised by a reasonably diligent person with:

(a) the general knowledge, skill and experience that may reasonably be expected of a person carrying out the functions carried out by the director; and
(b) the general knowledge, skill and experience that the director has.

This provides for an objective standard but one raised by the actual knowledge, skill and experience of a particular director if this is greater.

The old law was set out in *Re City Equitable Fire and Insurance Co Ltd (1925)*. The company had experienced a serious depletion of funds and the managing director, Mr Bevan, was convicted of fraud. The liquidator, however, sought to make other directors liable in negligence for failing to detect the frauds. Romer J, in what has become the classic exposition of directors' duties of care and skill, set out three propositions:

> There are, in addition, one or two other general propositions that seem to be warranted by the reported cases:
>
> (1) A director need not exhibit in the performance of his duties a greater degree of skill than may reasonably be expected from a person of his knowledge and experience. A director of a life insurance company, for instance, does not guarantee that he has the skill of an actuary or of a physician. In the words of Lindley MR, 'if the directors act within their powers, if they act with such care as is reasonably to be expected from them, having regard to their knowledge and experience, and if they act honestly for the benefit of the company they represent, they discharge both their equitable as well as their legal duty to the company': see *Lagunas Nitrate Co v Lagunas Syndicate (1899)*. It is perhaps only another way of stating the same proposition to say that the directors are not liable for mere errors of judgment.
> (2) A director is not bound to give continuous attention to the affairs of his company. His duties are of an intermittent nature to be performed at periodic board meetings and at meetings of any committee of the board upon which he happens to be placed. He is not, however, bound to attend all such meetings, though he ought to attend whenever in the circumstances, he is reasonably able to do so.
> (3) In respect of all duties that, having regard to the exigencies of business, and the articles of association, may properly be left to some other official, a director is, in the absence of grounds for suspicion, justified in trusting that official to perform such duties honestly...

### 12.5.1 Standard of care and skill

In relation to the first principle set out by Romer J, the decision in *Re Denham & Co (1883)* is illustrative. In this case a director recommended the payment of a dividend out of capital. As has been seen (Chapter 8), this is not something that is permissible! The director was held not liable in negligence. As was stated in the case, the director was a country gentleman and not an accountant. Although such cases resound with Victorian echoes, it was probably the case that little changed until the Companies Act 2006. Section 13 of the Supply of Goods and Services Act 1982 introduced a statutorily imposed implied term that the supplier of services would provide services of a reasonable standard. Directors were exempted from this provision before it even came into force by Statutory Instrument 1982/1771. In *Dorchester Finance Co Ltd v Stebbings (1989)* (a decision that was reached some 10 years before it was fully reported), Foster J held that the duties owed by non-executive directors were the same as those owed by executive directors. In this case, an executive director and two non-executive directors all had relevant accounting experience. The two non-executive directors signed blind blank cheques which the executive director then used to further his own ends and those of companies which he controlled. It was held that all three directors had been negligent.

There is some reason for believing that some movement in the law occurred prior to 2006. In s214 of the Insolvency Act 1986, an objective standard of care is introduced in relation to directors and shadow directors where the company is insolvent. Disqualification cases also demonstrate a move to an objective standard of care and skill for directors.

In *Norman v Theodore Goddard (1991)*, Hoffmann J accepted that the standard in s214 applied generally in relation to directors and that the relevant yardstick was what could be expected of a person in the position of the director carrying out those functions. The standard may well be different from what could be expected of that particular director. In the event, Hoffmann J held that the director of the property development company acted reasonably in accepting information from a senior partner in the city solicitors, Theodore Goddard.

In *Re D'Jan of London Ltd (1993)*, a director signed an insurance proposal without checking it. The information provided turned out to be wrong and the insurance company refused to pay up when the company's premises burnt down. It was held that the director had been negligent.

In both *Norman v Theodore Goddard* and *Re D'Jan of London Ltd*, Hoffmann J (later LJ) accepted that s214 set out the modern law regarding the duty of care and skill of directors.

In *Bishopsgate Investment Management Ltd v Maxwell (No 2) (1993)*, it was held that, where Ian Maxwell as a director of the company signed an instrument of transfer of shares in a pension fund which was for the company's employees and ex-employees, he could not rely on the opinion of fellow directors that the transfer was a proper one nor avoid liability by demonstrating that the transfer would have gone ahead without his concurrence.

In *Re Continental Assurance Co of London plc (1996)*, a leading disqualification case, a senior bank official was a non-executive director of the company and also its parent company. Both companies collapsed. The wholly owned subsidiary had made a number of cash advances to the parent company which were in breach of the provisions prohibiting financial assistance towards the purchase of shares.

The Secretary of State sought and obtained an order disqualifying him as his conduct rendered him unfit to hold office.

It was accepted that the director did not realise that there was indebtedness between the subsidiary and its holding company. However, it was reasonable that, given his background, he should have read and understood the company's statutory accounts.

He was disqualified for three years.

In many disqualification cases there was a movement towards a more rigorous standard. Thus in *Re Barings plc (No.5) (2000)* Jonathan Parker J, in a dictum endorsed by the Court of Appeal, spoke of a 'continuing duty to acquire and maintain a sufficient knowledge and understanding of the company's business…' to enable them properly to discharge their duties as directors. Furthermore, he stated 'whilst directors are entitled (subject to the Articles of Association of the company) to delegate particular functions to those below the management chain, and to trust their competence and integrity to a reasonable extent, the exercise of the power of delegation does not absolve the director from the duty to supervise the discharge of the delegated function'.

The judge further stated that there was no rule of universal application that could be formulated as to the duty in relation to supervision. The extent of the duty and the question whether it has been discharged, must depend on the facts of each particular case, including the director's role in the management of the company.

As noted the objective standard upheld in some cases is now of general effect, although it may be enhanced if the subjective knowledge, etc of the particular director is higher.

### 12.5.2 Continuous attention

In relation to Romer J's second proposition, *Re Cardiff Savings Bank, Marquis of Bute's Case (1892)* provides a stark example of this principle at play. In this case the Marquis of Bute was appointed president and director of the Cardiff Savings Bank when he was only six months old. At this age, clearly little could be expected from him in terms of corporate control. In the next 38 years, the Marquis only attended one board meeting and, during this time, massive frauds were perpetrated by another director. The court held that the Marquis was not liable for breach of duty in failing to attend board meetings as he had not undertaken to do so. This would not now stand.

### 12.5.3 Delegation

The third proposition set out by Romer J seems unexceptionable. It permits delegation to experts. Thus, in *Dovey and Metropolitan Bank (of England and Wales) Ltd v Cory (1901)*, where a director, John Cory, had delegated the task of drawing up the accounts to others, it was held that he was entitled to rely on those accounts in recommending the payment of a dividend which subsequently turned out to be illegal. This would stand under the new law.

It is now clear that *Re City Equitable* no longer represents good law. The statute makes it clear that a director must exercise the standard of care, skill and diligence of a reasonably diligent person in the director's position. This, therefore, introduces an objective standard, although it was noted that the law was probably moving in this direction anyway.

In addition, the section ensures that if the director's particular knowledge, skill and experience is greater than that of a reasonably diligent person in his position, then that higher standard of care will apply.

## 12.6 Fiduciary duties

In addition to the duty to act to promote the success of the company and to exercise reasonable care, skill and diligence, the Act provides for certain fiduciary duties that must be adhered to by a director.

Thus a director must avoid actual or possible conflicts of interest or duties (other than a conflict arising in relation to a transaction or arrangement with the company) unless the matter has been authorised by the independent directors, i.e. without interested directors counting for the vote or in the quorum (s175(6) CA 2006).

Additionally, a director must not accept benefits from a third party conferred by reason of his directorship unless the acceptance cannot reasonably be regarded as likely to give rise to a conflict (s176 CA 2006).

## 12.7 Use of corporate opportunities

Where directors place themselves in a position where their personal interest conflicts with their duty to the company, then obviously this brings the new duty in s175 into play.

The leading case in this area is the House of Lords' decision in *Regal (Hastings) Ltd v Gulliver (1942)*. Regal owned a cinema in Hastings. The company's solicitor considered that it would be a sound business move to acquire two other cinemas in the town. He suggested this to the directors. The company had insufficient funds. However, a scheme was hatched and a subsidiary was created for the purpose of acquiring the two other cinemas. The directors of Regal put up some money to subscribe for shares as did the company solicitor. The move proved to be a successful one and, ultimately, the shares of Regal and its subsidiary were sold to a purchaser. The directors made a profit on the sale as did the company solicitor. The company under its new management then proceeded to start an action against the former directors for damages in respect of the secret profit made on the sale of the shares. It was proved that the directors had acted from sound motives and there was no *mala fides*. The House of Lords held that the directors who acquired a beneficial interest in the shares were liable to disgorge their profits back to the company (that is, back to the purchaser who willingly paid the asking price for the business!) as this profit had been made at the expense of the company. The company's solicitor, as he was not a director, was not subject to any fiduciary duties and was therefore not liable to disgorge. It had, of course, been his idea in the first place!

The decision is in many ways a horrendous one. It is the triumph of form over substance. If the directors had obtained the consent of the company in general meeting to what they were doing, no complaint would have been possible. Furthermore, had the directors sold the business as a going concern rather than sold the shares, the purchaser would not have been in a position to bring the action as the company. The decision is a comedy or rather tragedy of errors! However, it does establish the very clear principle that directors should not let their personal positions conflict with their duties to the company.

Later cases illustrate the same point. In *IDC v Cooley (1972)*, Cooley was an architect with the East Midlands Gas Board. He left to become a director of IDC. He was subsequently approached by the Eastern Gas Board. They wished him to do some work for them by designing a gas holder at Ponders End! They did not wish to deal with IDC and made it quite clear that the offer was only applicable to Cooley in his personal capacity. Because Cooley was tied to IDC by contract, he went to his management and told them that he was desperately ill and sought leave to terminate his contract. This was agreed to. Whereupon Cooley convalesced by designing the gas holder! IDC then brought this action for disgorgement of profit. IDC was successful. One can in some ways sympathise with IDC. Clearly, Cooley was dishonest and the prospect of his profiting from his dishonesty is not an attractive one. The decision though must be questionable as it is unlikely that Cooley had here taken a corporate opportunity as the Eastern Gas Board was clear it did not wish to deal with IDC but only with Cooley. The judge, Roskill J, said that Cooley should have stayed with IDC and sought to convince the Eastern Gas Board to change its mind.

This approach was followed in *Re Bhullar (2003)*. The case concerned a grocery business run as a quasi partnership. Following a breakdown of the relationship of mutual trust, some directors seized an opportunity to buy property for themselves. This was at a time when the other directors had made it clear they were against further company expansion. Nevertheless it was held that the directors were in breach of fiduciary duty in that they took an opportunity personally which was that of the company. They did not disclose the opportunity to the company still less seek permission to take that opportunity.

Another interesting decision in this same line of cases is *Horcal Ltd v Gatland (1984)*. In this case, Gatland, who was a director, was nearing retirement. The board of directors other than Gatland had just decided to make a golden handshake payment to him on his retirement. Gatland subsequently, when a person rang up to arrange for some building work, diverted the contract to himself and undertook to execute it on his own account without putting it through the company books. Later, when the customer rang up to complain that the work was faulty after Gatland had retired from the company, it became obvious what he had done. Horcal Ltd then brought this action to (1) obtain disgorgement of the profit on the contract, and (2) obtain reimbursement of the golden handshake. The company was successful in obtaining disgorgement of the profit. That much is clear. However, the company was not successful in obtaining a return of the golden handshake. The judge said that at the time when the golden handshake payment was agreed to by the board, Gatland had evil thoughts but there had been no evil deeds! The decision on this point seems surprising. Surely, had the board known of these evil intentions, the golden handshake payment would not have been made.

Some cases present much simpler legal questions. In *Cranleigh Precision Engineering v Bryant (1964)*, the director concerned had been working on a revolutionary above ground swimming pool. He left the company taking the plans and designs with him and developed the swimming pool on his own. The company later brought this action to seek disgorgement of profits he had made from developing the swimming pool for his own purposes. It is clear that the company should succeed, as indeed it did.

In *Ball v Eden Project Ltd (2002)*, Ball applied to register the name Eden Project as a trademark. He was a founder and director of the company. It was held that the trademark was that of the company. There was a breach of director's fiduciary duty as he was trying to hold the company to ransom.

As noted under s175 CA 2006, the directors' action may be authorised by the independent directors in the case of a private company if there is nothing in the company's constitution which invalidates such authorisation, and in the case of a public company if the constitution includes provision for such authorisation.

By the same approach some breaches of directors' fiduciary duties are ratifiable (see s239 CA 2006). In *Regal (Hastings) v Gulliver (1942)*, it was open to the company as a matter of law to ratify what the directors had done. This did not happen as a matter of fact because control had passed to others. In other cases where fraud is involved, clearly ratification is not possible. Fraud cannot be ratified. Thus, in *Cook v Deeks*, where directors had diverted corporate opportunities to themselves contracts which they should have taken up on behalf of the company, ratification was not possible because it involved misappropriation of the company's property.

Questions of criminal law may also arise in such cases. Directors may well be guilty of theft in instances where they are appropriating company property to themselves (s1 of the Theft Act 1968).

If the board of directors considers a proposed activity or transaction and turns it down *bona fide* and then an individual director takes it up and exploits it, it is clear that this is not exploitation of a corporate opportunity. It has ceased to be a corporate opportunity when turned down by the company provided that the matter is decided independently of the directors with an interest in the matter (s175(4),(5), (6) CA 2006). See *Peso Silver Mines Ltd v Cropper (1966)*, from the Supreme Court of Canada. In *Island Export Finance Ltd v Umunna (1986)*, Hutchinson J said that the question of whether a director was liable to disgorge a profit to his former company from a corporate opportunity was to some extent a question of timing. Umunna had been managing director of the company and when he resigned the company had some hopes of doing business with the Cameroon authorities. Umunna resigned hoping to do business with the Cameroon authorities. At this time there were no specific corporate opportunities. It was held that Umunna could take it on his own account when such opportunities did arise some two years later.

## 12.8 Competing with the company

In a similar way, a director who competes with his company, either through the medium of another company or through another form of trading, either as an individual or in a partnership, is in a conflict position and this will involve a breach of his duties as set out in s175 CA 2006, unless it is sanctioned by the independent directors in the same way as in relation to use of corporate opportunities.

Strangely, the position in the case law is somewhat confused. From the position of strict logic it would seem that directors should not be directors of competing companies, nor to compete on their own account or through a partnership. They would be placed in invidious positions where corporate opportunities arose as to which of the two companies they should favour with the opportunity. As is so often predictably the case, the only British authority on the point indicates that there is no principle of law that prevents a director from being a director of two competing businesses: see *London and Mashonaland Exploration Co Ltd v New Mashonaland Exploration Co Ltd (1891)*. The decision is an old one and is open to question. Yet, the decision was approved by Lord Blanesburgh *obiter* in *Bell v Lever Brothers Ltd (1932)*. Commonwealth authority is inconsistent on the point. Some cases follow the *Mashonaland* case, others indicate that directors may not be directors of competing companies: see *Abbey Glen Property Corporation v Stumborg (1976)* from Canada. In other areas of the law, it seems that it is not possible for senior employees to compete by holding two employments in similar lines of business. Thus, in *Hivac Ltd v Park Royal Scientific Instruments Ltd (1946)*, senior employees engaged on sensitive work in wartime were prohibited from working for competing employers. They were normally engaged in work on midget valves for deaf aids. During the war, the work had wartime applications.

In partnership law, partners may not compete with their partnerships. The logical position should be that directors should not be able to compete with their company, either as directors of other competing businesses or as partners within a firm or indeed acting on their own account. The *Mashonaland* case is reviewed and criticised by Michael Christie in 'The director's fiduciary duty not to compete' (1992) 55 MLR 506.

In *Plus Group Ltd and Others v Pyke (2002)* the Court of Appeal missed the opportunity to overrule the Mashonaland decision.

Pyke and Plant each hold 50% of the shares in the Plus Group. They were the only directors and also the only directors of three subsidiaries. Constructive Interiors had an excellent relationship with Mr Pyke. They were the company's main customer. In 1996, Pyke suffered a stroke. He subsequent fell out with Plank and there was a complete rupture in the business relationship. Pyke was excluded from management of the company and denied remuneration and not allowed to draw on a loan account of the company. Pyke then incorporate John Pyke Interiors Ltd and carried out £200,000 worth of contractual work for Constructive. The question was whether Pyke had breached his duties. He had set up in competition and courted Plus' chief customer and used knowledge acquired as a director. The Court of Appeal unanimously held there was no breach of duty. It is not a breach of fiduciary duty, according to the court, for a director to work for a competing company where he has been excluded effectively from the company of which he is a director. The clear implication is that had the circumstances been different there would have been a breach of duty.

It is clear that in competing with the company, unless this is agreed to by directors independent of the competing director, there will be a breach of duty under s175 CA 2006.

## 12.9 Benefits from third parties

Clearly, where directors accept benefits from third parties, conferred by reason of the directorship, these actions will involve a breach of the duty under s176. Thus, in *Attorney General for Hong Kong v Regari (1994)* Privy Council from Hong Kong, in an analogous situation a solicitor who joined the legal service in Hong Kong and who accepted bribes to stifle prosecutions was ordered to pay Hong Kong $12.4m to the Crown.

Lord Templeman said that in law a gift from bribery belonged to the fiduciary and he became debtor to the person to whom he owed his duties.

If the acceptance cannot reasonably be regarded as likely to give rise to a conflict there is no breach. The exception would cover the donation of small gifts at Christmas time, or on other occasions, for example.

## 12.10 Personal liability of directors

In addition to liability to the company, directors may be directly liable to outsiders.

### 12.10.1 Contractual liability

Directors may be contractually liable as follows:

- **Breach of warranty of authority**
  If directors indicate to outsiders that they have authority to conclude a particular transaction on behalf of the company and no such authority exists, then

the director (or indeed other person) is liable for breach of the warranty of authority.

- **Collateral guarantee**

  Often, when directors conclude a contract on behalf of their company, they will also give a collateral guarantee. This is particularly the case where a company borrows money from its bank and the bank requires security from the company's officers. In such a situation, if the primary liability fails, the outsider may sue the guarantor on the collateral guarantee.

- **Pre-incorporation contracts**

  As has already been examined (see section 3.5), where a person (perhaps a future director) concludes an agreement on behalf of an as yet unformed company that person will be liable on the agreement unless there is an express contrary intention (s51(1) of the Companies Act 2006).

### 12.10.2 Tortious liability

Directors may be tortiously liable as follows:

- **Fraud**

  A director may be liable in fraud to subscribers and even purchasers on the open market in relation to statements made in a company prospectus or listing particulars under the principle in *Derry v Peek* (see section 4.8.2).

- **Negligent misstatement**

  In a similar way, a director may be liable in tort for the tort of negligent misstatement to subscribers and purchasers under the principle in *Hedley Byrne v Heller* for misstatements in a prospectus or listing particulars (see section 4.8.3).

- **Personal skill and care of directors**

  In rare circumstances, where a director has warranted his own personal skill and care, he may be liable to the outsider notwithstanding that the contract has been concluded with the company rather than with the director. Thus, in *Fairline Shipping Corporation v Adamson (1975)*, where Mr Adamson owned a refrigerated store used by a company of which he was managing director, he warranted to Fairline Shipping Corporation that the perishable goods stored in the company's refrigeration would be safe. In fact the goods were ruined. It was held that he was personally liable. The company itself could not pay damages as it had gone into liquidation.

A similar position was reached in *Williams v Natural Life Health Foods Ltd (1997)*. The company admitted that it had made negligent misstatements which had induced the plaintiffs to enter into a franchise agreement with the company, and to purchase a health food shop in Rugby. The figures produced for future sales were too optimistic and the business failed. The court held that the company was liable for the negligent misstatement and that the managing director was also personally liable. The company itself was insolvent.

On appeal, the Court of Appeal took the view that the director must have assumed personal responsibility for personal liability to result. The director in Williams had played a pivotal role in the production of the projections. By a majority of two to one, the Court of Appeal found the director personally liable.

However, the Court of Appeal decision was unanimously reversed by the House of Lords. The House of Lords held that a director of a limited company would only be personally liable for loss suffered as a result of negligent advice given by the company if the director had assumed personal responsibility for the advice, and if the other party had relied on that assumption of responsibility. The House of Lords took the view that the director, Richard Mistlin, did not assume personal responsibility for the representations relating to the business. The House of Lords further considered that there was no evidence that the plaintiffs believed that Mr Mistlin was undertaking such personal responsibility.

The normal rule remains that, when carrying out company business, directors are presumed to be acting for their company.

### 12.10.3 Statutory liability

Personal liability to outsiders may also arise under statute. For example, under the Financial Services and Markets Act 2000 s90(1) compensation for any untrue or misleading statement or omission from a prospectus or supplementary prospectus is payable by any person responsible, which includes every director of the company.

### 12.10.4 Other liability

There are, of course, other areas where there may be personal liability of directors in relation to company debts but these areas generally involve a contribution to the company's assets in liquidation rather than a direct payment to the outsider. Thus directors may be liable for fraudulent trading under s213 of the Insolvency Act 1986, for wrongful trading under s214 of the Insolvency Act 1986 and for acting in contravention of a disqualification order under s15 of the Company Directors Disqualification Act 1986.

## 12.11  Limiting the liability of directors

S232 of the Companies Act 2006 provides that any provision purporting to exempt a director of a company from any liability that would otherwise attach to him in connection with any negligence, default, breach of duty or breach of trust in relation to the company is void.

The section further provides that any provision by which a company directly or indirectly provides an indemnity for a director of the company, or of an associated company against any liability, attaching to him in connection with any negligence, default, breach of duty or breach of trust, is void except as permitted by ss233, 234 and 235 CA 2006.

### 12.11.1 Provision of insurance

S233 provides that it is permissible for a company to purchase and maintain for a director of a company, or an associated company, insurance against any such liability, as is mentioned in s232.

### 12.11.2 Qualifying third party indemnity provision

S234 provides that third party indemnity provision against liability incurred by a director to a person other than the company or an associated company is permitted, although it cannot cover any liability of the director to pay a fine in criminal proceedings, to pay a sum to a regulatory authority by way of penalty, or any liability incurred by a director in defending criminal proceedings in which he is convicted, or in defending civil proceedings where judgment is given against him or in connection with an application for relief in which the court refuses to grant him relief.

### 12.11.3 Qualifying pension scheme indemnity provision

S235 provides for pension scheme indemnity provision whereby a director of a company that is a trustee of an occupational pension scheme is idemnified against liability incurred in connection with the company's activities as trustee of the scheme. Once again this cannot extend to an indemnity against fines, sums payable to regulatory authorities, or liabilities incurred in defending criminal proceedings.

### 12.11.4 Relief from the court

Notwithstanding s232, it is open to the court to grant relief to an officer if it is proved that the officer acted honestly and reasonably and ought in all the circumstances to be excused in the whole, or in part, s1157 of the Companies Act 2006. This matter was discussed in *Re Duomatic Ltd (1969)*. The company in this case had three directors. The articles of the company required directors' remuneration to be determined by the general meeting. One director, Elvins, drew salary without the approval of the company in general meeting, assuming that it would be agreed at the subsequent annual general meeting. In fact, the company went into liquidation before the annual general meeting could be held. He also made a gratuitous payment to Hanley, another director, without complying with Companies Act provisions which requires disclosure of golden handshakes and approval of the payment by the company in general meeting, and in addition he drew in excess of the agreed limit on his drawings from the company.

It was held that Elvins would be relieved from liability for drawing the unauthorised salary as it was reasonable for him to follow the established practice. He was not relieved from liability in relation to the payment of the compensation payment as he should have sought legal advice in relation to this matter and he was also liable for the excessive drawings from the company. In relation to this last matter he had neither been honest nor reasonable.

An alternative course of action for the company where a director has acted in breach of duties (provided the breach of duty is not fraudulent) is to ratify what the director has done. This has the effect of negating any breach of duty. This is what occurred in *Hogg v Cramphorn* and *Bamford v Bamford* (see section 12.4.1). In relation to matters that are *ultra vires* the company, the possibility of ratification is now open to the company. The act itself must first be ratified and then the unauthorised act of the director must also be ratified.

In dealing with directors' liability, a sensible balance needs to be struck between, on the one hand dealing robustly with cases of gross negligence and dishonesty, and on the other ensuring that Britain has a diverse pool of high-quality individuals assuming the role of company director to take informed and rational risks.

### 12.11.5 Negating a breach of duty

Shareholders will be able to give authority by ordinary resolution after full disclosure of relevant details to what would otherwise be a breach of duty in circumstances where the common law already allows directors to do that (s180(4)(a) CA 2006).

S180(4)(b) CA 2006 provides that where a company's articles contain provisions for dealing with conflicts of interest, then there is no breach of a director's duties if the director acts in accordance with these provisions.

Ratification of directors acts is allowed by s239 CA 2006. Where the company ratifies the conduct of a director that amounts to negligence, default, breach of duty or breach of trust, then this must be conducted by resolution of the members of the company by way of ordinary resolution. If the resolution is proposed as a written resolution neither the director, if a member of the company, nor any member connected with him is an eligible member, and similarly the director and connected persons' votes are ignored in any meeting where a resolution is proposed.

## 12.12 Directors' contracts

S177 provides that it is the duty of a director to declare an interest in any proposed transaction or arrangement with his company, whether the interest is direct or indirect. He must declare the nature and extent of his interest to the other directors at a meeting of the directors or by notice to all of the directors either by notice in writing or by a general notice.

S182 requires a director to declare an interest in an existing transaction or arrangement in the same way. Thus, if an existing transaction or arrangement gives rise at a later stage to an interest of the director, then he must, at that stage, declare his interest to a meeting of the directors or by notice in writing or by general notice.

It is a breach of duty giving rise to criminal consequences for a director to fail to make a declaration of interest in an existing transaction or arrangement (s183 CA 2006).

S182 CA 2006 applies to shadow directors just as the other provisions contained in ss170–181 apply to shadow directors.

## 12.13  Substantial transactions

In addition to compliance with ss177 and 182, substantial property transactions requiring the approval of members are dealt with in s190 CA 2006.

The section provides that a company may not enter into an arrangement under which a director of the company, or of its holding company, or a person connected with such a director, acquires or is to acquire from the company substantial non-cash assets, or where the company acquires or is to acquire substantial non-cash assets from such a director or other person so connected. In both cases, whether directly or indirectly, unless the arrangement has been approved by a resolution of the members of the company or is condition on such approval being obtained.

S191 defines a substantial asset as an asset whose value:

(a) exceeds 10% of the company's asset value and is more than £5000, or
(b) exceeds £100,000.

S195 provides for the consequences of contravention. S195(2) states that the arrangement or transaction is voidable at the instance of the company unless:

(a) restitution is no longer possible;
(b) the company has been indemnified in pursuance of the loss or damage suffered; or
(c) rights acquired in good faith for value and without actual notice of the contravention by a person who is not a party to the arrangement or transaction, have intervened.

If the director or connected person is a director of the company's holding company, or a person connected with such a director, the arrangement must also have been approved by resolution of the members of the holding company or be conditional on such approval being obtained.

Whether or not the arrangement or transaction has been avoided, the following people will be liable to account to the company for any gain that has been made directly or indirectly by the arrangement or transaction, and jointly and severally with any other person to indemnify the company for any loss or damage resulting from the arrangement or transaction. The people liable are the director of the company or its holding company, any person who is connected with such a director, the director of the company or of its holding company with whom any such person is connected, and any other director of the company who authorised the arrangement or transaction entered into in pursuance of such an arrangement.

In *Re Duckwari plc (No.2) (1999)* demonstrates the severity of the section, applying as it does to direct and indirect gains.

It should be noted that the section applies to shadow directors in the same way as it applies to directors (s223 CA 2006).

Note: Solicitors who fail to advise of a potential s195 situation in advising clients on arrangements, may well be held to be negligent (see *British Racing Drivers Club Ltd v Hextall, Erskine and Co (a firm) (1996)*.

## 12.14 Control of political donations and expenditure

S362 makes provision in relation to political donations made by companies to political parties, to other political organisations and to independent election candidates, and to political expenditure incurred by companies. Trade unions are expressly excluded (s374 CA 2006).

S363 provides that this part of the Act (Part 14) applies to political parties that are registered under Part 2 of the Political Parties, Elections and Referendums Act 2000, or if the political party carries on or proposes to carry on activities for the purposes of or in connection with the participation of the party in any elections to public office held in a member State other than the United Kingdom.

S364 defines a political donation adopting the definition contained in ss50–52 of the Political Parties, Elections and Referendums Act 2000, and s53 of that Act applies in the same way for the purpose of determining the value of the donation. Donation is defined widely to include gifts, sponsorship, subscriptions, loans at uncommercial rates, and provision of property, services, facilities or personnel at uncommercial rates.

S365 defines political expenditure. In relation to a company this means expenditure incurred by a company on

(a) the preparation, publication or dissemination of advertising or other promotional or publicity material:

  (i) of whatever nature, and

  (ii) however published or otherwise disseminated
    that at the time of publication or dissemination, is capable of being reasonably regarded as intended to affect public support for a political party or other political organisation or an independent election candidate, or

(b) activities on the part of the company that are capable of being reasonably regarded as intended:

  (i) to affect public support for a political party or other political organisation or independent election candidate, or

(ii) to influence voters in relation to any national or regional referendum held under the law of a member State.

S366 provides for authorisation required for donations or expenditure. A company must not make a political donation to a political party or organisation or to an independent election candidate, or incur any political expenditure unless the donation or expenditure is authorised in accordance with this section.

The donation or expenditure must be authorised:

(a) in the case of a company that is not a subsidiary of another company by a resolution of the members of the company;
(b) in the case of the company that is a subsidiary of another company by:

    (i) a resolution of the members of the company, and
    (ii) a resolution of the members of any relevant holding company.
    It is further provided, however, that no resolution is required on the part of a company that is a wholly owned subsidiary of a UK company.

S367 provides that a resolution conferring authorisation with regard to political donations and political expenditure may relate to the company passing a resolution, one or more subsidiaries of that company, or the company passing the resolution and one or more subsidiaries of that company, and the resolution may authorise donations for expenditure under one or more of the following heads:

(a) Donations to political parties or independent election candidates;
(b) Donations to political organisations other than political parties;
(c) Political expenditure.

For each of the specified heads, the resolution must authorise donations or, as the case may be, expenditure up to a specified amount in the period for which the resolution has effect (see s369).

S368 provides that a resolution conferring authority has effect for a period of four years from the date the resolution is passed unless the directors determine, or the articles require, a shorter period of time.

S369 provides that where a company makes political donations or incurs political expenditure without authorisation, the directors in default are jointly and severally liable.

S370 provides that any liability of a person under s369 is enforceable by proceedings brought under this section in the name of the company by an authorised group of members of the company. This is in addition to being enforceable by proceedings brought by the company.

Those who may bring the proceedings as an 'authorised' group, means:

(a) the holders of not less than 5% in nominal value of the company's issued share capital;

(b) if the company is not limited by shares, not less than 5% of its members; or

(c) not less than 50 of the company's members.

S371 provides that the group may apply to the court for an order directing the company to indemnify the group in respect of costs.

In addition to trade unions that are exempt under s374, as they are not considered to be political organisations, trade associations are also exempt under s375, and all party parliamentary groups are exempt under s376.

S377 of the Companies Act 2006 provides that political expenditure may be exempted by order of the Secretary of State under the section. The order under the section is subject to affirmative resolution procedure.

S378 of the Companies Act 2006 further provides that donations not amounting to more than £5,000 in any 12 month period are exempt from the requirement for authority.

## SUMMARY

## Directors' duties

### Introduction

The law on directors' duties has now been codified although the 2006 Act makes it clear that existing case law exemplifying common law and equitable principles is still relevant in interpreting directors' duties.

Traditionally directors owed duties to the providers of capital (the shareholders) although the directors had to take account of the interests of employees (reforms introduced by the Companies Act 1980), and some cases suggested that directors should take account of the interests of creditors.

This has now been extended by statute in s172 CA 2006 so that directors must take account of the likely consequences of any decision in the long term. They must take account of the interests of the company's employees and the need to foster the company's business relationships with suppliers, customers and others. They must take account of the community and the environment, and of the desirability of the company maintaining a reputation for high standards of business conduct. The directors must lastly take account of the need to act fairly between members of the company.

This provision is said to reflect the 'enlightened shareholder value' approach to directors' duties.

### Duty of care and skill

The previous law in this area resounded with Victorian echoes. Little was expected of directors in terms of care and skill in the past, see *Re City Equitable Fire and Insurance Company Ltd (1925)*. More recently some cases suggested a movement towards an objective standard of care – see interpretation of s214 of the Insolvency Act 1986, and cases like *Norman v Theodore Goddard (1991)*.

S174 CA 2006 now introduces an objective standard of care geared up by the actual knowledge, skill and experience of a particular director if this is greater than the norm.

### Fiduciary duties

Traditionally, the standard expected of directors in relation to honesty, integrity and good faith is in stark contrast to the old approach in relation to care and skill.

Now the rules are statutory.

Directors must avoid actual or possible conflicts of interest or duties (s175). A director must not accept benefits from a third party conferred by reason of his directorship in general terms (s176 CA 2006).

Nominee directors must exercise independent judgment (s173 CA 2006).

Directors must exercise their powers for the purposes for which they are conferred and act in accordance with the company's constitution (s171 CA 2006).

Directors must declare an interest in any proposed transaction or arrangement. Additionally they must declare an interest in any existing transaction or arrangement which arises.

### Personal liability of directors to outsiders

Directors may, on occasion, be liable to outsiders in contract, in tort or by statute.

### Limiting directors' liability

S232 provides that any purported exemption of a director in a company's constitution from liability for negligence, default, breach of duty or breach of trust is void.

However, insurance is permissible under s233 as is qualifying third party indemnity provision under s234. Furthermore, s235 provides for qualifying pension scheme indemnity provision in appropriate circumstances. Additionally, s1157 permits the court, in appropriate circumstances, to grant relief to an officer if it is proved that the officer acted honestly and reasonably, and ought in all the circumstances to be excused in whole or in part.

### Political donations and expenditure

The Companies Act 2006 sets out restrictions on political donations and expenditure.

## Further reading

Bean, GMD, 'Corporate governance and corporate opportunities' (1994) 15 Co Law 266.

Beck, S, 'Saga of Peso Silver Mines: corporate opportunity reconsidered' (1971) 49 Can Bar Rev 80.

Berg, A, 'Company Law Review: Legislating directors duties' [2000] JBL 472.

Boyle, A, 'The common law duty of care and enforcement under s459' (1996) 17 Co Law 83.

Burridge, S, 'Wrongful rights issues' (1981) 44 MLR 40.

Christie, M, 'The director's fiduciary duty not to compete' (1992) 55 MLR 506.

Conaglen, M, 'The Nature and Function of Fiduciary Loyalty' (2005) 121 LQR 452.

Edmunds, R, and Lowry, J, 'The continuing value of relief for directors' breach of duty' (2000) MLR 195.

Finch, V, 'Company directors – who cares about skill and care?' (1992) 55 MLR 179.

Grantham, R, 'Can directors compete with the company?' (2003) MLR 109.

Hawke, N, 'Creditors' interests in solvent and insolvent companies' ([989] JBL 54.

Herzel, L, and Colling, DE, 'The Chinese wall' (1983) 4 Co Law 14.

Hicks, A, 'Directors' liability for management errors' (1994) LQR 390.

Hirt, H, 'The Law on Corporate Opportunities in the Court of Appeal' [2005] JBL 669.

Ipp, The Honourable Justice, 'The diligent director' (1997) 18 Co Law 162.

Keay, A, 'Directors' duties to creditors, contractors, or concerns relating to efficiency and over protection of creditors' (2003) MLR 665.

Koh, P, 'Directors' fiduciary obligations – a fresh look' [2003] CLJ 42.

Koh, P, 'Once a director always a fiduciary' [2003] CLJ 403.

Lowry, JP, '*Regal (Hastings)* 50 years on: breaking the bonds of the ancien regime?' (1994) 45 NILQ 1.

Lowry, J, 'Directorial self dealing: Constructing a regime of accountability' (1997) 48 NILQ 211.

Lowry, J, and Edmund, R, 'The corporate opportunity doctrine: Shifting boundaries of the duty and its remedies' (1998) 61 MLR 515.

Milman, D, 'Strategies for regulating managerial performance in the "twilight zone" – familiar dilemmas: new considerations' [2004] JBL 493.

Nakajima, C, 'Signing without reading' (1994) 15 Co Law 123.

Pettet, B, 'Duties in respect of employees under the Companies Act 1980' (1981) 34 CLP 199.

Prentice, D, 'The corporate opportunity doctrine' (1974) MLR 464.

Prentice, D, 'Creditors' interests and directors' duties' (1990) OJLS 265.

Rajak, H, 'Company directors – the end of an era' (1989) NLJ 1374, 1458.

Riley, C, 'Directors' duties and the interests of creditors' (1989) 10 Co Law 87.

Roach, L, 'Equitable Life and non-executive directors: Clarification from the High Court?' (2005) 26 Co Law 253.

Scott, S, 'The corporate opportunity doctrine and impossibility' (2003) MLR 852.

Sealy, L, 'Reforming the law on directors' duties' (1991) 12 Co Law 175.

Sealy, L, 'Bona fides and proper purposes in corporate decisions' (1989) Mon LR 265.

Wedderburn (Lord), 'Companies and employees: common law or social dimension?' (1993) 109 LQR 220.

Xuereb, PG, 'The limitation on the exercise of majority power' (1985) 6 Co Law 199.

Xuereb, PG, 'Remedies for abuse of majority power' (1986) 7 Co Law 53.

Xeureb, PG, 'Voting rights: a comparative review' (1987) Co Law 16.

# Insider dealing and market abuse

## 13.1 Introduction

It was only with the Companies Act 1980 that there was the first legislative intervention in the United Kingdom to combat insider dealing. Other jurisdictions came to this problem much earlier on, for example, the USA in the Securities Exchange Act 1934. Until recently, the relevant UK legislation was contained in the Companies Securities (Insider Dealing) Act 1985 and the Financial Services Act 1986.

Legislation has altered the law on insider dealing to take account of the EC Directive on Insider Dealing (89/592). The new law is contained in Pt V of the Criminal Justice Act 1993 and Sched 1 of that Act.

The securities covered by the legislation are set out in Sched 2. They include shares and gilts. The law for the most part only covers dealings on a regulated market so that the law does not generally extend to unlisted companies. Certain off market deals are caught.

There are two categories of insiders caught by the legislation – primary insiders and secondary insiders or tipees.

*Primary insiders* are persons who have information as an insider obtained through:

(a) being a director, employee or shareholder of an issuer of securities; or
(b) having access to the information by virtue of employment, profession or office.

Secondary insiders are those who have received or obtained information from a person who is an insider either directly or indirectly.

A person is not a secondary insider or tipee merely by virtue of being procured to deal in securities. He must have inside information and must know that it is inside information and he must know that it is from an inside source (s57).

The legislation prohibits dealing in securities by a person whether by himself or as an agent for another person. There is also a prohibition on encouraging or procuring another person to deal and also of disclosing information except in the performance of one's duties or on showing one did not expect the person to act upon the disclosure. Inside information is defined as specific information which is not in the public domain and which is unpublished. It must be information which, if published, would have an effect on the price of the securities (s56).

The legislation requires that there should be an intention to make a profit or to avoid a loss. The new law, however, tilts the balance towards the prosecution in that it is presumed that persons who deal in securities with the relevant knowledge have the intention to make a profit or avoid a loss. Thus the legislation places the burden on the defendant of disproving the intention. There are certain limited defences (s53 and Sched 1).

There is no civil remedy for insider dealing. The contract itself remains intact. The maximum criminal sanction that applies on indictment is seven years' imprisonment and/or an unlimited fine. On summary conviction, the maximum penalty is a fine and/or six months' imprisonment (s61).

Investigations may be set up under the Financial Services and Markets Act 2000 to investigate possible insider dealing (see section 22.5).

## 13.2   Criticisms

Various criticisms have been made of the UK law on insider dealing.

### 13.2.1   No civil remedy

The fact that there is no civil remedy is often the subject of criticism. By contrast, in the USA there has been a civil remedy ever since the Securities and Exchange Act whereby the person who has sold shares to an insider (or possibly bought from an insider) is able to sue for the profit made by the other or the loss avoided by the other. There is no civil remedy in the United Kingdom. It is possible that there may be an indirect remedy. Under the Powers of the Criminal Courts Act 1973 and, in Scotland, the Criminal Justice (Scotland) Act 1980, any victim of a criminal offence may be awarded compensation under the Act. This occurred, for example, in Scotland in *Procurator Fiscal v Bryce* in 1981.

In so far as directors profit from their use of inside information, there may be a remedy available to the company against the directors for breach of duty. It must be borne in mind, however, that insiders are wider than directors and also there may be difficulties with the company suing directors where the directors are in control of the company. In any event, as Suter notes, in *The Regulation of Insider Dealing in Britain*, 1989, London: Butterworths, p. 122:

> There is no reported decision in Britain on a claim by a company to recover insider dealing profits from an insider. Hence, the issue of whether insiders are accountable to their companies for such profits is unresolved.

### 13.2.2   No insider trading agency

A second major criticism made of the legislation in the United Kingdom is that there is no institution that has been set up specifically to deal with the matter of insider dealing. There is such an institution in the USA, namely the Securities and Exchange Commission. There have been calls from The Stock Exchange for an insider trading agency. At present most prosecutions are carried out by the Department of Trade on the basis of evidence gathered by The Stock Exchange.

### 13.2.3 Legislation only applies to quoted companies

A third criticism that is made is that the legislation only applies to quoted companies with one or two minor exceptions. There seems no real reason why the legislation should not apply to non-quoted companies as well. Clearly, the problem is more severe in relation to quoted companies, as in other cases a person would generally know that he is selling to or buying from an insider. However, it does seem that in circumstances where it can be shown that an insider has acted in contravention of the basic principle that influences the legislation, even in a non-quoted company, that person should be subject to some sanctions.

### 13.2.4 Enforcement is haphazard

A fourth criticism made of the Act is that enforcement is haphazard. There have been few prosecutions and very few convictions. Yet there is still evidence of widespread insider dealing. This is of some significance when it is the case that there is international competition between different stock exchanges and there are few sentences of imprisonment in relation to insider dealing in the United Kingdom. Although the maximum penalty was increased in 1988 from two years' imprisonment to seven years' imprisonment, at that stage, there had been very few convictions and there have been very few sentences of imprisonment imposed. This may be contrasted with the United States enforcement where early on Richard Whitney, the Head of the New York Stock Exchange, was despatched for a stay in Sing Sing in 1934.

## 13.3 Market abuse

The Stock Market can only work effectively where there is a level playing field in terms of those dealing, i.e. buying and selling shares and securities. Public confidence in the reliability of the Stock Exchange and the open nature of dealing will mean that the fairer the Stock Exchange is seen to be and the more reliable the market system, the more people will be inclined to use the relevant Stock Exchange.

In addition to laws combatting insider dealing, there are laws to combat market abuse.

S118 of the Financial Services and Markets Act 2000, as amended by SI2005/381, deals with market abuse, and market manipulation.

Market abuse is defined as behaviour, whether by one person alone or two or more persons jointly or in concert, which occurs in relation to qualifying investments admitted to trading on the prescribed market or qualifying investments in respect of which a request for admission to trading on such a market has been made, or certain behaviour in relation to related investments to such qualifying investments. This behaviour is where an insider deals or attempts to deal in a qualifying investment or related investment on the basis of inside information relating to the investment in question (insider dealing), or where an insider discloses inside information to another person other than in the proper course of the exercise of his employment profession or duties (improper disclosure).

These are two examples of market abuse. Another is set out in the section relating to insider dealing and is as follows:

Where the behaviour of any person is based on information not generally available to those using the market but which, if available to a regular user of the market, would be or would be likely to be regarded by him as relevant when deciding the terms on which transactions in qualifying investments should be effected (s118(4)(a)).

Behaviour which is based on such information will be market abuse if it does not pass the regular user test. It is likely to be regarded by a regular user of the market as a market abuse if there is a failure on the part of the person concerned to observe the standard of behaviour reasonably expected of a person in his position in relation to the market (s118(4)(b)) (misuse of information).

This form of market abuse is retained as originally enacted until 2008.

## 13.4 Insiders

Insiders are defined in s118B as any person who has inside information:

(a)   as a result of his membership of an administrative, management or supervisory body of an issuer of qualifying investments;
(b)   as a result of his holding shares in the capital of an issuer of qualifying investments;
(c)   as a result of having access to the information through the exercise of his employment profession or duties;
(d)   as a result of his criminal activities; or
(e)   where the person has obtained, by other means, and which he knows or could reasonably be expected to know is inside information.

## 13.5 Inside information

S118C defines inside information in relation to qualifying investments or related investments which are not commodity derivatives as information of a precise nature which:

(a)   is not generally available;
(b)   relates directly or indirectly to one or more issuers of the qualifying investments or to one or more of the qualifying investments; and

(c)  would, if generally available, be likely to have a significant effect on the price of the qualifying investments or on the price of related investments.

In relation to commodity derivatives, the third condition is that users of the markets on which the derivatives are traded would expect to receive the information in accordance with any accepted market practices on those markets. The other two conditions apply *mutatis mutandis*.

For a person charged with the execution of orders concerning any qualifying investments or related investments, inside information includes information conveyed by a client and related to the client's pending orders, which:

(a)  is of a precise nature;
(b)  is not generally available;
(c)  relates directly or indirectly to one or more issuers of qualifying investments or to one or more qualifying investments; and
(d)  would, if generally available, be likely to have a significant effect on the price of those qualifying investments or on the price of related investments.

Information is precise if it:

(a)  indicates circumstances that exist or may reasonably be expected to come into existence or an event that has occurred or may reasonably be expected to occur; and
(b)  is specific enough to enable a conclusion to be drawn as to the possible effect of those circumstances or that event on the price of qualifying investments or related investments.

It should be noted that the market abuse provisions depend upon information that is not generally available to those using the market, but which if available to a regular user of the market would be or would be likely to be regarded by him as relevant when deciding the terms on which transactions in qualifying investments should be effected.

## 13.6  Market manipulation as market abuse

The remaining courses of behaviour in s118 relate to market manipulation:

1.  Where the behaviour consists of effecting transactions or orders to trade, which:

    (a)  give or are likely to give, a false or misleading impression as to the supply of, or demand for, or the price of, one or more qualifying investments, or
    (b)  secure the price of one or more such investments at a normal or artificial level (manipulating transactions).

2. Where the behaviour consists of effecting transactions or orders to trade which employ ficticious devices or any other form of deception or contrivance (manipulating transactions).
3. Where the behaviour consists of the dissemination of information by any means which gives, or is likely to give, a false or misleading impression as to the qualifying investment by a person who knew or who could reasonably be expected to have known that the information was false or misleading (dissemination).
4. Where the behaviour (not covered by 1, 2, 3 above):

(a) is likely to give a regular user of the market a false or misleading impression as to the supply of, demand for or price or value of, qualifying investments (misleading information); or
(b) would be likely to be regarded by a regular user of the market as behaviour that would distort, or would be likely to distort, the market in a qualifying investment (distortion), and the behaviour is likely to be regarded by a regular user of the market as a failure on the part of the person concernerd to observe the standard of behaviour reasonably expected of a person in his position in relation to the market.

The last two forms of behaviour are retained until 2008.

## 13.7 Exceptions

Certain categories of behaviour are exempted by s118A(5) as follows:

1. If it conforms with a rule which includes a provision to the effect that behaviour of conforming with the rule does not amount to market abuse.
2. That it conforms with the relevant provisions of Commission Regulations (EC) 227/2003, 22 December 2003, implementing Directive 2003/6/EC, regarding exemptions to buy back programmes and stablisation of financial instruments.
3. If it is done by a person acting on behalf of a public authority in pursuit of monetary policies or policies with respect to exchange rates for the management of public debt or foreign exchange reserves.

## 13.8 Sanctions

S123(1)(A) of the Financial Services and Markets Act 2000 provides that if the Financial Services Authority is satisfied that a person is or has engaged in market abuse, it may impose a financial penalty or publish a statement to the effect that a person has engaged in market abuse. Similarly, if the Financial Services Authority is satisfied that a person has required or encouraged others to do something which would amount to market abuse, it may apply the relevant sanctions.

The standard of proof that is appropriate is on a balance of probabilities. The relevant transaction is not rendered void or unenforceable by reason of a penalty being imposed (s131 of the Financial Services and Markets Act 2000).

S381 of the Financial Services and Markets Act empowers the High Court to issue an injunction regarding continuing market abuse. It may also order a person to take steps to remedy or mitigate market abuse (s381(2) and (6)). The Financial Services Authority may make a restitution order against a person who has engaged in market abuse or encouraged another to do so (s384) or may apply to the High Court for it to make an order (s383).

The defences are available in relation to a financial penalty or restitution order if the Financial Services Authority or the Court is satisfied that:

(a)  the person concerned believed on reasonable grounds that his or her behaviour was not market abuse (or requirement or encouragement of market abuse); or
(b)  that the person took all reasonable precautions and exercised all due diligence to avoid engaging in market abuse or requiring or encouraging others to do so.

## SUMMARY

Legislation on insider dealing was not introduced in the United Kingdom until 1980. The law is now set out in the Criminal Justice Act 1993 which implements the EC Directive on Insider Dealing (89/592).

Criminal sanctions may be applied where an insider deals in securities of a quoted company on the basis of inside information. The law also prohibits secondary insiders (tipees) with insider information from dealing in the securities of quoted companies.

Various criticisms are levelled at the legislation:

(a)  no civil remedy is provided;
(b)  there is no institution specifically charged with investigating insider dealing;
(c)  the legislation does not generally extend to unquoted companies;
(d)  the enforcement of the law on insider dealing is haphazard.

The Financial Services and Markets Act 2000 also prohibits 'market abuse' by insider dealing, manipulation, use of fictitious devices, dissemination of misleading information and distortion. There are financial penalties that attach to breaches of the relevant provisions and the High Court can impose an injunction to prevent further abuse and a restitution order may also be made.

## Further reading

Alcock, A, 'Insider dealing – how did we get here?' (1994) 15 Co Law 67.
Jain, N, 'Significance of mens rea in insider trading' (2004) 25 Co Law 132.

McVea, H, 'What's wrong with insider dealing?' (1995) 15 LS 390.

McVea, H, 'Fashioning a system of civil penalties for insider dealing: ss61 and 62 of the Financial Services Act 1986' [1996] JBL 344.

White, M, 'The implications for securities regulation of new insider dealing provisions in the Criminal Justice Act 1993' (1995) 16 Co Law 163.

# Minority protection

## 14.1 The rule in *Foss v Harbottle*

Historically, the rule in *Foss v Harbottle (1843)* has been of the utmost significance in governing when shareholders can take action on behalf of the company in which they hold shares. The facts of the case were as follows:

Certain burghers in Manchester had got together to purchase park land to dedicate to the then heiress to the throne, Princess Victoria. The park opened to great acclamation but difficulties soon followed. It was alleged by some of the company's members that some directors had misapplied company property. The case was heard by Wigwram VC. He held that the action could not proceed as the individual shareholders were not the proper plaintiffs. If a wrong had been committed, the wrong had been committed against the company and the company was therefore the proper plaintiff. The rule in *Foss v Harbottle* has acted like a deadhand on minority protection in British company law. The rule is, to some extent, justifiable. It has sometimes been justified as preventing a multiplicity of actions and sometimes by the argument that the company can ratify what directors have done and that, therefore, litigation might well be pointless.

In *Stein v Blake (1998)*, the plaintiff and the defendant each owned 50% of the shares of the company. The defendant, who was the sole director of the company, transferred at an undervalue assets to companies under his control.

The plaintiff brought an action in his personal capacity alleging that the defendant had breached his director's duties. The Court of Appeal upheld the decision of the trial judge. Millet LJ quoted from the judgment of the Court of Appeal in *Prudential Assurance Co Ltd v Newman Industries (No 2) (1982)*: '... what [a shareholder] cannot do is to recover damages merely because the company in which he is interested has suffered damage'.

The rule in *Foss v Harbottle*, however, gave way to certain exceptions where a minority action may be brought by a member arguing that a wrong has been done to the company. Historically at common law, these exceptions were:

(a) *ultra vires* acts
(b) where a special majority is needed
(c) the personal rights exception
(d) fraud by those in control of the company.

## 14.2 Exceptions to the rule

Historically it has not been possible to bring an action as an exception to the princple in *Foss v Harbottle* as a derivative claim where the claim is one of negligence – at least where the directors have not profited from the negligence in question.

It is proposed to examine each of these exceptions to the principle in *Foss v Harbottle* and then to examine the change brought about by s260 CA 2006 which introduces a new statutory procedure for a 'derivative claim'.

### 14.2.1 Ultra vires acts

The principle that the company can ratify what had been done, converting an initial wrong into action that was legitimate, could not formerly apply to *ultra vires* activities. *Ultra vires* acts could not be ratified: see *Parke v The Daily News Ltd (1962)*; *Simpson v Westminster Palace Hotel Co (1868)*. Despite virtual abolition of the doctrine of *ultra vires*, it is still possible for shareholders to restrain companies from acting in an *ultra vires* way before a transaction has been concluded. The exception, therefore, to this extent remains (s40(4) CA 2006).

### 14.2.2 Where a special majority is needed

If the company's constitution stipulates that a special majority is needed before a particular course of conduct can be accomplished then, if the company seeks to fly in the face of this provision and not obtain the particular majority, a single shareholder may maintain an action as an exception to *Foss v Harbottle*. This is the basis of the decision in *Edwards v Halliwell (1950)*.

In fact, that action is a trade union case rather than a company case. The law in this particular is the same in both categories of law. The union was seeking to increase its subscriptions in contravention of the union rule book without obtaining the consent of the union members to the increase. Members of a branch of the union complained of this and were successful. The same principle would operate in company law. The case is an interesting one and the judgment of Jenkins LJ is particularly helpful in setting out lucidly the law in this area.

### 14.2.3 The personal rights exception

If the company denies a shareholder rights that are set out in the company's constitution, the shareholder can bring an action on behalf of himself and all other shareholders denied the right to enforce the rights that have been negated. Thus, in *Pender v Lushington (1877)*, a shareholder was able to enforce his right and that of other shareholders that they should be able to cast their votes and, in *Wood v Odessa Waterworks Co (1889)*, a shareholder was able to enforce his right to a dividend in cash rather than a dividend *in specie* (in the form of property) as provided for under the company's articles.

### 14.2.4 *Fraud by those in control*

One reason for restricting derivative claims to fraud was to prevent a multiplicity of claims where it was possible that the action complained of would be ratified by the company. The exception of fraud enabled a shareholder to bring an action on behalf of the company (a derivative action deriving from the company's right to sue) for a fraud perpetrated by somebody in control. Fraud can never be ratified so the ratification objection does not arise. In *Cook v Deeks (1916)*, a Privy Council case on appeal from Ontario, a shareholder was able to bring an action under this head complaining that directors had diverted corporate opportunities to themselves. The exception does not extend to cases of negligence: see *Pavlides v Jensen (1956)*, where the complaint was that the directors had been negligent in selling an asbestos mine in Cyprus at an undervaluation. The exception did not extend either to negligence tantamount to expropriation which was the way that the cause of action was pleaded in *Heyting v Dupont (1964)*. A particularly difficult case arose in *Daniels v Daniels (1978)*. In this case, a director had purchased property from a company at £4,250 and then re-sold it shortly afterwards for £120,000. The allegation was pleaded as one of negligence. The judge, Templeman J, allowed the action to proceed. This has sometimes been misinterpreted. The case is not authority for the proposition that where there has been gross negligence an action is possible as an exception to *Foss v Harbottle*. The judge specifically stated that:

> To put up with foolish directors is one thing; to put up with directors who are so foolish they make a profit of £115,000 odd at the expense of the company is something entirely different.

Clearly, the decision is exceptional. Templeman J is indicating that there is more to the case than meets the eye.

Another important decision in the area of fraud is that of *Prudential Assurance Co Ltd v Newman Industries Ltd (1980)*. The case dealt, *inter alia*, with the question of control. In this case, Vinelott J held that management control was sufficient and seemed to accept that the directors were in management control. The Court of Appeal took a different view as it considered it would need a trial to see if management control actually existed. Voting control on the other hand is easy to demonstrate. Vinelott J had erred in not considering as a preliminary issue whether the plaintiffs could bring a derivative action. A derivative action should be permitted, according to the view of the Court of Appeal, where the board of the company was shown to be under the control of the fraudsters, only then could the issue of fraud be considered.

S260 CA 2006 now allows a derivative claim to be brought in respect of a cause of action arising from an actual or proposed act or omission involving negligence, default, breach of duty or breach of trust by a director of a company.

The range of this remedy is clearly much wider than the pre-existing common law derivative action proceedure which required the director to have profited from the negligence.

It may be that this new procedure will increase claims against directors but the provisions do encompass some safeguards.

The safeguard is that a member of a company who brings a derivative claim must apply to the court for permission to continue with the claim (s261 CA 2006). The same applies where a member applies to take over an action that has been brought by a company where it is appropriate for the member to continue the claim as a derivative claim (s262 CA 2006).

If it appears to the court in either case that the evidence filed by the applicant does not disclose a prima facea case for giving permission for the continuation of the derivative claim, then the court should dismiss the application and make any consequential order that it considers appropriate.

The matters that are to be considered in determining whether permission is to be given or not are set out in s263 CA 2006.

Permission must be refused if the court is satisfied:

(a) that a person acting in accordance with s172 (duty to promote the success of the company) would not seek to continue the claim; or
(b) where the cause of action arises from an act or omsision that is yet to occur, that the act or omission has been authorised by the company; or
(c) where the cause of action arises from an act or omission that has already occurred that the act or omission:

   (i) was authorised by the company before it occurred; or
   (ii) has been ratified by the company since it occurred.

In general, in considering whether to give permission the court must take into account, in particular, the following:

(a) whether the member is acting in good faith in seeking to continue the claim;
(b) the importance that a person acting in accordance with s172 (duty to promote the success of the company) would attach to continuing;
(c) where the cause of action results from an act or omission that is yet to occur, whether the act or omission could be, and in the circumstances were likely to be:

   (i) authorised by the company before it occurs;
   (ii) ratified by the company after it occurs

(d) where the cause of action arises from an act or omission that has already occurred, whether the act or omission could be, and in the circumstances would be likely to be ratified by the company;
(e) whether the company has decided not to pursue the claim;
(f) whether the act or omission in respect of which the claim is brought gives rise to a cause of action that the member could pursue in his own right rather than on behalf of the company.

In considering whether to give permission, the court will have particular regard to evidence before it as to the views of members of the company who have no personal interest, whether direct or indirect, in the matter.

### 14.2.5 Shareholders' collateral actions

In *Johnson v Gore Wood & Co (2001)*, the House of Lords had to consider the extent to which a shareholder could bring a collateral claim where the company had already sued.

The case concerned an allegation that the defendant firm of solicitors had failed in its undertaking to serve efficaciously a notice to exercise an option to purchase land. The company which held the option had already sued the firm and obtained satisfaction of a large part of its claim. Before the settlement agreement was concluded the plaintiff, who owned all but two of the shares in the company, notified the firm that he too would be suing on the basis that the firm had contracted with, or otherwise assumed responsibility to him, as well as to the company. The settlement agreement contemplated the plaintiff retaining his right of action against the firm. The House of Lords struck out the plaintiff's claims to the extent that they reflected the loss suffered by the company. They left in place claims for consequential loss that the plaintiff may have suffered that were not so reflected.

This principle is entirely reasonable. A shareholder should not be able to reopen a case by seeking to pursue the defendant in a personal capacity where the company has already sued if his loss is merely reflective of the company's loss. As Lord Millett said in Johnson, 'Mr Johnson cannot be permitted to challenge in one capacity the adequacy of the terms he agreed to in another'.

The issue of reflective loss arose in *Giles v Rhind (2002)*. Giles and Rhind were both shareholders, employees and directors of SHS Ltd. Rhind left the company and diverted business away in breach of a shareholders' agreement. The company started proceedings against him but the proceedings were discontinued by the administrator as the company could not afford to continue. Giles then started an action in his personal capacity. Could he proceed as the company had a right of action against Rhind? Waller LJ, in the Court of Appeal, said it hardly seems right that a wrongdoer in breach of contract to a company and to a shareholder should be able to block an action by a shareholder where he had prevented the company pursuing an action by demanding costs from the company. The shareholder's action was allowed to proceed.

## 14.3 The statutory remedy

In many ways, minority protection is now the most active area of company law. Until the Companies Act 1980 and s75 of that Act, now ss994–996 CA 2006, minority protection was arguably the most stagnant area.

Section 210 of the Companies Act 1948 which provided relief where a minority was oppressed was introduced in response to the recommendations of the

Committee in 1945. The section was used very rarely in its 32 years of
n between 1948 and 1980.

s used successfully in *Scottish CWS v Meyer (1959)* where a shareholder
complained that the company's business was diverted away to another company
in which the petitioning shareholder had no interest. The petition was successful.
In another case, *Re HR Harmer Ltd (1958)*, the founding father of a stamp dealing company was ordered not to interfere in the affairs of the company. The petition was presented by his sons. The father aged 88 at the time of the action was
running the business as if it was his own personal business. He was tyrannical and
dictatorial. He defied board resolutions and appointed a private detective to spy
on some of his staff whom he wrongly suspected of stealing company assets. The
petition was successful.

### 14.3.1 Drawbacks of s210 of the Companies Act 1948

The old minority remedy section had various drawbacks. These were highlighted
by the Jenkins Committee in 1962. The drawbacks were as follows: an order
could only be made if the facts could be the basis for a winding up order on the
just and equitable ground. This meant that the section was very closely allied to
the rules relating to winding up:

(a) a single act was insufficient to justify a petition under s210. A course of conduct had to be shown to found a petition;

(b) the petitioner had to show that the conduct was oppressive. This meant 'bur-
densome, harsh and wrongful' (*Scottish CWS v Meyer (1959) per* Viscount
Simonds);

(c) a petition could not be based on omissions or on future conduct;

(d) it was generally thought that the old minority section could not encompass
personal representatives; however, Plowman J, in *Re Jermyn Street Turkish
Baths Ltd (1970)*, took the view that personal representatives could petition.

### 14.3.2 The remedy post 1980

These shortcomings were all remedied by s75 of the Companies Act 1980 (now
ss994–996 CA 2006). The link with winding up was swept away. A single act or
omission or threatened future conduct can be the basis for a petition. Personal representatives can now sue (see s994(2) of the Companies Act 206). Most importantly,
the new remedy applies in cases of unfair prejudice. This is obviously far easier to
demonstrate than oppression which requires a course of deliberate conduct. The
section now provides as follows:

> A member of a company may apply to the court by petition for an order under
> this part on the ground that the company's affairs are being or have been
> conducted in a manner which is unfairly prejudicial to the interests of its

members generally or of some part of its members (including at least himself) or that any actual or proposed act or omission of the company (including an act or omission on its behalf) is or would be so prejudicial.

### 14.3.3 Exclusion from management

The most common example of the minority seeking relief is where an undertaking to a member that he would have a say in the management of a company has been breached, usually by his removal from the board of directors. Under the old law, it was essential that the oppression was suffered *qua* member in the narrow sense. This requirement was strictly applied, so that a member complaining of exclusion from management would not have succeeded. The requirement of petitioning *qua* member has now, at least, been more broadly construed so that, for example, a founder member could well argue that a right to participate in the management of the company was a membership right.

Early on, it seemed that the old rule still applied, even under the reformed section. In *Re a Company (No 004475) (1983)*, Lord Grantchester QC held that prejudice had to be suffered *qua* member in the narrow sense. However, in an earlier unreported decision, *Re Bovey Hotel Ventures Ltd (1981, unreported)*, there had been a successful petition on the basis of exclusion from management. A husband and wife had operated a hotel company. They split up. The erstwhile husband excluded the former wife from participating in the management of the company. She successfully petitioned under the section and indeed was able to purchase the husband's shareholding as her remedy.

Another case involving exclusion from management is *Re RA Noble & Sons (Clothing) Ltd (1983)*. Here, the court accepted that exclusion from management could be the basis of a petition. However, it found that on the facts of the case the petitioner had brought the exclusion on himself by his disinterest. *Re London School of Electronics (1985)* provides a further example of exclusion from management. This case concerned a North London tutorial college where the petitioner complained of his de facto dismissal as a director. The other directors argued that the petitioning director, Lytton, had brought the exclusion upon himself by his own conduct. Nourse J held that the petitioner's conduct did not prevent him from bringing the petition. The alleged conduct, if proved, would be a factor in determining what relief should be available to the petitioning shareholder. It might also serve to demonstrate that the prejudice was not unfair.

In *Re a Company (No 002567 of 1982) (1983)*, Vinelott J took the view that the section would apply in an *Ebrahimi* type situation where a shareholder was wrongly excluded from management in a company. In *Re Bird Precision Bellows Ltd (1984)*, the petitioners, who were minority shareholders in Bird Precision Bellows Ltd, had been removed from the board of directors by the respondents. It was ordered by consent, without any admission of liability on the part of the respondents, that they had been responsible for unfairly prejudicial conduct, that the respondents should purchase the petitioners' shares at a price to be determined. Nourse J subsequently held that the exclusion was wrongful.

In *Richards v Lundy (2000)*, a remedy was granted where Richards was removed as an employee but remained a director of the Apollo Cleaning Services Company. The judge held he had expected to play an active management role.

The pattern is not absolutely uniform. Clearly, not every exclusion from management in a small private company is wrongful. In *Coulson, Sanderson and Ward Ltd v Ward (1986)*, Slade LJ considered that exclusion from management would not necessarily found a petition under s459. Furthermore, in *Re XYZ Ltd* (also under the name *Re a Company (No 004377 of 1986) (1986)*), it was similarly held that not every exclusion from management in a quasi-partnership company would ground a petition. It did not necessarily follow that there was always a legitimate expectation of management in such companies.

Whilst it is extremely unlikely that a petition can be presented under s994 for exclusion from a public company, still less a quoted company, the door does not seem absolutely closed on this possibility. In *Re Blue Arrow Plc (1987)*, the court held that although there was generally no room for implying a legitimate expectation of continued employment in a public company, special situations could arise where exclusion from management could be the basis for a petition in respect of a public company.

*Re Tottenham Hotspur plc (1994)* provides the type of situation where a director may be able to argue successfully that there has been an understanding that there should be a role for him in the management in a public company situation, although Terry Venables the chief executive failed to establish that in this case. He went on to become manager of the England team.

There must, however, be some membership nexus. Thus, in *Re JE Cade & Son Ltd (1992)*, the petitioning member was seeking to protect his interests as a landowner and failed as protecting such interests was held to be outside of the scope of the remedy, whilst in quasi-partnership situations a shareholder will be able to demonstrate that there was a clear understanding of a management role.

In *Exeter City AFC v The Football Conference Ltd (2004)*, the question involved was could a minority petition be stayed where the dispute was covered by an arbitration agreement. Judge Weeks QC believed that such an agreement could not preclude the section. This decision appears strange.

In *Fisher v Cadman (2005)*, Mrs Fisher was a minority shareholder and acquiesced in informality within the company. Later her attitude changed and she insisted on Annual General Meetings being held. The judge held following *Anderson v Hogg (2000)*, that a shareholder could acquiesce in informality and that this would not then constitute unfairness against that shareholder. Here, however, Mrs Fisher was able to 'revive' provisions in the articles and the judge found *inter alia* that the subsequent failure to hold AGMs was unfair to her.

It seems that a shareholder may petition on the grounds of unfair prejudice and recover as a creditor and not as a shareholder. The Privy Council took the view that to preclude this where the terms of a joint venture required shareholders to provide working capital would be inconsistent with the purpose of the section. See *Gamlestaden Fastigheter AB v Baltic Partners Ltd and others (2007)*. (On appeal to the Privy Council from Jersey).

### 14.3.4 Other grounds on which petitions have been based

There are various other grounds on which petitions have been based. These might include the following:

(a) the company failing to purchase the shares of a minority – *Re a Company (No 004475 of 1982) (1983)*, before Lord Grantchester QC. This petition was unsuccessful;

(b) the company changing its business. This was another ground for complaint in *Re a Company (No 004475 of 1982) (1983)*, before Lord Grantchester QC. This argument was also unsuccessful. The company had set up as an advertising agency and later diversified to become a wine bar and restaurant;

(c) a shareholder voting his shares in breach of an undertaking to the government – *Re Carrington Viyella Plc (1983)*. This was an unsuccessful petition;

(d) the provision of inadequate information and advice in recommending acceptance of a takeover bid. In *Re a Company (No 008699 of 1985) (1986)*, Hoffmann J held that circulars containing inadequate information in a takeover situation may ground a petition;

(e) calling a meeting to replace a director by a nominee of another company. This petition was successful in *Whyte Petitioner (1984)*;

(f) making a rights issue. This was a successful ground in *Re a Company (No 002612 of 1984) (1985)*, where Harman J granted an injunction to restrain a rights issue which would have reduced the petitioner's holding from one third to less than 5%, but unsuccessful in *Re a Company (No 007623 of 1984) (1986)*, where there had been no refusal by the respondents to buy the petitioner's shares at a fair valuation;

(g) a proposal to sell property belonging to the company. This was unsuccessful in *Re Gorwyn Holdings (1985)*;

(h) a proposal to sell the company's business substantially undervalued to connected persons. This allegation was not proved and the petition was unsuccessful in *Re Posgate and Denby (Agencies) Ltd (1987)*;

(i) delay in holding a meeting. This was the basis of a successful petition in *Re McGuinness and Another (1988)*. This petition was successful notwithstanding that the delay in holding the meeting was not contrary to the provisions of the Companies Act. The loophole was closed by para 9 of Sched 19 of the Companies Act 1989 (now s304 CA 2006);

(j) failure to lay accounts. This was a successful ground for the petition in *Re Nuneaton Borough AFC Ltd (1989)*;

(k) failure to pay dividends. There was previously some doubt as to whether this could be a ground for a petition because of the former requirement that some part of the membership be prejudiced. See *Re a Company (No 00370 of 1987) ex p Glossop (1988)*; *Re Sam Weller Ltd (1990)*. This difficulty has now been remedied by the amendment in para 11 of Sched 19 of the Companies Act 1989 which provides that the conduct must be unfairly prejudicial to the interest of the company's members generally or some part of the members. This is now incorporated into the Act (now s994 CA 2006);

(l) deletion of pre-emption rights. It was recognised that this may be a reason for a petition in *Re a Company (No 005685 of 1988) ex p Schwarz (1989)*;

(m) dilution of voting power. This was a successful ground for the petition in *Re DR Chemicals (1989)*;

(n) use of company assets for the family and friends of the controller of the company. This was the basis of the successful petition in *Re Elgindata Ltd (1991)*;

(o) the company operating at a loss with the directors taking excessive remuneration. Such a petition failed on the facts in *Re Saul D Harrison & Sons plc (1995)* as there was not excessive remuneration.

(p) mismanagement of the company. In *Re Elgindata (1991)*, the court said that it would refuse to intervene in relation to allegedly poor managerial decisions, accepting that there was a commercial risk of bad management. However, in *Re Macro (Ipswich) Ltd (1994)*, the court considered the mismanagement so serious that it granted a remedy to the petitioning shareholder.

## 14.4 The section in operation

In determining if a person can bring a petition, it is not necessary that he comes to court with clean hands. See *Re London School of Electronics (1985)*. However, if a petitioner has to some extent brought the conduct upon himself, this may be relevant in determining whether the prejudice is unfair and also in determining what remedy is available to the petitioner.

The question of unfair prejudice is an objective question and does not depend upon the intention of the respondents. See *Re RA Noble & Sons (Clothing) Ltd (1983)*.

In *Re Macro (Ipswich) Ltd (1994)*, Arden J considered that the question of prejudice was an objective one. If the prejudice was established, it then had to be demonstrated that there was unfairness. This was a matter of balancing different interests. The case involved allegations of exclusion from management and corporate mismanagement leading to a loss of value in the petitioner's shareholding. Unfair prejudice was made out.

The starting point in any case involving s994 is to focus upon the terms of the company's articles to determine whether the conduct of which the plaintiff complains is in contravention of the terms of the articles (see the judgment of Hoffmann LJ in *Re Saul D Harrison & Sons plc (1994)*).

Hoffmann LJ in *Re Saul D Harrison* went on to state that there are situations where the company's articles do not reflect all of the understandings on which the business is run. The section protects the legitimate expectations of shareholders.

The case concerned a petition presented by a minority shareholder seeking compulsory winding up of the company under s994 or an order that the petitioner's shares be purchased by the other shareholders. The company was in the business of converting waste textiles into cleaning and wiping cloths. The Court of Appeal held that there were no grounds for saying that it would be unfair for the board to act in accordance with the company's articles. Her legitimate expectations amounted to no more than that the board would run the company in compliance with their fiduciary obligations.

The first case on what is now s994 in the House of Lords was *O'Neill v Phillips (1999)*. Phillips was originally the sole director and shareholder of the company which stripped asbestos from buildings. O'Neill was originally a manual worker and was very talented. During the construction boom of the 1980's, O'Neill proved invaluable. Phillips promised him 50% of the profits and transferred 25% of the shares to him. He did, indeed, pay him 50% of the profits.

Phillips retired effectively making O'Neill managing director. Phillips also said, in principle, he would transfer 50% of the shares to O'Neill when the company's net asset value reached half a million pounds. There was no formal agreement to this effect.

Later there was a downturn in the business and O'Neill was effectively removed as managing director, and Phillips resumed in a managerial role. O'Neill remained on the board. O'Neill severed links later and brought a s994 petition, where he failed at first instance. The Court of Appeal, however, held that O'Neill had been forced out because of Phillips' action. The House of Lords, however, upheld unanimously Phillips' appeal. Lord Hoffmann said that legal rights were subject to equitable considerations but retreated from the 'legitimate expectations' phrase that he himself had used in *Re Saul D Harrison and Sons*.

The decision also makes it clear that unfairness may be negated by a reasonable offer such as to purchase the shares of the party who has suffered the unfairness.

The section does not provide a right for a disenchanted minority to ask to be bought out. In *Phoenix Office Supplies Ltd v Larvin (2003)*, the claimant was an employee and director of the company. He held a third of the shares as did two other directors. He resigned as an employee for personal reasons and said he would resign as a director on agreed terms. The other two shareholders offered to buy his shares at a substantial discount. He refused the offer and brought a s994 petition.

The judge held that the company was a quasi-partnership company and that the claimant director was entitlted to have his shares purchased for a third of the value of the company.

It was held on appeal in the Court of Appeal that s994 did not provide a shareholder who wished voluntarily to sever connections with a company the means of having his shares purchased (see Taylor, B, 'No Such Thing as a No Fault Corporate Divorce' (2003) NLJ 502).

## 14.5 Remedies

The court has power to make such order as it thinks fit for giving relief in respect of the matters complained of (s996(1) CA 2006). The court may make an order to regulate the conduct of the company's affairs in the future. It may require the company to refrain from doing or continuing to do an act complained of, or to do an act that the petitioner has complained it has omitted to do. The court may authorise civil proceedings to be brought in the name of the company. It may require the company not to make any, or any specified alterations, to its articles without the leave of the court. A very common remedy is where the court orders the purchase of the petitioners shares. As noted, the court has the power to award whatever relief it considers fit (s996(1) of the Companies Act 2006), and it may make an order to regulate the company's affairs or to restrict the company from acting in a particular way. It may order the company to do something or it may order civil proceedings to be brought in the name of the company. A very common remedy is where the court orders the purchase of the petitioner's shares.

On occasion, it may be an order that the respondent sell his shares to the petitioner, as in *Re Bovey Hotel Ventures Ltd*. It is rare for the court to order that the minority buy out the majority. Such an order was made in *Re Brenfield Squash Racquets Club Ltd (1996)*. If the court does order the purchase of shares, problems of valuation arise. There is no rule in s996 regarding share valuation. As Oliver LJ said in *Re Bird Precision Bellows Ltd (1985)*:

> It seems to me that the whole framework of the section ... is to confer on the court a very wide discretion to do what is considered fair and equitable in all the circumstances of the case...

Generally, where a minority shareholding is sold, there is a discount applied as a percentage of the company's value. This rule only applies, however, if a sale is a willing sale, see *dicta* of Nourse J in *Re Bird Precision Bellows Ltd (1986)*.

What has become the classic situation of exclusion from management in a quasi-partnership company arose in *Quinlan v Essex Hinge Co Ltd (1997)*. The petitioner had been working for the company which manufactured hinges in excess of 30 years. For 27 years he had been production director. The managing director had joined the company in 1936 and was extremely autocratic. The company did not pay dividends but, instead, paid bonuses to the company's directors. After a dispute, the managing director dismissed the petitioner.

The court held that this amounted to exclusion from management and that the petitioner was entitled to have his shares bought with no discount being made for their being a minority holding. (See also *Richards v Lundy (2000)*.)

On the other hand, a discounted valuation might be appropriate if the petitioner brought the exclusion upon himself.

Another moot point is the date of the valuation. Once again, there is no fixed rule to apply. If the petitioner refused a reasonable offer for his shares, the date of valuation may well be the date of the hearing: see *Re a Company (No 002567 of 1982) (1983)*.

On the other hand, if a fair offer is not made and the conduct of the majority causes the value of the company's shares to fall, the court may order a valuation at the date the unreasonable conduct began: see *Re OC (Transport) Services Ltd (1984)*.

This seems to be the most logical date for valuing the shares.

The old minority remedy was very much a fly-swatter or pea-shooter of a remedy compared to the blunderbuss of the present remedy. It consistently failed to meet the needs of wronged minorities and prompted the Jenkins Committee on Company Law to recommend in 1962 that a broader remedy of unfair prejudice should be introduced (Cmnd 1749, para 205). Under the present remedy, companies must consider carefully the effect that their actions and inactions will have on all of their members. The possibility is now that the pendulum has swung too much in the opposite direction and that, from a position of too little protection for shareholders, we have now moved to a position of too much.

## 14.6 Just and equitable winding up

A company may be wound up by the court if the court is of the opinion that it is just and equitable that the company should be wound up (s122(1)(g) of the Insolvency Act 1986). (The procedure on a winding up will be considered in Chapter 23.) Before the advent of ss459–61 of the Companies Act 1985, just and equitable winding up was sometimes the only possible remedy for a disenchanted minority shareholder. It was this remedy that was sought and obtained in *Ebrahimi v Westbourne Galleries*. The remedy is a sledgehammer remedy. Since the advent of what is now ss994–996, it has been less common. Indeed, s125(2) of the Insolvency Act 1986 provides that, if the court is of the opinion that there is some other remedy that is available to the petitioners, and that they are acting unreasonably in seeking to have the company wound up instead of pursuing that other remedy, then the court should refuse the petition. Yet, in *Virdi v Abbey Leisure Ltd (1989)*, the Court of Appeal considered that, where a minority shareholder sought a winding up order rather than utilising the mechanism under the articles to have his shares purchased at a fair valuation the minority was not acting unreasonably. The Court of Appeal took the view, reversing Hoffmann J at first instance, that the minority might legitimately object to the mode of valuation for valuing his shares.

In *Ebrahimi v Westbourne Galleries (1973)*, the House of Lords made the point that the categories of conduct where just and equitable winding up might be ordered were not closed. It will be attempted here to classify the cases into certain areas. There is nothing magic in this categorisation.

Jonathan Parker J held in *Re Guidezone Ltd (2000)* that a petition to wind up on the just and equitable ground could only be granted if a petition based on unfairly prejudicial conduct would have been successful. This view is highly questionable and at odds with *Re R A Noble (Clothing) Ltd*. The decision in *Re Guidezone Ltd* is criticised by Acton S in 'Just and Equitable Winding Up: The Strange Case of the Disappearing Jurisdiction' (2001) 22 Co Law 134.

### 14.6.1 Exclusion from management

Apart from *Ebrahimi* itself, exclusion from management has featured in other cases. In *Re A & BC Chewing Gum Ltd (1975)*, the petitioning shareholder had put up a third of the capital of the company and had been promised a say in the management of the company. The court granted the petitioning shareholder's petition where he had been excluded from management. In *Tay Bok Choon v Tahansan Sdn Bhd (1987)*, in similar circumstances, a shareholder who had put up a considerable amount of capital and who was excluded from management was held entitled to wind the company up.

### 14.6.2 Destruction of the substratum of the company

If the main and overriding purpose for which the company has been formed is destroyed so that the company cannot achieve its main objective, then a petition to wind the company up on the just and equitable ground will be successful. In *Re German Date Coffee Co (1882)*, the company had been formed to obtain a German patent to manufacture coffee from dates. A request for a patent was refused. It was held that a petition to wind the company up would be successful. It must be that all of the company's main activities are incapable of achievement before such a petition can succeed. In *Re Kitson & Co Ltd (1946)*, the company's engineering business had ceased when it was sold. The company had other activities, however, that were still capable of achievement. A petition to wind the company up was therefore not granted.

It is interesting to note that a petition will not succeed merely because a company is making a loss. In order to succeed, it must be demonstrated that the company is incapable of making a profit: see *Re Suburban Hotel Co (1867)*.

### 14.6.3 Deadlock

If there is deadlock within the company and there is no way of breaking that deadlock by some mechanism in the articles or by the shareholders resolving the problem by appointing a director or removing a director, then a petition will be granted. In *Re Yenidje Tobacco Co Ltd (1916)*, the company had two shareholders with an equal number of shares who were each directors. They could not agree on how the company should be managed. There was no provision for breaking the deadlock and a petition to wind the company up on the just and equitable ground was granted.

### 14.6.4 Lack of probity of the directors

If a petitioning shareholder can demonstrate a lack of probity and integrity on the part of directors, this will be sufficient ground for winding up the company. In *Re Bleriot Manufacturing Aircraft Co (1916)*, the court held that where directors had misappropriated company property, a winding up order could be made. In *Loch v John Blackwood Ltd (1924)*, a Privy Council decision on appeal from the Court of Appeal of the West Indies (Barbados), where directors had failed to supply corporate information to shareholders and to hold company meetings and in general ran the company as if it was their own property, a winding up order was granted. Similarly, in *Re Lundie Brothers Ltd (1965)*, Plowman J granted a winding up petition in a situation where the directors ran the company as if it was their own business without any account being taken of the interests of shareholders. In addition, the petitioner had been excluded from management.

### 14.6.5 Breakdown of trust and confidence

This category overlaps with exclusion from management; indeed, in many of the cases, some of the factors set out in the different areas may be present. In *Re Zinotty Properties Ltd (1984)*, it was held that one of the founding shareholders of a business was entitled to assume he would participate in the management. He was excluded from the management. Furthermore, it had been understood that once the company had developed a particular site, the company would be dissolved. This did not happen. Some of the company's money was lent to another business in which one of the directors had an interest. The petition brought by the excluded shareholder was successful.

It may thus be seen that the remedy of just and equitable winding up is available in a variety of circumstances, although its popularity has decreased since the remedy in ss994–996 has been on the scene as selling company property in a liquidation generally means obtaining a discounted price for the company's assets which is not in the interests of any of the shareholders.

### 14.6.6 Self-help

One of the recommendations in the consultation before the Act is to be included in new model articles. This is the possible exit route for a shareholder exercisable by notice to the company. The exit route could be exercisable, for example, where there is a removal of a shareholder/director from office.

Most respondents were against including regulations in the company's articles relating to arbitration or the valuation of shares.

# SUMMARY

## Minority protection

### The rule in Foss v Harbottle and s260 CA 2006

Historically, the decision in *Foss v Harbottle* has meant that, where the company suffers harm, the company is the proper plaintiff so that shareholders cannot generally sue for wrongs done to the company.

### Exceptions

There were certain exceptions:

(a) where there is an *ultra vires* act;
(b) where a special majority is needed;
(c) where personal rights are infringed;
(d) where fraud had been committed by those in control.

S260 CA 2006 now provides that a derivative claim may be brought in respect of a cause of action arising from an actual or proposed act or omission involving negligence, default, breach of duty or breach of trust by a director of a company.

This is a broader remedy but there are certain safeguards which apply, so that permission to bring proceedings may be refused if there has been authorisation or ratification or if this is likely, for example.

### The statutory remedy

Before ss994–996 of the Companies Act 2006, the old remedy, s210 of the Companies Act 1948, had certain serious defects:

(a) an order could only be made if a winding up order could have been made on the just and equitable ground;
(b) a single act was insufficient to found a petition;
(c) the petitioner had to show that the conduct was oppressive;
(d) a petition could not be based on omissions or on future conduct;
(e) probably personal representatives could not present petitions.

Under what is now ss994–996, all of these defects are remedied. In particular, a petitioner needs now to demonstrate unfair prejudice and does not need to show oppression.

The 2006 Act remedy covers a wide range of situations. The courts have interpreted the remedy liberally and it is not necessary for a petitioner to confine his petition to membership matters in the narrow sense and may, for example, in appropriate circumstances complain of exclusion from management. The court has a total discretion as to what remedy to award a successful petitioner although the usual remedy is a purchase of the petitioner's shares.

### Just and equitable winding up

'Just and equitable' winding up may not look like a membership remedy at first sight but it is.

A disenchanted member will usually only seek this remedy where all other possible remedies have been exhausted. Just and equitable winding up under s122(1)(g) of the Insolvency Act 1986 is a sledgehammer remedy and the court should refuse it if there is some other remedy which is appropriate which the petitioner is unreasonable in not seeking.

Just and equitable winding up may be granted in various situations and the categories are not closed. The situations include:

(a)  exclusion from management;
(b)  destruction of the substratum of the company;
(c)  deadlock;
(d)  lack of probity of management;
(e)  breakdown of trust and confidence.

## Further reading

Acton, S, 'Just and Equitable Winding Up: the strange case of the disappearing jurisidiction' (2001) 22 Co Law 134.

Boyle, AJ, 'The new derivative action' (1997) 18 Co Law 256.

Cheffins, B, and Dine, J, 'The statutory protection of minority shareholders: S459 of the Companies Act 1985 (1992) 13 Co Law 83.

Chesterman, MR, 'The 'just and equitable' winding up of small private companies' (1973) 36 MLR 129.

Ferran, E, 'Litigation by shareholders and reflective loss' [2001] CLJ 245.

Griffin, S, 'Defining the scope of a membership interest' (A casenote on Re J E Cade & Son Ltd [1992] BCLC 213), (1993) 14 Co Law 64.

Hirt, H, 'In what circumstances should breaches of directors' duties give rise to a remedy under s459–461 of the Companies Act 1985' (2003) Co Law 100.

Lowry, J, 'Reconstructing shareholder actions: a response to the Law Commission's Consultation Paper' No 142 (1997) 18 Co Law 247.

Lowry, J, 'The elasticity of unfair prejudice: stretching the ambit of Companies Act 1985, s459' [1995] LMCLQ 337.

Moran, LJ, 'Missing links and missed opportunities' (1997) 18 Co Law 264.

Mukwiri, J, 'S459 on parent and subsidiary companies' (2005) 26 Co Law 75.

Mukwiri, J, 'The No Reflective Loss Principle' (2005) 26 Co Law 304.

Payne, J, 'Clean hands in derivitive actions' [2002] CLJ 76.

Payne, J, 'S459 and Public Companies' (1999) 114 LQR 368.

Payne, J, and Prentice, D, 'S459 and the House of Lords View' (1999) 114 LQR 587.

Prentice, DD, 'The theory of the firm: minority shareholder oppression and sections 459–61 of the Companies Act 1985' (1988) OJLS 55.

Prentice, DD, 'Winding up on the just and equitable ground: the partnership analogy' (1973) 89 LQR 107.

Prentice, D, 'Shareholder actions: the rule in Foss v Harbottle' (1988) 104 LQR 341.

Rider, BAK, 'Partnership and its impact on domestic companies' [1979] CLJ 148.

Riley, CA, 'Contracting out of company law: s459 of the Companies Act and the role of the courts' (1992) 55 MLR 782.

Riley, CA, 'The values behind the Law Commission's Consultation Paper' (1997) 18 Co Law 260.

Roberts, P, and Poole, J, 'Shareholder remedies – efficient litigation and the unfair prejudice remedy' [1999] JBL 38.

Rolls, P, and Warwick, M, 'Unfair prejudice – how buy out offers can be used to end petitions based on unfairly prejudicial conduct' (2003) Sol Jo 735.

Sealy, L, 'The rule in Foss v Harbottle: the Australian experience' (1989) 10 Co Law 52.

Simm, G, 'Shareholders in dispute' (2003) NLJ 876.

Sugarman, D, 'Reconceptualising company law: reflections on the Law Commission's Consultation Paper on Shareholder Remedies' (1997) 18 Co Law 226 and 274.

Taylor, B, 'No such thing as a no fault corporate divorce' (2003) NLJ 502.

Watts, P, 'The shareholder as co-promisee' (2001) 117 LQR 388.

# Company meetings

There are two types of members' meetings: annual general meetings and general meetings.

## 15.1 Annual general meetings

S336 of the Companies Act 2006 provides that every public company must hold a general meeting at its annual general meeting in each period of six months beginning with the day following the accounting reference date. Failure to comply with this requirement is an offence committed by every officer of the company who is in default.

S337 provides that a notice calling an annual general meeting of a public company must state that the meeting is an annual general meeting.

S338 of the 2006 Act provides that the members of a public company may require the company to give to members of the company entitled to receive notice of the next annual general meeting, notice of a resolution which may properly be moved and is intended to be moved at that meeting.

The company is required to give notice of a resolution once it has received a request to do so:

(a) from members representing at least 5% of the total voting rights of the members who have a right to vote on a resolution at the AGM to which the requests relate; or

(b) at least 100 members who have a right to vote on the resolution at the AGM to which the request relates, and hold shares in the company on which there has been paid up an average sum per member of at least £100 (s338(3) CA 2006).

S339 provides that public companies must circulate resolutions that are submitted in accordance with the above conditions, and s340 provides that the expenses of the company in complying with the section are those of the company if the resolution is submitted to the company before the end of the financial year preceeding the meeting. Otherwise, the expenses in complying with the section must be paid by the members unless the company resolves otherwise and unless the company has previously so resolved, it is not bound to comply with the section unless there is deposited with it not later than six weeks before the AGM to which the request relates, or if later, the time at which notice is given of that meeting, a sum reasonably sufficient to meet the expenses in complying with the section.

Prior to the 2006 Act, private companies could opt out of the requirement to hold AGMs if their members unanimously agreed. Since the 2006 Act, private companies are not required to hold AGMs at all although they may do so if they wish.

## 15.2 General meetings

### 15.2.1 Members

S303 provides for the members' power to require directors to call meetings. The directors are required to do so if members who hold at least 10% of the paid up capital of the company carry voting rights at general meetings, except in the case of a private company where more than 12 months has elapsed since the end of the last general meeting, in which case the required percentage is 15%.

S304 provides that it is the directors' duty to call meetings that are required by members under s303. They must call the meeting within 21 days of receiving the request and the meeting must be held not more than 28 days after the date of the notice convening the meeting (s304(1) (a), (b) CA 2006).

S305 provides that the members may call a meeting at the company's expense if the directors are required under s303 to call a meeting and have not done so in accordance with s304 CA 2006. The meeting must be called for a date not more than three months after the date on which the directors become subject to the requirement to call a meeting (s305(3)). Any reasonable expenses incurred by the members requesting the meeting by reason of the failure of the directors duly to call a meeting must be reimbursed by the company (s305(6)).

### 15.2.2 The court

S306 provides for the court to order a meeting. The section applies if, for any reason, it is impracticable:

(i) to call a meeting of the company in any manner in which meetings of the company may be called; or
(ii) to conduct the meeting in the manner prescribed by the company's articles or the Act (s306(1) CA 2006).

The court may either, of its own motion or on the application:

(i) of a director of the company; or
(ii) of a member of the company

who would be entitled to vote at a meeting, order a meeting to be called, held and conducted in any manner the court thinks fit (s306(2)).

A previous similar provision was often used in the case of deadlock where a company perhaps has two members and one member is refusing to attend a meeting, for example see *Re Sticky Fingers Restaurant Ltd (1992)*. In this case, one member of the company had presented a petition claiming of unfairly prejudicial conduct. The other member, Bill Wyman of the Rolling Stones, was allowed to hold a meeting with the quorum fixed at one for the purpose of appointing additional directors, provided that any such directors would not act to the prejudice of the other shareholder pending the outcome of the minority protection proceedings. The section was used in a similar way in *Re Whitchurch Insurance Consultants Ltd (1993)* where Mr Rudd wished to remove the other member, Mrs Rudd, as a director. In *Re the British Union for the Abolition of Vivisection (1995)*, application was made to the court under s306 to give directions for the calling of a meeting to avoid anticipated disruption. There had been disorder at a previous meeting and what was therefore sought was the convening of a small meeting consisting only of members of the committee, with no other members being entitled to attend in person but to vote by postal means.

S306 cannot be used to affect substantive voting rights or to shift the balance of power between different shareholders.

The Court of Appeal allowed an appeal in *Ross v Telford and another (1997)*, where the judge had ordered a meeting which would have had the effect of enabling one 50% shareholder and his solicitor to out vote the other 50% shareholder. Ross and Telford, during the course of their marriage, had carried on business as electrical contractors through the medium of a small group of companies.

They had equal shareholdings in one company (PLB) although Ross had effectively more shares in another company (L). The shareholdings in L were held as to 50% by Ross and as to 50% by PLB.

Ross alleged that Telford had forged his name on company cheques. He caused the company (L) to start proceedings against T. He applied for, and obtained, an order under s371 that a meeting of the board of L (Ross and Telford were the only directors) could be called, and that one member should be deemed to be a quorum. This was granted by court order; the judge ordering that a meeting be held for the purpose of considering and voting upon a resolution for the appointment of a representative of Ross' solicitors as a third director of the company, and that the representative of the solicitors might attend at the meeting and vote on behalf of PLB.

The effect of the order made by the judge was to regulate the affairs of PLB by authorising a representative of Mr Ross' solicitors to be appointed to represent the company at a general meeting of L. Such an appointment would normally be made at a board meeting of PLB. The effect of the order was to break the deadlock in PLB.

The Court of Appeal held that what is now s306 did not empower the court to break a deadlock at either a board or general meeting of a company.

The court cannot make an order so as to permit a 50% shareholder to override the wishes of the other 50% shareholder.

This case is clearly distinguishable from cases such as *Re Sticky Fingers Restaurant Ltd (1992)*, where the court was determined to prevent the quorum provisions from being abused by minority shareholders.

### 15.2.3 Directors

S302 provides that the directors may call general meetings.

### 15.2.4 Auditors

S518 CA 2006 provides that an auditor may deposit with a notice of resignation a signed requisition calling on the directors of the company forthwith duly to convene a general meeting of the company for the purpose of receiving and considering such explanation of the circumstances connected with the resignation as the auditor may wish to place before the meeting.

### 15.2.5 Serious loss of capital

The directors of a public company are obliged to call an extraordinary general meeting where the net assets of the company are half or less of its called up share capital (s656 CA 2006).

The directors must call a general meeting of the company to consider what steps, if any, should be taken to deal with the situation. They must do so not later than 28 days from the earliest day on which that fact is known to a director of the company. The meeting must be convenened for a date not later than 56 days from that date.

Failure to convene a meeting as required constitutes an offence by any director who knowingly authorises or permits the failure or after the relevant period knowingly authorises or permits the failure to continue.

## 15.3 Class meetings

In addition to meetings of the company, meetings may also be held of different classes of shareholders. Such meetings may be necessary, for example, to consider a proposed variation of class rights (see section 6.5). Most of the rules that apply in relation to company meetings also apply in relation to class meetings (see ss334–335 CA 2006).

## 15.4 Notice

The Companies Act 2006 lays down periods of notice required for general meetings.

S307 provides the notice required for a general meeting of a private company is at least 14 days notice.

In relation to a public company, the notice required is in the case of an annual general meeting at least 21 days and in any other case at least 14 days (s307(2) CA 2006).

Shorter notice may be agreed to by the members (s307(4)), though this does not apply to an annual general meeting of a public company. In the case of an annual general meeting of a public company, *all* of the members must agree to the giving of short notice (s337(2) CA 2006).

The waiving of short notice must be done purposefully and cannot be done simply by all of the members turning up to the meeting without realising that there should have been a longer period of notice provided to the members: see *Re Pearce Duff (1960)*.

The shorter notice period must be agreed to by a majority in number of the members having the right to attend and vote at the meeting, being a majority who together hold not less than the requisite percentage in nominal value of the shares with a right to attend and vote, or, in the case of a company not having a share capital, together represent not less than the requisite percentage of the total voting rights at that meeting. The requisite percentage is:

(a)  in the case of a private company 90% or such higher percentage (not exceeding 95%) as may be specified in the articles; and
(b)  in the case of a public company, 95% (s307(5) and (6) CA 2006).

Notice may be given in hard copy form, in electronic form or by means of a website (s308 CA 2006).

In relation to a website notice, s309 provides as follows.

The website notification must:

(a)  state that it concerns a notice of a company meeting;
(b)  specify the place, time and date of the meeting; and
(c)  in the case of a public company, state whether the meeting will be an annual general meeting.

The notice must be available on the website throughout the period, beginning with the date of the notification and ending with the conclusion of the meeting (s309(3) CA 2006).

Notices must be sent to every member of the company and every director (s310(1) CA 2006).

In relation to members this includes any person entitled to a share in consequence of death or bankruptcy of a member (s310(2) CA 2006).

The notice of a general meeting of a company must state:

(a)  the time and date of the meeting; and
(b)  the place of the meeting.

Notice of a general meeting of a company must state the general nature of the business to be dealt with at the meeting (s311 CA 2006).

### 15.4.1 Special notice

Where by any provision of the Companies Act special notice is required of a resolution, the resolution is not effective unless notice of the intention to move it has been given to the company at least 28 days before the meeting at which it is moved (s312(1) CA 2006).

The company must, where practicable, give its members notice of any such resolution in the same manner and at the same time as it gives notice of the meeting. If that is not practicable, the company must give its members notice at least 14 days before that meeting:

(a) by advertisement in a newspaper having appropriate circulation; or
(b) in any other manner allowed by the company's articles (s312(2) and (3) CA 2006).

It is provided that if after notice of the intention to move such a resolution has been given to the company, a meeting is called for a date 28 days or less after the notice has been given, the notice is deemed to have been properly given though not given within the time required (s312(4) CA 2006).

### 15.4.2 Accidental failure to give notice

S320 CA 2006 provides for accidental failure to give notice of a resolution or meeting.

Where a company gives notice of:

(a) a general meeting; or
(b) a resolution intended to be moved at a general meeting

any accidental failure to give notice to one or more persons shall be disregarded for the purpose of determining whether notice of the meeting or resolution (as the case may be) is duly given.

It is important to realise the effect of this provision. The accidental failure to send notice where there was an oversight did not render the meeting invalid in *Re West Canadian Collieries Ltd (1962)*. The error arose here because the dividend payment had been made separately to certain members and their addressograph plates had therefore been kept in a separate place. They were, therefore, omitted when notices were sent out. By contrast, the failure to send notice in *Musselwhite v Musselwhite & Son Ltd (1962)* was quite deliberate. It was considered that the members concerned did not have a right to vote at the meeting as they had agreed to sell their shares. This was a genuine mistake but the failure to send notice was deliberate and therefore the meeting was invalid.

### 15.4.3 Members may require statements to be circulated

S314(1) provides that the members of a company may require the company to circulate to members of the company entitled to receive notice of the general meeting a statement of not more than 1000 words with respect to:

(a) a matter referred to in a proposed resolution to be dealt with at that meeting; or
(b) other business to be dealt with at that meeting.

A company is required to circulate a statement if it receives a request to do so from:

(a) members representing at least 5% of the total voting rights of all members who have a relevant right to vote; or
(b) at least 100 members who have a relevant right to vote and hold shares in the company on which there has been paid up an average sum per member of at least £100.

If a company fails to circulate a member's statement under s314, then an offence is committed by every officer of the company who is in default (s315 CA 2006).

The expenses of circulating members' statements need not be paid by the members who requested the circulation of the statement if:

(a) the meeting to which the requests relate is an Annual General Meeting of a public company; and
(b) requests sufficient to require the company to circulate the statement are received before the end of the financial year preceding the meeting (s316(1) CA 2006).

Otherwise the expenses of the company in complying with the section must be paid by the members who requested the circulation unless the company resolves otherwise, and unless the company has previously so resolved, it is not bound to comply with that section unless there is deposited with, or tended to it, not later than one week before the meeting a sum reasonably sufficient to meet its expenses in doing so (s316(2) CA 2006).

A company is not required to circulate a statement under s322 if, on an application by the company or another person who claims to be aggrieved, the court is satisfied that the rights conferred by s314 and that section (s315) are being abused.

The court may order the members who requested the circulation of the statement to pay the whole or part of the company's costs on such an application, even if they are not parties to the application (s317(2) CA 2006).

## 15.5 Quorum at meetings

S318 provides that in the case of a company limited by shares or guarantee, and having only one member, one qualifying person present at a meeting is a quorum (s318(1) CA 2006).

In any other case, subject to the company's articles, two qualifying persons present at a meeting are a quorum, unless:

(a) each is a qualifying person only because he is authorised under s323 to act as the representative of the corporation in relation to the meeting, and they are representatives of the same corporation; or
(b) each is a qualifying person only because he is appointed as proxy of a member in relation to the meeting and they are proxies of the same member (s318(2) CA 2006).

Problems sometimes arise over the matter of a quorum. The *Oxford Concise Dictionary* defines a meeting as an assemblage of persons. This implies that there should be more than one person present and that they should be in each other's physical presence. Each of these features tends to cause problems.

At common law, a meeting must be made up of more than one person. In *Sharp v Dawes (1876)*, a meeting of a stannary mining company governed under the Stannaries Acts (which governed tin mining companies set up in Cornwall) was called for the purpose of making a call on shares. Only one member, Silversides, turned up at the meeting, together with the company secretary who was not a member. Lord Coleridge CJ said in the Court of Appeal '... the word "meeting" *prima facie* means a coming together of more than one person'. The court held that there was no meeting here. Lord Coleridge CJ did acknowledge that on occasion the word 'meeting' could have a different meaning but found there was nothing here to indicate that that was the case.

The same principle applies where one member present has proxies for the other company members: see *Re Sanitary Carbon Company (1877)*. The same principle was applied in *Re London Flats Ltd (1969)*, where all but one member had left the room when the vote was taken. The court held that there could be no meeting. Plowman J considered that there would need to be special circumstances present to displace the usual rule. In *MJ Shanley Contracting Ltd (in voluntary liquidation) (1979)*, the court held there was no meeting where the chairman present at the meeting held a proxy for his wife and had the consent of the other member to voting in favour of voluntary liquidation (although there was no meeting, the decision to put the company into liquidation was upheld on the basis of the assent principle, which is discussed below at para 15.10.5). In the Scottish case of *James Prain & Sons Ltd, petitioners (1947)*, the Court of Session declined to confirm a reduction of capital that had been authorised at a meeting where only one person was present.

This principle that one person cannot constitute a meeting has to give way to certain exceptions.

Sometimes, as has been noted, it is necessary to hold a class meeting, for example to consider a proposed variation of class rights. It may be that there is only one shareholder of the class in question. In these circumstances clearly the quorum for the class meeting cannot be set higher than one: see *East v Bennett Bros (1911)*.

This now also applies in relation to companies which only have one member (s318(1) CA 2006).

As noted above (section 15.2.2), under s306 of the CA 1985, the court may order an extraordinary general meeting to be held and may fix the quorum at one. In *Re El Sombrero Ltd (1958)*, the company had three members. The applicant had 90% of the shares and he wished to remove the other two shareholders as directors. They held 5% of the shares each. They refused to attend meetings where this was to be proposed. The applicant, therefore, applied to the court for a meeting to be ordered under s306 and for the quorum to be fixed at one. This was done. The decision in *Re El Sombrero Ltd* was followed in *Re HR Paul & Son (1973)*. In this case, the matter at issue was not the removal of directors but the alteration of the articles where the majority shareholder wished to alter the articles and the minority shareholders were blocking his wishes. In *Re Sticky Fingers Restaurant Ltd (1992)*, deadlock in a small private company was again featured. The restaurant was owned jointly by Bill Wyman of Rolling Stones fame and a Mr Mitchell. Wyman owned 66 shares and Mitchell owned 34. Wyman sought to remove Mitchell under s168 but Mitchell refused to attend meetings. Mitchell was also petitioning under s994 of the Act. Wyman sought an order under s306 of the Act requiring a meeting to be convened at which the quorum could be fixed at one. The court ordered this, subject to the proviso that any outcome of such a meeting would be stayed until the s994 matter had been resolved.

Problems relating to quorum abound. On occasion, the acquiescence of those entitled to attend a meeting is sufficient to validate the action taken.

*Hood Sailmakers v Axford and Another (1997)* involved a board meeting which purported to make pension arrangements for the company. A and B, two directors, sought their share of a pension fund from the company following their dismissal. The company resisted on the ground that A had changed the pension arrangements by written resolution following a board meeting of which no notice had been given to the then only other director, H. (H was succeeded by W and B.) H resided in the USA and played no part in the management of the company.

The Pensions Ombudsman held that the resolutions were valid under reg 106, Table A of the Companies Act 1948, since they were in writing and all directors entitled to receive notice had done so (H was not so entitled as he was abroad). The Pensions Ombudsman so held despite the fact that reg 99 provides for a quorum of two directors.

The Queen's Bench Division dismissed the appeal. Written resolutions made at board meetings which did not meet the quorum requirements were invalid. However, W had acquiesced in the new pension scheme so that it was unconscionable for the company to deny the validity of the resolutions.

A second problem referred to in relation to a quorum at a meeting is the matter of whether a meeting can be held where members are not in each other's physical presence. This becomes a very real problem in a time of technological change and given the possibility of video and audio link ups. In *Re Associated Color Laboratories (1970)*, a Canadian decision held that it was not possible to hold a meeting by telephone link between California and Vancouver. McDonald J took the view that a meeting meant that the participants were in each other's presence. The decision was, however, reversed by s109(9) of the Canada Business Corporations Act. In Britain, *Byng v London Life Association Ltd (1990)* considered the matter of the audio and visual link system of holding meetings. The court held that a meeting may be validly held even though people at the meeting are not together in the same room where there is some audio visual link up. The decision seems a sensible one.

## 15.6 Chairman

A member may be elected to be chairman of a general meeting by a resolution of the company passed at the meeting (s319(1) CA 2006).

On a vote on a resolution at a meeting on a show of hands, a declaration by the chairman that the resolution:

(a) has or has not been passed; or
(b) passed with a particular majority

is conclusive evidence of that fact without proof of the number or proportion of the votes recorded in favour of or against a resolution (s320(1) CA 2006).

## 15.7 Polls

A provision of a company's articles is void insofar as it would have the effect of excluding the right to demand a poll at a general meeting on any question other than:

(a) the election of the chairman; or
(b) the adjournment of the meeting (s321(1) CA 2006).

A provision of a company's articles is void insofar as it would have the effect of making ineffective a demand for a poll on any such question which is made:

(a) by not less than 5 members having the right to vote on the resolution; or
(b) by a member or members representing not less than 10% of the total voting rights of all the members having the right to vote on the resolution; or
(c) by a member or members holding shares in the company conferring a right to vote on the resolution being shares on which an aggregate sum has been

paid up equal to not less than 10% of the total sum paid up on all the shares conferring that right (s321(2) CA 2006).

S322 provides for voting on a poll. On a poll taken at a general meeting of a company, a member entitled to more than one vote need not, if he votes, use all his votes or cast all the votes he uses in the same way.

S323 CA 2006 provides for representation of corporations at meetings.

## 15.8 Proxies

S324 provides for the right to appoint proxies. A member of a company is entitled to appoint another person as his proxy to exercise all or any of his rights to attend, speak and vote at a meeting of the company.

In the case of a company with share capital, a member may appoint more than one proxy in relation to a meeting, provided that each proxy is appointed to exercise the rights attached to a different share or shares held by him or (as the case may be) to a different £10 or multiples of £10 of stock held by him (s324(2) CA 2006).

In every notice calling a meeting of a company there must appear, with reasonable prominence, a statement informing a member of his rights under s324, and any more extensive rights conferred by the company's articles to appoint more than one proxy (s325 CA 2006).

S326 CA 2006 provides that if there are issued at the company expense invitations to members to appoint as proxy a specified person or a number of specified persons, the invitations must be issued to all members entitled to vote at the meeting.

The notice required of the appointment of a proxy is dealt with in s327. Any provision in the company's articles is void insofar as it would have the effect of requiring any such appointment or document to be received by the company or another person earlier than the following time:

(a) in the case of a meeting or adjourned meeting, 48 hours before the time for the holding of the meeting or adjourned meeting;
(b) in the case of a poll taken more than 48 hours after it was demanded, 24 hours before the time appointed for the taking of the poll;
(c) in the case of a poll taken not more than 48 hours after it was demanded, the time at which it was demanded (s327(2) CA 2006).

In calculating the periods, no account should be taken of any part of a day that is not a working day.

S328 provides that a proxy may be elected to be the chairman of the general meeting by a resolution of the company passed at the meeting subject to any provision of the company's articles which states who may or may not be chairman.

The appointment of a proxy to vote on a matter at a meeting of a company authorises the proxy to demand or join in demanding a poll on that matter (s329 CA 2006).

In relation to termination of a proxy's authority, unless the company receives notice of the termination before the commencement of the meeting it does not affect:

(a)  whether he counts in deciding whether there is a quorum at a meeting;
(b)  the validity of anything he does as chairman of the meeting;
(c)  the validity of a poll demanded by him at a meeting.

The termination of authority does not affect the validity of a vote given by that person unless the company receives notice of the termination:

(a)  before the commencement of the meeting or adjourned meeting at which the vote is given; or
(b)  in the case of a poll taken more than 48 hours after it was demanded before the time appointed for taking the poll (s330 CA 2006).

S331 provides that nothing in the Act prevents a company's articles from conferring more extensive rights on members or proxies than are conferred by the Act.

## 15.9 Electronic communications

S340 provides that where a company has given an electronic address in a notice calling a meeting it is deemed to have agreed that any document or information relating to proceedings at the meeting may be sent by electronic means to that address.

## 15.10 Resolutions

The Companies Act lays down stringent rules in relation to resolutions.

S281 of the Companies Act 2006 deals with resolutions.

S281(1) provides that a resolution of the members or a class of members of a private company must be passed:

(a)  as a written resolution in accordance with Chapter 2 of Part 12 of the Act; or
(b)  at a meeting of the members (see Chapter 3 of Part 12 of the Act).

S281(2) provides that a resolution of the members or a class of members of a *public company* must be passed at a meeting of the members.

### 15.10.1 Ordinary resolutions

S282 CA 2006 deals with ordinary resolutions. An ordinary resolution is defined as one that is passed by a simple majority.

S282(2) provides that a written resolution is passed by a simple majority if it is passed by members representing a simple majority of the total voting rights of eligible members.

S282(3) provides that a resolution is passed at a meeting on a show of hands if it is passed by a simple majority of:

(a)  the members who, being entitled to do so, vote in person on the resolution, and
(b)  the persons who vote on the resolution as duly appointed proxies of members entitled to vote on it.

S282(4) provides that a resolution passed on a poll taken at a meeting is passed by a simple majority if it is passed by members representing a simple majority of the total voting rights of members who vote in person or by proxy on the resolution.

### 15.10.2 Special resolutions

S283 provides that a special resolution of the members or a class of members of a company means a resolution passed by a majority of not less than 75%.

S283(2) provides a written resolution is passed by a majority of not less than 75% if it is passed by members representing not less than 75% of the total voting rights of eligible members. (As noted in section 15.10.4, this is not available to public companies.)

S283(3) provides that where a resolution of a private company is passed as a written resolution:

(a)  the resolution is not a special resolution unless it stated that it was proposed as a special resolution; and
(b)  if the resolution so stated, it may only be passed as a special resolution.

S283(4) provides that a resolution passed at a meeting on a show of hands is passed by a majority of not less than 75% if it is passed by not less than 75% of:

(a)  the members who, being entitled to do so, vote in person on the resolution; and
(b)  the persons who vote on the resolution as duly appointed proxies of members entitled to vote on it.

S283(5) provides that a resolution passed on a poll taken at a meeting is passed by a majority of not less than 75% if it is passed by members representing not less than 75% of the total voting rights of the members who (being entitled to do so) vote in person or by proxy on the resolution.

Extraordinary resolutions have been abolished by the Companies Act 2006. It should also be noted that special resolutions no longer require 21 days notice (s283 CA 2006).

### 15.10.3 Votes on resolutions

S284 CA 2006 provides for the position in relation to the general legal position on votes.

S284(1) provides that on a vote on a written resolution:

(a) in case of a company having a share capital, every member has one vote in respect of each share or each £10 worth of stock held by him; and
(b) in any other case every member has one vote.

S284(2) provides that on a vote on a resolution on a show of hands at a meeting:

(a) every member present in person has one vote; and
(b) every proxy present who has been duly appointed by a member entitled to vote on a resolution also has one vote.

S284(3) provides that on a vote on a resolution on a poll taken at a meeting:

(a) in the case of a company having a share capital, every member has one vote in respect of each share or each £10 of stock held by him; and
(b) in any other case, every member has one vote.

S284(4) provides that this is all subject to any provision of the company's articles (which could provide for weighted voting).

S285(1) provides that where a member entitled to vote on a resolution has appointed one proxy only, and the company's articles provide that the proxy has fewer votes in a vote on a resolution on a show of hands taken at a meeting than the member would have if he were present in person:

(a) the provision about how many votes the proxy has on a show of hands is void; and
(b) the proxy has the same number of votes on a show of hands as the member who appointed him would have if he were present at the meeting.

S285(2) provides that where a member has appointed more than one proxy, sub-section 1 above applies as if the references to the proxy were references to the proxies taken together.

In a similar fashion in relation to a resolution required or authorised by an enactment, if a private company's articles provide that a member has a different number of votes in relation to a resolution, when it is passed as a written resolution, and when it is passed on a poll taken at a meeting:

(a) the provision about how many votes a member has in relation to the resolution passed on a poll is void; and
(b) a member has the same number of votes in relation to the resolution when it is passed on a poll as he has when it is passed as a written resolution (s285(3)).

### 15.10.4 Written resolutions

S288 CA2006 provides in relation to written resolutions of private companies.
Certain resolutions may not be passed as written resolutions:

(a) a resolution under s168 removing a director before the expiration of his period of office;
(b) a resolution under s510 removing an auditor before the expiration of his term of office (s288(2)).

S288(3) provides a resolution may be proposed as a written resolution:

(a) by the directors of a private company (s291); or
(b) by the members of a private company (ss292–295).

Eligible members are those in relation to a resolution proposed as a written resolution, who would have been entitled to vote on the resolution on the circulation date of the resolution (s289).

S291 provides in relation to circulation of written resolutions proposed by directors.

S291(2) provides the company must send or submit a copy of the resolution to every eligible member.

The copy of the resolution must be accompanied by a statement informing the member:

(a) how to signify agreement to the resolution (s296); and
(b) as to the date by which the resolution must be passed if it is not to lapse (s297).

In the event of default in complying with this section, an offence is committed by every officer who is in default (s291(5)).

S292 provides that members of a private company may require the company to circulate a resolution that may properly be moved and is proposed to be moved as a written resolution (s292(1)).

Resolutions may be moved as written resolutions unless:

(a) it would, if passed, be ineffective whether by reason of inconsistency with any enactment or the company's constitution or otherwise;
(b) it is defamatory of any person;
(c) it is frivolous or vexatious (s292(2)).

Where the members require a company to circulate a resolution they may require the company to circulate with it a statement of not more than 1000 words on the subject matter of the resolution (s292(3)).

A company is required to circulate the resolution and any accompanying statement once it has received requests that it is to do so from members not representing not less than the requisite percentage of the total voting rights of all members entitled to vote on the resolution (s292(4)).

The requisite percentage is 5% or such lower percentage as is specified for this purpose in the company's articles (s292(5)).

S293 provides that a company that is required under s292 to circulate a resolution must send or submit to every eligible member:

(a)  a copy of the resolution; and
(b)  a copy of any accompanying statements.

S295(1) provides that a company is not required to circulate a member's statement under s293 if, on an application by the company or another person who claims to be aggrieved, the court is satisfied that the rights conferred by s292 and that section are being abused.

S296 provides the procedure for signifying agreement to a written resolution. A member signifies agreement when the company receives from him an authenticated document:

(a)  identifying the resolution to which it relates; and
(b)  indicating his agreement to the resolution.

The document must be sent to the company in hard copy form or in electronic form. A member's agreement to a written resolution, once signified, may not be revoked.

S297 provides the period for agreeing to a written resolution proposed as a written resolution lapses if it is not passed before the end of:

(a)  the period specified for this purpose in the company's articles; or
(b)  if none is specified the period of 28 days beginning with the circulation date.

The agreement of a member to a written resolution is ineffective if signified after the expiry of that period (s297).

S298 provides for the sending of documents relating to written resolutions by electronic means.

S299 provides for the publication of a written resolution on a website. The section applies where a company sends:

(a)  a written resolution; or
(b)  a statement relating to a written resolution to a person by means of a website.

S299(2) provides that the resolution or statement is not validly sent for the purposes of this part of the act unless the resolution is available on the website throughout the period, beginning with the circulation date and ending on the date on which the resolution lapses under s297.

It is now possible for private though not public companies to pass written resolutions by the same majority that they would be passed at actual meetings. Thus written resolutions will require only a simple majority in the case of an ordinary resolution, or 75% if a special resolution is required.

### 15.10.5 De facto resolutions – the assent principle

Quite independently of the Companies Act 2006, on occasion the courts have been willing to recognise certain acts, irrespective of the fact that no proper meeting has been called on the basis of the company's unanimous consent. Thus, in *Re Express Engineering Works Ltd (1920)*, where all the members agreed at a board meeting rather than at a general meeting, the assent principle was applied.

The principle has also been applied in *Parker and Cooper Ltd v Reading (1926)*, *Re Bailey Hay & Co Ltd (1971)* and *Cane v Jones (1980)*. The position has not been uniform, though, and in some cases the courts have been unwilling to recognise the unanimous assent of members as a substitute for a resolution at a meeting: see *Re Barry Artists Ltd (1985)*. The written resolution procedure makes this principle of less significance but it may remain important, particularly for public companies.

### 15.10.6 Records of resolutions and meetings, etc

S355 CA 2006 provides that every company must keep records comprising copies of all resolutions, minutes of all proceedings of general meetings, and details provided to the company in accordance with s357 (decision of the sole member). The records must be kept for at least 10 years from the date of the resolution, meeting or decision as appropriate (s355 (2) CA 2006).

It is provided in s356 that where there is a record of a resolution or of minutes of proceedings of a general meeting, then the record of a resolution passed otherwise than at a general meeting, if purported to be signed by a director of the company or by the company secretary, is evidence of the passing of the resolution.

Where there is a record of a written resolution of a private company, the requirements of the Act with respect to the passing of the resolution are deemed to be complied with unless the contrary is proved, and the minutes of proceedings of the general meeting, if purported to be signed by the chairman of that meeting or by the chairman of the next general meeting, are evidence of the proceedings at the meeting.

Where there is a record of proceedings of a general meeting, then until the contrary is proved, the meeting is deemed duly held and convened, the proceedings are deemed to have duly taken place, and all appointments at the meeting are deemed valid (s356).

S357 deals with records of decisions by a sole member. Where the member takes any decision that may be taken by the company in a general meeting and has effect as if agreed by the company in a general meeting, then he must provide the company with details of the decision. Failure to do so is an offence (s357 CA 2006).

The company must, at all times, keep available for inspection records of resolutions, etc relating to the previous 10 years and open those records to inspection by any member without charge. Any member is entitled, on payment of such fee as may be prescribed, to be furnished with a copy of any of those records (s358 CA 2006).

### 15.10.7 Amendments

Resolutions may be amended at the meeting provided that the amendment is within the general notice of the business that has been sent out to members. This principle does not apply if the resolution has to be set out verbatim. In the case of extraordinary and special resolutions, no amendment can be permitted which alters the substance of the resolution contained in the notice: see *Re Moorgate Mercantile Holdings Ltd (1980)*. An amendment to a resolution would be permitted to resolve an ambiguity or to correct a grammatical mistake without the notice usually necessary.

If the chairman improperly rejects an amendment and the unamended resolution is then passed, that resolution is then invalid: see *Henderson v Bank of Australasia (1890)*.

Where amendments are proposed, the amendment is first put to the vote. If that is passed the amended resolution is then voted upon.

## 15.11 Additional requirements for quoted companies

There are additional requirements for quoted companies.

S341 provides that where a poll is taken at a general meeting of a quoted company, the company must ensure that the following information is made available on a website:

(a) the date of the meeting;
(b) the text of the resolution or, as the case may be, a description of the subject matter of the poll;
(c) the number of votes cast in favour;
(d) the number of votes cast against.

S353 provides that the information must be made available on a website that is maintained by, or on behalf of, the company and identified as the company in question.

Access to the information on the website and the ability to obtain a hard copy of the information from the website must not be conditional on the payment of a fee or otherwise restricted, and the information must be made available as soon as is reasonably practicable and must be kept available throughout the period of two years, beginning with the date on which it is first made available on a website in accordance with this section.

S342 CA 2006 provides that members of a quoted company may require the directors to obtain an independent report on any poll taken or to be taken at a general meeting of a company.

The directors are required to obtain an independent report if they receive requests from:

(a) members representing not less than 5% of the total voting rights of all the members who have a right to vote on the matter; or

(b) not less than 100 members who have a right to vote on the matter to which the poll relates and hold shares of the company on which there has been paid up on average not less than £100 per member.

A request may be made in hard copy or in electronic form, and must identify the poll or polls to which it relates and must be authenticated by the person or persons making it, and must be received by the company not later than one week after the date on which the poll is taken.

S343 provides that directors who are required under s342 to obtain an independent report must appoint a person they consider to be appropriate (an independent assessor) to prepare a report for the company on it or them. The appointment must be made within a week after the company being required to obtain the report. The directors must not appoint a person:

(a) who does not meet the independent requirement (s344) or

(b) who has another role in relation to any poll on which he is to report (including in particular a role in connection with collecting or counting votes or with the appointment of proxies).

S344 CA 2006 provides that a person may not be appointed as an independent assessor if he is an officer or employer of the company, or a partner or employee of such a person, or a partnership of which such a person is a partner, or if he is an officer or employer of an associated undertaking of a company or a partner or employee or such a person or a partnership of which such a person is a partner. However, an auditor of a company is not regarded as an officer or an employer of the company for this purpose. S345 and s346 deals further with the application of the independence requirement.

S347 provides for an independent assessor's report which must state whether:

(a) the procedures adopted in connection with the poll or polls are adequate;

(b) whether the votes cast including proxy votes were fairly and accurately recorded and counted;

(c) whether the issue of the validity of members' appointed proxies was fairly assessed;

(d) whether the notice of the meeting complied with the relevant requirements; and

(e) whether s326 in relation to company's sponsored invitations to appoint proxies was complied with in relation to the meeting.

If he is unable to form an opinion on any of these matters, the report must record that fact and state the reasons for it. The report must state the name of the independent assessor (s347 CA 2006).

An independent assessor who has been appointed to report on a poll is entitled to attend the meeting at which the poll is taken and any subsequent proceedings in connection with the poll (s348 CA 2006). He is also entitled to be provided by the company with a copy of the notice and any other communication relating to it.

S349 provides that the independent assessor is entitled to access the company's records relating to any poll on which he is to report and the meeting at which the poll or polls may be or were taken.

He can require anyone who, at any time, was a director, secretary of the company, employee or accountable for the company's records, a member of the company or agent of the company, to provide him with relevant information of explanations for the purpose of preparing his report.

A person who fails to comply with a requirement under s349, unless it was not reasonably practicable for him to provide the relevant information, commits an offence (s350 CA 2006).

Where an independent assessor has been appointed to report on a poll the company must ensure that the following information is made available on a website: the fact of his appointment, his identity, the text of the resolution that he is looking at, and a copy of any report by him (s351 CA 2006).

The provisions relating to results of a poll to be made available on a website by a quoted company (s341) and the provision of an independent report on a poll (ss342–351) apply in relation to class proceedings mutatis mutandis. (Ss352–353 CA 2006.)

## SUMMARY

## Company meetings

### Meetings

Public companies must hold annual general meetings, private companies need not do so. Companies may hold general meetings between annual general meetings.

The Companies Act 2006 and the company's articles set out the rules which companies must follow.

## Notice

The minimum period of notice is 21 days' notice for annual general meetings of public companies, and for other general meetings 14 days' notice if the company is limited. On occasion, short notice may be sufficient.

Notices must go to members and directors.

## Chairman

The company's articles will generally specify who is to act as chairman. In the event that the articles make no provision, the members must act to fill the vacuum and elect one of their number.

The chairman's role is to take the meeting through the agenda, put matters to the vote and keep order.

## Quorum

The rules on quorum are generally set out in the company's articles. They must be followed to the letter, although if members are deliberately boycotting meetings then the Secretary of State may seek the calling of an annual meeting with a lower quorum or there may be an application to the court for the holding of an extraordinary general meeting with a lower quorum.

## Resolutions

If a special resolution is to be put to the vote at a meeting, then it should be set out verbatim in the notice as should any amendment. In practice, ordinary resolutions are also set out verbatim in the notice. Any substantive amendment should also be set out in the notice.

There are provisions to permit private companies to resolve matters by written resolutions without the need for a meeting.

## Votes

Initially, a vote is taken on a show of hands. This is not conclusive of the matter, however, except in two instances where the articles may state that a vote on a show of hands is decisive – namely, election of the chairman and adjournment of the meeting. In every other circumstance, a poll may be demanded by not less than five members or by members representing 10% of the voting rights, or by members holding shares in the company conferring a right to vote at the meeting being shares on which an aggregate sum has been paid up equal to not less than 10% of the total sum paid up on all the shares conferring that right.

Where a vote is taken on a poll, the outcome overrides the outcome on a show of hands.

## Proxies

A member entitled to attend and vote at a meeting of a company with share capital may appoint somebody else to attend and vote in his place as a proxy. The notice sent to members must set out their right to appoint a proxy.

The proxy may speak.

## Adjournment

The chairman of the meeting may adjourn the meeting if it is appropriate to do so – for example, to preserve order – and he must do so if so directed by the company.

## Minutes

Companies must cause minutes and records of resolutions of general meetings to be kept.

## Quoted companies

Additional requirements apply to quoted companies in relation to the publication of poll results on a website and the right of members to require an independent report on a poll taken at a general meeting.

## Further reading

Baker, C, 'Amending special resolutions' (1991) 12 Co Law 64.
Birds, JR, 'The deregulation provisions of the Companies Act 1989' (1990) 11 Co Law 142.
Grantham, R, 'The unanimous consent rule in company law' [1993] CLJ 245.
Higginson, HW, 'Written resolutions of private companies' (1993) 109 LQR 16.
Jaffey, P, 'Contractual obligations of the company in general meeting' (1996) 16 LS 27.

# Accounts and returns

## 16.1 Accounts and reports

Part 15 of the 2006 Act deals with accounts and reports. S380 provides that this part of the Act applies to accounts and reports in relation to each financial year of a company.

### 16.1.1 Accounting records

S386 provides that every company must keep adequate accounting records. This means accounting records that are sufficient:

(a) to show and explain the company's transactions;
(b) to disclose with reasonable accuracy, at any time, the financial position of the company at that time;
(c) to enable the directors to ensure that any accounts required to be prepared comply with the requirements of the Act (and, where applicable, of Article 4 of the IAS Regulation).

The accounting records must contain entries from day to day of sums received and expended, and a record of the assets and liabilities of the company.

If the company's business involves dealing in goods, the accounting records must contain statements of stock held by the company at the end of each financial year, statements of stock takings and, excepting goods sold by way of ordinary retail trade, statements of goods sold and purchased.

If a company fails to comply with the provisions of s386 then every officer of the company in default is liable.

S388 provides that accounting records must be kept at the company's registered office or such other place as the directors may think fit, and must, at all times, be open to inspection by the company's officers. In the case of a private company, they must be kept for three years, and in the case of a public company, for six years from the date on which they were made.

S389 provides that failure to comply with maintenance of the records for these periods results in liability on every officer of the company in default.

### 16.1.2 Small companies

S381 relates to companies that are subject to the small companies regime. Companies that are subject to the small companies regime are sometimes treated differently, e.g. they are not subject to s399 (duty to prepare group accounts), and are, subject to s477, exempt from audit. The small companies regime for accounts and reports applies to companies for the financial year in relation to which the company:

(a) qualifies as small (ss382–383); and
(b) is not excluded from the regime (s384).

A small company qualifies as small in its first financial year if it fulfils the following qualifications:
  It must fulfil two or more of the following requirements:

1.  Turnover of not more than £5.6m.
2.  Balance sheet total not more than £2.8m.
3.  Number of employees not more than 50 (s382).

S383 provides further that a parent company qualifies as a small company in relation to a financial year only if the group headed by it qualifies as a small group.

(a) a company qualifies as small in relation to a subsequent financial year if the qualifying conditions are met in that year and the preceeding year;
(b) if the qualifying conditions are met in that year and the company qualified as small in relation to the preceeding financial year;
(c) if the qualifying conditions were met in the preceding financial year and the company qualified as small in relation to that year.

A group qualifies as a small group in relation to the parent company's first financial year if the qualifying conditions are met in that year. These are that the group must satisfy two or more of the following requirements:

1.  Aggregate turnover of not more than £5.6m net or £6.72m gross.
2.  Aggregate balance sheet of not more than £2.8m net or £3.36m gross.
3.  Aggregate number of employees not more than 50.

Net means after any set offs and other adjustments made to eliminate group transactions, gross means without those set offs and other adjustments.
  A group qualifies as small in relation to a subsequent financial year of the parent company:

(a) if the qualifying conditions are met in that year and the preceding financial year;
(b) if the qualifying conditions are met in that year and the group qualified as small in relation to the preceding financial year;

(c) if the qualifying conditions were met in the preceding financial year and the group qualified as small in relation to that year.

S384 provides that certain companies are excluded from the small companies regime. The small companies regime does not apply to a company that is, or was, at any time within the financial year to which the accounts relate:

(a) a public company;
(b) a company that

    (i) is an authorised insurance company, a banking company, an e-money issuer, an ISD investment firm or a UCITS management company, or
    (ii) carries on insurance market activity, or

(c) is a member of an ineligible group.

A group in ineligible if any of its members is:

(a) a public company;
(b) a body corporate (other than a company) whose shares are admitted to trading on a regulated market in an EEA state;
(c) a person who has permission under Part 4 of the Financial Services and Markets Act 2000 to carry on a regulated activity; or
(d) a small company that is an authorised insurance company, a banking company, an e-money issuer, an ISD investment firm or a UCITS management company; or
(e) a person who carries on insurance market activity.

### 16.1.3 Medium sized companies

S465 provides that a company qualifies as medium sized in relation to its first financial year if the qualifying conditions set out in s465 (3) are met (see below).
    It qualifies as a medium sized company in relation to a subsequent financial year if:

(a) the qualifying conditions are met in that year and the preceding financial year;
(b) if the qualifying conditions are met in that year and the company qualified as medium sized in relation to the preceding financial year;
(c) if the qualifying conditions were met in the preceding financial year and the company qualified as medium sized in relation to that year.

S465(3) provides that the qualifying conditions that must be satisfied by a company are two or more of the following requirements:

1. Turnover not more than £22.8m.
2. Balance sheet total not more than £11.4m.
3. Number of employees not more than 250.

S466 defines the companies that qualify as medium sized companies where they are parent companies.

S466(1) provides a parent company qualifies as a medium sized company in relation to a financial year only if the group headed by it qualifies as a medium sized group.

A group qualifies as medium sized in relation to the parent company's first financial year if the qualifying conditions are met in that year, and the group qualifies as medium sized in relation to a subsequent financial year of the parent company:

(a) if the qualifying conditions are met in that year and the preceding financial year;
(b) if the qualifying conditions are met in that year and the group qualified as medium sized in relation to the preceding financial year;
(c) if the qualifying conditions were met in the preceding financial year and the group qualified as a medium size in relation to that year.

The qualifying conditions which must be satisfied to at least two of the three, are as follows:

1. Aggregate turnover not more than £22.8m net (or £27.36m gross).
2. Aggregate balance sheet not more than £11.4m net (or £13.68m gross).
3. Aggregate number of employees not more than 250.

S467 deals with certain companies that are excluded from being treated as medium sized.

A company is not entitled to take advantage of the provisions of this part of the Act if it is:

(a) a public company
(b) a company that

    (i) has permission under Part 4 of the Financial Services and Markets Act 2000 to carry on a regulated activity; or
    (ii) carries on insurance market activity; or

(c) a member of an ineligible group.

A group is ineligible if any of its members is:

(a) a public company;
(b) a body corporate other than a company whose shares are admitted to trading on a regulated market;
(c) a person other than a small company who has permission under Part 4 of the Financial Services and Markets Act 2000 to carry on a regulated activity;

(d)  a small company that is an authorised insurance company, a banking company, an e-money issuer, an ISD investment firm, or a UCITS management company, or

(e)  a person who carries on insurance market activity.

Medium sized companies enjoy certain exceptions in relation to the links obligations (s445 CA 2006).

### 16.1.4  Quoted and unquoted companies

Quoted and unquoted companies are defined in s385.

For the purposes of Part 15 of the Act, a company is a quoted company in relation to a financial year if it is a quoted company immediately before the end of the accounting reference period by reference to which that financial year was determined.

A quoted company means a company whose equity share capital:

(a)  has been included in the official list in accordance with the provisions of Part 6 of the Financial Services and Markets Act 2000; or

(b)  is officially listed in an EEA state; or

(c)  is admitted to dealing on either the New York Stock Exchange or the exchange known as Nasdaq.

An unquoted company is a company that is not quoted (s385(3) CA 2006). Quoted companies are sometimes subject to additional rules, e.g. s420 (duty to prepare directors' remuneration report), s428 (form and contents of summary financial statement: quoted companies).

### 16.1.5  A company's financial year

S390 deals with a company's financial year. A company's first financial year begins with the first day of its first accounting reference period and ends with the last day of that period, or a date not more than seven days before or after it, as the directors may determine.

Subsequent financial years begin with the day immediately following the end of the previous financial year, and end with the last day of the next accounting reference period or such other date not more than seven days before or after the end of that period, as the directors may determine.

The company's accounting reference period is determined according to its accounting reference date in each calendar year (s391).

S392 provides for alteration of a company's accounting reference date. This may be done by giving notice to the registrar specifying a new accounting reference date, having effect in relation to:

(a)  the company's current accounting reference period and subsequent periods; or

(b)  the company's previous accounting reference period and subsequent periods.

The notice must state whether the current or previous accounting reference period is to be shortened or extended, and a notice extending a company's current or previous accounting reference period is not effective if given less than five years after the end of an earlier accounting reference period of the company that was extended under this section.

A company's accounting reference period may not be extended so as to exceed 18 months, and a notice under this section is ineffective if the current or previous accounting reference period as extended in accordance with the notice would exceed that limit.

## 16.2 Annual accounts

S393 of the Companies Act 2006 provides that the directors of a company must not approve accounts for the purposes of the Act unless they are satisfied that they give a true and fair view of the assets, liabilities, financial position and profit or loss:

(a) in the case of a company's individual accounts, of the company;
(b) in the case of a company's group accounts of the undertakings included in the consolidation as a whole, so far as concerns members of the company.

It is further provided that the auditor of a company in carrying out his functions under the Act must have regard to the directors' duty under the section.

### 16.2.1 Individual accounts

S394 provides that the directors of every company must prepare accounts for the company for each financial year. These accounts are referred to as the company's individual accounts.

S395 sets out the appropriate accounting framework for the accounts, and s396 provides that individual accounts must comprise:

(a) a balance sheet as at the last day of the financial year; and
(b) a profit and loss account.

The accounts must, in the case of the balance sheet:

(a) give a true and fair view of the state of affairs of the company as at the end of the financial year;
(b) in the case of the profit and loss account, give a true and fair view of the profit or loss of the company for the financial year.

### 16.2.2 Group accounts

S399 provides that companies not subject to the small companies regime are liable to prepare group accounts if the company is part of a group.

S400 provides that a company is exempt from the requirement to prepare group accounts if it is itself a subsidiary undertaking and its immediate parent undertaking is established under the law of an EEA state in the following cases:

(a) where the company is a wholly owned subsidiary of that parent undertaking;
(b) where that parent undertaking holds more than 50% of the allotted shares in the company and notice requesting the preparation of group accounts has not been served on the company by shareholders holding in aggregate

  (i) more than half of the remaining allotted shares in the company; or
  (ii) 5% of the total allotted shares in the company.

Additionally, the company, in order to be able to claim exemption:

(a) must be included in consolidated accounts for a larger group drawn up to the same date or to an earlier date in the same financial year by a parent undertaking established under the law of an EEA state;
(b) those accounts must be drawn up and audited and that parent undertaking's annual report must be drawn up according to that law:

  (i) in accordance with the provisions of the Seventh Directive as modified where relevant by the provisions of the Bank Accounts Directive or the Insurance Accounts Directive; or
  (ii) in accordance with international accounting standards.

S401 provides that a company is exempt from the requirement to prepare group accounts if it is itself a subsidiary undertaking and its parent undertaking is not established under the law of an EEA state in the following cases:

(a) where the company is a wholly owned subsidiary of that parent undertaking;
(b) where that parent undertaking holds more than 50% of the allotted shares in the company and notice requesting the preparation of group accounts has not been served on the company by shareholders holding in aggregate

  (i) more than half of the remaining allotted shares in the company; or
  (ii) 5% of the total allotted shares in the company.

S402 provides that a parent company is exempt from the requirement to prepare group accounts if under s405 all of its subsidiary undertakings could be excluded from consolidation in Companies Act group accounts.

S403 sets out the applicable accounting framework for group accounts, and s404 provides that the group accounts must comprise a consolidated balance sheet and a consolidated profit and loss account.

S405 provides that subsidiary undertakings may be excluded from consolidation if the inclusion is not material for the purpose of giving a true and fair view (two or more undertakings may be excluded only if they are not material taken together), or if severe long-term restrictions substantially hinder the exercise of the parent company's rights over the assets or the management of that undertaking.

Furthermore, subsidiaries are exempted from inclusion if the information can only be acquired at disproportionate expense or undue delay. Subsidiaries are also excluded if the parent company's interest is only held with a view to subsequent resale.

S407 provides that the directors of a parent company must secure that the individual accounts of:

(a)  the parent company; and
(b)  each of its subsidiary undertakings

are all prepared using the same financial reporting framework, except to the extent that in their opinion there are good reasons for not doing so.

### 16.2.3 Notes to the accounts

Ss409–410 provide that the Secretary of State may make provision by regulations requiring information about related undertakings to be given in notes to a company's annual accounts.

S411 provides that information about employee numbers and costs must be included in notes to the company's accounts except in the case of companies that are subject to the small companies regime.

The information given should show the average number of persons employed by the company in the financial year and the average number of persons so employed within each category of persons employed by the company.

S412 provides that the Secretary of State may make provision by regulations requiring information to be given in notes to the company's annual accounts about directors' remuneration. Such a requirement extends to persons connected with a director or a body corporate controlled by a director.

S413 provides that in the case of a company that does not prepare group accounts, details of advances and credits granted by the company to its directors and guarantees of any kind entered into by the company on behalf of its directors must be shown in the notes to its individual accounts. In the case of a parent company that prepares group accounts, details of advances and credits and guarantees must be shown in the notes to the group accounts. The details required of an advance or credit include the amount, the interest rate, the conditions and any amounts repaid. In relation to guarantees, the details required include the main terms, the amount of the maximum liability that may be incurred, any amount paid and any liability incurred by the company for the purpose of fulfilling the guarantee.

S408 provides that where notes to the company's individual balance sheet show the company's profit or loss for the financial year, and the companies concerned prepare group accounts, then there is no need to supply the information specified in s411 (employee numbers and costs).

### 16.2.4 Approval of the accounts

S414 provides that a company's annual accounts must be approved by the board of directors and signed on behalf of the board by a director of the company. The signature must be on the company's balance sheet.

## 16.3  Directors' report

The directors of a company must prepare a directors' report for each financial year (s415).

If the company is a parent company, and the directors of the company prepare group accounts, the directors' report must be a consolidated report relating to the undertakings included in the consolidation.

The directors' report for the financial year must state the names of the persons who, during the financial year, were directors of the company, and the principal activities of the company in the course of the year (s416).

Unless the company is subject to the small companies regime, the directors, report must contain a business review (s417). The business review must contain a fair review of the company's business and a description of the principal risks and uncertainties facing the company.

The review requires a balanced and comprehensive analysis of:

(a)  the development and performance of the company's business during the financial year; and
(b)  the position of the company's business at the end of the year

consistent with the size and complexity of the business.

In the case of a quoted company, the business review must, to the extent necessary for an undertaking of the development, performance or position of the company's business include:

(a)  the main trends and factors likely to affect the future development, performance and position of the company's business; and
(b)  information about

(i)  environmental matters, including the impact of the company's business on the environment,
(ii)  the company's employees, and
(iii)  social and community issues

including information about any policies of the company in relation to those matters and the effectiveness of those policies.

S418 provides that the directors' report must contain a statement to the effect that in the case of each of the persons who are directors at the time a report is approved:

(a)  so far as the director is aware there is no relevant audit information of which the company's auditor is unaware; and

(b) he has taken all the steps that he ought to have taken as a director to establish for himself that any relevant audit information has been made known to the auditor.

S419 provides for the approval and signing off of a directors' report by the board of directors on behalf of the board by a director or the secretary of the company.

If the report is prepared in accordance with the small companies regime it must contain a statement to that effect in a prominent position above the signature.

If a directors' report is approved that does not comply with the requirements of the Act, every director of the company who:

(a) knew that it did not comply or was reckless as to whether it complied; and
(b) failed to take reasonable steps to secure compliance with those requirements, or as the case may be to prevent the report from being approved,

commits an offence.

### 16.3.1 Quoted companies – directors' remuneration report

S420 provides that the directors of a quoted company must prepare a directors' remuneration report for each financial year. Failure to do so constitutes an offence.

S421 provides for the content of the report. The Secretary of State may make provision by regulations as to the information that should be in the report and how it is to be set out, and what is to be the auditable part of the report.

S422 provides that the directors' remuneration report must be approved by the board of directors and signed on behalf of the board by a director or the secretary of the company.

If a directors' report is approved and does not comply, then every director who knew of non-compliance or was reckless as to whether it complied, and who failed to take reasonable steps to secure compliance, or as the case may be to prevent the report from being approved, commits an offence.

## 16.4 Publication of accounts and reports

S423 provides that every company must send a copy of its annual accounts and reports for each financial year to:

(a) every member of the company;
(b) every holder of the company's debentures; and
(c) every person who is entitled to receive notice of general meetings.

The time allowed for sending out copies of the annual accounts and reports is as follows.

A private company must send them out not later than the end of the period for filing accounts and reports, or, if earlier, the date on which it actually delivers its accounts and reports to the registrar.

In the case of a public company, the information must be given not later than 21 days before the relevant accounts meeting. If accounts are sent out later than that date, they shall, despite that, be deemed to have been duly sent if so agreed by all the members entitled to attend and vote at the relevant accounts meeting (s424).

S425 provides for the situation in default. If there is a failure to comply with the sections above, the company and every officer of the company who is in default is guilty of an offence.

S426 provides the option of providing a summary financial statement. This is available to companies that may be specified in regulations by the Secretary of State and providing any conditions specified are complied with.

S427 sets out the form and contents of summary financial statements for unquoted companies. The information must be derived from the company's annual accounts and be prepared in accordance with s427 and regulations made under it.

S428 provides for the form and contents of summary financial statements for quoted companies.

If there is a failure in relation to any of these sections then the company and every officer in default is guilty of an offence.

A quoted company must ensure its annual accounts and reports are available on a website and remain so available until the annual accounts and reports for the company's next financial year are made available (s430 CA 2006).

S431 provides for the rights of members or debenture holders to copies of accounts and reports for unquoted companies, and S432 deals with the similar right for members and debenture holders of quoted companies.

In each case the member, debenture holder, etc, is entitled to the company's last annual accounts, the last directors' report and the auditor's report on the accounts, and in addition in the case of quoted companies, is also entitled to the last directors' remuneration report and the auditor's report on these reports.

S434 provides that where a company publishes any of its statutory accounts, they must be accompanied by the auditor's report unless the company is exempt from audit and the directors have taken advantage of that exemption.

If a company produces non-statutory accounts it must publish a statement stating they are non-statutory, and whether statutory accounts have been delivered to the registrar, and whether an auditor's report has been made on the company's statutory accounts, and if so, whether the report is qualified or unqualified or includes a reference to any matters to which the auditor draws attention by way of emphasis without qualifying the report or contained a statement under s498(2) (records or returns inadequate, or accounts or directors' remuneration report not agreeing with records or returns), or s498(3) (failure to obtain necessary information and explanations) (s435 CA 2006).

### 16.4.1 Public companies: laying of accounts and reports

S437 of the Companies Act 2006 provides that the directors of a public company must lay before the company in general meeting copies of its annual accounts and reports.

S438 provides that it is an offence to fail to lay the accounts and the reports, although it is a defence for a person charged with such an offence to prove that he took all reasonable steps to secure that the requirements would be complied with before the end of the relevant period.

### 16.4.2 Quoted companies – members' approval of directors' remuneration report

S439 provides that a quoted company must, prior to the accounts meeting, give to the members of the company notice of the intention to move at the meeting an ordinary resolution approving the directors' remuneration report for the financial year.

S440 provides that it is an offence to fail to comply with this section, although it is a defence for a person charged with an offence to prove he took all reasonable steps to secure that the resolution was put to the vote of the meeting.

### 16.4.3 Filing of accounts and reports with the registrar

S441 provides that the directors of a company must deliver to the registrar for each financial year the accounts and reports required by:

(a) s444 (filing obligations of companies subject to small companies regime);
(b) s445 (filing obligations of medium sized companies);
(c) s446 (filing obligations of unquoted companies); or
(d) s447 (filing obligations of quoted companies).

This is subject to s448 (unlimited companies exemption from filing obligations).

S442 provides the period for filing accounts. The period is, for a private company, nine months from the end of the relevant accounting reference period, and, for a public company, six months from the end of that period.

S444 provides that the directors of a company subject to the small companies regime:

(a) must deliver to the registrar for each financial year a copy of the balance sheet drawn up as at the last day of that year; and
(b) may also deliver to the company:

  (i) a copy of the company's profit and loss accounts for that year; and
  (ii) a copy of the directors' report for that year.

The directors must also deliver to the registrar a copy of the auditors' report on the accounts (and on the directors' report).

There is provision for delivery of abbreviated accounts (s444(3) CA 2006).

S445 provides for the filing obligations of medium sized companies. The directors of such a company must deliver to the registrar a copy of:

(a)  the company's annual accounts; and
(b)  the directors' report.

They must also deliver a copy of the auditor's report on those accounts and on the directors' report.

There is again provision for delivery of abbreviated accounts (s445(3) CA 2006).

In relation to both small companies and medium sized companies, the obligations do not apply if the company is exempt from audit and the directors have taken advantage of that exemption.

S446 provides for the filing obligations of unquoted companies. The directors of an unquoted company must deliver to the registrar for each financial year of the company a copy of:

(a)  the company's annual accounts; and
(b)  the directors' report.

They must also deliver to the registrar a copy of the auditor's report on those accounts and the directors' report. Once again this does not apply to companies exempt from audit and where the directors have taken advantage of that exemption.

S447 provides for the filing obligations of quoted companies. The directors of a quoted company must deliver to the registrar for each financial year of the company a copy of:

(a)  the company's annual accounts;
(b)  the directors' remuneration report; and
(c)  the directors' report.

They must also deliver a copy of the auditor's report on the accounts and on the directors' remuneration report and the directors' report.

S448 provides for the exemption of unlimited companies from obligation to file accounts. The directors of an unlimited company are not required to deliver accounts and reports to the registrar in respect of a financial year if the following conditions are met.

These conditions are that at no time during the relevant accounting reference period:

(a)  has the company been, to its knowledge, a subsidiary undertaking of an undertaking which was then limited; or
(b)  have there been, to its knowledge, exercisable by or on behalf of two or more undertakings which were then limited, rights which, if exercisable by one of them, would have made the company a subsidiary undertaking of it, or:

(c) has the company been a parent company of an undertaking, which was then limited.

### 16.4.4 Abbreviated accounts

S449 provides that where the directors of a company deliver abbreviated accounts to the registrar, and the company is not exempt from audit or the directors have not taken advantage of such an exemption, they must deliver to the registrar a copy of the special report of the company's auditor, stating that in his opinion:

(a) the company is entitled to deliver abbreviated accounts; and
(b) the abbreviated accounts are properly prepared in accordance with regulations under that section.

The auditors' report on the company's annual accounts need not be delivered, but:

(a) if the report was qualified the special report must set out that report in full together with any further material necessary to understand the qualification; and
(b) if that report contained a statement under:

  (i) s498(2)(a) or (b) accounts, records or returns inadequate or accounts not agreeing with records and returns; or
  (ii) s498(3) failure to obtain necessary information and explanations,

the special report must set out that statement in full.

S450 provides for the approval and signing of abbreviated accounts, they must be approved by the board of directors and signed on behalf of the board by a director of the company. The signature must be on the balance sheet.

If abbreviated accounts are approved that do not comply with the requirements of regulations under the relevant section, every director of the company commits an offence if he knew that they did not comply or was reckless as to whether they complied and failed to take reasonable steps to prevent them from being approved.

## 16.5 Failure to file accounts and reports

S451 provides for the situation where there is default in filing accounts and reports.

It is an offence to fail to file accounts and reports, and every person who immediately before the end of the period was a director of the company, commits an offence. It is a defence for a person charged with such an offence to prove that he took all reasonable steps to secure that the requirements would be complied with before the end of the period.

S452 provides for default in filing accounts and reports and a court order. If there is non-compliance with filing accounts and reports, and the directors of the company fail to make good the default within 14 days after the service of a notice on them requiring compliance, the court may, on the application of any member or creditor of the company, or of the registrar, make an order directing the directors or any of them to make good the default within such time as may be specified in the order.

S433 provides for a civil penalty for failure to file accounts and reports. The liability falls on the company and the amount of the penalty is to be determined in accordance with regulations made by the Secretary of State by reference to the length of period between the end of the period for filing and the day on which the requirements are complied with, and whether the company is a private or public company.

The penalty may be recovered by the registrar and is to be paid into the Consolidated Fund.

### 16.5.1 Liability for false or misleading statements in reports

S463 deals with this situation.

The reports to which the section applies are:

(a)  the directors' report;
(b)  the directors' remuneration report; and
(c)  a summary financial statement so far as it is derived from either of those reports.

It is provided that a director of a company is liable to compensate the company for any loss suffered by it as a result of any untrue or misleading statement in a report, or the omission from a report, to which the section applies, of anything required to be included in it.

He is liable only if he knew the statement to be untrue or misleading, or was reckless as to whether it was untrue or misleading, or knew the omission to be a dishonest concealment of a material fact.

### 16.5.2 Preparation and filing of accounts in euros

S469 (1) provides that the amount set out in the annual accounts of a company may also be shown in the same accounts translated into euros.

## SUMMARY

## Accounting Records

Companies have to keep adequate accounting records.

## Audit

Small companies are excempt from audit. Small companies are defined by reference to turnover, balance sheet total and the number of employees. Medium sized companies which are larger than small companies but defined by reference to the same three factors enjoy certain exemptions otherwise companies' individual accounts are subject to audit.

## Group Accounts

Companies in a group must submit group accounts each year with a consolidated balance sheet and a consolidated profit and loss account.

## Directors' Report

The directors of a company must generally submit a directors report each year setting out a business review of the company.

## Directors' Remuneration Report

Every quoted company must prepare annually a directors' remuneration report.

# Auditors and annual return

## 17.1 Audit

Part 16 of the 2006 Act deals with audit. Chapter 1 deals with the requirement for audited accounts. S475 provides that a company's annual accounts for a financial year must be audited unless the company is exempt from audit under s477 (small companies), s480 (dormant companies), or unless it is exempt under s482 (non profit making companies subject to public sector audit).

If a company is so exempt, it must include a statement to that effect in its balance sheet (S475(2)).

The statement must be to the effect that the members have not required the company to obtain an audit of its accounts for the year in question under s476, and the directors acknowledging their responsibilities for complying with the requirements of the Act with respect to accounting records and the preparation of accounts.

S476 provides that the members of the company may require an audit. The members who wish for an audit must hold not less in total than 10% in nominal value of the company's issued share capital or any class of it, or if the company does not have a share capital, must constitute not less than 10% in number of the members of the company.

S477 provides for exemption from audit for small companies, provided that the company qualifies as a small company in relation to that year and that its turnover in the year is not more than £5.6m and its balance sheet total for the year is not more than £2.8m.

S478 provides for exclusion from the small companies exemption of a public company, a company that is an authorised insurance company, a banking company, an e-money issuer, an ISD investment firm or a UCITS management company, a company carrying on insurance market activity. A special register body within s117(1) of the Trade Union and Labour Relations (Consolidation) Act 1992, or an employers' association under s122 of the same Act, are similarly not exempt.

S479 provides that small companies are not entitled to exemption in the case of group companies unless the conditions in the section are complied with.

These are that the group must qualify as a small group and must not at any time in the year be an ineligible group, and that the group's aggregate turnover in the year is no more than £5.6m net or £6.72m gross, and the balance sheet total for that year is not more than £2.8m net or £3.36m gross.

S480 deals with dormant companies which are themselves exempt from audit.

### 17.1.1 Appointment of auditors

S485 provides that an auditor or auditors of a private company must be appointed for each financial year of the company unless the directors reasonably resolve otherwise on the ground that audited accounts are unlikely to be required. Part 42 CA 2006 provides for the qualification of such auditors.

S486 deals with the appointment of auditors of a private company and the default power of the Secretary of State. If a private company fails to appoint an auditor in accordance with s485, the Secretary of State may do so in order to fill the vacancy.

An auditor or auditors of a private company hold office in accordance with the terms of their appointment (s487).

S489 deals with the appointment of auditors of a public company. These must be appointed for each financial year of the company unless the directors reasonably resolve otherwise on the ground that audited accounts are unlikely to be required.

In default, once again, the Secretary of State may appoint somebody to fill the vacancy (s490).

S491 provides that the term of office of auditors of a public company is in accordance with the terms of their appointment.

S492 deals with the fixing of the auditor's remuneration. This must be fixed by the members by ordinary resolution or in such manner as the members may, by ordinary resolution, determine.

S493 provides that the Secretary of State may make provision by regulations for securing the disclosure of the terms of appointment of the companies' auditors, their remuneration and their duties.

S494 provides that the Secretary of State may make provision by regulation for securing the disclosure of the nature of any services provided for a company by the company's auditor whether as auditor or otherwise, or by his associates, and the amount of any remuneration received or receivable in this regard.

### 17.1.2 Functions of the auditor

S495 provides that a company's auditor must make a report to the company's members on all the annual accounts of the company which are sent out to the members in the case of a private company, and in the case of a public company, which are laid before the company in general meeting.

The report must state clearly whether in the auditor's opinion the annual accounts give a true and fair view, and have been properly prepared in accordance with the relevant financial reporting framework, and have been prepared in accordance with the requirements of the Act and, where applicable, article 4 of the IAS Regulation.

The auditor's report must be either unqualified or qualified, and must include a reference to any matters to which the auditor wishes to draw attention by way of emphasis without qualifying the report (s495(4) CA 206).

The auditor's report should include an introduction identifying the annual accounts that are the subject of the audit and the financial reporting framework that has been applied, and a description of the scope of the audit identifying the auditing standards in accordance with which the audit was conducted (s495(2)).

S496 provides that the auditor is to report on the directors' report. The auditor must state in the report on the company's annual accounts whether, in the opinion of the auditors, the information given in the directors' report for the financial year for which the accounts are prepared is consistent with those accounts.

S497 provides for an auditor's report on the auditable part of the directors' remuneration report.

If the company is a quoted company the auditor must report to the company's members on the auditable part of the directors' remuneration report and state whether, in his opinion, that part of the directors' remuneration report has been properly prepared in accordance with the Act.

### 17.1.3  Auditor's statutory duties

S498 provides that a company's auditor in preparing his report must carry out such investigations as will enable him to form an opinion as to:

(a) whether adequate accounting records have been kept by the company and returns adequate for their audit have been received from branches not visited by him; and
(b) whether the company's individual accounts are in agreement with the accounting records and returns; and
(c) in the case of a quoted company whether the auditable part of the directors' remuneration report is in agreement with the accounting records and returns.

If the auditor is of the opinion that adequate records have not been kept or that the company's individual accounts are not in agreement with the records and returns, or in the case of a quoted company that the auditable part of the directors' remuneration report is not in agreement with the accounting records and returns, the auditor shall state that fact in his report (s498(3) CA 2006).

S499 provides for the auditor's general right to information from the company in relation to the company's books, accounts and vouchers, and his right to require any officer or employee or person accountable for any of the company's books, accounts or vouchers, any subsidiary undertaking, any officer, employee or auditor of a subsidiary undertaking, or anybody who fell within the previous categories at a time to which the information or explanations required by the auditor relates or relate, then the auditor may require such persons to provide him with such information or explanations as he thinks necessary for the performance of his duties as auditor.

S500 deals with the auditor's right to information from overseas subsidiaries.

S501 deals with offences. A person commits an offence who knowingly or recklessly makes to an auditor of a company a statement that conveys or purports to convey information that is misleading, false or deceptive in a material particular.

S502 provides for auditor's rights in relation to resolutions and meetings. In relation to a written resolution proposed to be agreed by a private company, the company's auditor is entitled to receive all such communications relating to the resolution, as are required to be supplied to a member of the company.

The company's auditor is entitled to receive all notices and other communications relating to general meetings which a member of a company is entitled to receive, and is entitled to attend any general meeting of the company and to be heard at any general meeting which he attends on any part of the business of the meeting which concerns him as auditor.

### 17.1.4 Disclosure in the auditor's report

The senior statutory auditor must sign the report in his own name on behalf of the audit firm (if it is an audit firm) (s503 CA 2006).

The name of the individual who is the senior statutory auditor, as well as the name of the firm, must appear in all copies of the audit report (s505 CA 2006).

There is an exemption from disclosing the name of the person who signed as senior statutory auditor if the company, on reasonable grounds, believes that a statement of the name would create, or be likely to create, a serious risk that the auditor or senior statutory auditor or any other person who would be subject to violence or intimidation. If this is the case, the company must resolve that the name should not be stated and must give notice of the resolution to the Secretary of State disclosing who the senior statutory auditor is.

### 17.1.5 Offences in connection with the auditor's report

S507 provides that in relation to any matter that is misleading, false or deceptive in a material particular, or where the company's report omit a statement that is required, then the auditor is guilty of an offence under this section.

This is a new criminal offence.

### 17.1.6 Auditors' liabilities – the case law

#### 17.1.6.1 Conduct of the audit

The starting point of any survey of auditor's liability is the famous *dictum* of Lopes LJ in *Re Kingston Cotton Mill (1896)*, that 'an auditor is not bound to be a detective ... he is a watchdog but not a bloodhound'. The auditors in this case had taken on trust a management assessment of the amount of yarn in stock, failing to make a physical check themselves. The assessments were frauds, which had been perpetrated by a manager to make the company appear to flourish by exaggerating the quantity and value of cotton and yarn in the company's mills.

The auditors took the entry of the stock in trade at the beginning of the year from the last preceding balance sheet, and they took the values of the stock-in-trade at the end of the year from the stock journal.

The book contained a series of accounts under various heads purporting to show the quantities and values of the company's stock in trade at the end of each year and a summary of the accounts which was adopted by the auditors.

The auditors always ensured that the summary corresponded with the accounts but they did not enquire into the accuracy of the accounts. The auditors were held not liable; the court concluded they were entitled to accept the certificate of a responsible official. This is a decision that would almost certainly be reversed today. The *dictum* of Lopes LJ, however, still finds approval and has fossilised into an immovable principle of law, though it is now generally accepted that an auditor is a watchdog which must bark loudly and relentlessly at any suspicious circumstance.

At the outset of the audit, an auditor must familiarise himself with the company's memorandum and articles of association, so that he can ensure that payments shown in the accounts have been properly incurred. It will be no defence to assert that he has not read these company documents.

In *Leeds Estate Building and Investment Co v Shepherd (1887)*, the terms of the articles had not been carried out, and it was held that it was no excuse that the auditor has not seen them. As a result of this neglect dividends, directors' fees and bonuses were improperly paid and the auditor was therefore held liable for damages.

An auditor is required to investigate suspicious circumstances. In *Re Thomas Gerrard (1967)*, Pennycuick J noted that 'the standards of reasonable care and skill are, upon the expert evidence more exacting than those which prevailed in 1896' (*Re Kingston Cotton Mill*). Here, in addition to an overstatement of stock, there had been fraudulent practice in changing invoice dates to make it appear that clients owed money within the accounting period, when in fact it was due outside of it and to make it appear that suppliers were not yet owed money for goods when such liability did exist.

In holding Kevans, the auditors, to be liable, Pennycuick J considered that the changed invoice dates should have aroused suspicion:

> I find the conclusion inescapable, alike on the expert evidence and as a matter of business common sense that at this stage (of discovering the altered invoice dates) he ought to have examined the suppliers' statements and where necessary have communicated with the suppliers.

### 17.1.6.2 The USA experience

In the absence of much British authority, transatlantic experience is instructive for the accounting standards adopted in Britain and the USA being similar.

In the USA, in 1939, there occurred a case of far-reaching significance, *McKesson and Robins*, which involved the most ingenious of frauds. The fraud was engineered by four brothers who were operating under different names and who accomplished a massive deception in the operation of a wholly fictitious crude drug business.

Purchases were claimed to have been made by the McKesson company from Canadian vendors who, it was alleged, sold the goods on to customers. The firms to whom it was alleged that the goods had been sold were real but had done no business of the type claimed. The Canadian vendors were either fictitious or blinds used to support the fictitious transactions. The fraud was supported by fictitious invoicing, advice notes and records of communication. The auditors, Price Waterhouse, failed to discover the fraud. The stocks and debtors of the company were consequently overstated by $23 million.

The US Securities and Exchange Commission was extremely critical of the practice of the auditors, emphasising the need for physical contact with the inventory and the case led to a general change in auditing practice.

The report stated:

> It is unusually clear to us that, prior to this case, many independent public accountants depended entirely too much upon the verification of cash as the basis for the whole auditing programme and, hence, as underlying proof of the authenticity of all transactions. Where, as here, during the final three years of the audit, physical contact with the operations of a major portion of the business was limited to examinations of supposed documentary evidence of transactions carried on completely off-stage through agents unknown to the auditors ... it appears to us that the reliability of these agents must be established by completely independent methods.

Another notorious US case is also instructive. This is the *Salad Oil Swindle* case of 1963. De Angelis, an Italian American had built up a massive vegetable oil empire. He was able to negotiate warehouse receipts from American Express to commodity brokers on the basis of his stock.

The stocktaking exercise affords an illustration of the ludicrous acceptance of fiction as fact. De Angelis' employees would climb to the top of each tank to make a depth sounding of the oil, which would be shouted down to the American Express man below, who would slavishly take down the figures. While the team moved from one vat to the next the oil would be pumped from one tank to the adjacent one and this process would continue throughout the warehouse.

The case has had a salutary effect on auditing practice in the USA and in England. The importance of a physical stock check is now established. An auditor is unwise to take anything on trust from his client, it is advisable to treat any management statement or assertion with healthy suspicion. Thus a check should be made of petty cash held (random checks for large firms are probably sufficient). Thus, in *London Oil Storage Co Ltd v Seear Hasluck & Co (1904)*, where the auditors failed to check the petty cash which, according to the books, amounted to £760 but which, in fact, amounted to £30, they were held liable in damages.

The balance of moneys in the bank should be verified by a bank statement (*Fox v Morrish (1918)*) and similarly certificates of investments held should be examined (*Re City Equitable Fire Insurance Co Ltd (1925)*).

It may thus be seen that auditing practice has blown the sails of legal practice on a fresh tack so that now the standard expected of an auditor is much higher than at the time of *Re Kingston Cotton Mill*. An auditor might still not be a blood-hound but he must be a watchdog at the very peak of his performance and must never go to sleep on the audit – even with one eye open!

### 17.1.6.3 The auditor's contractual liability

Liability may arise in contract. The auditor will be liable for failing to perform properly what he has undertaken to do. The other party to the contract – the company – is the only person who can sue the auditor under this head of liability.

The extent of the auditor's liability will be to pay damages resulting from the breach of contract if the damages are in the contemplation of the parties; for instance, if the breach is for failure to detect fraud, damages will be awarded to compensate for further fraud that has been perpetrated after the date when the fraud should have been detected.

### 17.1.6.4 The auditor's tortious liability

An auditor may be liable in negligence to his client or in the tort of negligent mis-statement to third parties. Formerly, it was the law that there was no duty owed to third parties to exercise care in drawing up accounts. In *Candler v Crane Christmas & Co (1951)*, the auditors prepared inaccurate accounts which were relied upon by the plaintiff as the basis of investing money in the company. A major-ity of the Court of Appeal refused to allow an action in such circumstances.

However, in an historic decision in *Hedley Byrne and Co. Ltd. v Heller and Partners Ltd (1964)*, the House of Lords overruled the *Candler* decision. Liability could henceforth arise where an auditor knew or ought to have known that his report would be relied upon and he was negligent in preparing it. Initially, the pre-cise scope of an auditor's liability was not clear. The Institute of Chartered Accountants amongst others took an optimistic view that it was limited to those persons whom the auditor specifically knew would rely upon the audited accounts.

This view was blown sky high by *JEB Fasteners Ltd v Marks Bloom & Co (a firm) (1981)*, affirmed on other grounds (1983). In 1975, the defendants had audited the accounts of JEB Fasteners. The audited accounts massively overvalued the company's stock. JEB Fasteners had read the negligently audited accounts. Woolf J held that the defendants owed a duty to the plaintiffs. In the event, there was no liability as the judge held that the negligently audited accounts did not induce the purchase. Woolf J relied on his judgment in an earlier unreported English case,

*Grover Industrial Holdings Ltd v Newman Harris & Co (1976)* and the judgment of Stocker J in that case, as well as two Commonwealth authorities, the Canadian case of *Haig v Bamford, Hagan, Wicken and Gibson (1976)* and the New Zealand case of *Scott Group Ltd v McFarlane (1978)*. Both resulted in liability being placed on auditors in similar circumstances to *JEB Fasteners*.

In the later Scottish case of *Twomax Ltd v Dickson, McFarlane and Robinson (1982)*, Twomax had acquired a majority stake in a private company, Kintyre Knitwear Ltd. Twomax claimed that in purchasing shares in the company it had relied upon the accounts negligently prepared by the defendants. The court held that the audit was perfunctory and negligent and the auditors were held liable in damages to the plaintiffs.

In *Caparo Industries plc v Dickman and Others (1990)*, the House of Lords considered the position of the liability of an audit firm. The third defendants were the auditors Touche Ross. The first and second defendants were the chairman and chief executive of a company called Fidelity. The contention of the plaintiff, Caparo, was that it was misled by the fraudulent misrepresentations of the first and second defendants which the third defendants, the auditors, had been negligent in failing to detect and report. The House of Lords considered the possible liability of the auditors. It was held in the circumstances that the auditors did not have liability. The auditors owed a duty to the company and not to individual shareholders.

It is clear post-*Caparo* that liability is restricted to cases where the auditor knows of the user and the use to which he will put the information – see *Morgan Crucible Co plc v Hill Samuel Bank Ltd (1991)*. Even here, an auditor will not be liable in tort if he reasonably believes that the user will also seek independent advice: see *James McNaughten Paper Group Ltd v Hicks Anderson and Co. (1991)*.

In *Barings plc v Coopers & Lybrand (1997)*, the Court of Appeal accepted the argument that in principle the auditor of a subsidiary company can owe a duty of care to the parent company.

In this case, Barings sought to lay responsibility for the collapse of Barings on the auditors for failure to report on Nick Leeson's fraud in unauthorised futures trading. These activities were carried out through a subsidiary, Barings Securities Ltd. Coopers & Lybrand prepared the consolidated group accounts for Barings, and Coopers & Lybrand, Singapore, audited Barings Securities' consolidation schedules.

The auditors argued that they owed no duty of care to Barings and that the damages being claimed by Barings as a shareholder in its subsidiaries ought to be claimed by the subsidiary.

The Court of Appeal held that Barings had a right of action independent of the company. The court stressed that Coopers & Lybrand, Singapore, knew that their report on Barings Securities' consolidation schedules were required by Barings to enable Barings to demonstrate that the group accounts should give a true and fair view of the group's business.

In the Scottish decision of *The Royal Bank of Scotland plc v Bannerman Johnstone Maclay (2005)*, Lord MacFadyen in the Scottish Court of Session (Outer House) had to consider the extent of tortious liability of auditors.

The defendants had audited the accounts of APC Ltd. The bank which advanced money to the company brought an action alleging that a duty was owed to them as the defendant chartered accountants knew that the company required a substantial overdraft facility for the bank and that the bank required to see monthly management accounts and relied on the annual audited accounts. The defendant argued that for a duty of care to arise there had to be an intention on their part that the bank should rely on the audited accounts. Lord MacFadyen held that intention was not essential and that knowledge of reliance was sufficient. His Lordship stated that it was open to the defendants to attach a disclaimer of responsibility to the bank which they had not done. The decision did not deal with the question of whether any loss suffered by the bank fell within the duty. This was not dealt with in this action. The bank had to produce evidence to show negligence.

### 17.1.6.5. Limiting liability

The Institute of Chartered Accountants of England and Wales recommends that auditors clearly limit their duty to the company's members as a body. Thus, the class of persons to whom an auditor may be liable is somewhat larger than originally envisaged.

If liability is proved, damages are awarded to compensate the plaintiff for the loss he has sustained by reason of the negligence of the auditor in so far as the losses that they compensate are forseeable consequences of the auditor's breach of duty.

S532 provides for the voidness of provisions protecting auditors from liability which would otherwise attach to them in connection with any negligence, default, breach of duty or breach of trust in relation to the company, occurring in the course of the audit of accounts, or by which a company directly or indirectly provides an indemnity for an auditor of the company or an associated company against any such liability.

Any such provision is void except as permitted by s533 (indemnity for costs of successfully defending proceedings) or ss534–536 (liability limitation agreements).

SS534–536 provide for liability limitation agreements. These are agreements that purport to limit the amount of a liability owed to a company by its auditor in respect of any negligence, default, breach of duty or breach of trust, occurring in the course of the audit of accounts. The liability limitation agreement must not apply in relation to more than one financial year and must specify the financial year in relation to which it applies.

The Secretary of State may by regulations require liability limitation agreements to contain specified provisions or provisions of a specified description, and may prohibit liability limitation agreements from containing specified provisions or provisions of a specified description.

S536 provides that a liability limitation agreement is authorised by the members of the company if it is authorised under the section (to be effective a liability limitation agreement must be authorised). It is provided that a liability limitation agreement between a private company and its auditor may be authorised by the company passing a resolution before it enters into the agreement, waiving the need for approval, or by the company passing a resolution before entering into the agreement approving the agreement's principal terms, or by the company passing a resolution after entering into the agreement approving the agreement itself.

In relation to a public company's auditor, the agreement may be authorised by the company passing a resolution before it enters into the agreement approving the principal terms, or after the agreement is entered into approving the agreement itself.

S537 provides that a liability limitation agreement is not effective to limit the auditor's liability to less than such amounts as is fair and reasonable having regard to the auditor's responsibilities, the nature and purpose of the auditor's contractual obligations, and the professional standards expected of him.

S538 provides that a company which has entered into a liability limitation agreement must make such disclosure in connection with the agreement as the Secretary of State may require by regulations.

### 17.1.6.6 The auditor's statutory liability

An auditor may be liable in a winding up for misfeasance or breach of duty to the company (s212 of the Insolvency Act 1986). If this were to be so, the court will order whatever compensation it thinks fit.

### 17.1.7 Removal resignation, etc, of auditors

S510 provides for the removing of an auditor from office. The members of a company may remove an auditor from office at any time. S511 provides that this power is only exercisable after special notice has been served (section 15.4.1). The company must then send a copy of the notice to the person proposed to be removed.

The auditor proposed to be removed may make, with respect to the intended resolution, representations in writing to the company and request their notification to members of the company and the company must circulate those representations.

If the representations are not circulated, then the auditor may require them to be read out at the meeting and this is without prejudice to the auditor's right to be heard at the meeting in any event.

S514 deals with the failure to reappoint an auditor and the special procedure that is required if this is to be done by written resolution.

If such a resolution is proposed as a written resolution, and its effect would be to appoint a person as auditor other than a person whose term of office has expired or is to expire, then the company must send a copy of the proposed resolution to the person proposed to be appointed and to the outgoing auditor, and the outgoing auditor may, within 14 days of the notice, require that written representations should be circulated to members of the company, and the company must then circulate those representations. If any requirement of the section is not complied with, the resolution is ineffective.

S515 deals with the failure to reappoint an auditor at a meeting. The section applies to a resolution at a general meeting whose effect would be to appoint somebody other than the retiring auditor whose term of office has ended.

In such a situation, special notice is required in the case of a private company if no period for appointing auditors has ended since the outgoing auditor's ceased to hold office, or such a period has ended and an auditor or auditors should have been appointed but were not.

In the case of a public company, where there has been no accounts meeting of the company since the outgoing auditor ceased to hold office, or there has been an accounts meeting at which an auditor or auditors should have been appointed but were not, in such situations special notice is required.

The outgoing auditor may require his written representations to be circulated and the company must then circulate those written representations.

S516 deals with the resignation of an auditor. An auditor may resign by depositing a notice to that effect at the company's registered office. S517 provides for the notice to the registrar of the resignation of an auditor.

S518 deals with the rights of a resigning auditor. He may deposit with the notice a signed requisition calling on the directors to convene a general meeting for the purpose of receiving and considering such explanation of the circumstances connected with his resignation as he may wish to place before the meeting, and he may request the company to circulate to its members before the meeting a statement in writing of the circumstances connected with his resignation.

S519 provides that where an auditor of an unquoted company ceases for any reason to hold office, he must deposit at the company's registered office a statement of the circumstances connected with his ceasing to hold office unless he considers there are no circumstances in connection with the ceasing to hold office that need to be brought to the attention of members or creditors of the company, and if that is the case he must deposit at the company's registered office a statement to that effect.

S520 provides that within 14 days of the deposit of such a statement, the company must send a copy of it to every person entitled to be sent copies of the accounts or apply to the court and if it applies to the court it must notify the auditor of the application.

S521 provides that a copy of the statement must also be sent to the registrar.

S522 provides that it is the duty of the auditor to notify the appropriate audit authority where, in the case of a major audit, an auditor ceases for any reason to hold office, or in the case of an audit that is not a major audit, ceases to hold office before the end of his term of office.

S523 similarly provides that it is the duty of a company to notify the appropriate audit authority where an auditor ceases to hold office before the end of his term of office and this statement must be accompanied by a statement by the company of the reason for his ceasing to hold office, or, if a copy of the statement deposited by the auditor at the company's registered office in accordance with s519 contains a statement of the circumstances in connection with the ceasing to hold office, must annex that statement.

S524 provides that the information given to the audit authority must then be passed to the accounting authorities and may, if the appropriate audit authority considers it appropriate, forward to those authorities a copy of the statement or statements accompanying the notice.

The accounting authorities are the Secretary of State and any other person authorised by him under s456.

### 17.1.8 Quoted companies and the rights of members to raise audit concerns at accounts meetings

S527 provides that members of a quoted company may require the company to publish on a website a statement setting out any matter relating to the audit of the company's accounts or any circumstances connected with the auditor of the company ceasing to hold office since the previous accounts meeting, that the members propose to raise at the next accounts meeting.

To exercise rights under the section, members must represent at least 5% of the total voting rights of all members who have a relevant right to vote, or at least 100 members who have a relevant right to vote and hold shares in the company on which there has been paid up an average sum per member of at least £100.

S528 deals with website availability. The information must be made available on a website that is maintained by or on behalf of the company, and identifies the company in question, and access to the information on the website and the ability to obtain a hard copy of the information from the website must not be conditional on the payment of a fee or otherwise restricted. The statement must be made available within three working days of the company being required to publish it on a website, and must be kept available until after the meeting to which it relates.

S529 provides that a quoted company must, in the notice it gives of the accounts meeting, draw attention to the possibility of placing a statement on the website and the effect of the provisions of the Act.

S530 provides it is an offence for any company officer to fail to comply with these website requirements.

## 17.2 Annual return

S853 provides that every company must deliver to the registar sucessive annual returns, each of which is made up to a date, not later than the date that is, from time to time, the company's return date.

The company's return date is the anniversary of the company's incorporation, or if the company's last return delivered in accordance with the Act was made up to a different date, the anniversary of that date.

S855 provides for the contents of the annual return. The following information must be detailed:

(a)  the address of the company's registered office;
(b)  the type of company it is and its principal business activities;
(c)  the prescribed particulars of:

   (i)  the directors of the company, and
   (ii) in the case of a private company with a secretary or a public company, the secretary or joint secretaries.

(d)  If the register of members is not kept available for inspection at the registered office, the address of the place where it is kept available for inspection, and if there is a register of debenture holders which is not kept available for inspection at the company's registered office, the address of where it is kept available for inspection.

(e)  The annual return should also set out a statement of the company's capital and the total number of shares, the aggregate nominal value of the shares, and the rights attaching to different classes of shares, together with the aggregate nominal value of shares of that class. It should also set out the amount paid and the amount, if any, unpaid on each share. Clearly these provisions only apply if the company has a share capital.

(f)  The return must also set out prescribed particulars of every person who is a member of the company or who ceased to be a member of the company during the period since the last return. It must also state the number of shares held by each member of the company at the date the return is made up and the number of shares that have been transferred since the date of the last return by each member or person who has ceased to be a member.

S858 provides that if a company fails to deliver an annual return before the end of the period of 28 days after the return date, this constitutes an offence by the company, and every director of the company and every secretary of the company and every officer of the company who is in default.

## SUMMARY

## Auditors and annual return

### Auditors

All companies except dormant companies and certain exempt private companies must appoint auditors. The auditors have statutory protection if they are to be removed from office. They also have rights to bring matters to the attention of members where they resign.

Auditors must be qualified with a recognised body.

The auditor must adopt a strict approach in conducting the audit. There is a statutory obligation to report to the company on the accounts. There will also be contractual duties owed to the company flowing from the contract concluded between the company and the auditors.

Auditors also owe a duty of care to third parties whom they know are going to rely on the audited accounts for specific purposes without the benefit of other independent advice.

Auditors may, subject to restrictions, limit their liability.

Members of a quoted company may require the company to publish their audit concerns on a website.

### Annual return

Every company must file an annual return concerning information about the company's activities, officers, shares and debentures. There is now a simplified 'shuttle return' procedure for updating existing information.

## Further reading

Chua, S, 'The auditor's liability in negligence in respect of the audit report' [1995] JBL 1.

Cohen, H, 'Auditors' liability of negligence: a time for reform?' (1993) 8 JIBL 133.

Hemraj, M, 'Audit failure due to negligent audit: lessons from DTI investigations' (2003) Co Law 45.

Morris, PE, and Stevenson, J, 'Accountancy: auditors, negligence and incorporation' (1996) 176 Bus LR 54.

# Company secretary

## 18.1 Introduction

One hundred years ago, a company secretary would have found his powers were few. The question of the authority of the company secretary was considered many years ago in *Barnett Hoares & Co v South London Tramways Co (1887)*.

In this case, the South London Tramways Co had made an agreement with Messrs Green and Burleigh who were contractors to construct part of the tramline. The company, as is common in building and construction contracts, retained a certain percentage of the amounts for which their engineer had certified completion, since Green and Burleigh were to maintain the line for a period of time. The retention money was payable to the contractors at the end of this period. The contractors had applied to the bankers, Barnett Hoares & Co, for a loan and had given them as security a letter which purported to assign to them to retention money of £2,000 under the contract.

The bankers had then written to the Tramway company's secretary for the confirmation that £2,000 was held and the required confirmation had been given. When Barnett Hoares were not paid back by the contractors, they had claimed the retention money. They then discovered that only £675 was held as retention money, despite the written assurances of the secretary. The issue in the case they brought against the company concerned the authority of the company secretary. Had he had the authority to bind the company?

The outcome in the case was clear and unequivocal: the company secretary had not had the authority to bind the company.

As Lord Esher MR said:

> A secretary is a mere servant; his position is that he is to do what he is told and no person can assume that he has any authority to represent anything at all, nor can anyone assume that statements made by him are necessarily to be accepted as trustworthy without further enquiry ...

Things have changed. In 1971, the Court of Appeal again considered the role and significance of the company secretary in *Panorama Developments (Guildford) Ltd v Fidelis Furnishing Fabrics Ltd (1971)*.

Panorama Developments (Guildford) Ltd ran a car hire business which was called Belgravia Executive Car Rental. The company fleet comprised limousines which included Rolls-Royces and Jaguars. Fidelis Furnishing Fabrics Ltd was a company of good repute, and its managing director was a man of integrity. However, its company secretary RL Bayne was not of the same cloth. He told Panorama that Fidelis wished to hire cars so that he could meet important customers at Heathrow Airport. He claimed that he took these customers to the company's office and the company's factory in Leeds.

This was not true. No customers were met at Heathrow and the company did not have a factory in Leeds. The cars had been used by Bayne personally. Panorama sued Fidelis Fabrics for their hire charges.

As in the earlier *Barnett* case, the defendants argued that they were not bound by the acts of their company secretary, who fulfils a very humble role and has no authority to make any contracts or representations on behalf of the company. However, the Court of Appeal decided that, on the contrary, the company secretary had bound the company. In considering the *Barnett* case, Lord Denning MR said:

> But times have changed. A company secretary is a much more important person nowadays than he was in 1887. He is an officer of the company with extensive duties and responsibilities. This appears not only in the modern Companies Acts, but also by the role which he plays in the day-to-day business of companies. He is no longer a mere clerk. He regularly makes representations on behalf of the company and enters into contracts on its behalf which come within the day-to-day running of the company's business. So much so that he may be regarded as held out as having authority to do such things on behalf of the company. He is certainly entitled to sign contracts connected with the administrative side of a company's affairs, such as employing staff, and ordering cars, and so forth. All such matters now come within the ostensible authority of a company secretary.

Today, then, the company secretary is one of the principal officers of the company and he is the agent through whom much of the company's administrative work is done. Indeed, when making contracts on behalf of the company, it is advisable for the secretary to ensure that he does so as agent of the company to avoid any personal liability.

As an officer, the secretary will be liable to a default fine for contravention along with directors under many provisions of the Companies Acts. The Department of Trade brings many prosecutions for offences under the Companies Acts, especially concerning failures to lodge documents with the registrar of companies.

The company secretary will in all probability be an employee, entitled as a 'clerk or servant' to rank as a preferential creditor and as such will be paid off first in a liquidation. However, secretaries who do not give their whole time to the company and perform their duties through a deputy are not within the scope of the provision. This was decided in the case of *Cairney v Back (1906)*.

In this case, the company secretary of Consolidated Mines Ltd had to attend directors' meetings, deal with the correspondence and callers and keep the minute book. Mr Justice Walton considered that, if the evidence had stopped there, then the defendant would have been a clerk or servant. However, although the defendant was generally at the office from 12 pm to 2 pm, he had no particular hours of attendance. He also paid a clerk who worked regularly from 10 am to 5 pm. In other words, the general work of the company falling within his purview was really done by the clerk. The defendant did not, therefore, exactly serve the company. Rather he provided services, attending himself occasionally when required. So he was not an employee.

With the Companies Act 2006 it is no longer necessary for a private company to have a secretary (s270 CA 2006). If it choses to have one it will still have to enter particulars in its register of secretaries and send details of any changes to Companies House as with the secretary of a public company (s276 CA 2006).

A company secretary will henceforth be able to register a service address which, just as in the case of directors, may be stated as the company's registered office so that a secretary, just as a director, does not have to disclose his home address (s277 CA 2006).

## 18.2 Duties of the secretary

As an officer, the secretary owes fiduciary duties to the company and is liable for any secret gain made from the company. An illustration of this principle is *Re Morvah Consols Tin Mining Co (1876)*. A James Hammon sold a tin mine in Cornwall to a certain McKay, who set up a company to purchase the mine. McKay became company secretary. Hammon was to be paid partly in cash and partly in shares, and McKay was to receive some shares for setting up the deal. The company knew nothing of this.

Later, the company was wound up by the Stannary Court. (The tin mines of Devon and Cornwall, or Stannaries, were formerly subject to a special legal regime. The jurisdiction is now exercised by the Cornish County Court.) McKay was ordered to pay over the value of the shares to the liquidator because he was in breach of his fiduciary duty.

## 18.3 Responsibilities of the secretary

Formerly, when companies tended to be smaller, their affairs less complex and the legal requirements less onerous, the company secretary was typically a clerk who was employed to perform routine work under orders. Today, the responsibilities of the company secretary would usually include the following:

(a) the preparation and keeping of minutes of board and general meetings (s248 and s355 of the Companies Act 2006);

(b)  dealing with share transfers and issuing share and debenture certificates;

(c)  keeping and maintaining the register of members and debenture holders (s113 and s743 of the Companies Act 2006) (in large public companies, a professional share registrar often maintains these registers as well as dealing with share transfers);

(d)  keeping and maintaining the register of directors and secretary (s162 and s275 of the Companies Act 2006);

(e)  the registration of charges and the maintaining of the company's register of charges (s860 and ss875–876 of the Companies Act 2006);

(f)  maintaining directors' contracts (s228 of the Companies Act 2006);

(g)  keeping and maintaining the register of share interests (s808 of the Companies Act 2006);

(h)  sending notices of meetings, copies of accounts, etc;

(i)  keeping the company's memorandum and articles up to date;

(j)  preparation and submission of the annual return (s854 of the Companies Act 2006);

(k)  filing with the registrar of numerous returns and documents;

(l)  preparation of the numerous returns required by government departments and official bodies;

(m)  witnessing documents, that is, signing as witness (together with a director) against the company seal or otherwise;

(n)  payment of dividends and the preparation of dividend warrants.

Depending on the size of the headquarters staff, the company secretary may also be the chief accounting officer, have charge of staff employment and pension matters, obtain legal advice from solicitors and confer with the auditors. If the company is quoted, he or she may also deal with The Stock Exchange. It is entirely possible that still other responsibilities may be placed upon the secretary by the company's articles.

## 18.4  Qualifications

Because of the great welter of statutory duties and the increasing responsibilities placed on company secretaries, it was inevitable that a company secretary should have to possess a relevant qualification. Although there are no mandatory qualifications for a company secretary of a private company, there are for a public company. According to s273 of the Companies Act 2006, it is the duty of directors of a public company to take all reasonable steps to ensure that the secretary or each joint secretary of the company is a person with the requisite knowledge and experience and who:

(a)  was the secretary of a public company for at least three of the five years immediately preceding the appointment as secretary; or

(b)  is a member of one of the following professional bodies:

- The Institute of Chartered Accountants in England and Wales;
- The Institute of Chartered Accountants of Scotland;
- The Association of Certified Accountants;
- The Institute of Chartered Accountants in Ireland;
- The Institute of Chartered Secretaries and Administrators;
- The Institute of Chartered Management Accountants;
- The Chartered Institute of Public Finance and Accountancy;

or

- is qualified in the United Kingdom as a barrister, or an advocate or a solicitor; or
- is a person who by virtue of holding or having held any other position or being a member of any other body, appears to the directors to be capable of discharging the functions of a secretary.

It should be noted that the obligation is a continuing one so that, for example, if a person ceases to hold an appropriate qualification, the directors should reconsider his appointment.

It is somewhat ironic that there should be minimum qualifications for the company secretary of a public company but not for directors. Nothing could better illustrate the change in the role of the company secretary and the law's perception of this.

## SUMMARY

## Company secretary

### Responsibilities

Responsibilities include: the preparation and keeping of minutes of board and general meetings; dealing with share transfers and issuing share and debenture certificates; keeping and maintaining the register of members and debenture holders; keeping and maintaining the register of directors and secretary; the registration of charges and the maintaining of the company's register of charges; keeping and maintaining the register of directors' share interests); sending notices of meetings, copies of accounts; keeping the company's memorandum and articles up to date; preparation and submission of the annual return; payment of dividends and the preparation of dividend warrants.

### Duties

The secretary owes fiduciary duties to the company and is liable for any secret gain made from the company: *Re Morvah Consols Tin Mining Co (1876)*.

## *Qualifications*

Private companies are not required to have a secretary, but may do so.

In a public company, a company secretary must possess a recognised qualification. A company secretary may be a director but need not be one.

## Further reading

Severn, R, 'Protection and respect are due to the company secretary' (1996) 43 IHL 21.

# 19

# Debentures and the law of mortgages

Debentures are, in general, subject to the same principles as ordinary mortgages. Equitable principles protect mortgagors against 'clogging the equity of redemption', that is, making it difficult to redeem or placing some restriction on redemption. These clogs may include making the mortgage irredeemable or redeemable only after a long time or providing some commercial advantage to the lender of money as against the borrower of the money. In relation to debentures, there is no rule prohibiting debentures from being irredeemable or redeemable only after a long period of time. S739 of the Companies Act 2006 provides that:

> A condition contained in debentures, or in a deed for securing debentures, is not invalid by reason only that the debentures are made irredeemable or redeemable only on the happening of a contingency (however remote), or on the expiration of a period (however long), any rule of equity to the contrary notwithstanding.

In *Knightsbridge Estates Trust Ltd v Byrne (1940)*, a company which had secured a loan by mortgaging its property to the lender of the money, argued that the provision that the mortgage would last for 40 years was void as an unreasonable restriction on the mortgagor. The court held that the mortgage constituted a debenture within the Companies Act and, therefore, was not void. Other restrictions placed upon the mortgagor may well be invalid. Thus, in *Kreglinger v New Patagonia Meat & Cold Storage Co Ltd (1914)*, the court recognised that requiring the borrower to sell sheepskins to the lender of finance for a period of time could constitute an unfair clog on the equity of redemption. In the event, on the facts of the particular case, it was held not to be unreasonable. The agreement provided that for five years the borrower should sell the skins to the lender so long as the lender was willing to buy at the best price offered by any other person.

## 19.1 Types of debentures

Every trading or commercial company has an implied power to borrow for the purposes of its business. Thus, for example, an auctioneers was held to have the implied power to borrow money in *General Auction, Estate and Monetary Co v Smith (1891)*.

Clearly, any company incorporated under the Companies Act 2006 without any restriction on its objects may do so. Companies with objects clauses will be able to borrow money to achieve their objects unless there is some express prohibition in the objects clause.

A company's articles may restrict the company's powers to borrow money. There was such a provision in Table A of the Companies Act 1948, but there is no similar provision in the 1985 Table A.

The term debenture is used in many senses. Usually, debentures are secured but they need not be. A debenture is generally under the company seal, but once again need not be.

There may be a single debenture; typically, a secured loan from a bank. By contrast there may be an issue of debenture stock where a loan is raised, usually by means of an offer to the public via The Stock Exchange. Where there is debenture stock, there will be a debenture trust deed. The trust deed will set out the terms of the loan. There may also be a debenture trust deed where there is a series of debentures, that is to say, several separate loans made to people that rank for payment *pari passu* (equally one with the other).

By virtue of s738 of the Companies Act 2006, a debenture covers any form of borrowing by a company whether secured or unsecured. The definition reads as follows:

> 'Debenture' includes debenture stock, bonds and any other securities of a company, whether constituting a charge on the assets of the company or not.

In practice, the term debenture is used to describe a secured borrowing. A mortgage that is created by a company is also a debenture: see *Knightsbridge Estates Trust Ltd v Byrne (1940)*.

## 19.2 Debentures compared with shares

Debentures and shares have certain similarities. They are both collectively termed securities. Dealings in debentures on The Stock Exchange are carried out in much the same way as dealings in shares. Prospectus rules are applicable to both shares and debentures in much the same way. There are certain distinctions between shares and debentures, however.

The main distinctions are as follows:

(a) the essential distinction between the two is that a debenture holder is a creditor of the company whereas a shareholder is a member of the company;
(b) the company is free to purchase its own debentures;
(c) debentures may be issued at a discount whereas shares cannot, see s580 of the Companies Act 2006;
(d) interest on a debenture when due is a debt which can be paid out of capital. There is no automatic right to a dividend and dividends are payable out of profits.

## 19.3  Debenture trust deeds

Where there is a debenture trust deed, which there will be if debenture stock has been issued, the trustee acts as the company's creditor. He acts on behalf of all debenture holders. It is his duty to ensure that the terms of the debentures are enforced.

The trustee of debentures may, for example, act to appoint an administrative receiver on behalf of all the debenture holders where there has been a breach of the terms of the debenture. The receiver (see Chapter 20) will be responsible for taking possession of the property which is the subject of the charge with a view to realising the property and paying off the debenture holders. This process is explained in Chapter 20 (see section 20.3, 20.4).

Certain conditions are uniform:

(a) a covenant to repay the amount of the loan at the appropriate time and to pay interest upon the due dates. In default of either of these requirements, the whole loan becomes immediately repayable;
(b) the creation of a floating charge over some or all of the company's assets;
(c) the creation of a fixed charge over the company's fixed assets;
(d) on the happening of certain events, the whole amount of the loan to become immediately repayable, for example the company ceasing business;
(e) a covenant to keep the company's property insured;
(f) a covenant to keep the company's property in good repair;
(g) the powers and the duties of the debenture trustee will also be set out in the debenture trust deed.

The advantages of a debenture trust deed are clear. It enables the company to deal with the trustee for debenture holders on behalf of all of the debenture holders and thus to act expeditiously. The trustee of debentures will be supplied with information by the company on the state of the company's business. The trustee of debentures would generally be somebody expert in business and he will thus be able to act with alacrity and with expert knowledge where the debenture holders may lack the appropriate knowledge and would in any event find it difficult to act as promptly as the trustee for debenture holders.

Once it was common to exonerate trustees of debentures in advance for any breach of trust by a provision in the trust deed. Now such provisions are generally void (s750 of the Companies Act 2006). Debenture holders may give a release to a trustee for past defaults at a meeting of debenture holders for the class of debenture holders by special resolution (s750(2) of the Companies Act 2006).

S751 CA 2006 also provides for the continuation of certain earlier provisions relieving trustees of debentures from liability.

## 19.4  A fixed charge

Although technically, under s738 of the Companies Act 2006, any form of borrowing by a company is a debenture, in practice the term is used to describe a secured borrowing. The borrowing may be secured in one or both of two different ways. The debenture may be secured by a fixed charge. This is similar to an ordinary mortgage. The charge attaches to the property subject to the charge at the time of its creation. A fixed charge over land is the most common form of fixed charge. A fixed charge may be created over other assets, however. Thus a fixed charge may be created over investments held by the company. It seems in addition that a fixed charge may be created over a company's book debts provided that these book debts are paid into a separate bank account: see *Siebe Gorman & Co Ltd v Barclays Bank Ltd (1979)*; *Re Keenan Bros Ltd (1986)*. In *Re New Bullas Trading Ltd (1993)*, Knox J held that a charge over the company's book debts constituted a floating charge.

In *Re New Bullas Trading Ltd (1994)*, the charge was over book debts which also provided that money paid was to be paid into an account at a named bank. It was then for the chargee to direct how the money was to be used but, in default, the money was removed from the fixed charge and became subject to a floating charge. The Court of Appeal held that uncollected debts were subject to a fixed charge.

In the Privy Council appeal from the Court of Appeal from New Zealand, *Agnew v Commissioner of Inland Revenue (Re Brumark) (2001)*, the case concerned a debenture which was closely modelled on the *New Bullas* debenture.

Lord Millett, delivering the judgment of the board in *Agnew*, held that the critical feature distinguishing a floating charge from a fixed charge lay in the chargor's ability, freely and without the chargee's consent, to control and manage the charge assets and withdraw them from the security. The Privy Council considered that *New Bullas* had been wrongly decided and the decision in *Siebe Gorman* was treated in guarded terms as a case in which Slade J had found sufficient restrictions on the use to which the chargor could put the collected debt payments to warrant that the charge was a fixed charge.

The issue arose once again in the House of Lords decision in *Re Spectrum Plus Ltd (in liquidation) (2005)*. Here a charge over present and future book debts, where the chargor was required to collect and place the debts in a designated account with the chargee bank, but where the chargor was free to draw on the account for its business purposes provided the overdraft limit was not exceeded, was held in law to be a floating charge, even if it was expressed as being a fixed charge.

The House of Lords held that the unrestricted use by the chargor of the proceeds in the account was inconsistent with the creation of a fixed charge since it allowed the debt and its proceeds to be withdrawn from the security.

The House of Lords held, following the Privy Council decision of Agnew in which *New Bullas* had been held to be wrongly decided, that *Siebe Gorman* was wrong and should be overruled. Although the decision in *Re Spectrum* overruled long standing authority which had been relied upon for many years by banks and other commercial lenders, the House of Lords felt that it was inappropriate to depart from the normal circumstances in which a decision has retrospective effect and did not feel that this was an appropriate case for a decision that only had prospective effect.

## 19.5  A floating charge

The second type of security is called a floating charge. The ability to create a floating charge is one of the advantages of incorporation, however, since the impact of the Enterprise Act 2002; holders of floating charges created on or after 15 September 2003, with few exceptions, will not be able to appoint an administrative receiver (a narrow category of specialist financing transactions are exempted from this general prohibition – see ss72B–72G of the Insolvency Act 1986). The floating charge enables a company to raise finance by mortgaging its entire assets and undertaking back to the provider of the finance and yet continue to trade. A floating charge does not attach to the property which is the subject of the charge until the charge crystallises. Until this time, the company is free to carry on trading with the property that is the subject of the charge. The characteristics of the floating charge are set out in *Re Yorkshire Woolcombers Association Ltd (Illingworth v Houldsworth and Another) (1904)*. These are that the floating charge is over a class of assets present and future; that the company can continue to do business and to dispose of the assets in the course of that business and that the assets within the class of assets subject to the floating charge will fluctuate and change as the company trades.

In the House of Lords, the Lord Chancellor the Earl of Halsbury described a floating charge thus:

> In the first place, you have that which in a sense I suppose must be an element in the definition of a floating security, that it is something which is to float, not to be put into immediate operation, but such that the company is to be allowed to carry on its business. It contemplates not only that it should carry with it the book debts which were then existing, but it contemplates also the possibility of those book debts being extinguished by payment to the company, and that other book debts should come in and take the place of those that had disappeared. That, my Lords, seems to me to be an essential characteristic of what is properly called a floating security.

In *Re GE Tunbridge Ltd (1995)*, the charge was expressed to be a fixed charge over all the company's assets other than land or trading stock. This would have included office equipment and book debts. Since the characteristics of a floating charge, as set out in *Re Yorkshire Woolcombers Association*, were present, these were held to be subject to a floating charge.

Generally, if the company is able to deal with the charged property in the normal course of business, the charge is a floating charge but, in *Re Cimex Tissues (1994)*, although the company had a limited power to deal with the charged machines, the charge was still held to be a fixed one.

A floating charge will crystallise in certain circumstances:

(a) if the company goes into liquidation;
(b) if a receiver is appointed either by the court or under the terms of the debenture;
(c) if there is cessation of the company's trade or business: *Re Woodroffes (Musical Instruments) Ltd (1986)*;
(d) if an event occurs which by the terms of the debenture causes the floating charge to crystallise.

There is doubt as to whether the happening of an event specified in the debenture would cause automatic crystallisation of the charge or whether the happening of the event merely permits the debenture holders to act to bring about crystallisation. In *Re Manurewa Transport Ltd (1971)*, the New Zealand court held that crystallisation could occur automatically on the happening of the specified event. This view was approved *obiter* by Hoffmann J in *Re Brightlife Ltd (1986)* and confirmed by him in *Re Permanent House (Holdings) Ltd (1989)*.

## 19.6 Registration of charges

The charges that require registration are set out in s860 of the Companies Act 2006. They are:

(a) a charge on land or an interest in land other than a charge for rent;
(b) a charge on goods or any interest in goods;
(c) a charge on intangible movable property which includes:

- goodwill;
- intellectual property;
- book debts;
- uncalled share capital of the company or calls made but not paid;
- a charge for securing an issue of debentures;

(d) a floating charge on the company's property or undertaking;
(e) a charge on a ship or aircraft, or any share in a ship.

The Secretary of State may amend the categories of registerable charges by regulation (s894 of the Companies Act 2006).

Ss860–862 of the Companies Act 2006 require registration of prescribed particulars of these charges within 21 days of their creation. Failure to register the prescribed particulars of a charge renders the charge void under s874. It does not affect the validity of the debt, of course. The charges that involve registration include charges on land, charges created to secure an issue of debentures and floating charges on the company's property or undertaking. The obligation to register the prescribed particulars of the charge is an obligation placed upon the company and therefore failure to register a charge constitutes an offence by the company and any officer who is involved. Since the creditor has an interest in registering the prescribed particulars of the charge, it may well be that he will undertake to effect the registration (s860(2) CA 2006).

The Act requires that the prescribed particulars are delivered to the registrar of companies for registration.

The obligation to register prescribed particulars also extends to the situation where the company acquires a piece of property that is already mortgaged (s862 CA 2006). Failure to register particulars of such a charge, however, does not render the charge invalid but merely results in the liability of the company and any officer in default (s862(4) and see s874). Provision is made in s873 for late delivery of particulars to the registrar after the 21 days time limit has passed. Rectification of the register of charges may be made on application of the company or a person interested and on such terms and conditions as seen to the court just and expedient. If the court is satisfied that the failure to register the charge before the end of the permitted period or the omission of any particuar:

(i)  was accidental or due to inadvertence or to some other sufficent cause; or

(ii) is not of a nature to prejudice the position of creditors or shareholders of the company, or alternatively that on other grounds it is just an equitable grant relief.

If at the time of delivery of the particulars, the company is unable to pay its debts as they fall due, or subsequently becomes unable to do so as a result of the transaction involving the charge and insolvency proceedings begin before the end of the relevant period, then the charge is void against the administrator, liquidator or other person. The relevant time period is two years in the case of a floating charge in favour of a connected person, one year in the case of a floating charge in favour of an unconnected person, and six months in any other case (see section 24.2).

## 19.7 Discharge of charges

S872 CA 2006 provides for entries of satisfaction and release.

This statement is delivered to the registrar verifying with respect to a registered charge that the debt for which the charge was given has been paid or satisfied in whole or in part, with the part of the property or undertaking charged had been released from the charge, then the registrar may enter on the register a memorandum of satisfaction in whole or of the fact that part of the property or undertaking has been released from the charge or ceased to form part of the company's property, as the case may be.

Where the registrar enters a memorandum of satisfaction in whole, the registrar, shall it require, send the company a copy of it.

## 19.8 Priorities amongst charges

As has been noted, a fixed charge applies to the property it covers from the point of creation. A fixed charge will usually take priority over a subsequent fixed charge and over any floating charge no matter when created. This is, however, subject to the proviso that, if a floating charge is created prior to a fixed charge, and the floating charge prohibits the creation of any subsequent charge with priority over that floating charge, and this condition is actually registered with the prescribed particulars at the company's registry, then that floating charge will take ahead of a subsequent fixed charge.

A floating charge attaches to the property which it covers when it crystallises. Generally, a floating charge will take priority over a subsequent floating charge: see *Re Benjamin Cope & Sons Ltd (1914)*. An exception to this general principle is if a company retains the power to create a later floating charge which covers only a particular class of assets enjoying priority over an earlier floating charge: see *Re Automatic Bottle Makers (1926)*. The company here manufactured glass bottles and other glassware. The company issued a series of debentures and by a debenture trust deed created a general floating charge over all its undertaking and assets present and future. The company retained the power to create in priority to that charge such mortgages or charges as the company should think proper 'by the deposit of any dock warrants, bills of lading, or other similar commercial documents, or upon any raw materials, or finished or partly finished products and stock for the purpose of raising moneys in the ordinary course of the business of the company'. In pursuance of this, Automatic Bottle Makers charged documents, material and stock to raise money by way of floating charge to rank ahead of the floating charge created by the trust deed.

The Court of Appeal held that the company had the power to create a second specific floating charge with priority over the first general floating charge.

## 19.9 Special circumstances affecting priorities

In relation to floating charges, three particular situations need to be noted:

(a) a judgment creditor in all probability takes priority over a floating charge if he has been paid at the time the charge crystallises or if the company's goods have been seized and sold, even though the proceeds are still retained by the bailiff;
(b) a landlord may retain goods belonging to the company and any subsequent proceeds from the sale of those goods where he is distraining for rent before the floating charge has crystallised;
(c) any preferential debts of the company are to be paid out of assets that are subject to a floating charge if there are no other assets free of the charge sufficient to pay off the preferential debts. Preferential debts are examined in detail below in section 24.4.

Furthermore, a floating charge may be invalid in certain circumstances. Under s245 of the Insolvency Act 1986, a floating charge which is created in favour of a connected person within the period two years before the onset of insolvency is invalid, except to the extent that it is made for good consideration or within 12 months of the onset of insolvency if it is made in favour of an unconnected person. If it is made in favour of an unconnected person, it also needs to be demonstrated that at the time that the charge was created the company was unable to pay its debts.

The following are connected with a company:

(a) a director or shadow director of the company;
(b) an associate of a director or shadow director of the company; and
(c) an associate of the company.

An associate includes a person's spouse, relatives, partners and their spouses and relatives, employers, employees and companies which the person and his associates control.

This condition does not apply where the charge was created in favour of a connected person.

The charged property cannot be used for paying certain debts but the debts are still payable.

In *Re Fairway Magazines Limited (1992)*, also considered below, a floating charge was created in favour of a director. The company subsequently went into insolvent liquidation, and the liquidator argued that the charge constituted a preference under s239. He also argued that £15,000 had been paid in advance of the creation of the charge and was not protected by s245(2)(a) in so far as it was argued by the liquidator that it was not for money paid or goods or services supplied at the same time or after the creation of the charge. Mummery J considered that the advance of cash could pre-date the creation of the charge, saying that as a matter of common sense it was impossible for the two to be made simultaneously and that there would inevitably be a gap between payment and the creation of the charge. What was necessary was to look at the substance of the transaction.

In *Re Shoe Lace Ltd, Power v Sharp Investments Ltd (1992)*, however, Hoffmann J thought the wording of the section required one to ask whether a reasonable businessman would consider that the money was paid at the same time as the charge was created.

In *Re Shoe Lace Ltd, Power v Sharp Investments Ltd (1993)*, in the Court of Appeal, it was decided that, where there was a gap between the advance of cash and the creation of the charge, s245 would come into play unless it was the briefest of delays. Any delay in the execution of the debenture will result in invalidity unless it really is *de minimis*.

It is also possible that a fixed or floating charge may be found to be invalid under s239 of the Insolvency Act 1986 as a preference. If it is made in favour of a connected person, once again, the period of time is two years preceding the onset of insolvency. If it is made in favour of a connected person, the period is six months ending with the onset of insolvency.

One of the guiding principles behind the insolvency legislation is to achieve equal treatment for like creditors. Therefore, preferring some creditors to others has to be tackled. In *Re Beacon Leisure Limited (1992)*, rent was paid to a director before the due date by the company. The date of payment had not arrived and the assets of the company were diminished by the payments. However, the judge accepted that there was no preference. On the face of it, the decision seems somewhat surprising.

In *Re Fairway Magazines Limited (1992)*, Mummery J held that there was no preference where a director of a company which was in financial difficulties and who had guaranteed the company's overdraft agreed to extend the borrowing facility to the company in return for a floating charge over the company's assets. It was held that the creation of the charge was part of a scheme which would enable the company to continue to do business. This was not a case of asset depletion but rather of survival of the company. It was held that the transaction was not inspired by a desire to prefer (see, also, section 24.2).

### 19.9.1 Reservation of title

There are certain additional features which need to be borne in mind in relation to priority of charges (the same features will need to be borne in mind in relation to liquidations). If a company has goods that are let out under a hire purchase agreement, or are leased, and, therefore, do not belong to the company, the owner of the goods clearly retains title to them. A similar principle applies where there is a valid reservation of title clause. In *Aluminium Industrie Vaassen BV v Romalpa Aluminium Ltd (1976)*, we have a classic exposition of the law in relation to reservation of title. The supplier of aluminium foil in the Netherlands supplied aluminium foil to the company in the United Kingdom. The aluminium foil was supplied on credit terms. The supplier expressly reserved title in the goods until they were paid for. The supplier required the purchaser to store the aluminium foil separately and imposed fiduciary obligations upon the purchaser in relation to the property. Mocatta J held that there was an effective reservation of title. He was upheld unanimously by the Court of Appeal. The relevant clause of the contract of sale provided:

> The ownership of the material to be delivered by [AIV] will only be transferred to [Romalpa] when [it has] met all that is owing to [AIV]. Until the date of payment [Romalpa could be required] to store the material in such a way that it is clearly the property of [AIV].

Three particular features were stressed in the case:

(a) there must be a clear and unambiguous reservation of the title in the property;
(b) the goods must not be inextricably linked with other goods and must be capable of being separated from other people's property;

(c) a fiduciary obligation must be placed on the purchaser by the supplier. In *Romalpa*, agency and bailment relationships had been created.

The principles in the *Romalpa* case (interestingly Romalpa was the company suffering from the so called *Romalpa* clause which was actually a clause in the supplier's terms and conditions) were applied in subsequent cases. In *Borden (UK) Ltd v Scottish Timber Products Ltd (1979)*, the supplier of resin reserved title in the resin. This was problematic because, although the resin had not been paid for, it was inextricably linked with chipboard. It was held that the supplier of the resin could not effectively reserve title where the resin was mixed with other products and could not be separated out. As Templeman LJ said:

> When the resin was incorporated in the chipboard, the resin ceased to exist, the seller's title to the resin became meaningless and the seller's security vanished. There was no provision in the contract for the buyers to provide substituted or additional security. The chipboard belongs to the buyers.

In *Re Bond Worth Ltd (1979)*, there is an object lesson in how not to create a valid retention of title (or *Romalpa* clause). Acrilan Fibre had been supplied by Monsanto Ltd to Bond Worth. It was to be used in the manufacture of carpets. The sale agreement reserved 'equitable and beneficial ownership' of the fibre. Slade J held that the effect of such a reservation was to create the necessary implication that legal title had not been reserved by the supplier. The effect of this was that the supplier was creating a charge over the property rather than reserving effective title. As such, the charge required registration. It was not registered and was, therefore, void. Similarly, in *Stroud Architectural Systems Ltd v John Laing Construction Ltd (1994)*, the plaintiffs supplied glazing units on terms where they reserved the equitable and beneficial ownership in the goods. This was held to create a floating charge as they have not reserved the legal title or full title. In *Re Peachdart Ltd (1983)*, the supplier of leather reserved title in the leather. This leather was used in the manufacture of handbags. Once again, there was an inextricable mixing of the different properties and therefore there could be no valid reservation of title in such circumstances. The provision concerned created a charge and this charge was void for lack of registration. In *Re Clough Mill Ltd (1984)*, there was a valid reservation of title in relation to yarn. The Court of Appeal restated the requirements of a valid reservation of title which had been earlier expressed in the *Romalpa* case. In *Chisholm Textiles v Griffiths and Others (1994)*, the supplier of cloth to a dress manufacturer sought to reserve title in dresses into which the fabric had been incorporated. The judge held that this created a charge over the manufactured articles which was void for non-registration.

An interesting case on reservation of title is *Hendy Lennox (Industrial Engines) Ltd v Graeme Puttick Ltd (1984)*. In this case, the supplier of diesel engines had sought to reserve title in them. The engines were installed into generators. It was contended that there could be no valid reservation where such mixing had taken place. The court held, however, that there was no inextricable linking in such a situation as the engine could be removed from the generator.

A rather curious situation arose in *Chaigley Farms Ltd v Crawford, Kaye and Grayshire (t/a Leylands) (1996)*.

In this case, the retention of title clause was over livestock. The judge considered that the exchange of correspondence made it clear that the reservation of title was over live animals. It was held that animals that had been slaughtered were not within the clause.

### 19.9.2 Liens

Another feature which should be watched for in insolvency situations, whether involving the enforcement of charges or a liquidation, is the situation involving liens. A lien is the situation that exists where a person who has done work for another retains property belonging to that other, for example, a car repairer or a watch repairer.

In circumstances where a person holds property belonging to the company where that property is subject to a charge (or would otherwise come under the direct control of a liquidator if the company is in liquidation), the holder of the property must be paid off first so that the lien is discharged before the property becomes subject to the control of the administrative receiver or liquidator. Thus, in *George Barker (Transport) Ltd v Eynon (1974)*, a transport contractor was held entitled to retain possession of a consignment of meat belonging to the company until it had been paid in respect of money owed to it. Once paid, the lien is released and the property then becomes subject to the control of the administrative receiver (or liquidator). In fact, in *George Barker*, the transport contractors had a specific provision in their contract giving them a lien – a contractual lien. Some liens such as repairers liens arise by operation of law. The transporting company in fact released the meat to the company's receiver without prejudice to any lien that it had.

### 19.9.3 Overseas companies

The principal change in the provisions relating to company charges is that charges created by overseas companies have now been replaced by a regulation making power to require registered overseas companies to register charges over property in the United Kingdom (s1052 CA 2006).

## SUMMARY

## Debentures and the law of mortgages

### Debentures

Technically, a debenture is any form of borrowing by a company but, in practice, a debenture is a secured borrowing. A debenture may be a single loan, for example, from a bank or one of an issue of debentures made to the public. An issue of debentures to the public is very similar in many respects to an issue of shares to the public. However, a debenture holder is a lender to the company not a member of the company. Debentures and shares issued to the public are collectively called securities.

Where debentures are issued to the public, there must be a debenture trust deed and, in other cases of lending, there may be. The debenture trustee who is given the task of guarding the debenture holders' interests will act to enforce the security in appropriate situations and will ensure that the terms of the lending are honoured.

## Charges

The security given to a company's borrowings may take one of two forms. It may be in the shape of a *fixed charge* which is basically similar to an ordinary mortgage and may be granted over the fixed assets such as land, investments, etc. It seems it may also be granted over a company's present and future book debts where these are paid into a separate bank account.

The other type of charge is a *floating charge* which is unique to company law and which a company may grant over its entire assets and undertaking. Unlike a fixed charge, a floating charge is not effective from the date of its creation but rather when it crystallises upon the happening of certain events. Crystallisation may occur if the company goes into liquidation, if a receiver is appointed, if the company ceases business and possibly on the happening of an event specified in the debenture agreement – automatic crystallisation.

## Registration of charges

Particulars of most, but not all, charges have to be registered within 21 days of their creation at the companies' registry. Failure to register the prescribed particulars of the charge renders it void against an administrator, liquidator or a person who acquires an interest or right over the charged property.

Late registration is permitted but subject to any rights acquired in the meantime.

In respect of matters required to be placed on the register of charges with the companies' registry, deemed notice still operates.

When a charge is discharged, an entry of satisfaction and release to that effect should be registered with the registrar of companies.

## Priorities

Fixed charges are generally paid off ahead of all floating charges and later fixed ones.

A first floating charge will generally take ahead of a subsequent floating charge unless the first preserves the possibility of a subsequent limited floating charge taking ahead of the earlier one.

*Points to note on priorities*

In determining priorities in relation to floating charges, certain creditors will take ahead of floating chargees. These are judgment creditors, landlords distraining for rent and preferential creditors.

On occasion, floating charges may be held to be invalid where a company goes into liquidation or an administration order is made and fixed or floating charges, if created as preferences (over other creditors), may also be found to be invalid where a company goes into liquidation or an administration order is made.

It is important to watch out for valid reservation of title clauses. If there are such clauses the property concerned does not belong to the company.

Where a person has a valid lien over company property, for example, a repairer's lien over lorries belonging to a company which are with the repairer following work being done on them, then the lien must be released by payment before the receiver or liquidator can take control of the property in question.

## Further reading

Berg, A, 'Charges over book debts: a reply' [1997] JBL 433.

Berg, A, 'Brumark Investment Ltd and the inominate charge' [2001] JBL 531.

Capper, D, 'Fixed charges over book debts – back to basics but how far back' [2002] LMCLQ 246.

Ferran, E, 'Floating charges – the nature of the security' [1988] CLJ 213.

Goode, R, 'Charges over book debts: a missed opportunity' (1994) 110 LQR 592.

Gregory, R, and Walton, P, 'Book debt charges – the saga goes on' (1999) 115 LQR 14.

Lawson, M, 'The reform of the law relating to security interests in property' [1989] JBL 287.

Naser, KJ, 'The juridical basis of the floating charge' (1994) 15 Co Law 11.

Pennington, RR, 'The genesis of the floating charge' (1960) 23 MLR 630.

Turing, D, 'Retention of title: how to get value from a bad penny' (1995) 16 Co Law 119.

Worthington, S, 'Floating charges – an alternative theory' [1994] 53 CLJ 81.

Worthington, S, 'Fixed charges over book debts and other receivables' (1997) 113 LQR 562.

# 20

# Receivership

Since the advent of the Enterprise Act 2002, for all new floating charges (save exceptional floating charges involving financial market operations), administration and not receivership has been the appropriate vehicle of enforcement. Banks and other trade crediitors that have floating charges created before 15 September 2003 may however continue to enforce them in the traditional way. It is unlikely that an examiner will seek more than an outline knowledge of the law of receivership. Because of this fundamental change in the law, the matter is covered here only for the sake of completeness without going into undue detail.

Where it is sought to enforce the terms of a debenture where there has been a default, the appropriate remedy used generally to be to secure the appointment of a receiver. If it is sought to appoint a person under the terms of a floating charge, the person appointed was generally an administrative receiver who had to be a qualified insolvency practitioner: see s388 of the Insolvency Act 1986. Since the coming into force of the Enterprise Act 2002, generally holders of floating charges created on or after 15 September 2003 have not been able to appoint administrative receivers. Exceptionally, in special circumstances in relation to specialist financing transactions, administrative receivers may still be appointed (see ss72B–72G of the Insolvency Act 1986).

Where an administrative receiver is appointed over the entire assets and undertaking of the company, he will need to act as manager as well as receiver. It is likely where there are substantial contracts that the receiver will also be appointed as manager, as the company will wish to continue its business during the receivership.

## 20.1 Appointment

An administrative receiver may, if the debenture is issued under the common seal of the company, be appointed where the company is in default under s101(1) of the Law of Property Act 1925. In such a circumstance, the debenture holder or a trustee for debenture holders has the opportunity to appoint a receiver of the company's income.

An alternative course of action is to enforce any express power given by the debenture to install a receiver.

In the last resort, the debenture holder can apply to the court for an order of sale of the property, foreclosure, delivery of possession or the appointment of a receiver of the property that is subject to the charge. The court will generally only appoint a receiver if the principal sum or interest is in arrears, if the company has gone into liquidation or if the security is in some way jeopardised. A receiver will not be appointed merely because it can be demonstrated that the company's assets will on realisation be insufficient to meet the amount of the secured debt: see *Re New York Taxi Cab Company (1913)*.

## 20.2 Procedure on appointment

The appointment of an administrative receiver will be in writing unless it is by court order. The debenture holder or person appointing must, within seven days, give notice that he has appointed an administrative receiver to the registrar of companies (s409 of the Companies Act 1985). The person who it purports to appoint as administrative receiver must agree to the appointment.

The person appointed as administrative receiver must notify the company of his appointment and all of the company's creditors so far as their addresses are known to him. This must be done within 28 days of the appointment (s46(1) of the Insolvency Act 1986).

In addition, administrative receivers must ensure that there is a statement of their appointment contained in the *London Gazette* (s46(1) of the Insolvency Act 1986). (The *London Gazette* is used to publicise certain matters in the administration of companies. It is read by financiers and credit agencies.)

In every receivership, there must be publicity given to the fact that there is a receivership. This must be stated on every invoice, order for goods or business letter issued by or on behalf of the company or the receiver or manager where the company's name appears (s39 of the Insolvency Act 1986).

## 20.3 The course of the administrative receivership

On the appointment of an administrative receiver, the administrative receiver will require the directors of the company to produce a statement of affairs of the company giving details of the company's assets, debts, liabilities (the names and addresses of creditors), any securities held by the creditors and the dates those securities were given (s47 of the Insolvency Act 1986). The administrative receiver should send a report to the registrar of companies, to any trustees for secured creditors and to all secured creditors for whom he has an address. The report should detail:

(a) the events leading up to his appointment;
(b) the disposal and proposed disposal of property by him;
(c) the carrying on or proposed carrying of any business by him;

(d) sums owed to debenture holders and preferential creditors;
(e) the amount, if any, likely to be available to pay other creditors (s48 of the Insolvency Act 1986).

In the course of this report, the administrative receiver is likely to comment on the content of the statement of affairs.

It should be the aim of the administrative receiver to get in the property that is subject to the charge and generally convert it to cash for payment of the sums owed to chargeholders and, where appropriate, to pay off any preferential creditors.

It may well be that, in seeking to achieve this aim, the administrative receiver elects to carry on running the business. In relation to existing contracts, the appointment of an administrative receiver would generally have no effect on the liability under such contracts. An administrative receiver is not the agent of the person appointing him, rather he is the company's agent (s44(1)(a) of the Insolvency Act 1986). The administrative receiver may conclude new contracts and will be personally liable on them (s44(1)(b) of the Insolvency Act 1986) but is entitled to an indemnity out of the assets of the company in respect of that liability (s 44(1)(c) of the Insolvency Act 1986).

When an administrative receiver is appointed by the court, he will need the approval of the court for most of his actions. Since such an administrative receiver has been appointed by the court, he is an officer of the court and interference with his functions will therefore constitute a contempt of court. Such an administrative receiver is, therefore, not an agent of the debenture holders or of the company, rather he is an officer of the court. He still has a right of indemnity out of the company's assets in the same way as an administrative receiver appointed out of court.

The powers of administrative receivers are set out in s42 and Sched 1 of the Insolvency Act 1986 and these powers include taking possession of the property, selling it, borrowing money, bringing or defending legal proceedings, appointing agents, carrying on the company's business, etc. The powers are extensive. A person dealing with an administrative receiver in good faith and for value is not concerned to enquire whether the receiver is acting within his powers (s42(3) of the Insolvency Act 1986).

In general, therefore, it may be seen that administrative receivers owe duties to the persons appointing them where they are appointed out of court and when they are appointed in court, the administrative receivers are officers of the court. It is clear from a recent case that administrative receivers also owe duties to other people. In *Downsview Nominees Ltd and Another v First City Corporation and Another (1993)*, a Privy Council case on appeal from New Zealand, it was held that a duty was owed by a receiver and manager to a second debenture holder to act in good faith for proper purposes in conducting the receivership, although the primary duty was to realise the assets for the benefit of the debenture holders. Liability was based on a breach of duty in equity rather than on negligence.

## 20.4 Priority of payments in an administrative receivership

The priority of payments in an administrative receivership is as follows:

(a) it is first necessary to pay the expenses of the administrative receivership including the administrative receiver's remuneration;
(b) where the charge is a floating charge and there are preferential creditors, these preferential creditors should be paid off out of the proceeds of the sale of property subject to the floating charge before the secured creditors are paid off (preferential creditors are considered below in section 24.4);
(c) paying off the debenture debt and interest that is due.

## 20.5 Termination of administrative receivership

Where an administrative receiver has completed his task, he may vacate office. He must give notice forthwith to the registrar of companies that he is ceasing to act (s45(4) of the Insolvency Act 1986).

An administrative receiver may also be removed by an order of the court (s45(1) of the Insolvency Act 1986). Once again, here, the administrative receiver would need to serve notice under s45(4) of the Insolvency Act 1986. Similarly, an administrative receiver may resign from office. He must give notice to his appointer and the company of his intention to resign. The notice must be of at least seven days' duration. There must be notice given to the registrar under the Companies Act 1985 and the Insolvency Act 1986.

An administrative receiver must also vacate office if he ceases to be qualified to act as an insolvency practitioner (s45(2) of the Insolvency Act 1986) and also if an administration order is made in respect of the company (s11(2) of the Insolvency Act 1986).

### SUMMARY

### Administrative receivership for floating charges created before 15.9.2003

Where there is a default in honouring the terms of a debenture, a receiver may be appointed. If a receiver is appointed under a floating charge over all of the company's assets and undertaking, he will generally act as receiver and manager (managing the company's business) and he is termed an administrative receiver. He must be a qualified insolvency practitioner. Where a person is appointed under a fixed charge, he is a receiver and need not be a qualified insolvency practitioner.

It is the role of the administrative receiver to realise the assets subject to the floating charge and to pay off in priority the charges of the receivership, preferential creditors and money owing to chargees.

## Further reading

Berg, A, 'Duties of a mortgagee and a receiver' [1993] JBL 213.

Grantham, R, 'The purpose of a company receiver's powers' (1993) Conv 401.

Hogan, A, 'Receivers revisited' (1996) 17 Co Law 226.

Lightman, Mr Justice, 'The challenges ahead: address to the Insolvency Lawyers' Association' [1996] JBL 113.

# Voluntary arrangements and administration

## 21.1 Voluntary arrangements

Part I of the Insolvency Act 1986 (ss1–7) provides a simple procedure whereby a company which is in financial difficulties may enter into a voluntary arrangement with its creditors. This arrangement may involve either: a composition in satisfaction of its debts, that is, provision for creditors to receive a percentage of what is due to them, or a scheme of arrangement of its affairs.

The voluntary arrangement must be supervised by a person, 'the nominee', who must be a qualified insolvency practitioner. The proposal for a voluntary arrangement may be made by the directors of a company or where an administration order is in force by the administrator or where the company is being wound up by the liquidator (s1 of the Insolvency Act 1986).

If the nominee is not the company's administrator or liquidator, then the proposal should be submitted to him, together with a statement of the company's affairs containing particulars of the company's assets, creditors, liabilities and debts. The nominee must then submit a report to the court stating: whether, in his opinion, meetings of the company and of its creditors should be summoned to consider the proposal, and if, in his opinion, such meetings should be summoned, the date on which and place at which they should be held (s2 of the Insolvency Act 1986).

If the nominee is the company's liquidator or administrator, he should summon meetings of the company and of its creditors to consider the proposal (s3(2) of the Insolvency Act 1986).

The meetings summoned must then determine whether to approve the proposed voluntary arrangement with or without modifications. A meeting may not approve:

(a) any proposal which affects the right of a secured creditor of the company to enforce his security except with his consent;

(b) the withdrawal of the priority of a preferential debt over other debts, except with the consent of the creditor;

(c) the payment of a proportion of preferential debts to a preferential creditor which is a smaller proportion than is to be received by other preferential creditors except with the consent of the creditor.

The proposal must be approved by three quarters in value of the creditors present and voting and by a simple majority of the members, according to the Insolvency Rules.

If the voluntary arrangement is approved, then, if the company is being wound up or if an administration order is in force, the court may stay the winding up proceedings or discharge the administration order or it may give such directions as it thinks appropriate to facilitate the implementation of the voluntary arrangement (s5 of the Insolvency Act 1986). There is a period of 28 days from the date when the nominee reports the results of the meetings' consideration to the court (s4(6) of the Insolvency Act 1986) for members, creditors and others to object to the court.

On the application of a member, contributory creditor, nominee or, if appropriate, liquidator or administrator, the proposal may be challenged on the ground that it unfairly prejudices the interests of a creditor, member or contributory of the company or that there has been some material irregularity at or in relation to either of the meetings. This section in part echoes s459 of the Companies Act 1985 (see para 14.3), just like s27 of the Insolvency Act 1986 in relation to administration (see para 20.4) (s6 of the Insolvency Act 1986).

Once the proposal for the voluntary arrangement has taken effect, the nominee becomes the supervisor of the composition of the voluntary arrangement. The supervisor may apply for a winding up to be ordered or for an administration order to be made.

If any creditor or some other interested party is dissatisfied with any act, omission or decision of a supervisor, he may apply to the court to give the supervisor directions or to alter the decision, etc in question (s7 of the Insolvency Act 1986).

The voluntary arrangement procedure is a valuable one. It was added to British company law at the behest of the Cork Committee (paras 400–403) which considered that companies, like individuals, should be able to enter into binding arrangements with their creditors.

On 6 April 1995, the government announced proposals for a new form of procedure for dealing with companies in financial trouble (Revised Proposals for a New Company Voluntary Arrangement Procedure). The directors of a company would be given 28 days to put together a rescue plan. During this moratorium the company would be supervised by a licensed insolvency practitioner.

There are safeguards for lenders and creditors. There has to be a reasonable prospect of success in the opinion of the insolvency practitioner before the plan can be put into force. There must be a creditors' meeting within 28 days of the commencement of the moratorium. If more than 75% of the creditors in value support the proposals, it is binding on all creditors. The creditors can reject the entire project. They can also extend it.

## 21.2 Administration

Following the report of the Review Committee on Insolvency Law and Practice – the Cork Report (Cmnd 8558, 1982) – a government white paper (A Revised Framework for Insolvency Law (Cmnd 9175, February 1984)) echoing some of its recommendations set out a procedure to facilitate the rehabilitation or reorganisation of a company. This process was the administration process and it was incorporated into the Insolvency Act of 1985, which was in turn consolidated in the Insolvency Act 1986. In essence, the scheme of administration is to make possible the rescue of a company by placing its management in the hands of an administrator. For as long as the administration is in force, it is not possible to commence winding up proceedings or any other process against the company or to enforce any charge, hire purchase or retention of title provision against the company without the leave of the court.

The corporate insolvency provisions of the Enterprise Act 2002, which came into force on 15 September 2003, made fundamental changes to the law of insolvency.

Henceforth the holder of a floating charge created on or after 15 September 2003 cannot appoint an administrative receiver but must instead appoint an administrator. The court-based administrative procedure of Part II of the Insolvency Act 1986 is replaced by a new system. There are henceforth three ways of appointing an administrator:

(a)   by the Court
(b)   out of Court by the company or its directors
(c)   out of Court by the holder of a floating charge.

The powers and role of an administrator are now set out in the Insolvency Act 1986 Sch.B1 para 3 (inserted by the Enterprise Act 2002).

The administrator must now seek to rescue the company and maintain it as a going concern. If this is not reasonably practicable then the administrator should seek to achieve a better result with the company's creditors than would be likely if the company were to be put into liquidation. If neither of these is reasonably achievable, then the administrator, without unnecessarily harming the interests of creditors, should seek to realise the company's property to make a distribution to one or more secured or preferential creditors.

## 21.3 Appointment by the Court

Appointment by the Court may be made at the behest of the company by ordinary resolution or unanimous written resolution, by the company's directors by a majority, or by one or more creditors. Additionally, a holder of a floating charge may seek appointment of an administrator by the court. For this to be successful, the floating charge must be a 'qualifying floating charge'.

A floating charge is a 'qualifying floating charge' if it satisfies the requirements set out in the Enterprise Act 2002 Sch 16, inserting Sch B1 to the Insolvency Act 1986. It must either state that the relevant paragraph applies to the floating charge making it a 'qualifying floating charge' or purport to give the holder of the floating charge the power to appoint an administrator or an administrative receiver. It should be noted that this last provision means that even those pre-Enterprise Act 2002 floating charges, where there was the power given to appoint an administrative receiver, will fall within the scope of this part of the Act allowing the floating charge holder to apply for an administration order.

Additionally, the floating chargeholder must hold security that relates to the whole or substantially the whole of the company's property.

It is worth noting that a 'qualifying floating chargeholder' can intervene where others apply to the Court for an order to seek the appointment of an administrative receiver (if it is an appropriate case where he is entitled to do so) or of an administrator.

A 'qualifying floating chargeholder' seeking to enforce the floating charge in obtaining an administration order need only show that the charge is enforceable. Others who seek a court administration order must demonstrate that the company is or is likely to become unable to pay its debts, and that the court order is likely to achieve the purpose of administration.

On appointment the administrator must advertise the court order in the London Gazette and in a newspaper that circulates in the area of the company's principal place of business and additionally send a copy of the court order to the Registrar of Companies.

In relation to an application to the court for the appointment of an administrator by the company or by one or more of the company's creditors, inability to pay debts has to be demonstrated.

## 21.4 Appointment by the company or the company's directors

If the appointment is to be made by the company or its directors, five written business days' notice must be given of the intention to appoint to those persons with the right to appoint an administrative receiver (in the exceptional case where this applies) or to persons having a right to appoint an administrator under the Act.

Additionally, a notice of the appointment must be filed in court, together with a statutory declaration by the appointer that he is entitled to make the appointment and that it is made under the Act. The administrator must additionally file a statement that he consents to the appointment and that the purpose of the administration is reasonably likely to be achieved in his opinion.

## 21.5 Appointment by a qualifying floating chargeholder

An appointment may be made out of court by a qualifying floating chargeholder. The qualifying floating chargeholder must give two written business days' notice to any prior qualifying charge holder unless such earlier qualifying chargeholder has consented to the appointment.

The notice of intention may be filed in court. The qualifying chargeholder must file in court a notice of the appointment and a statutory declaration that he is a qualifying floating chargeholder and that the floating charge is enforceable. Additionally, the administrator must file a statement that he has consented to the appointment and that in his opinion the purpose of the administration is reasonably likely to be achieved.

## 21.6 The administrator's proposals

However the administrator is appointed, the following steps apply.

Within eight weeks of the company entering administration, and as soon as is reasonably practicable, the administrator must file proposals as to how the purpose of the administration is to be achieved. This is sent to the Registrar of Companies as well as creditors and members of the company.

An initial creditors' meeting must be called within ten weeks, and as soon as is reasonably practicable, to consider the administrator's proposals. This meeting need not be convened if the administrator considers there is insufficient property to make a distribution to unsecured creditors above the ring-fenced amount that they are guaranteed under the Act (see section 24.4). In any event, creditors whose debts amount to at least 10% of the company's debts may require a meeting of the creditors.

At the creditors' meeting the creditors must vote on the administrator's proposals. A simple majority in value of debts is decisive of the issue.

In relation to secured creditors, the relevant amount relating to their vote is in terms of any shortfall between their debt and the value of their security. However, the administrator's proposals cannot include action that is detrimental to their rights unless this has been agreed.

'Inability to pay debts' is determined by s123 of the Insolvency Act 1986. This provides that inability to pay debts may be demonstrated by one of the following:

(a) if a creditor is owed a debt exceeding £750 for three weeks after making a written request for payment of that debt;
(b) execution or process issued on a judgment is returned unsatisfied in whole or in part (in practice, the minimum sum owed must exceed £750);
(c) if it is proved to the satisfaction of the court that the company is unable to pay its debts as they fall due (in practice, the same minimum sum applies);
(d) if the company's assets are worth less than the amount of its liabilities, taking account of contingent and prospective liability (in practice, the same minimum sum applies);
(e) in Scotland, a charge for payment on an extract decree or extract registered bond or extract registered protest have expired without payment being made (in practice, the same minimum sum applies);
(f) in Northern Ireland, a certificate of unenforceability has been granted in respect of a judgment against the company (in practice, the same minimum sum applies).

## 21.7 Effects of administration

The effect of an application for an administration order is set out in Sch B1 of the Act. Once a petition has been presented for an administration order and during the currency of an administration, none of the following may occur:

(a) no resolution may be passed or order made to wind up the company;
(b) no steps can be taken to enforce any security of the company's property or to repossess goods in the company's possession under any hire purchase or leasing agreement except with the leave of the administrator and the court and subject to such terms as the administrator or the court may impose (note that hire purchase agreements are defined to include retention of title agreements in this part of the Insolvency Act 1986);
(c) no other proceedings and no execution or other legal process may be commenced or continued and no distress may be levied against the company or its property except with the leave of the court, and once again subject to such terms as it may impose.

Once a petition for an administration order has been made, and during the currency of an administration order, a landlord's right to re-enter for forfeiture of the lease is not possible except with the permission of the court or the administrator.

## 21.8 Powers of the administrator

The person appointed to administer the company must be a qualified insolvency practitioner (see s388d, the Insolvency Act 1986). He is given wide powers of management to do what is necessary for the management of the affairs, business and property of the company. These powers include taking possession of the property, selling and otherwise disposing of it, raising or borrowing money, appointing a solicitor or accountant, bringing or defending legal proceedings, effecting and maintaining insurances, appointing agents, carrying on the business of the company, establishing subsidiaries, granting or accepting surrender of a lease or tenancy and power to do all such things that are incidental to these powers.

## 21.9 Contracts of employment and the Enterprise Act 2002

The appointment of an administrator does not affect the dismissal of the company's employees. The administrator acts as agent of the company.

S19 of the Insolvency Act 1986 provided that nothing done or omitted to be done within fourteen days of the appointment of an administrator, shall be construed as adoption of employment contracts by the administrator. This provision created some doubt as to whether failing to act within those fourteen days could be construed as adoption of employment contracts.

Sch B1 of the Insolvency Act 1986, as inserted by the Enterprise Act 2002, provides that in relation to administrations on or after 15 September 2003, action taken within the period of fourteen days after an administrator's appointment shall not be taken to amount or contribute to the adoption of a contract of employment. The clear effect of this is to indicate that an omission to act cannot amount to adoption. The decision in *Powdrill v Watson (1995)* is thus unambiguously endorsed by this provision.

## 21.10 Fair dealing

The Insolvency Act makes provision for certain transactions at an undervalue (s238), preferences (s239), extortionate credit transactions (s244) and floating charges to be invalidated where an administration order has been made. These are considered in more detail below (see section 24.2).

## 21.11 Termination of administration

Administration is terminated automatically twelve months after the effective date of appointment. This period may be extended on a single occasion for a period of an additional six months with the consent of the creditors, or any number of times by the court on the application of the administrator for such period as the court deems appropriate. In relation to creditor consent there must be the consent of at least half in value of the unsecured creditors and all of the secured creditors.

If the company is rescued in accordance with the provisions of the Act, then the administration will terminate.

Additionally, if there are funds available after secured and preferential creditors have been paid, the company may go into creditors' voluntary winding up. The administrator would, in these circumstances, become the liquidator, unless the creditors make a different choice.

If there are no funds available for distribution to creditors, the administrator must give notice to that effect to Companies House unless the court orders otherwise. The company will then be deemed dissolved after three months of the giving of the notice unless the court orders otherwise.

## SUMMARY

### Voluntary arrangements

In response to recommendations made by the Cork Committee, Pt I of the Insolvency Act 1986 makes provision for companies in financial difficulties to come to voluntary arrangements with their creditors agreeing to pay a percentage of debts that are due. A proposal for a voluntary arrangement may be made by a company's directors, liquidator or administrator. The supervisor charged with implementing the proposal must be a qualified insolvency practitioner.

## Administration

First introduced in 1985 at the behest of the Cork Committee, administration enables a company's survival – often though not always where it has been unable to pay its debts or is likely to become unable to do so.

Since the Enterprise Act 2002, the administration procedure has taken over from administrative receivership as the main method of enforcement of rights for holders of floating charges. The Enterprise Act 2002 has introduced a massive shift in the nature of insolvency law, putting, as it does, the emphasis on the survival and rescue of the company rather than on its dissolution.

## Further reading

Green, T, 'The process of administration – a potted summary, (1994) 10 IL & P 77.

Milman, D, 'Rescuing corporate rescue' (1993) 14 Co Law 82.

Phillips, M, 'The administration procedure and creditors' voluntary arrangements: the case for radical reform' [1996] 17 Insolv L 14.

Walters, A, 'Corporate Insolvency after the Enterprise Act 2002, (2004) 25 Co Law 1.

# Investigations

Minority remedies have already been considered. On occasion, powers are given to the Department of Trade and Industry which buttress the minority remedies which are available. In particular, investigations, or inspections (as they are sometimes called), may be held into companies.

## 22.1 Production of documents

If it believes that there is good reason to do so, the Department of Trade and Industry may require a company to produce documents at such time and place as is specified or it may authorise an officer of the Department or any other competent person to require a company to produce to him any documents which may be specified (s447 of the Companies Act 1985 as amended by s21 of the Companies (Audit, Investigation and Community Enterprise) Act 2004). The power extends to requiring production of documents from any person who appears to be in possession of documents but without prejudice to any lien that may be held over the documents.. The section also provides for the Secretary of State to require questions to be answered and not just those relating to any papers handed over. The power is reinforced by a power of entry and search of premises set out in s448 and ss453A and 453B of the Act. Section 450 of the Act provides a punishment for destroying, mutilating or falsifying a document and the offence is punishable by imprisonment and/or a fine. S453C of the Act makes it an offence treatable as contempt of court to fail to comply with the requirements of s447. It is usual for an officer of the Department to arrive to inspect documents to prevent destruction of the documents.

## 22.2 Investigation of affairs of company

In addition to the power to require the production of documents, the Department of Trade and Industry can in certain situations appoint inspectors to investigate the affairs of a company. Very often, the investigation is preceded by requiring the production of documents which may then demonstrate that a full-blooded investigation is appropriate. Section 431 of the Act provides that the Secretary of State may appoint one or more inspectors to investigate the affairs of a company and to report on them in such manner as he may direct. The appointment may be made in the case of a limited company with share capital on the application of not less than 200 members or members holding one tenth of the issued shares and in the case of a company without share capital on the application of one fifth of the members of the company and in any case an investigation may be held on the application of the company. In general two joint inspectors are appointed – one is usually a senior solicitor or barrister and the other is usually a senior accountant. For the sake of convenience here, the appointment will be referred to as an appointment of an inspector. The appointment of an inspector to investigate into the affairs of the company is not a judicial proceeding but an administrative one and the decision of the Department of Trade and Industry is final and cannot be challenged provided that the power is exercised *bona fide*: see *Norwest Holst Ltd v Secretary of State for Trade and Industry (1978)*. It was stated in this case that an investigation is an administrative act and that the full rules of natural justice did not therefore apply. In the case of such an application, it should be supported by such evidence as the Secretary of State may require to demonstrate that there is good reason for requiring the investigation. The Secretary of State may before appointing an inspector require the applicant or applicants to give security for the costs of the investigation.

Section 432 provides that an investigation must be held into the affairs of a company where it is ordered by the court (s432(1) of the Companies Act 1985). Furthermore, the Secretary of State may order that an investigation should be held if there are circumstances suggesting:

(a) that the company's affairs are being or have been conducted with intent to defraud creditors or otherwise for a fraudulent or unlawful purpose or in a manner which is unfairly prejudicial to some part of the members; or
(b) that an actual or proposed act or omission is or would be so prejudicial or that the company was formed for any fraudulent or unlawful purpose (note that the wording of the section was not amended by the Companies Act 1989 when s459 was amended to permit petitions where all of the members have been prejudiced. The odd result is that it would seem that an investigation cannot be ordered if all of the members are prejudiced);
(c) that persons connected with the company's formation or management have been guilty of fraud, misfeasance or other misconduct toward the company or its members; or
(d) the company's members have not been given all the information with respect to the company's affairs which they might reasonably expect (s432(2) of the Companies Act 1985).

Section 432(2A) provides that inspectors may be appointed under s432(2) on terms that their report is not for publication. In every other case, the Secretary of State may if he thinks appropriate provide that the report is to be published.

## 22.3 Investigation of ownership or control

Section 442 of the Companies Act 1985 provides that the Secretary of State may order an investigation into the ownership or control of a company to find out who the true owners of the company are if he feels there is good reason to do so. He must order an investigation if an application is made by 200 or more members or by members holding 10% or more of the company's issued shares unless he feels that the investigation is vexatious or that it would be sufficient to carry out an investigation under s444 (this provides for information being given direct to the Secretary of State without the need for the appointment of inspectors).

If the difficulty in obtaining information about any shares appears due to the non-cooperation of persons, then the Secretary of State may make an order that:

(a) any transfer of the shares will be void;
(b) voting rights in respect of the shares may not be exercised;
(c) additional shares may not be issued in respect of those shares;
(d) sums due on the shares will not be paid except in a liquidation (s454 of the Companies Act 1985).

An aggrieved person may appeal against such an order (s456 of the Companies Act 1985).

## 22.4 Investigation of directors' share dealings

In every case where an inspector is appointed under s431, 432 or 442, the inspector may investigate any other company in the group.

## 22.5 Investigation into insider dealing

Section s97 and ss167–169 of the Financial Services and Markets Act 2000 confer on the FSA and the Secretary of State power to set up investigations.

## 22.6 Consequences of inspections

As well as a final report made by the inspector, there may be interim reports. This will particularly be the case if there is a long and complex investigation. Generally speaking, the reports will be published without delay but, occasionally, there will be a time lag. A delay was challenged unsuccessfully in *Rv Secretary of State for Trade ex p Lonrho Plc (1989)*.

Some of the more important consequences of the report or the inspection of documents under the Companies Act may include the following:

(a) the Secretary of State may petition under s124(4) of the Insolvency Act 1986 if he considers it is expedient in the public interest to wind the company up on the just and equitable ground. The matter does not have to be considered personally by the Secretary of State but may be considered by an official: see *Re Golden Chemical Products Ltd (1976)*. The report will be evidence in the proceedings, see *Re Tower and Holiday Clubs Ltd (1967)*. The report itself, however, is open to challenge and other evidence may need to be adduced: see *Re Koscot (Interplanetary) (UK) Ltd (1972)*;

(b) if it appears to the Secretary of State that in the case of a company which has received a report under s437 CA 1985 (Inspectors Report), or where the Secretary of State has exercised his powers under s447 or s448 of that Act, powers to require documentation and information or to enter and search premises, or the Secretary or the Financial Services Authority has exercised powers under Part 11 of the Financial Services and Markets Act 2000 (information gathering and investigations), or the Secretary of State has received the report from an investigator appointed by him or the Financial Services Authority, then the Secretary of State may, if it appears to him that the company's affairs are being or have been conducted in a manner that is unfairly prejudicial to the interests of members generally or some part of the members, or that an actual or proposed act or omission of the company, including an act or omission on its behalf would be so prejudicial, then he may apply to the court for a petition under s995 in relation to unfairly prejudicial conduct. He may do this in addition to or instead of presenting a petition for the winding up of the company (s995 CA 2006);

(c) an application may be made for a disqualification order against any person who is or has been a director or shadow director of any company if it appears to the Secretary of State from the report or from information gleaned from documents that have been disclosed that a disqualification order should be made in the public interest. The maximum period for such a disqualification is 15 years.

If matters come to light during the course of an investigation which suggest that a criminal offence has been committed and those matters are referred to the appropriate prosecuting authority, the Secretary of State can halt the inspection or confine it to specific matters (s437(1A) of the Companies Act 1985).

## 22.7 Expenses of investigation

The expenses of investigation are borne by the Department of Trade. It may, in appropriate cases, recover them from persons, particularly those convicted as a result of prosecutions consequent upon a report.

## 22.8 Impact of the Companies Act 2006

The 2006 Act makes some minor amendments to the law on company investigations.

The Inspector may now be given general directions by the Secretary of State under s446(a) with regard to exercising his functions. He may also be asked to take no further steps in the investigation s44B (s1035 CA 2006).

The 2006 Act also makes provision in relation to the resignation, removal and replacement of Inspectors (s1036 CA 2006), and the power to obtain information from former inspectors (s1037 CA 2006).

## SUMMARY

### Investigations

The Department of Trade and Industry is given various powers to investigate the affairs, ownership or directors' share dealings within a company. There are also powers to investigate insider dealing.

As a prelude to an investigation, the Department of Trade and Industry may order a company to disclose specified documents to it. This may conclude the matter by revealing what action should be taken or that nothing is amiss or it may be the prelude to a full-blooded investigation. Where inspectors are appointed, one is generally a senior lawyer and one a senior accountant. Their report may be published. The inspection is an administrative proceeding not a judicial one.

As a consequence of the inspection, the Secretary of State may do one or more of the following:

(a)  initiate winding up proceedings on the just and equitable ground;
(b)  petition on the grounds of unfair prejudice;
(c)  apply for a disqualification order against a director or shadow director.

### Further reading

Mitchard, P, 'Judicial review of DTI inspectors appointed under s 432(2) of the Companies Act 1985' [1985] 1 CJRB 6.

# Takeovers, reconstructions and amalgamations

Certain terms are used repeatedly in this area of 'takeovers'.

## 23.1 Takeovers

The term 'takeover' is generally used to describe the situation where one company acquires the shares of another company (target company). The acquiring or bidding company becomes the holding company of the acquired or target company which therefore becomes a subsidiary. Takeovers may be accomplished by agreement or a takeover bid may be a 'hostile' bid.

## 23.2 Reconstructions

A reconstruction is generally accomplished where the shareholders of the transferring company and the shareholders of this company to which the business has transferred are the same. The people who are carrying on the reconstructed business are thus generally the same as those who carried it on before. Reconstructions may involve an external element such as where a particular company sells its business and assets to another company in exchange for shares in that company; alternatively reconstructions may be internal within a particular group where the capital structure within the group is altered.

## 23.3 Amalgamations

The term 'amalgamation' is usually used where two companies are brought together. The two companies may become one new company, for example, X Plc and Y Plc becoming Z Plc, or alternatively X Plc may be subsumed by Y Plc or vice versa. Here, clearly, there is an overlap with the term 'takeover'.

## 23.4 Takeovers directive

The United Kingdom was obliged to take action in relation to takeovers by virtue of the EU Takeovers Directive (2004/25/EC). This had to be implemented in the UK by 20 May 2006. In consequence the government made the Takeovers

Directive (Interim Implementation) Regulations 2006 (SI/2006/1183). These regulations came into force on 20 May 2006. The provisions in the regulations have been replaced by the relevant provisions of the Companies Act 2006.

## 23.5 Key changes

The key changes relate to new statutory rules that have been introduced and also to revisions in The City Code on Takeovers and Mergers.

The new statutory rules generally apply to companies whose shares are admitted to trading on an EEA regulated market, whilst the Code has been amended to bring its provisions into line with the Takeovers Directive for all companies and for all transactions that come within the Panel's jurisdiction.

The new statutory rules include a requirement for directors' reports every year containing detailed information on the share and management structures of the company (s992 CA 2006); a new offence for failure to comply with the Code's rules on documentation in relation to takeover bids (s953 CA 2006); changes relating to compulsory purchase of outstanding shares where there is a takeover offer ('squeeze-out' and 'sell-out') (Part 28 Chapter 3 of the 2006 Act), as well as provisions enabling companies to 'opt in' to the 'breakthrough' provisions which have the effect of removing pre-bid defences for opting in companies (s966 CA 2006).

Most of the new statutory rules only apply where there is a takeover bid within the Directive. It is important therefore to understand what takeover bids are captured by the Directive. The jurisdiction only relates to a public offer for the transferable securities of an EEA company where the securities carry voting rights and are admitted to trading on an EEA regulated market provided that the bid's object is control of the company or where control has already been acquired.

Voting rights are defined as votes in a general meeting including rights that may only arise in certain circumstances.

## 23.6 Directors' reports

The statutory rules require additional disclosure in directors' reports if the company had securities carrying voting rights admitted to trading on a regulated market at the end of the financial year, whether or not the company is presently subject to a takeover bid. The aim is to ensure transparency in relation to the share and management structures of companies that may become subject to a bid within the terms of the Directive (s992 CA 2006).

## 23.7 The new offence relating to bid documentation

The Act introduces a new criminal offence for failure to comply with rules relating to the documentation on a takeover bid. This applies if there is a bid within the terms of the Directive to which the Code's rules apply. If the document does not comply with the document rules then an offence is committed.

In relation to an offer document, the offence could be committed by a company or by a company's directors, officers or shareholders. In relation to a response document responding to a bid, the offence could be committed by any of the target directors or other officers but not the target company itself.

Liability would only lie where the person knew or was reckless as to the non-compliance of the relevant documents and where that person failed to take all reasonable steps to ensure that the document did comply (s953 CA 2006).

## 23.8 'Squeeze-out' and 'sell-out' rules

The offeror has to reach the relevant 90% threshold before and cannot give a 'squeeze-out' notice after the end of the period of three months after the closure of the last date on which the offer can be accepted. It should be remembered that the purpose of the provisions is to ensure that where an offer is made to acquire all the shares or shares of a class that the offeror does not already hold, then if the offer is accepted by 90% in value of shareholders then the offeror can give notice to acquire the other 10%. Similarly there is reciprocity in that the remaining percentage of 10% or less can serve notice to be acquired. These are the 'squeeze-out' and 'sell-out' principles in the Act and existed in the 1985 Act although they have now been amended (Part 28 Chapter 3 of the 2006 Act).

## 23.9 'Opting in' and 'opting out' in relation to pre-bid defences

The Takeover Directive provides for the cancellation of companies' pre-bid defences. The pre-bid defences are where minority shareholders can issue disproportionate voting rights and where they have restrictions on the transfer of shares in the company's articles or in separate contractual agreements. The Act permits UK companies to 'opt in' to a regime which has the effect of cancelling these pre-bid defences. A company may 'opt in' by passing a special resolution. It can 'opt out' again by passing similarly a further special resolution (s966 CA 2006).

If a person suffers loss by reason of the rendering invalid of a pre-bid defence, that person is entitled to such just and equitable compensation as may be ordered by the court (s968(6) CA 2006).

## 23.10 Changes to the code

S942 CA 2006 provides the definition of the panel, i.e. the Panel on Takeovers and Mergers, which has functions in relation to the supervision of takeovers and mergers within the Takeovers Directive and beyond.

The panel is responsible for issuing Principles, Rules, Rulings and Directions. The Act makes provision for this in ss943–946 CA 2006.

S952 provides for sanctions in relation to breach of rules issues by the Panel.

Furthermore, s953 provides that it is an offence for failure to comply with rules about bid documentation within this section, and s954 provides that rules may confer power on the Panel to order a person to pay such compensation as it thinks just and reasonable if he is in breach of a rule, the effect of which is to require the payment of money.

S955 provides for enforcement by the court on the application of the Panel, if the court is satisfied there is a reasonable likelihood that a person will contravene a rule of the Panel or contravene an order requiring disclosure of information or documents under s947.

It is further provided however by s956 that contravention of a rule or disclosure reuqirement does not give rise to any right of action for breach of statutory duty.

Provision is made in ss957–959 for funding the Panel's activities.

A prime change in the law relates to the scope of the Code's jurisdiction. Previously the Code's jurisdiction limited the Panel's ability to act in relation to takeover bids, but now the jurisdiction has been extended to cover all takeover bids within the Takeover Directive where there is a United Kingdom element in terms of registered office or where the securities of the company are traded on a UK regulated market.

Sometimes there will be shared jurisdiction as to where the registered office is in the United Kingdom but the regulated market is in a different EEA member state.

If the target company has its registered office in the United Kingdom, the Isle of Man or the Channel Islands, and its securities are regulated on a UK regulated market or on any stock exchange in the Isle of Man or the Channel Islands, then the Code applies to that company, whether or not the main place of management is within the United Kingdom, the Isle of Man or the Channel Islands. The law in applying the provisions to the Isle of Man and the Channel Islands goes beyond the scope of the Directive which does not require this (s965 CA 2006).

Other companies are also within the jurisdiction if the registered office and the main place of management is within the United Kingdom but the securities are admitted to trading on a regulated market elsewhere within the EEA, then the companies are subject to the jurisdiction of the Panel within the Code.

In certain cases there is shared jurisdiction as where the target company has its registered office in an EEA state and securities are admitted to trading on a regulated market in another EEA member state and the UK is one of those states in one or the other situation. If there is shared jurisdiction then only part of the Code applies dependent on whether it is a matter of the company's registered office being within the UK or the company's securities being traded in the UK. If there is shared jurisdiction then, in those cases, the Code would only cover takeover bids within the meaning of the Directive. If, however, the jurisdiction is not shared then the Code will continue to regulate transactions that were previously covered. These are takeover bids and mergers, together with other transactions where the objective is obtaining or consolidating control as well as partial (and tender) offers. However, it would only regulate these additional transactions if the company is a UK, Isle of Man or Channel Islands company, or it is the type of public or private company that it regulated previously.

## 23.11  General principles, definitions and rules

New general principles contained in the Directive have now been enacted.

A major change to the definitions is the extension of the definition of acting 'in concert'. This has been extended to include a person who co-operates with the target company to frustrate the bid.

There are certain rule changes as well to bring the Code into line with the requirements of the Directive. Some of these rule changes involve detailed provisions relating to the contents of offer documents. There are also more detailed rules regarding the disclosure of the offeree board's views.

## 23.12  Substantial Acquisition Rules abolished

The Substantial Acquisition Rules, which were introduced in response to the dawn raid syndrome, and which required those establishing significant shareholdings in companies above 15% to declare this, have now been abolished.

It is worth noting that stakeholders must still disclose within two days of acquiring an interest of 3% or above, and within an offer period those 'interested' in 1% or more of a company's securities are required to disclose their dealings under the Code.

## 23.13  Arrangements and reconstructions

Part 26 of the Companies Act 2006 deals with arrangements and reconstructions.

Ss895–901 deal with compromise or arrangements between a company and its creditors or any class of them or its members or any class of them (s895 CA 2006).

However, these provisions essentially apply to arrangements and reconstructions of private companies. Part 27 of the Companies Act 2006 deals with mergers and divisions of public companies and there are more onerous rules to be followed in relation to these companies.

With respect to private companies, however, application should be made to the court under s896 to order a meeting of the creditors or class of creditors or members or class of members to be summoned as the court may direct to consider the proposed arrangement.

Where a meeting is summoned under s896, the notice summoning the meeting must explain the effect of the compromise or arrangement and in particular state any material interests of the directors, whether as members or as creditors of the company, and the effect on those interests of the compromise or arrangement that is proposed.

S899 provides that if a majority in number representing 75% in value of the creditors or class of creditors or members or class of members (as the case may be) present and voting, either in person or by proxy, agree a compromise or arrangement, the court may, on an application under this section, sanction the compromise or arrangement.

The application to the court may be made by the company or any creditor or member of the company, or if the company is being wound up, or an administration order is in force in relation to it, the liquidator or administrator.

As noted, Part 27 of the Act deals with mergers and divisions of public companies. S903 provides that the requirements applicable to a merger for public companies are specified in ss905–914, and that certain of these requirements modify or exclude the provisions of Part 26.

Furthermore, the requirements applicable to a division are specified in ss920–930 and similarly these requirements modify or exclude in some respects the provisions of Part 26 by ss931–934.

S904 defines the mergers that are affected by Part 27 of the Act.

S905 provides that a draft of the proposed terms of the scheme must be drawn up and adopted by the directors of the merging companies. These draft terms must be published and published to the registrar (s906).

The scheme must be approved by a majority in number representing 75% in value of each class of members present and voting (s907).

The directors of each of the merging companies must draw up or adopt reports explaining the effect of the compromise or arrangement and must adopt this report. Furthermore, s909 provides that an expert's report must be drawn up on behalf of each of the merging companies. The report that is required is the written report on the draft terms to the members of the company. The expert's report must indicate the methods to be used in arriving at the share exchange ratio, describing the valuation difficulties that may have arisen, giving an opinion of the method or methods used, and stating whether they consider the share exchange ratio to be reasonable.

S910 provides that the last annual accounts of any of the merging companies are to be supplemented by an accounting statement if there are more than seven months before the first meeting of the company summoned to consider and possibly approve the scheme.

S911 provides for inspection of the documents relating to merger, setting out the draft terms, the directors' explanatory report, the expert's report and the company's annual accounts and reports, supplemented, if appropriate.

S912 provides for articles of the new company to be approved by ordinary resolution of the transferor company or each of the transferer companies, and s913 provides for protections of holders of special rights attaching to securities.

Ss915–918 provides for some circumstances where particulars in reports are not required. In particular s916 provides that meetings or members of a transferee company is not required where the merger is one by absorption when 90% or more of the relevant securities of the transferer or company are held by or on behalf of the transferee company, and s917 provides that no meetings are required if conditions are met regarding disclosure of documents where minority members of not less than 5% of the paid up capital of the company would have been able, during the period, to require a meeting of each class of members and did not require such.

In a similar way, Chapter 3 of Part 27 deals with division of companies where the scheme involves a division where under the scheme the undertaking properties and liabilities of the company in respect of which the compromise or arrangement is proposed, are to be divided among and transferred to two or more companies, each of which is either an existing public company or a new company, whether or not a public company.

In such a situation, draft terms of the scheme must be drawn up and adopted by the directors (s920 CA 2006) and the draft terms must be published by the directors, delivering a copy of the draft terms to the registrar (s921 CA 2006).

The members must approve the division by 75% in value of each class of members of the company present in voting in person or by proxy (s922 CA 2006).

The directors of the transferor company and each existing transferee company must draw up and adopt an explanatory report which sets out the legal and economic grounds for the draft terms, and details of the criteria for the allocation to members of shares in the transferee company (s923 CA 2006).

S924 CA 2006 provides for an expert's report to be drawn up on behalf of each company involved in the division, setting out the methods used to arrive at the share exchange ratio, describing any special valuation difficulties that have arisen, describing the method or methods used for valuation, and stating whether in the expert's opinion the share exchange ratio is reasonable.

S925 provides for a supplementary accounting statement if the last annual accounts ended more than seven months before the first meeting of the company summoned for the purposes of approving the scheme.

S926 provides that members of the company must be able, during the period before the scheme is adopted, to be able to inspect the following documents: the draft terms, the directors' explanatory report, the expert's report, the company's annual accounts and reports, and, if appropriate, any supplementary accounting statement that has been required by s925.

Once again, there are circumstances in which meetings of members of a transferee company may not be required. One such is if documents are appropriately disclosed and there is the right for members representing 5% or more of paid up capital to require a meeting and no such meeting has been required (s932 CA 2006).

Furthermore, s933 provides that all of the members may agree to dispense with the requirements of certain reports such as the directors' explanatory report, the expert's report, and the supplementary accounting statement.

S934 provides for the power of the court to exclude certain requirements where conditions regarding disclosure of documents and publication of draft terms have been complied with.

## 23.14 Sale of assets in return for shares

Another way of accomplishing a reconstruction is under ss110 and 111 of the Insolvency Act 1986. This involves the following procedure. The company that is to be transferred is in the course of a voluntary winding up or being proposed for voluntary winding up. The company in voluntary liquidation sells its assets in exchange for shares in the transferee company. The transferee company's shares are then distributed to the former members of the transferor company. Section 111 of the Insolvency Act provides that dissentient members of the transferor company who did not vote in favour of the special resolution placing the company in voluntary liquidation may, within seven days, by writing to the liquidator, require that their interests be purchased for cash.

There is no need to apply to the court here. The main disadvantage for the transferee company is the provision that dissentients may require that their interests be purchased for cash. Indeed, the right of a dissentient member to dispose of his shares for cash is sacrosanct and cannot be excluded by the company's constitution: see *Bisgood v Henderson's Transvaal Estates Ltd (1908)*.

## SUMMARY

### Takeovers, reconstructions and amalgamations

The Companies Act 2006 makes provision for the compulsory acquisition of up to 10% of a target company's shares where the bidding company has acquired 90%. The acquisition of the minority holding would be ordered on the same terms as the majority was acquired. Not only does the majority have a right to acquire the minority but the minority has a corresponding right to be acquired.

The Act also provides for schemes of arrangement to be made between a company and its creditors or members. These provisions are usually utilised where there is an internal reconstruction. The procedure involves application to the court on two occasions so it can be costly. There are additional requirements if the reconstruction involves the merger of at least one public company or a division where at least one of the companies is a public company or a new company.

A straightforward procedure for merger is presented by the Insolvency Act where a company goes into voluntary liquidation. The liquidator accepts shares from a transferee company in exchange for the assets of the company. The shares are then distributed to the former members of the transferor company. A dissentient in the transferor company can insist on his interest being purchased for cash.

Where there is a takeover involving a quoted company, the City Code on Takeovers and Mergers is of crucial importance. It is extra-statutory but policed by the City Panel on Takeovers and Mergers. The City Code is made up of general principles and detailed rules governing the conduct of takeovers.

### Further reading

Adenas, M, 'European takeover directive and the city' (1997) 18 Co Law 101.
Calcutt, D, 'Company law lecture – the work of the takeover panel' (1990) 11 Co Law 203.
Oditah, F, 'Takeovers, share exchanges and the meaning of loss' (1996) 112 LQR 424.

# 24

# Liquidation

It is beyond the scope of this work to give a detailed survey of the law on liquidation. This area of law is a complex one. Not only is the Insolvency Act 1986 devoted in part to the law on liquidation (or winding up), but this is supplemented by detailed insolvency rules governing the practice of insolvency (Insolvency Rules 1986).

The law on winding up as well as personal bankruptcy was updated by the Insolvency Act 1985 following the Report of the Review Committee on Insolvency Law and Practice (the Cork Report – Cmnd 8558, 1982). The Committee had been appointed as long ago as 1977 with the allotted task of making proposals to reform the law on personal bankruptcy and corporate insolvency. This was then consolidated in the Insolvency Act 1986. The Enterprise Act 2002, as has been noted, makes some fundamental changes to insolvency law (Chapter 20).

## 24.1 Types of winding up

There are essentially two types of winding up. There is compulsory winding up – a winding up by court order, and voluntary winding up – winding up initiated by the members of the company. Voluntary winding up then splits into two types:

(a) members' voluntary winding up which is largely under the control of the members where the directors swear a statutory declaration of solvency; and
(b) creditors' voluntary winding up which is largely under the control of the creditors as the directors have seen fit not to swear a statutory declaration of solvency.

### 24.1.1 Compulsory winding up

Section 122(1) of the Insolvency Act 1986 sets out the grounds of compulsory winding up. They are as follows:

A company may be wound up if:

(a) the company has by special resolution resolved that the company be wound up by the court;

(b) that the company is a public company which has registered as such on initial incorporation but has not been issued with a certificate to do business under s117 of the Companies Act and more than a year has expired since it was so registered;

(c) the company is an old public company within the meaning of the Consequential Provisions Act;

(d) the company has not commenced business within a year of incorporation or suspends business for a year;

(e) the number of members is reduced below two unless it is a private company to which the exemption relating to a membership of one now applies;

(f) the company is unable to pay its debts;

(g) the court is of the opinion that it is just and equitable that the company should be wound up.

The court clearly has a discretion as to whether or not to grant a petition. This point receives support from s125 of the Insolvency Act 1986 which provides that the court may dismiss a petition or adjourn the hearing conditionally or unconditionally or make an interim order or any other order that it thinks fit.

Only the last two grounds in s122(1) are of great importance. The inability to pay debts is 'fleshed out' in s123 of the Act. This has been covered above (section 21.6). In considering the various grounds that demonstrate inability to pay debts, the court will take account of any disputed debts and if it feels that there is a bona fide dispute concerning a debt, no winding up order will be granted unless it is clear that more than £750 is owed by the company.

In *Re Welsh Brick Industries Ltd (1946)*, the Court of Appeal held that a judge was competent to grant a petition on the basis of the evidence before him even though unconditional leave to defend the debt had been given to the company.

Even if it is demonstrated that there is a dispute concerning the debt, a winding up petition may be granted if it is established that at least £750 is owing. Thus, it was established in *Re Tweeds Garages Ltd (1962)* that the garage owned at least the minimum amount then required by the Act and the petition was granted.

Yet, the existence of a debt of the requisite amount is not sufficient of itself to force a winding up petition. The court has a discretion and will consider the views of contributories and especially of other creditors. In *Re ABC Coupler and Engineering Co Ltd (1961)*, a judgment creditor with a debt of in excess of £17,500 petitioned for an order that the company be compulsorily wound up. The petition was not supported by any other creditor and was opposed by a number of them. The company had extensive goodwill and a considerable excess of assets over liabilities. The petition was not granted.

The various grounds on which a petition to wind the company up on the just and equitable ground may be granted have also been considered above (see para 14.6). The petition here is presented by a member or contributory as he is termed in a liquidation situation (see s124(2) of the Insolvency Act 1986). The presence of the remedy of just and equitable winding up is a clear demonstration of the fact that winding up is available in situations other than where the company is in financial difficulties. The appellation insolvency as applied to the Insolvency Act is in some ways misleading. Indeed, it seems that the contributory whose shares are fully paid must show that he has an interest in the winding up which means that he must demonstrate that assets will be available for distribution. The question was left open in *Re Rica Gold Washing Co (1879)*.

In addition, s124(2) of the Insolvency Act 1986 provides that a contributory may only present a petition if the number of members is reduced below the statutory minimum or he holds shares which were originally allotted to him, or have been transmitted to him on the death of a former holder or he has held the shares for at least six months from the previous 18 months before the commencement of the winding up.

The progress of a compulsory liquidation is that the petition is presented, for example, by a creditor if it is on the ground of inability to pay debts or by a contributory if it is on the ground that it is just and equitable that the company should be wound up.

The Secretary of State for Trade and Industry may also present a petition on grounds (b) or (c) above and also if, following a report made or information received in relation to company investigations or information obtained under s2 of the Criminal Justice Act 1987 in relation to fraud investigations or under s83 of the Companies Act 1989 in relation to assisting overseas regulatory authorities, he thinks that it is expedient in the public interest that a company should be wound up.

Once the petition has been presented, it is then for the court to decide whether the case has been made out. If it has been made out, the petition may be granted at the court's discretion and an order to wind the company up may be made. The commencement date of the liquidation is the date the petition is presented, that is, retrospectively the date of the commencement of liquidation is the date of the petition. This is material in many situations as certain acts or transactions may be rendered invalid within certain time limits.

As has been noted, s125 of the Insolvency Act 1986 provides that on hearing a winding up petition the court can grant the petition or adjourn the hearing conditionally or unconditionally or make an interim order. It should not refuse to grant a winding up petition solely on the ground that the company's assets have been mortgaged equal to or in excess of the company's assets or on the basis that the company has no assets.

Once a winding up petition has been presented, the company or any creditor or contributory can apply to the court for a stay of proceedings where proceedings are pending in the High Court or Court of Appeal and in any other case may apply to restrain further proceedings (s126 of the Insolvency Act 1986). The actual making of the order operates to stay all proceedings but this provision enables action to be taken to stay proceedings upon presentation of the petition.

Once a winding up petition has been presented, any disposition of the company's property and any transfer of shares or alteration of its status is void unless the court orders otherwise where it has been committed after the commencement of the winding up (s127 of the Insolvency Act 1986). Since the commencement date of a winding up is the presentation of the petition, this renders void dispositions after the presentation of the petition.

Section 127 includes payments that are made into and out of a company's bank account, see *Re Gray's Inn Construction Co Ltd (1980)*. The principles on which dispositions may be validated were discussed by the Court of Appeal in *Re Gray's Inn Construction Co Ltd*. Buckley LJ said that in general the interests of the unsecured creditors will not be prejudiced in making any validation decision. He went on to say that a disposition carried out in good faith in the course of business at a time when the parties are unaware that a petition has been presented would normally be validated by the court.

Where a winding up order is granted, the court will appoint a provisional liquidator and that liquidator will be the official receiver (s136(2)). The official receiver may require some or all of the company's officers, those involved in its formation within the previous year, those in its employment or previous employment within the last year, or those who are officers or in the employment of a company which was within the previous year an officer of the company, to provide a statement of affairs to the official receiver setting out the company's assets, debts, liabilities, names and addresses of its creditors, securities held by them and the dates on which the securities were given.

Section 139 provides that separate meetings of creditors and contributories may be called for the purpose of choosing a permanent liquidator. The creditors and the contributories at their respective meetings may nominate a person to be liquidator. The liquidator will be the person nominated by the creditors in the event of any conflict. Yet, the contributories may go to court to overturn the decision seeking the appointment of the person nominated by them. The same meetings of creditors and contributories may nominate people to a liquidation committee. The purpose of the liquidation committee will be to liaise with the liquidator during the course of the winding up. The liquidation committee is not able or required to function whilst the official receiver is liquidator.

Certain powers of the liquidator in a compulsory winding up can only be exercised with the sanction of the liquidation committee (see s167(1)(a) of the Insolvency Act 1986).

It is the function of the liquidator to realise the company's property for cash during the liquidation. The proceeds should then be distributed to the company's creditors and if there is a surplus to the persons entitled to it, generally the contributories (class rights are again relevant here – see Chapter 6): s143 of the Insolvency Act 1986.

The liquidator takes into his custody and places under his control all the company's property and things in action (s144 of the Insolvency Act 1986).

### 24.1.2 *Voluntary liquidation*

Voluntary liquidation may commence in the following ways:

1 If a fixed period has been settled for the duration of the company and the fixed period has now passed or if the company is to come to an end, after a certain event, then the company may be wound up by ordinary resolution.
2 If the company resolves to be wound up voluntarily by special resolution.
3 If the company resolves by extraordinary resolution to be wound up on the basis that it cannot by reason of its liabilities continue its business.

(Section 84 of the Insolvency Act 1986.)

Notice of any resolution to wind up should be published in the *London Gazette* within 14 days (s85(1) of the Insolvency Act 1986).

In a voluntary winding up, the winding up commences on the date that the resolution is passed (s86 of the Insolvency Act 1986).

If the directors of the company or a majority of them swear a statutory declaration of solvency to the effect that the company will be able to pay its debts in full together with interest within the next 12 months, then this represents a statutory declaration of solvency. If such a declaration is made, then the declaration should be delivered to the registrar of companies. Where there is such a declaration, the liquidation proceeds as a members' voluntary winding up as the interests of creditors are supposedly protected by the statutory declaration of solvency that has been sworn. The statutory declaration of solvency should be passed within the five week period immediately before the resolution to wind up (ss89–90 of the Insolvency Act 1986).

If the winding up proceeds as a members' voluntary winding up, then there will be a general meeting of members or contributories to pass a resolution to wind up and to appoint somebody as liquidator.

If no statutory declaration of solvency is sworn then the liquidation proceeds as a creditors' voluntary winding up. In such a situation, a general meeting of members is needed to resolve to wind up, to nominate a liquidator and to appoint members (up to five) for the liquidation committee.

(Note that a liquidation committee implies a compulsory winding up or a creditors' voluntary winding up. No liquidation committee is appointed in a members' voluntary winding up as it is believed that the interests of creditors are protected by the statutory declaration of solvency. In a compulsory winding up and a creditors' voluntary winding up, there may be a liquidation committee.)

In the creditors' voluntary winding up, a meeting of creditors will be called to appoint a liquidator and if the creditors so wish to appoint up to five creditors' representatives on to a liquidation committee. In the event of a dispute on the choice of liquidator, the creditors' choice will prevail unless the court orders otherwise (ss100–101 of the Insolvency Act 1986).

## 24.2 Fair dealing

Certain matters that should be watched for in relation to a liquidation have already been noted: see invalidity of floating charges (s245 of the Insolvency Act 1986) and invalidity of preferences (s239 of the Insolvency Act 1986) (see section 19.10).

There are other provisions in the Insolvency Act concerned with the adjustment of prior transactions (administration and liquidation). These are the so-called fair dealing provisions.

Section 238 of the Insolvency Act 1986 provides that an administrator or liquidator may apply to the court for an order of restitution where the company has entered into a transaction at an undervalue as where it makes a gift of property or receives significantly less consideration for property than its true value. The court will not make an order if it is satisfied that the company entered into the transaction in good faith and for the purpose of carrying on its business and that at the time it did so there were reasonable grounds for believing that the transaction would benefit the company.

An order may be made, just as in the case of preferences, if the transaction is in favour of a connected person, within two years of the onset of insolvency or, if in favour of an unconnected person, within six months of the onset of insolvency. (The onset of insolvency means the date of presentation of a petition to appoint an administrator or the date of commencement of the winding up. Any transaction between the presentation of a petition for administration and the granting of the order is also caught.)

In *Re MC Bacon Ltd (1990)*, the court had to consider whether the granting of a floating charge in favour of a bank amounted to a preference or a transaction at an undervalue, or neither.

The company imported bacon. Its main customer withdrew and two of the company's directors retired; one of them was obese and could not perform the manual work required of him. The bank was worried at the decline in the company's fortunes. It sought and obtained a floating charge to secure the company's overdraft. The directors knew they needed the continued support of the bank. Subsequently, the company went into insolvent liquidation and the liquidator sought to set aside the charge and the appointment of an administrative receiver. The judge considered that the decision to grant the floating charge to the bank had been made to prevent the bank calling in its overdraft. Furthermore, he considered that the transaction was not at an undervalue.

Payments made to three directors (husband, wife and son) from accounts which each held with the company less than three months before the company went into administration were held to be preferences in *Re Exchange Travel (Holdings) Ltd (In Liq) (1996)*.

Extortionate credit transactions where credit is supplied to the company on terms where the payments are grossly exorbitant or where the terms otherwise grossly contravene ordinary principles of fair dealing are also caught (s244 of the Insolvency Act 1986). The time limit here is a transaction within the three year period terminating with the date of the administration order or the date when the liquidation commenced (s244(2) of the Insolvency Act 1986).

The court may order the transaction to be set aside or some part of it. It may vary the terms or order the surrender of money or property or order accounts to be taken. It may order any combination of these.

## 24.3 Malpractice

Another area of law of importance in a liquidation concerns the penalisation of directors and officers for malpractice. Section 212 of the Insolvency Act 1986 provides a summary remedy in winding up where a person who has been an officer, liquidator, administrator or administrative receiver or concerned in the promotion, formation or management of the company has misapplied or retained or become accountable for the company's money or property or been guilty of any misfeasance or breach of any fiduciary or other duty in relation to the company. The court may order repayment of money or restoration of property or such contribution for breach of duty as the court thinks just. It would appear that s1157 of the Companies Act 2006 enabling the court to give relief to any officer does not cover liquidators, administrators or administrative receivers (see section 12.11.4).

A provision of some importance enables the court on the application of the liquidator to declare that any persons knowingly party to the carrying on of the business of a company with intent to defraud creditors or for a fraudulent purpose be ordered to contribute to the company's assets. This is the so called 'fraudulent trading' section (s213 of the Insolvency Act 1986). The Cork Committee had recommended that, whilst retaining the high standard of proof for criminal proceedings (now s993 of the Companies Act 2006), a lower standard of proof founded on unreasonable behaviour should become the basis for civil liability. In the event, a new provision – s214 of the Insolvency Act – based on unreasonable behaviour – wrongful trading – supplements rather than replaces s213 of the Act.

Under s213, actual deceit on the part of the person carrying on the business must be shown. In *Re Gerald Cooper Chemicals Ltd (1978)*, it was said that where the company received forward payment for the supply of indigo knowing that it could not continue to trade because of insolvency and used this to pay off part of a loan, the company was carrying on business fraudulently. The person receiving the money was stated to be liable if he accepted money which he knew full well to have been obtained by the carrying on of a business with intent to defraud creditors.

When an order is made on the application of the liquidator, the sum which the person is ordered to pay will generally contain a punitive element as well as a compensatory one: see *Re William C Leitch Bros Ltd (1932)*; *Re a Company (No 001418 of 1988) (1991)*.

S213 was considered in *Morphitis v Bernasconi (2003)*. The case concerned Transmetal Chimica Ltd, who were hauliers operating from a trading estate in Sandwich. Bernasconi was a director of the company. The company misleadingly claimed that a certain payment of £10,000 would be made when it was known that it could not be made and the company carried on incurring debts that the company knew would never be paid (these included rents owed to Ramac Holdings Ltd). The liquidator brought a claim under s213 IA86 which provides for payments where a company is indulging in fraudulent trading. At first instance Antony Ellery QC held that there was liability. The Court of Appeal reversed this holding that it does not follow that because a person has defrauded in the course of a company's business that the business was carried on with intent to defraud.

Savirimuthu criticises the Court of Appeal for failure to provide a coherent explanation of the basis of liability in s213 (A. Savirimuthu, Casenote on *Morphitis* (2005) 26 Co Law 245).

Section 214 of the Insolvency Act 1986 extends liability for directors or shadow directors who should know or ought to have concluded that there was no reasonable prospect that the company would avoid going into insolvent liquidation. The section is therefore more limited in catchment than s213 as s213 applies to any person knowingly party to the carrying on of the business. Furthermore, s214 has no corresponding criminal sanction.

It seems that only the liquidator can bring proceedings under s214.

In *Re Oasis Merchandising Services Ltd (1997)*, the liquidator had entered into an agreement with a specialist litigation support service. The service was to fund the litigation as the company had no funds. In exchange for this, the liquidator was to sell and assign the fruits of the action. The litigation service was given a significant degree of control over the proceedings.

The Court of Appeal held that the liquidator had no power to enter into such an agreement and that, although the liquidator had power to sell any of the company's property, this did not extend to the fruits of any litigation bought by the liquidator under s214.

The section was considered in *Re Produce Marketing Consortium Ltd (No 2) (1989)*. The liquidator of the company sought an order under s214 of the Insolvency Act 1986 against two directors. The auditors of the company, which was in the business of importing fruit, had warned the directors of the company's serious financial position. The judge found the directors liable to contribute £75,000. In determining how to decide whether directors ought to have known of the company's position, Knox J had this to say:

> The knowledge to be imputed in testing whether or not directors knew or ought to have concluded that there was no reasonable prospect of the company avoiding insolvent liquidation is not limited to the documentary material actually available at the given time. This appears from s214(4) which includes a reference to facts which a director of a company not only should know but those which he ought to ascertain, a word which does not appear in s214(2)(b). In my judgment this indicates that there is to be included by way of factual information not only what was actually there, but what given reasonable diligence and an appropriate level of general knowledge, skill and experience, was ascertainable.

In *Re Purpoint Ltd (1991)*, Vinelott J held a director of the company liable under s214 where it should have been plain to him that the company could not avoid going into insolvent liquidation. The purpose of an order under s214 is to ensure that any depletion of the company's assets which occurs after a time when there is no reasonable prospect of the company's avoiding an insolvent winding up is made good. The company's business is being conducted at such a time at the risk of creditors.

In *Re Hydrodam (Corby) Ltd (1994)*, the extent to which wrongful trading may extend to others was at issue. Liability is imposed under s214 on shadow directors (s741(2) defines a shadow director as 'a person in accordance with whose directions or instructions the directors of the company are accustomed to act'. The sub-section continues: 'However, a person is not deemed a shadow director by reason only that the directors act on advice given by him in a professional capacity').

Hydrodam was a wholly owned subsidiary of Eagle Trust plc. The liquidator made a claim for wrongful trading against Eagle Trust plc, one of Eagle Trust's subsidiaries, and all of Eagle Trust's directors. Two of Eagle Trust plc's directors applied to have the claim struck out. The company had duly appointed directors, two Channel Island companies. Millett J was prepared to assume that Eagle Trust could be a shadow director. He did not accept, however, that it followed that Eagle Trust's directors were also shadow directors. Although they attended the ultimate holding company's board meetings, they were still not thereby without other factors shadow directors. Millett J held that no case had been made out against either of the defendants.

Previously, it had been thought that banks and substantial creditors ran risks when they gave instructions to companies in financial difficulties. *Re Hydrodam* makes it very clear that cogent evidence will be needed of giving instructions to those people running the company before the shadow directorship is made out.

A person is only liable for wrongful trading if the court is not satisfied that he took every step with a view to minimising the potential loss to the company's creditors as (assuming him to have known that there was no reasonable prospect that the company would avoid going into insolvent liquidation) he ought to have taken. Directors should therefore raise concerns with other board members and urge action, such as discontinuing trading, as is appropriate. This appears to be the only defence available under s214. Section 727 of the Companies Act 1985 was considered and rejected as a defence in *Re Produce Marketing Consortium Ltd (No 2) (1989)*.

As well as the potential liability of directors for matters occurring before the liquidation commences, there are various offences of fraud and deception which may be committed during a liquidation. These include:

(a) fraud, etc, in anticipation of a winding up (s206 of the Insolvency Act 1986);
(b) past or present officers making gifts or transfers of or charges on company property (s207 of the Insolvency Act 1986);

(c) misconduct by past or present officers during the course of the winding up (s208 of the Insolvency Act 1986);

(d) falsification, destruction, mutilation, etc of the company's books, papers, etc (s209 of the Insolvency Act 1986);

(e) material omission from the statement relating to company's affairs (s210 of the Insolvency Act 1986).

## 24.4 The conduct of the liquidation

Whilst it is not intended to go into the minutiae of the conduct of the liquidation, it is proposed here to mention one or two miscellaneous facets of the process of liquidation and to consider the priority of payments in a liquidation.

Section 233 of the Insolvency Act implementing a recommendation of the Cork Committee, provides that suppliers of gas, water, electricity and telephone services cannot make it a condition of continued supply, where there is an administration, administrative receivership, voluntary arrangement or liquidation, that all moneys owing be paid. The section is a recognition of the dominant bargaining position of such utility suppliers and it prevents them using their 'economic muscle'. The supplier can, however, insist on a personal guarantee in relation to continued supplies.

Another matter to consider in a liquidation is the right of the liquidator to disclaim onerous property under s178 of the Insolvency Act 1986. Onerous property means any unprofitable contract and any other property of the company which is unsaleable or not readily saleable such as a wasting lease. This power must be exercised within 12 months of the commencement of the liquidation. Where it is exercised, any person sustaining loss or damage is deemed a creditor and can prove for the extent of the loss or damage in the winding up.

Another matter that may arise in a liquidation situation concerns the re-use of company names. Section 216 of the Insolvency Act 1986 deals with the so called 'phoenix syndrome' and places certain limitations on the re-use of company names. The section provides that the old name or a similar one cannot be used by the directors or shadow directors for a period of five years from the commencement of the liquidation. In *Thorne v Silverleaf (1994)*, the defendant was a director of two companies which had gone into liquidation, Mike Spence (Reading) Ltd and Mike Spence (Motor Sport) Ltd. He had personally guaranteed their overdrafts. The defendant established and became a director of a third company, Mike Spence Classic Cars Ltd. The company dealt in vintage cars. The plaintiff provided the company with finance. The company's financial position deteriorated and the plaintiff complained that the defendant was personally liable for its debts since the company had a name so similar to the two previous companies to suggest an association with them. The court held that this was so and the defendant was held personally liable under s216 of the Insolvency Act 1986. However, the old name may well have a value and the court can give leave to a director of a failed company to buy-over the old name (see *Re Bonus Breaks Ltd (1991)*).

In *Re Lightning Electrical Contractors Ltd (1996)*, leave was granted respecting a company which was already trading. This was not a 'phoenix syndrome' situation. The liquidating company's administrative receivers supported the application and it was not opposed by the Secretary of State.

When the liquidator has realised the company's assets, he is faced with paying off the company's debts. Many features of priority which applied in relation to receivership also apply here (see section 20.4). The order of priority is as follows:

(a)  the costs of the liquidation, including the liquidator's remuneration;
(b)  preferential creditors are paid off next.

The categories of preferential debts are set out in Sched 6 of the Insolvency Act 1986 as amended by the Enterprise Act 2002. The categories rank equally and are as follows:

- any sums owing to occupational and state pension schemes;
- wages due to employees for the four month period before liquidation up to £800 per employee;
- any accrued holiday pay owed to employees.

Note that any sum advanced by a bank, etc, for paying salaries and accrued holiday pay which would otherwise have been preferential becomes preferential by subrogation.

(c)  charges secured by floating charges are paid off next (subject to the ring-fencing provisions of the Enterprise Act 2002). The Enterprise Act provides for ring-fencing of assets where there is a floating charge to provide funds for unsecured creditors. Currently the following provisions determine the amount that is ring-fenced:

 (i)  if the amount available for distribution is less than £10,000 and it is considered thanks that the cost of making provision for the unsecured creditors would be disproportionate, then no assets are available;
 (ii)  50% of the first £10,000 realised, and thereafter 20% of further realisations.
 (iii)  a maximum ring-fenced fund of £600,000 (Insolvency (Prescribed Part) Order 2003)

d)  ordinary trade creditors who have no security (subject to the Enterprise Act 2002 provisions);
(e)  any deferred debts such as dividends which have been declared but not paid.

If there is a surplus of assets (many liquidations are solvent ones), the surplus will be distributed amongst the company's members according to their class rights (see Chapter 6).

Liquidations (or winding ups) fall into two basic categories: compulsory by court order and voluntary initiated by the members of the company. Voluntary liquidations are of two types: members' voluntary winding up under the control of the members where the directors have sworn a statutory declaration of solvency, and creditors' voluntary winding up. In the latter case, there has been no statutory declaration of solvency and the predominant interest of the creditors is recognised.

In a liquidation, certain prior transactions may be re-opened if they are made at an undervalue, or if they are extortionate credit agreements or if they constitute preferences. Floating charges made in the run up to a liquidation may also be held to be invalid.

If the company has been trading when it was known that it could not pay its debts, those trading will be civilly and possibly criminally liable. Directors and shadow directors may even be civilly liable where they ought to have known that the company could not survive. There are also various areas of liability for officers during a liquidation such as falsification of a company's books, transferring company property during a liquidation, etc.

The suppliers of utility services – gas, water, electricity and telephone – cannot insist on payment of moneys due as a condition for continued service. During the liquidation, the liquidator may disclaim onerous property such as a lease or an unprofitable contract but the other party may then prove as a creditor in the liquidation.

There is a set order for payment of debts – liquidation expenses, preferential debts, floating charges, ordinary debts and the deferred debts. If there is a surplus this should be distributed to members taking account of their class rights.

## SUMMARY

Companies may be wound up or, as it is sometimes phrased, put into liquidation. Liquidation may be by court order (compulsory winding up), or by resolution of creditors and/or members.

The most common forms of compulsory winding up are where the company is unable to pay its debts or where the court is of the opinion that it is just and equitable that the company should be wound up.

Provisions in the Insolvency Act called the 'fair dealing' provisions protect against forward or sharp practice.

There are further provisions to control wrongful trading and fraudulent trading. When those within the company's directorate, in the case of wrongful trading, carry on trading negligently when the company is insolvent or, in the case of fraudulent trading, when anyone in a trading position carries on trading when they know the company is insolvent.

Detailed rules provide for the conduct of the liquidation and for priorities in paying off debts.

## Further reading

Doyle, LG, 'Anomalies in the wrongful trading provisions' (1992) 13 Co Law 96.
Ferran, E, 'Timing requirements of the companies and insolvency legislation, [1994] 53 CLJ 37.

Finch, V, 'Doctoring in the Shadows of Insolvency' [2005] JBL 690.

Hooke, T, and Hicks, A, 'Wrongful trading – predicting insolvency' [1993] JBL 338.

Keay, A, 'What Future for Liquidation in the light of the Enterprise Act Reforms?' [2005] JBL 143.

Nolan, R, 'Less equal than others – maxwell and subordinated unsecured obligations' [1995] JBL 485.

Oditah, F, 'Wrongful trading' [1990] LM CLQ 205.

Oditah, F, 'Assets of the treatment of claims in insolvency' (1992) 108 LQR 459.

Prentice, DD, 'Preferences and defective floating charges' (1993) 109 LQR 371.

Savirimuthu, A, 'Morphitis in the Court of Appeal: some reflections' (2005) 26 Co Law 245.

Turnbull, S, and Crofts, S, 'Directors in danger' (1992) 110 Accountancy 115.

Ulph, J, and Allen, T, 'Transactions at an undervalue, purchasers and the impact of the Human Rights Act 1998' [2004] JBL 1.

Wheeler, S, 'Swelling the assets for distribution in corporate insolvency' [1993] JBL 256.

# 25

# Corporate governance

Corporate governance developments in the United Kingdom are of relatively recent date. As has been seen in company law in the United Kingdom, the interests of shareholders have generally predominated until the first statutory intervention in the Companies Act 1980 to broaden the duties of directors to include a duty to employers.

Increasingly, however, it has been recognised that other stakeholders have an interest in the governance of companies. Particular concern attached to larger companies and specifically to listed companies. Companies' scandals at the end of the last century such as BCCI, Polypeck and Maxwell heightened concerns.

Current thinking on corporate governance recognises a corporation's obligations to society generally in the form of stakeholders. Corporate governance is concerned with issues such as:

*   the effectiveness of a company's operations
*   the reliability of a company's financial reporting
*   compliance with laws and regulations
*   the safeguarding of corporate assets.

Corporate governance has recently become increasingly focussed on corporate failures, auditor independence, excessive remuneration for directors and other executives, ineffective non-executive directors, and the representation of large investors in public companies.

The origins of the corporate governance debate are in the need to respond to the problems that are caused by the separation of ownership and control in companies dating back to the formation of joint stock companies in the middle of the 19th century. Then, as now, the owners of companies were not necessarily involved in day-to-day operational matters. That is why shareholders were originally centre stage in the corporate governance debate. Now, however, as noted, it is recognised that a corporations's obligations run more widely to society generally in the form of stakeholders.

It is widely recognised in the United Kingdom that a large number of financial failures have been caused by breakdowns in internal control. This is true also in the United States. The Tredway Commission in the US found that in nearly 50% of cases of corporate breakdown, fraudulent financial reporting was a contributory issue.

## 25.1 The Cadbury Committee

The Committee on the Financial Aspects of Corporate Governance (the Cadbury Committee) published its final report in December 1992. This report contained a Code of Practice which was aimed at achieving the very highest standards of corporate behaviour.

The Committee was set up in May 1991 by the Financial Reporting Council, the London Stock Exchange and the accountancy profession. It adopted as its terms of reference: to consider the following in relation to financial issues arising from financial reporting and accountability and to make recommendations on good practice:

(a) the responsibilities of executive and non-executive directors for reviewing and reporting on performance to shareholders and other financially interested parties; and the frequency, clarity and form in which information should be provided;
(b) the case for audit committees of the board, including their composition and role;
(c) the principal responsibilities of auditors and the extent and value of the audit;
(d) the links between shareholders, boards and auditors;
(e) any other relevant matters.

The Cadbury report in December 1992 attracted considerable attention. The concern about financial reporting and accountability was no doubt heightened by recent company scandals.

The Committee's recommendations are for the most part centred upon the control and reporting functions of boards and the role of auditors. This reflects the Committee's main aim which was to review those aspects of corporate governance related to financial reporting and accountability.

At the core of the Committee's recommendations was a Code of Best Practice which was designed to achieve the necessary high standards of corporate behaviour. The London Stock Exchange is to require all listed companies registered in the United Kingdom, as a continuing obligation of listing, to state whether they were complying with the Code and to give reasons for any points of non-compliance.

The Code was thus directed to listed companies. The principles upon which the code was based were principles of openness, integrity and accountability.

Many of the key recommendations of the Committee are incorporated into the code. Some of the key recommendations were as follows:

(a) there should be a clearly defined split of responsibilities at the head of a company to ensure a balance of power and authority between executive and independent non-executive directors;

(b) there should be a schedule of matters specifically reserved for board decision so that it is clear that the company's control and direction are firmly in its hands;

(c) there should be an agreed procedure for directors in the furtherance of their duties to take independent professional advice if necessary, at the company's expense;

(d) ideally, the posts of Chairman and Chief Executive should be kept separate;

(e) executive directors' service contracts should not exceed three years;

(f) executive directors' pay should be subject to the recommendations of a remuneration committee made up wholly or mainly of non-executive directors;

(g) non-executive directors should be appointed for specified terms and reappointment should not be automatic;

(h) non-executive directors should be selected through a formal process and this should be a matter for the board as a whole;

(i) the board should establish an audit committee of at least three non-executive directors with written terms of reference;

(j) the directors should report on the effectiveness of the company's internal controls;

(k) there should be full disclosure of fees paid to audit firms for non audit work.

### 25.1.1 Critique

Various criticisms were made of the Cadbury Committee report. Some people criticised the lack of statutory teeth. This criticism was rejected by Sir Adrian Cadbury who felt that the report had given companies a checklist and shareholders an agenda to improve the effectiveness of corporate governance in Britain. Yet, some of the recommendations did not 'go the whole hog'. Thus, the report urged, *generally*, there should be a split of the Chairmanship and post of Chief Executive between different people.

Another criticism that was levelled at the Cadbury report was that it failed to address itself to long term solutions of encouraging long term incentives for management and a long term view of the investment by investment institutions, despite its statement in the opening paragraph of the report: 'The country's economy depends on the drive and efficiency of its companies'.

## 25.2 The Greenbury Committee

The governance of companies remained a favourite topic of debate. Following the Cadbury Committee report, a further Committee was set up by the CBI under the Chairmanship of Sir Richard Greenbury. The aim of this Committee was to consider issues relating to directors' remuneration and emoluments. The Committee report, which was published in 1995, once again set out a Code of Best Practice. This Code was annexed to the listing rules and every listed company must state, in its annual report and accounts, whether it has secured compliance with the Code. If it has failed to comply with the Code, it must explain why this is so.

Basically, the Code requires that directors of a listed company should establish a remuneration committee made up of non-executive directors to determine policy on remuneration packages for executive directors. The remuneration committee should have access to independent professional advice and the committee chairman, or alternatively another member of the committee, should attend the company's AGM to be available to answer questions on remuneration.

## 25.3 The Hampel Committee

A further committee on corporate governance under the Chairmanship of Sir Ronald Hampel was set up in November 1995. This was at the behest of the Financial Reporting Council.

The Hampel Committee was asked:

(a) to review the Cadbury Code and its implementation to ensure that its purposes were being achieved and to suggest amendments to the code as necessary;
(b) to review the role of directors;
(c) to pursue any relevant matters arising from the report of the Greenbury Committee;
(d) to address, as necessary, the role of shareholders and auditors in corporate governance issues;
(e) and to deal with any other relevant matters.

The Hampel Committee published its preliminary report on 5 August 1997. The Committee:

(a) rejected the principle of stakeholder democracy and a two tier board system;
(b) rejected the government's idea for a standing panel on governance;
(c) asserted that companies are more concerned with accountability than business prosperity. The Committee indicated that it wanted to see this imbalance corrected;
(d) proposed a set of general principles rather than a detailed corporate governance blue print and rejected the 'tick-box' attitude to compliance pursued by Cadbury and Greenbury;
(e) stated that companies should include a statement in the annual report on compliance with broad corporate governance principles.

Following consultation, the Committee resisted pressure from the government to 'beef up' its proposals.

Sir Ronald Hampel, Chairman of the Committee and Chairman of ICI, indicated that the Committee had stuck to the fundamental principle of corporate prosperity before accountability.

Some criticisms have been made that the report dilutes the Cadbury guidelines in that, for example, it concludes that companies need not separate the roles of

Chairman and Chief Executive although this goes against a key principle of the Cadbury guidelines.

The Hampel Committee report (1998) considered that, in the debate on corporate governance, too much stress had been laid on accountability and not enough on business prosperity.

The report urged that companies should include in their annual report a description of how corporate governance is being applied in relation to their business. The Hampel Committee produced a set of principles and a Code which comprehends the work of the Cadbury, Greenbury and Hampel Committees – the Combined Code.

Companies should have a Nomination Committee to make recommendations for appointments to the board. Remuneration Committees should be made up of independent directors to consider remuneration packages and their application. Institutional investors are said to have a responsibility to use their vote sensibly and the key role of shareholders at the AGM is acknowledged.

Every company should establish an Audit Committee made up of at least three non-executive directors.

The final Hampel report contained a proposal that each Board should have a lead non-executive director. He or she would be a focal point of contact for shareholders.

Some critics (for example, CA Riley in 'Whither UK corporate governance?', *Amicus Curiae*, October 1997) argue that the approach to corporate governance raises a deeper and more troubling problem. This is that the debate on corporate governance has been semi-privatised and carried out through the medium of relatively small and unrepresentative committees championing a narrow range of interests.

The Secretary of State announced that she did not intend to legislate on the Hampel recommendations, but preferred that they should be established by best practice: 'There are those who would say the government has a responsibility to legislate for good corporate governance. However, while the legal system can be used to enforce aspects of best practice, I believe that the very best will adopt even better practice because they see its value, and will do so more readily of their own accord than if it is forced on them. That is why I would prefer to see many of the recommendations … embodied in good practice rather than enshrined in legislation'.

## 25.4 The Turnbull Report

The Turnbull Committee was set up by the Institute of Chartered Accountants in England and Wales. The report of the committee – 'Internal Control: Guidance for Directors on the Combined Code' was published in 1999 and sets out how directors of listed companies should comply with the UK's Combined Code requirements in respect of internal controls. The guidance was supported and endorsed by the London Stock Exchange.

## 25.5  The Higgs Report

In April 2002, the Secretary of State for Trade and Industry and the Chancellor of the Exchequer appointed Derek Higgs to lead a short independent review of the role and effectiveness of non-executive directors. Derek Higgs published his report in January 2003.

The Higgs Report considered the position of non executive directors. Among its recommendations were the need for a fuller discussion of the role and responsibilities of non executives, a requirement to disclose attendance at board meetings, the need for the provision of training and for non executives to meet major investors as part of their induction and for the senior independent director to meet shareholders regularly.

## 25.6  The Smith Report

The Smith Review, chaired by Sir Robert Smith and set up by the Financial Reporting Council, considered the guidance for audit committees. The Smith Report was published in January 2003. The committee recognised that the main role and responsibility of audit committees should be to monitor the integrity of the company's financial statements and to review its internal financial controls.

The audit committee should be given written terms of reference by the board of directors tailored to the particular circumstances of the company. It should review annually its terms of reference and its effectiveness and recommend any necessary changes to the board.

The audit committee should be comprised solely of independent non executive directors, the term independent is as defined by the Higgs report as a director who is independent in character and judgement and has no relationships or circumstances which affect his judgement. It is stipulated that the chairman of the company should not be an audit committee member.

The audit committee should, at least annually, meet the external and internal auditors without management being present to discuss issues arising from the audit. The audit committee should be provided with sufficient resources to undertake its duties.

Appropriate training should be given to members of the audit committee.

The chairman of the audit committee should be present at the Annual General Meeting to answer questions through the chairman of the board on the audit committee's activities and matters within the scope of the audit committee's responsibilities.

## 25.7  The Combined Code on Corporate Governance 2003

In July 2003, a new version of the Combined Code on Corporate Governance was issued. This code supersedes and replaces the Combined Code issued by the Hampel Committee on Corporate Governance in 1998. The new code derives from a review of the role and effectiveness of non executive directors by Derek Higgs (January 2003) and a review of audit committees by a group led by Sir Robert Smith (January 2003), as well as provisions on internal control derived from the Turnbull Committee (September 1999).

The Combined Code applies to reporting years beginning on or after 1 November 2003. The Financial Services Authority has annexed the code to the listing rules and made consequential rule changes.

All companies incorporated in the UK and listed on the London Stock Exchange are required under the Listing Rules to report on how they have applied the Combined Code in their annual report and accounts. This requirement does not apply to AIM companies.

The code contains both main and supporting principles and provisions. Listed companies have to make a disclosure statement in two parts in relation to the code. In the first part of the statement, companies need to report on how they apply the principles and provisions of the code. Companies should set out their governance policies and any special circumstances that apply to them. In the second part of the statement companies have to confirm that they comply with the code's provisions or, if they depart from them, to provide an explanation. This 'comply or explain' approach has been in operation since the Cadbury code was adopted and has been generally welcomed by companies and investors.

Whilst it is recognised that most listed companies will comply with the code's provisions most of the time, it is recognised that sometimes departure from the provisions of the code may be justified. Every company must review every provision carefully and provide an explanation if it departs from the code's provisions. Smaller listed companies, especially those that are new to listing, may feel that some of the provisions are disproportionate or less relevant in their case. Some of the provisions do not apply to companies below FTSE 350. Such companies may, however, feel that it is right to adopt the general approach of the code and are encouraged to consider this option.

The 2003 code does not include material from the previous code on the disclosure of directors' remuneration. This is because the Directors' Remuneration Report Regulations 2002 are now in force and supersede the earlier code provisions.

The code, as has been noted, is made up of main principles together with supporting principles and provisions.

The Financial Reporting Council reviewed the present code in 2005. Some minor amendments were proposed and these came into force in November 2006.

### 25.7.1 The code - Section 1: Companies

*A: Directors*

A1: THE BOARD

The main principle is that every company should be headed by an effective board which is collectively responsible for the success of the company. Supporting principles provide for the board's role in the provision of entrepreneurial leadership of the company, setting strategic aims, ensuring appropriate financial and human resources are in place, and reviewing management performance. It is noted that all directors should take decisions objectively in the interests of the company.

Non-executive directors should constructively challenge proposals on strategy. They should scrutinise the management performance and satisfy themselves regarding the integrity of financial information. They are also responsible for determining remuneration levels of executive directors and have a leading role in their appointment and, if appropriate, their removal.

Code provisions include the need for regular meetings of the board; an annual report indicating how the board operates, identifying the chairman, deputy chairman (if there is one), the chief executive, and senior independent director, and the chairman and members of the nomination audit and remuneration committees. It should also set out the number of meetings of the board and its committees, together with attendance records.

The chairman should hold meetings with non-executive directors without executive directors being present. The non-executive directors led by the senior independent director should, at least, annually appraise the chairman's performance in the absence of his presence.

Directors who have concerns about the running of the company should ensure their concerns are reported in the board minutes and on resignation a non-executive director should provide a written statement to the chairman for circulation to the board if he has any such concerns.

The company should arrange appropriate insurance cover in respect of legal action against its directors.

### A2: CHAIRMAN AND CHIEF EXECUTIVE

The main principle provides that there should be a clear division of responsibilities at the head of the company between executive responsibility and chairing responsibility.

The supporting principle recognises the chairman's responsibility for leadership of the board and that the chairman should facilitate the effective contribution of non-executive directors in particular, and ensure constructive relations between executive and non-executive directors.

The code provides that the roles of the chairman and chief executive should not be exercised by the same individual. The chairman should be independent. The chief executive should not go on to be the chairman of the same company. If this happens exceptionally, the board should consult major shareholders in advance and should set out its reasons to shareholders at the time of the appointment and in the next annual report.

### A3: BOARD BALANCE AND INDEPENDENCE

The main principle provides that the board should include a balance of executive and non-executive directors. No individual or small group of individuals should dominate the board's decision taking. This is backed up by supporting principles that the board should not be too large so as to be unwieldy, yet should be of sufficient size to accommodate the balance of skills and experience appropriate for the requirements of the business. There should be a strong presence on the board of both executive and non-executive directors, and undue reliance should not be placed on particular individuals in relation to chairmanship and membership of committees. No one other than the committee chairman and members is entitled to be present at a meeting of the nomination, audit or remuneration committee, but others may attend at the invitation of the committee.

Code provisions provide that the board should identify in the annual report each non-executive director it considers to be independent. It should set out any factors that it feels may affect a directors' judgement and if it considers that despite the existence of a relationship or circumstance that may be relevant in relation to the directors' independence that the director is still independent. Such factors include past employment in the last five years, any material business relation within the last three years, remuneration other than directors' fees or share options, performance related pay or involvement in a pension scheme, close family ties, a significant shareholding or having served on the board for more than nine years since first election.

Except for smaller companies, at least half of the board, excluding the chairman, should be made up of non-executive directors determined by the board to be independent. (A smaller company is one outside of the FTSE 350 in the whole of the year preceding the reporting year.)

The board should appoint one of the independent non-executive directors to be the senior independent director. That director should be available to shareholders if they have concerns which contact through the chairman, chief executive or finance director has failed to resolve.

### A4: APPOINTMENTS TO THE BOARD

The main principle is that there should be a formal, rigorous and transparent procedure for appointment of new directors to the board.

Appointments to the board should be made on merit and against objective criteria. The board should ensure there are plans to ensure an orderly succession for appointments to the board providing the right balance of skills and experience.

The provisions of the code state that there should be a nomination committee dealing with board appointments, and a majority of the members of the nomination committee should be independent non-executive directors. The chairman or an independent non-executive director should chair the committee but the chairman should not chair the nomination committee when it is dealing with the appointment of a successor to the chairmanship.

The chairman's other significant commitments should be disclosed to the board before appointment and included in the annual report. Changes to such commitments should also be reported as they arise and included in the next annual report.

No individual should be appointed to the chairmanship of more than one FTSE 100 company.

The terms and conditions of appointment of non-executive directors should be made available for inspection. The letter of appointment should set out the expected time commitment and non-executive directors should undertake that they will have sufficient time to meet the commitments that are required of them. Their other significant commitments should be disclosed to the board before appointment, with a broad indication of the time involved. The board should also be informed of subsequent changes.

The board should not agree to a full time executive director taking on more than one non-executive directorship in a FTSE 100 company, nor the chairmanship of such a company.

## A5: INFORMATION AND PROFESSIONAL DEVELOPMENT

It is provided that the board should be supplied in a timely manner with information to enable it to discharge its duties effectively. All directors should receive induction on joining the board, together with regular updates and assistance to refresh their skills and knowledge.

The chairman of the company is stated to be responsible for ensuring directors receive accurate, timely and clear information. He should ensure that directors continually update their skills and knowledge. The company secretary under the direction of the chairman should ensure that information flows within the board and its committees, and between senior management and non-executive directors.

The chairman should ensure new directors receive full formal and tailored induction on joining the board and should also offer major shareholders the opportunity to meet new non-executive directors. The board should ensure that directors, especially non-executive directors have access to independent professional advice at the company's expense where they judge it necessary to discharge their responsibilities as directors. Committees should be provided with appropriate resources to undertake their duties.

## A6: PERFORMANCE EVALUATION

The board should undertake a formal and rigorous annual evaluation of its own performance and that of its committees and individual directors.

Individual evaluation should aim to show whether each director continues to contribute effectively and demonstrate commitment to the relevant role including commitment of time. The chairman should act on the results of the performance evaluation by recognising the strengths and addressing the weaknesses of the board and, where appropriate, proposing new members be appointed to the board, or seeking the resignation of existing directors.

The board should state in the annual report how performance and evaluation of members of the board and of committees is conducted. The non-executive directors should be responsible for performance evaluation of the chairman.

### A7: RE-ELECTION

All directors should be submitted for re-election at regular intervals, subject to continued satisfactory performance. The board should provide for planned and progressive changes to the board.

All directors should be subject to election by shareholders at the first Annual General Meeting after appointment, and to re-election thereafter at intervals of no more than three years.

Non-executive directors should be appointed for specified terms subject to re-election, and to Companies Acts provisions relating to the removal of directors. The board should indicate in papers sent out to shareholders why they consider that a non-executive director should be elected. The chairman should confirm to shareholders when proposing re-election that following performance evaluation the individual's performance continues to be effective. Any term beyond six years for a non-executive director should be subject to a particularly rigorous review and should take into account the need for progressive changes of the membership of the board. Non-executive directors may serve longer than nine years subject to annual re-election.

As noted above, serving for more than nine years could be relevant to the determination of a non-executive director's independence.

## B: Remuneration

### B1: THE LEVEL AND MAKEUP OF REMUNERATION

The main principle is that levels of remuneration should be sufficient to attract, retain and motivate directors of the quality required to run the company successfully but without paying more than is necessary for this purpose. The remuneration committee should judge where to position their company relative to other companies. They should use comparisons with caution, however, in view of the risk of an upward ratchet of remuneration levels with no corresponding improvement in performance.

The performance-related elements of remuneration should form a significant proportion of the total remuneration package of executive directors and should be designed to align their interests with those of shareholders and to give them incentives to perform to the highest levels.

Levels of remuneration for non-executive directors should reflect the time commitment and responsibilities of the role that they fill. Remuneration for non-executive directors should not include share options. If they are granted, exceptionally shareholder approval should be sought in advance and any shares acquired by exercise of the options should be held until at least one year after the non-executive director leaves the board of directors.

Where a company releases an executive director to serve as a non-executive director elsewhere, the remuneration report should include a statement as to whether or not the director will retain such earnings, and if so what the remuneration is.

The remuneration committee should carefully consider what compensation commitments, including pension contributions and all other elements their directors' terms of appointment would entitle them to in the event of early termination. Notice or contract period should be set at one year or less. If it is necessary to offer longer notice or contract periods to new directors recruited from outside, such periods should reduce to one year or less after the initial period.

### B2: PROCEDURE

There should be a formal and transparent procedure for developing policy on executive remuneration and for fixing the remuneration packages of individual directors. No director should be involved in deciding his or her own remuneration.

The remuneration committee should consult the chairman and/or chief executive about their proposals relating to the remuneration of other executive directors. The remuneration committee should also be responsible for appointing any consultants in respect of remuneration. The chairman of the board should ensure that the company maintains contact as required with its principal shareholders about remuneration in the same way as for other matters. The remuneration committee should consist of at least three, or in the case of smaller companies two members, who should all be independent non-executive directors. The remuneration committee should make available its terms of reference.

The 2006 Combined Code amendments amend the existing restriction on the company chairman serving on the remuneration committee to permit this where he or she is considered independent, although it is recommended that this should not extend to chairing the committee.

The board, itself or, where required by the Articles of Association, the shareholders should determine the remuneration of the non-executive directors within the limits set in the Articles of Association. Where permitted by the Articles, the board may, however, delegate this responsibility to a committee which might include the Chief Executive.

### C: Accountability and audit

#### C1: FINANCIAL REPORTING

The board should present a balanced and understandable assessment of the company's position and prospects.

#### C2: INTERNAL CONTROL

The board should maintain a sound system of internal control to safeguard shareholders' investments and the company's assets. This system of internal control should be reviewed at least annually to ensure that it is effective.

## C3: AUDIT COMMITTEE AND AUDITORS

The board should establish formal and transparent arrangements for considering how they should apply the financial reporting and internal control principles and for maintaining an appropriate relationship with the company's auditors.

The board should establish an audit committee of at least three, or in the case of smaller companies, two members who should all be independent non-executive directors. At least one member of the audit committee should have recent and relevant financial experience.

It is the main role of the audit committee to monitor the integrity of the financial statements of the company to review internal financial controls and to monitor and review the effectiveness of the company's internal audit function. The audit committee should also make recommendations about appointment, re-appointment and removal of external auditors and of their remuneration. The audit committee should review their effectiveness, independence and objectivity.

The terms of reference of the audit committee should be made available, and a separate section of the annual report should describe the work of the committee in discharging its responsibilities.

## D: Relations with shareholders

### D1: DIALOGUE WITH INSTITUTIONAL SHAREHOLDERS

It provides that there should be dialogue with shareholders based on the mutual understanding of objectives. The board as a whole has responsibility for ensuring that a satisfactory dialogue with shareholders takes place.

The board should keep in touch with shareholder opinion in whatever ways are most practical and efficient. It is for the chairman to ensure that the views of shareholders are communicated to the board as a whole. The chairman should discuss governance and strategy with major shareholders. Non-executive directors should be offered the opportunity to attend meetings with major shareholders and are expected to attend such meetings if requested by major shareholders. The senior independent director should attend sufficient meetings with a range of major shareholders to listen to their views, to help develop a balanced understanding of the issues and concerns of major shareholders.

The board should state in its annual report the steps taken to ensure that members of the board, and especially non-executive directors, develop an understanding of the views of major shareholders.

### D2: CONSTRUCTIVE USE OF THE AGM

The board should use the Annual General Meeting to communicate with investors and to encourage their participation.

The company should count all proxy votes and, except where a poll is called, should indicate the level of proxies lodged on each resolution and the balance for and against the resolution and the number of abstentions after the matter has been dealt with on a show of hands.

Further, as modified in 2005, all proxy forms should include a 'vote withheld' option where shareholders want to register that they have reservations.

The chairman of the company should arrange for the chairmen of the audit, remuneration and nomination committees to be available to answer questions at the Annual General Meeting.

The notice of the Annual General Meeting and related papers should be sent to shareholders at least 20 working days before the meeting.

### 25.7.2 The code - Section 2: Institutional shareholders

*E: Institutional shareholders*

E1: DIALOGUE WITH COMPANIES

Institutional shareholders should enter into a dialogue with companies based on the mutual understanding of objectives.

E2: EVALUATION OF GOVERNANCE DISCLOSURES

When evaluating companies' governance arrangements, particularly those relating to board structure and composition, institutional shareholders should give due weight to all relevant factors that are drawn to their attention. They should consider carefully explanations given for departure from the code and make reasoned judgements in each case. If they disagree with the company's approach, they should say so giving reasons and should avoid a box ticking approach to assessing a company's corporate governance.

E3: SHAREHOLDER VOTING

Institutional shareholders have a responsibility to make considered use of their votes. They should, on request, make available to their clients information on the proportion of resolutions on which votes are cast, and non discretionary proxies lodged. Major shareholders should attend Annual General Meetings where appropriate and practicable, and companies and registrars should facilitate this.

## 25.8 Alternative Investment Market companies

The Combined Code does not apply to companies quoted on the Alternative Investment Market. To fill this lacuna the Quoted Companies Alliance published guidelines for AIM companies. The guidelines are made up of a code of best practice.

## 25.9 International corporate governance

In recent times, well known global companies have experienced financial collapses and this has eroded global confidence in them – most notably Enron and WorldCom.

Multi-lateral bodies like the World Bank and the Organisation for Economic Co-operation and Development have contributed to the corporate governance debate on an international basis.

The World Bank and the OECD established a global governance forum in 2001 to contribute to governance reform on an international basis. This forum has helped develop initiatives in emerging economies and identified areas for the reform of corporate governance. The OECD has developed Principles of Corporate Governance to help develop frameworks for corporate governance rules. The principles are non-binding and are broadly drawn but they have helped in the promotion of appropriate standards of corporate governance world-wide. They provide guidance on the basis of an effective framework for corporate governance, the treatment of shareholders and their rights, the role of stakeholders in corporate governance, and board responsibilities.

## 25.10 European Commission

At the same time the European Commission has set up a European Corporate Governance Forum to encourage the co-ordination of national codes. This could well lead to harmonisation of corporate governance rules and accordingly the Companies Act 2006 by Part 43 gives the Financial Services Authority the power to make rules to implement any such Directive. It is not intended to introduce a European Corporate Governance Code, however, it considers that the EU should adopt a common approach to governance.

## 25.11 The US

In the US, the Sarbanes-Oxley Act 2002 applies to companies that have a listing in the US. It was introduced post the Enron and WorldCom collapses (the so-called 'pinstripe-plunder'), and imposes criminal liabilities on officers of companies who knowingly sign off false financial statements.

The Sarbanes-Oxley reforms have led to improvements in the corporate governance performance of large companies in the US. However, the reforms have had their critics too. The cost of compliance, especially with regard to s404, requiring outside audit of a company's internal control systems have often been severely criticised as being disproportionate.

### SUMMARY

Since the early 1990s, increased attention has been paid to corporate governance, particularly in the case of listed companies in the United Kingdom.

In 1992, the Cadbury Committee on the Financial Aspects of Corporate Governance published its final report. It was looking at the responsibilities of executive and non-executive directors, the case for audit committees, principal responsibilities of auditors, and the links between shareholders, board and auditors, as well as other relevant matters. The report contained a Code of Practice. Listed companies were required to comply with the Code of Practice.

The Greenbury Committee looked at directors' remuneration. Once again, it published a Code of Best Practice which was annexed to the listing rules. It reported in 1995.

The Hampel Committee was set up in November 1995 to review the Cadbury code, to review the role of directors, and to pursue any matters arising from the Greenbury Committee, and to address, as necessary, the role of shareholders and auditors in relation to corporate governance. It published its preliminary report in 1997 and its final report in 1998.

The Turnbull Committee published a report in 1999 setting out how directors of listed companies should comply with the code, and this guidance was endorsed by the London Stock Exchange.

In April 2002, Derek Higgs was asked to lead a review into the role and effectiveness of non-executive directors. He published his report in 2003.

The Smith Review, chaired by Sir Robert Smith, looking at the position of audit committees also published its report in 2003.

In July 2003, a new version of the Combined Code on Corporate Governance was issued. This replaced the Combined Code issued by the Hampel Committee in 1998, which had combined its own recommendations together with the substance of the earlier codes from the Cadbury and Greenbury Committees.

The new code takes full account of the reports of Derek Higgs and Sir Robert Smith, as well as the provisions on internal control derived from the Turnbull Committee.

In 2005, a review of the implementation of the 2003 version of the Combined Code was effected which brought in minor amendments.

## Further reading

Alcock, A, 'Corporate governance: a defence of the status quo' (1995) 58 MLR 898.

Belcher, A, 'Regulation by the market: the case of the Cadbury Code and Compliance Statement' [1995] JBL 321.

Dine, J, 'The governance of governance' (1994) 15 Co Law 73.

Finch, V, 'Board performance and Cadbury on corporate governance' [1992] JBL 581.

Hemraj, M, 'Corporate Governance: rationalising stakeholder doctrine in corporate accountability' (2005) 26 Co Law 211.

Riley, CA, 'Corporate management – UK and US initiatives' [1994] LS 244.

Villiers, C, 'Draft report by the Cadbury Committee on the financial aspects of corporate governance' (1992) 13 Co Law 214.

# Index